THE NEW ERA OF REGULATORY ENFORCEMENT

A Comprehensive Guide for Raising
the Bar to Manage Risk

RICHARD H. GIRGENTI
TIMOTHY P. HEDLEY

New York   Chicago   San Francisco   Lisbon   Athens   London
Madrid   Mexico City   Milan   New Delhi   San Juan   Seoul
Singapore   Sydney   Toronto

1 2 3 4 5 6 7 8 9 0   DOC/DOC   1 2 1 0 9 8 7 6

ISBN   978-1-259-58459-6
MHID   1-259-58459-3

e-ISBN   978-1-25-958460-2
e-MHID   1-259-58460-7

This publication is designed to provide accurate and authoritative information in regard to the subject matter covered. It is sold with the understanding that neither the author nor the publisher is engaged in rendering legal, accounting, securities trading, or other professional services. If legal advice or other expert assistance is required, the services of a competent professional person should be sought.

—From a Declaration of Principles Jointly Adopted by a Committee of the American Bar Association and a Committee of Publishers and Associations

Library of Congress Cataloging-in-Publication Data

Names: Girgenti, Richard H., author. | Hedley, Timothy P., author.
Title: The new era of regulatory enforcement : a comprehensive guide for raising the bar to manage risk / Richard H. Girgenti and Timothy P. Hedley.
Description: New York : McGraw-Hill, [2016]
Identifiers: LCCN 2015051014| ISBN 9781259584596 (alk. paper) | ISBN 1259584593 (alk. paper)
Subjects: LCSH: Fraud—Prevention. | Corporations—Corrupt practices—Prevention. | Trade regulation. | Consumer protection.
Classification: LCC HV6691 .G57 2016 | DDC 363.25/963—dc23 LC record available at http://lccn.loc.gov/2015051014

McGraw-Hill Education books are available at special quantity discounts to use as premiums and sales promotions or for use in corporate training programs. To contact a representative, please e-mail us at bulksales@mheducation.com.

This book represents the views of the authors only and does not necessarily represent the views or professional advice of KPMG LLP.

Contents

About the Editors/Authors

Richard H. Girgenti, Principal, KPMG

Rich Girgenti is the U.S. and Americas leader for KPMG LLP's Forensic Advisory Services and a member of the firm's Global Forensic Steering Group. He has more than 40 years of experience, both nationally and globally, conducting investigations; helping clients assess, design, and implement compliance programs; and providing fraud risk management advisory services to public and private corporations, as well as federal and state government entities and not-for-profit organizations.

Rich has served as a member of the board of directors for KPMG LLP and the Americas region. He has chaired the board's Governance Task Force, as well as the Professional Practice, Ethics and Compliance committees.

Prior to joining KPMG, Rich held a number of high-level legal and law enforcement positions. He served as New York State Director of Criminal Justice and Commissioner of the Division of Criminal Justice Services, where he oversaw and coordinated the policies and initiatives of all the state's criminal justice agencies and worked closely with all federal and state law enforcement agencies. He is a former veteran state prosecutor in the Office of the Manhattan District Attorney, where he handled investigations, trials, and appeals in both the state and federal courts, including investigations and prosecutions of white-collar, violent, and major narcotics organized crime cases.

Rich holds a bachelor's degree from Seton Hall University and a J.D. from Georgetown University Law Center. He is a Certified Fraud Examiner.

Rich publishes extensively on a wide range of criminal justice, white-collar, and fraud-related topics. He lectures frequently and conducts training programs and workshops on all aspects of fraud investigations and on the evaluation, development, and implementation of integrity programs. Along with Tim Hedley, he is the co-author of *Managing the Risk of Fraud and Misconduct: Meeting the Challenges of a Global, Regulated, and Digital Environment* (The McGraw-Hill Companies, Inc., March 2011).

Timothy P. Hedley, Partner, KPMG

Tim Hedley is a partner in KPMG's Forensic practice where he serves as global lead for the firm's Fraud Risk Management network. He provides clients with a wide range of forensic services by assisting with the prevention of, detection of, and response to fraud and misconduct. Tim also directs the development of methodologies and tools to assess the effectiveness of anti-fraud, corporate compliance, and integrity programs for multinational business organizations.

Tim has significant experience working with both public and private companies across a broad range of industries to respond to allegations of fraud or misconduct, including, among others, allegations involving earnings management, counterfeiting, bribery and kickbacks, construction, potential Ponzi schemes, and employee theft. He conducts fraud and compliance risk assessment and designs and conducts fraud awareness and compliance training programs. Tim assists clients with benchmarking their anti-fraud and compliance efforts against recognized industry practices and with designing, implementing, and evaluating corporate fraud investigative units. He also coordinates detailed internal audit testing of identified fraud, compliance, and integrity risk areas, including, among other areas, cash, FCPA, conflicts of interest, equal treatment, and antitrust.

Tim has served on KPMG's Legal and Compliance Committee, chairing the Code of Conduct task force and the Investigative Process Enhancement task force.

Tim is a Certified Public Accountant and a Certified Fraud Examiner and is certified in financial forensics. He holds a bachelor's degree from Siena College and a master's degree from the State University of New York at Albany, both in accounting. He completed his Ph.D. in public management (accounting and control) from Rockefeller College, State University of New York at Albany.

Tim is an adjunct associate professor at Fordham University. He publishes and lectures extensively on fraud, misconduct, and compliance-related topics.

Contributors

The authors would like to thank the following individuals for their invaluable contributions.

Sara Jacobs Beard
Richard J. Bergin
Laurence Birnbaum-Sarcy
John F. Caruso
Regina G. Cavaliere
Ori Ben-Chorin
Joy Cohen
Nicholas D'Ambrosio
Kelly A. Dynes
Einar B. Gitterman
Laurie M. Hatten-Boyd
Nigel Holloway
Jack C. Lenzi
Melinda M. Lesko
Karen A. Lynch
Sean P. Macdonald
Mary A. Mallery
Amy S. Matsuo
Brian J. McCann

Jonathan Meyer
Marc L. Miller
Glen E. Moyers
Pamela J. Parizek
Teresa A. Pesce
Nathan B. Ploener
Charles A. Riepenhoff
Michael S. Rudnick
Cliff R. Saffron
Mark C. Scallon
Howard A. Scheck
Jennifer A. Shimek
Joel E. Simkins
Karen S. Staines
Charlie M. Steele
Adam C. Susser
Kathy Tench
Gurhan Uslubas
Richard L. Zimmerer

Authors' Acknowledgments

When we decided to work on a second book to discuss and analyze the new era of regulatory enforcement, we knew, with the benefit of our experience working on our first book, *Managing the Risk of Fraud and Misconduct,* that we were embarking on a daunting task and would need to rely on the help of many others if we were to fulfill our ambition. As with our first book, we were fortunate to be able to draw upon a team of subject matter experts from KPMG to share their expertise and experience serving our clients to author many of the book chapters. They, in turn, were supported by an even larger number of KPMG professionals who working under constant deadlines, often late into the evening after work and on weekends, tirelessly and selflessly helped with the research, drafting and editing of this book. We could not have completed this book without their efforts and we cannot adequately express our gratitude to them. We have listed all of the authors and contributors in the list of contributors and attempted to acknowledge them as well in each of the chapters.

In addition to these terrific professionals, there were a number of others whose exceptional efforts and contributions were critical to the completion of this book and we wish to acknowledge separately their special contributions.

To begin, particular thanks is due to Ori Ben-Chorin who was a critical part of this effort from the beginning as he was for our first book. Ori played a critical role in moving the book from a concept to a chapter structure framing the overall approach of the book. Ori's expertise in compliance was critical to drafting the chapter that provides a framework for raising the bar to manage the risks in the new era of regulatory enforcement.

Nigel Holloway deserves our acknowledgment and appreciation as well. Nigel supported our efforts in editing and proofreading each of the chapters and assisting with the research. Nigel also provided critical thinking, often asking the basic questions that we needed to answer to bring our ideas to light.

A very special debt of gratitude is owed to Joy Cohen. We knew immediately when Joy skeptically asked if we really intended to put the time and effort into a second book that we were indeed willing, but only under one condition— and that condition was that we could persuade Joy to provide the incredible support on this book as she had with our first book. Once she was on board, we knew we could get the book done. Day in and day out, Joy relentlessly followed up with the chapter authors, kept the drum beating to ensure that we would meet our various deadlines, served as our liaison with our publisher, proofread all of the chapters, and arranged the numerous calls, meetings, and brainstorming sessions required to bring this project from start to completion. In short, there would be no book without Joy.

Finally, we want to acknowledge our appreciation to our families and their willingness to tolerate once again the late nights and lost weekends and holidays required to complete this book. Thank you, Catherine, Matthew, Christopher and Amy Girgenti, and Grant and Mason Hedley for not giving up on us. We promise that we will think long and hard before embarking again on an endeavor of this magnitude.

Richard and Tim

Introduction

Richard H. Girenti

In 2011, Tim Hedley and I, with the help of many highly experienced forensic professionals at KPMG, completed a book titled *Managing the Risk of Fraud and Misconduct: Meeting the Challenges of a Global, Regulated, and Digital Environment*.[1] The book was intended to serve as a practical primer on a variety of forms of corporate fraud and misconduct, providing a framework for an effective compliance program and a model for managing the risk of fraud and misconduct. It was written for a wide audience that included board members, C-level executives, managers, auditors, compliance professionals and others responsible for, and interested in, maintaining the integrity of an organization.

As we were completing the book, the U.S. Congress passed, and the president signed, two historic pieces of legislation, the Patient Protection and Affordable Care Act (PPACA, popularly known as Obamacare) and the Dodd-Frank Wall Street Reform and Consumer Protection Act (Dodd-Frank). At the same time, a wave of reforms swept through a number of industries, especially financial services, marking the dawn of a new era of aggressive government enforcement. With the ink barely dry, the implications of these new laws and reforms were yet to be determined.

We noted at the time that much had happened in the first decade of the twenty-first century before these new laws and reforms were put in place. There was the passage, in 2001, of the USA Patriot Act, which, among other things, changed the way the government attempted to address terrorist financing and money laundering. The Sarbanes-Oxley Act of 2002 established necessary reforms in the wake of a financial reporting crisis. There was a renewed focus on global corruption, with the stronger enforcement of the U.S. Foreign Corrupt

Practices Act (FCPA, passed in 1977) and the adoption of anti-bribery legislation around the world. Enhancements were made in 2004 and 2010 to the
Federal Organizational Sentencing Guidelines. These placed the responsibility
on corporate executives and boards to ensure that organizations have a culture of
integrity and that compliance programs were designed and operated effectively.

Despite these measures, it became quickly apparent that the first decade of
this century would not end with a dance to celebrate the success of corporate
reform. As we noted in 2011, much of the progress that was made in the area
of corporate governance and integrity was soon overshadowed by the worst
economic downturn in 75 years. After the financial crisis meltdown, fresh
debates emerged over what had caused this crisis and how it had gone unnoticed
or unmanaged, or perhaps both. This debate led to new legislation and more
aggressive enforcement efforts, creating a new era of regulation and enforcement
that goes far beyond the financial sector.

In the past few years, government enforcement has reached unprecedented
levels. We have witnessed the demise of such storied institutions as Bear Stearns
and Lehman Brothers, the takeover by the government of AIG, record fines and
penalties for nearly every major financial institution, from Citigroup, JPMorgan
Chase, BNP Paribas, and HSBC, to pharmaceutical giants, such as Pfizer and
GSK, and to global energy companies, such as BP, and many others. The list
includes many of the most respected companies in the United States and abroad.
Of the top 100 companies worldwide by revenue, 20 of them paid fines totaling
$72 billion in the 45 month period ending September 2015.[2]

In this book we have, once again, called upon a number of experienced
subject matter professionals at KPMG to help the reader understand the new
regulatory and enforcement landscape and how it has evolved since the publication of *Managing the Risk of Fraud and Misconduct*. What we have witnessed
since our last book is nothing less than a seismic shift in the role of enforcement,
with more aggressive government enforcement efforts and tactics. At the same
time, a wide range of local, state, federal, and global agencies have established
enforcement jurisdiction, often bringing parallel proceedings on the same set of
transactions and incidents, resulting in record fines and penalties.

Combined with the speed and volume of regulatory change over the past
15 years, there has been a proliferation of digital data, the evolution of new tools
and techniques to manage and analyze data, reliance upon the Internet and
social media to conduct business, and the availability of a range of new technologies. It therefore comes as little surprise that the risks now faced by organizations
are unprecedented. The bar by which the integrity of an organization is judged
has never been higher.

Our objective in the following pages is to help the reader deal with this
heightened level of risk by answering some important questions:

1. What are some of the more significant areas of risk that individuals and companies face with the dizzying array of laws and regulations enacted in the past decade and a half?
2. What are the policies driving the increased enforcement activity, and what are the government's expectations for organizational compliance and integrity?
3. What are the tools and techniques deployed by the government to identify, investigate, and ensure organizational compliance?
4. What steps can prudent and diligent organizations take to prevent, detect, and, as necessary, respond to the regulatory risks that are the heightened focus of enforcement activity?

To accomplish these objectives, we have not attempted to identify all conceivable risks that companies face, but rather, we have selected nine areas that, in our view, have dominated the enforcement landscape. Each of these nine risk areas is the subject of an individual chapter.

In Chapters 1 and 2, Tim Hedley and I attempt to develop a common understanding of the new regulatory enforcement landscape and a compliance framework for managing regulatory risk, resulting from the changed enforcement environment.

In Chapter 3 on bribery and corruption, Pam Parizek discusses the evolution of enforcement, both in the United States and globally, in the area of anti-bribery and corruption. Specifically, she analyzes the laws and approaches being taken in four jurisdictions, the United States, the United Kingdom, Brazil, and China. The aim is to identify a global approach to compliance that may be simpler and more effective than a country-by-country approach.

Chapter 4 is devoted to money laundering. Since the terrorist attacks of 9/11, the subject of terrorist financing has been shaped by the war on terror. Here, Terry Pesce and John Caruso discuss the continuing evolution of enforcement activity surrounding a company's anti-money laundering (AML) program and the severity of regulatory responses when programmatic weaknesses are identified. Of particular note is the expansion of AML scrutiny beyond traditional financial institutions into new areas such as the alternative investment industry, investment advisors, money service businesses, cyber currency companies, innovative payment technologies, and retail companies offering financing. The chapter also discusses the four pillars of an effective AML compliance program.

Chapter 5 covers the subject of economic and trade sanctions, which is closely related to AML regulations. In light of events in North Korea, Iran, Cuba, the Ukraine, and Russia, there can be no question that the subject of economic and trade sanctions is an arm of foreign policy. In this chapter, Charlie Steele discusses sanctions implementation and enforcement in the United States by providing a history, as well as a forward-looking perspective, of sanctions in the United States. He then moves to a discussion of the unique efforts a company must make to prevent, detect, and effectively respond to violations.

In Chapter 6, the subject of market manipulation and insider trading is covered by Richard Bergin, Nathan Ploener, and Tim Hedley. This includes a broad discussion of the topics of market abuse that have dominated the headlines in the wake of the recent financial crisis. Perhaps no area has garnered more attention since the passage of Dodd-Frank than the government's efforts to curb insider trading and the manipulation of markets, most notably in the vigorous prosecution of banks and individuals responsible for the fraudulent manipulation of LIBOR (London Interbank Offered Rate) and forex (foreign exchange).

The chapter discusses how these enforcement efforts may intensify as government agencies expand their investigations into other areas of commodity trading. The chapter also provides recommendations regarding the ways in which companies may develop an effective compliance program to prevent, detect, and respond to the risks of market abuse and insider trading.

Chapter 7 focuses on the topic of financial reporting fraud. More than a decade has passed since the financial reporting scandals of the early 2000s. While the instances of enforcement activity in the area of financial reporting fraud declined steadily since just prior to the financial crisis, the U.S. Securities and Exchange Commission (SEC) in 2014–15, in a number of pronouncements, has expressed its intention to refocus on this area. As a result, there were increases in 2014 in accounting and disclosure related enforcement actions for the first time since 2011. And, there have been continuing increases in 2015. In this chapter, Howard Scheck and Tim Hedley take a fresh look at the issue of financial reporting fraud. Using a current perspective, they identify the ways in which companies may be at risk as a result of the new enforcement focus and how they can shape their compliance efforts to manage the risk.

The topic of consumer financial fraud is covered in Chapter 8. The financial crisis unearthed a large number of abusive and unethical business practices in the area of consumer financing, from fraud in the origination and servicing of mortgages to the issuing and financing of student loans. Many of these abusive practices are cited as factors contributing to the financial crisis. Dodd-Frank attempted, among other things, to address these abusive practices by creating a new agency, the Consumer Financial Protection Bureau (CFPB), and providing it with sweeping new enforcement powers. In this chapter, Amy Matsuo looks at the history of government activity in protecting consumers from unfair, deceptive, and abusive practices. She discusses the authority, implications, and activities of the CFPB since its inception in 2010, as well as the role of other government agencies. As with the earlier chapters, Chapter 8 covers in detail the sort of compliance activities that are required to manage the risk of consumer fraud.

Curbing offshore tax evasion has become a government priority over the past few years, and Chapter 9, authored by Laurence Birnbaum-Sarcy, is devoted to understanding the regulatory focus in this area. Tax evasion is not a new area of government enforcement. However, the vigor of recent enforcement activity with regard to offshore tax evasion has made it abundantly clear that this is a high priority for the government, with implications for individuals and financial institutions. The level of risk has grown exponentially with the passage in 2010 of the Foreign Account Tax Compliance Act (FATCA). This imposes a new tax reporting and withholding regime that ultimately affects bank secrecy laws in the United States and elsewhere. The chapter discusses the compliance challenges faced by financial institutions and offers a course of action that these institutions should take to mitigate the risk of offshore tax evasion.

In Chapters 10 and 11, we take a slightly different approach from the one adopted in Chapters 3 through 9. We examine two industries, healthcare and life sciences, and some of the most important risks that these heavily regulated sectors face from government enforcement activity. We discuss a variety of risks in these industries rather than looking at a specific risk area.

In Chapter 10, Glen Moyers explains that the PPACA raised the level of regulatory scrutiny in the healthcare industry, but that the attempt to curtail fraudulent payments in the industry is not a new phenomenon. This chapter focuses on the risks and challenges faced by healthcare providers as pressure increases to deliver higher-quality care at lower costs in a changing regulatory environment. The chapter then provides insights into how healthcare providers can prevent, detect, and respond to the risk of noncompliance in an environment of significant enforcement activity.

The life sciences industry has been the subject of much of the enforcement focus over the past few years. In Chapter 11, Mark Scallon, Regina Cavaliere, and Rick Zimmerer discuss the different practices in life sciences that have been the subject of enforcement activity. These enforcement actions and the subsequent settlement agreements have fundamentally reshaped the business practices and compliance programs in the industry. This chapter will discuss how the industry's practices have been reshaped and the ways in which the industry is working to avoid these and other risks in the future.

The challenges facing companies today in the new era of regulatory enforcement have never been greater. While we do not have a crystal ball that will enable us to predict the next new crisis or event and what it will bring, we can say with a high degree of certainty that companies can be better prepared than they have been in the past. This book is intended for a range of people, from members of corporate boards and C-suite executives to others within an organization who are responsible for compliance and risk. It is also intended for those who are tasked with providing assurance on the effectiveness of a company's internal controls, whether as part of the external or internal audit function. And, of course, it should provide a useful guide for others who may want to know more about the risks organizations face in this new era of regulatory enforcement. We hope that this book will improve our readers' understanding of these risks and provide them with the insights and approaches necessary to respond to these risks. The simple imperative is that getting it right will not only preserve the hard-earned value of the company but also help improve its chances for sustainable business success, for the benefit of all of its stakeholders, whether they are employees, shareholders, customers, or the public at large.

Richard H. Girgenti

Chapter 1

The New Era of Regulatory Enforcement

Richard H. Girgenti

The New Regime

Since the outset of the twenty-first century, there has been a relentless flow of events and circumstances that has given birth to a new regulatory and enforcement landscape. Over the past decade and a half, we have had front row seats to the launching of the war on terror in the wake of the 9/11 attack; the financial reporting crisis of the early 2000s; the changing dynamics of emerging global economies; the financial recession of 2008 with the resulting economic uncertainty and lingering global financial instability; healthcare reform and escalating costs; and the proliferation of digital data, social media, and cyber attacks. These events, each in their own unique way, have profoundly altered the government's approach to regulation and enforcement.

Fueled by a powerful mix of constant media attention, growing resentment toward business and financial executives, and ever-increasing regulation, companies in today's global economy find themselves in a continuously evolving and increasingly complex, volatile, and risky regulatory environment. None of this has been lost on those who function in the C-suite or on corporate boards. The new terrain has rapidly changed the way executives think about and conduct business. Not surprisingly, a 2015 survey[1] of U.S. CEOs by KPMG found that global economic growth and the regulatory environment are the two issues that have the most impact on their companies.

As organizations attempt to navigate this changing regulatory landscape, they face new risks and uncertainty resulting from a new regime of government enforcement that is now global in nature and unprecedented in its aggressiveness. With broader mandates and authority, enforcement agencies are employing new strategies, tactics, and weapons and are using the latest technology tools. Those organizations that fail to effectively manage the risks presented by this new regime find themselves facing harsher penalties and sanctions than anything experienced before.

The list of billion-dollar fines levied by regulatory authorities continues to lengthen. In 2014, Bank of America agreed to pay a record settlement of $16.5 billion with the U.S. Department of Justice (DOJ), resulting from mortgage lending abuses that arose from its acquisition of Countrywide Financial in 2008 and Merrill Lynch in the following year. This settlement, the largest ever, was a capstone to a legal journey that can be traced back to the dark days of the financial crisis.

In January 2016, Goldman Sachs agreed to a $5 billion settlement resulting in the largest regulatory penalty in its history, and resolving U.S. and state claims stemming from the firm's sale of mortgage bonds heading into the financial crisis.[2] In November 2013, JPMorgan Chase agreed to a $13 billion settlement for U.S. mortgage mis-selling. Other financial services settlements include BNP Paribas ($9 billion for U.S. sanctions violations); Citigroup ($7 billion for misselling mortgage-backed bonds); Credit Suisse ($2.5 billion for aiding tax fraud); HSBC ($1.9 billion for money laundering lapses); and UBS ($1.5 billion for manipulation of the London Interbank Offered Rate—LIBOR).

Fines and penalties are only part of the cost to the financial sector. The Conduct Costs Project, an independent research foundation, estimated that in the five years to the end of 2013, the total legal cost of misconduct by 10 major international banks totaled $250 billion, after including legal fees as well as fines and other penalties.[3] As a further indication of the aggressiveness of regulators in the past few years, five banks were the subject of criminal charges and agreed to plead guilty to manipulating the global foreign exchange market, an almost unprecedented outcome.

The financial services sector was not the only industry to be heavily fined. The array of billion-dollar penalties since 2012 includes life sciences company GlaxoSmithKline (GSK), which paid $3 billion for the unlawful promotion of some of its drugs and failure to report safety data. Johnson & Johnson (J&J) agreed to pay a $2.2 billion fine to resolve criminal and civil allegations relating to three prescription drugs. In the energy sector, BP, in July 2015, agreed to pay $18.7 billion to settle all federal and state claims arising from the 2010 Deepwater Horizon oil spill.[4] This included a civil penalty of $5.5 billion, the largest pollution settlement under the federal Clean Water Act. The settlement added at least $10 billion to the roughly $44 billion BP had already incurred in legal and cleanup costs.

The risks of regulatory enforcement are particularly acute in highly regulated sectors such as financial services, healthcare, and energy. There are, though, certain regulatory regimes, such as anti-bribery and corruption, anti-money laundering (AML), and trade sanctions that affect all industries where enforcement is not just a national effort, but is the subject of long-arm jurisdiction and global cooperation among enforcement authorities. Examples of international enforcement include EU fines of a number of banks totaling $2.3 billion for manipulating the European Interbank Offered Rate. Also, Swiss and British regulators have worked together to investigate collusion in the foreign exchange markets. In charging Hewlett-Packard with Foreign Corrupt Practices Act (FCPA) violations in 2014, U.S. Securities and Exchange Commission (SEC) chair Mary Jo White acknowledged the "great support" the commission had received from regulators in Australia, Guernsey, Liechtenstein, Norway, Canada, Switzerland, and the UK.[5]

The War on Terror

Events since 2000, many unforeseen, have been drivers over the past decade and a half of new laws and regulations and a re-ordering of priorities for enforcement authorities. A shock wave was started at the beginning of the past decade with the September 2001 attack on the Twin Towers in New York City. With the onset of the war on terror and terrorist financing, a new regime of AML enforcement activity began that extended far beyond the original intent of the USA Patriot Act, designed primarily as a tool to fight terrorism.

The enforcement of the AML laws has continued unabated since then. In the early days of the USA Patriot Act, enforcement was focused on discrete programmatic deficiencies, such as failures to report suspicious activities. It has since grown to become a steady and institutionalized regime of enforcement that challenges every aspect of a firm's AML compliance program, including oversight, customer due diligence, monitoring, reporting, and independent testing. Just as significantly, AML regulators have broadened their focus from traditional banks to include the alternative investment industry, money service businesses, investment advisors, cyber-currency companies, innovative payment technologies, and retail companies offering financing.

The post 9/11 enforcement regime, designed to combat terrorist financing, has been a two-front attack. In addition to AML enforcement, government regulators unleashed the power of economic and trade sanctions against individuals, entities, and countries suspected of terrorist ties. A time-honored weapon of foreign policy was now deployed by the U.S. Department of the

Treasury's little-known Office of Foreign Assets Control (OFAC) as part of the war on terror. The result has been that many U.S. companies (e.g., Weatherford International and American Express) and foreign firms (e.g., BNP Paribas, ING, and HSBC) have found themselves the target of enforcement efforts and subjected to heavy fines and penalties. The risks of economic and trade sanctions are not likely to go away any time soon and have kept companies on their toes, as events in the Ukraine, Russia, Iran, North Korea, and other rogue nations have required organizations to constantly reevaluate their risk profiles.

The Financial Reporting Crisis of 2001-02 and the 2008-09 Financial Recession

Just as the United States and the rest of the world were coming to grips with the reality of global terrorism, a new event, the financial reporting crisis of 2001-02, erupted within weeks of 9/11 and shook people's confidence in the capital markets as profoundly as the Twin Towers attack had shaken confidence in U.S. national security. There was a bubble created by the confluence of earnings pressure, grey areas of accounting, and rationalizations that justified reporting high earnings at all cost. When it burst, it brought down companies and individuals whose successes were too good to be true. The result was the passage of new laws and regulations, most notably the U.S. Sarbanes-Oxley Act and amendments to the U.S. Federal Sentencing Guidelines for Organizational Defendants (the FS Guidelines). These measures were designed to revamp fundamental principles of corporate governance, risk management, compliance, and practices around financial reporting. Along with the passage of Sarbanes-Oxley came a wave of enforcement actions involving both companies and individuals accused of an array of wrong-doing including, among other forms of misconduct, improper revenue recognition, earnings management, stock options backdating, and misstated loan reserves.

These and other reforms, and the resulting onslaught of enforcement activity that followed, began a process of rebuilding confidence that we had turned the corner into a new era of improvements in corporate governance that would protect the public from future corporate misdeeds. That is, until the next shock wave hit—the dramatic economic downturn of 2008-09—that nearly reached Great Depression proportions and once again called into question the soundness of U.S. laws, regulations, and economic policies, as well as the reliability of government enforcement efforts. With the economic recession came the unraveling of massive and well-publicized Ponzi schemes, such as those perpetrated by Bernie Madoff and Allen Stanford, further eroding public confidence. And, as with the previous events, the implications were felt around the world. With the downward spiral of stock prices and home values and the loss of jobs, anger and resentment toward those believed responsible turned to a fevered pitch that still lingers in the public discourse, whether in the media or on the campaign trail, further fueling demands for new laws and regulations and setting the agenda for more aggressive enforcement.

"Too big to fail" became the catchphrase in the days following the start of the financial crisis. Nonetheless, historic institutions such as Bear Stearns, Lehman Brothers, AIG, Merrill Lynch, Wachovia, and others collapsed, were sold off, or turned to government bailouts for their very survival. As with the financial reporting crisis of a few years earlier, Congress and the president were quick to react. Congress passed the Emergency Economic Stabilization Act of 2008, authorizing trillions of dollars to shore up the economy, stabilize weakened financial institutions, and purchase troubled assets. A new watchdog, the Office of the Special Inspector General for the Troubled Asset Relief Program (TARP), was created with enforcement powers to oversee part of the program. Soon after, Congress passed the American Recovery and Reinvestment Act of 2009, which created new federal programs and authorized hundreds of billions of dollars in new federal funding. There was also the Fraud Enforcement and Recovery Act (FERA) of 2009, which was intended to strengthen regulatory controls and help prevent and detect potential fraud, waste, and abuse.

All of these new laws, regulations, and enforcement activity were just the opening act for the most sweeping and comprehensive financial regulatory reform since the Great Depression, the Dodd-Frank Wall Street Reform and Consumer Protection Act (Dodd-Frank).[6] This historic piece of legislation once again dramatically altered the regulatory landscape. In addition to many significant changes to the structure of federal financial regulation and wide-ranging provisions covering numerous reforms from corporate governance to executive compensation, Dodd-Frank also greatly altered the enforcement landscape. It contained a number of provisions, both procedural and substantive, that were designed to facilitate enforcement of the securities laws and expand the scope of remedies available to regulators.

The enforcement powers of two agencies, the SEC and the Commodities and Futures Trading Commission (CFTC), in particular, were greatly increased. One such change was in the area of whistleblowers. Dodd-Frank established monetary awards for whistleblowers in any SEC or CFTC enforcement action resulting in a sanction of more than $1,000,000, with award amounts determined as a percentage of the recovery. It also created a private right of action for whistleblowers against employers who retaliate. The CFTC's mission was also expanded, for the first time, to include oversight of the swaps market.[7]

Dodd-Frank also strengthened the SEC's enforcement powers in several key respects. It enabled the SEC to impose monetary penalties under certain circumstances against any person, rather than just regulated entities, in cease-and-desist proceedings. And it expanded federal court jurisdiction for the SEC to bring enforcement actions against persons for activity outside of the United States when an individual takes "significant steps in furtherance" of a violation and the conduct has a foreseeable impact within the United States.

The result of these post–financial crisis laws and regulations has been nothing short of dramatic. The passage of Dodd-Frank and the new powers of the SEC and the CFTC opened the door for a new era of regulatory enforcement focused on restoring the integrity of the capital markets. Since then there has been aggressive enforcement against market abuses and manipulation and insider trading. More particularly, the CFTC, with its newfound enforcement powers, became a major player in enforcement actions for manipulation of LIBOR and the foreign exchange rate (forex), along with other agencies with jurisdiction including the SEC and DOJ. There was also a new round of investigations into the possible manipulation of precious metal prices.

The first wave of investigations and enforcement actions focused on activities of banks falsely inflating or deflating their average interest rates so as to profit from trades. In the United States, LIBOR is used as a benchmark in the derivatives markets, thereby bringing the CFTC into the picture. What followed was one of the most expensive scandals to hit Wall Street since the financial crisis. By the time the dust had settled, as of May 2015, global banks had paid more than $9 billion in fines to U.S. and European regulators. More than 100 traders or brokers have been fired or suspended, 21 have been charged, and several bank executives have been forced out.[8]

The second wave of investigations focused on the manipulation of foreign exchange rates and led to guilty pleas by four global banks: Citigroup, JPMorgan Chase, Barclays, and Royal Bank of Scotland (RBS).[9] Although it was not charged criminally, a fifth bank, UBS, was also accused of foreign currency manipulation. The accusations resulted in the DOJ voiding an earlier non-prosecution agreement (NPA) and requiring UBS to plead guilty to a previous charge of LIBOR manipulation. A sixth bank, Bank of America, while not found guilty, agreed to a fine of $204 million for unsafe practices in foreign markets. All told, the six banks were fined $5.6 billion for their role in the rigging of foreign exchange markets. This was in addition to fines paid in November 2014, when the CFTC fined Citigroup and JPMorgan Chase $310 million each, RBS and UBS $290 million each, and HSBC $275 million for their roles in attempting to manipulate global foreign exchange benchmark rates to benefit their traders' positions.

Also in the past year, the CFTC and DOJ launched a third wave of new investigations of 10 major financial institutions, including Barclays, Bank of Nova Scotia, Deutsche Bank, Credit Suisse, Goldman Sachs, HSBC, JPMorgan Chase, UBS, Société Générale, and Standard Bank, for possible price-fixing in the precious metal markets[10] (which includes gold, silver, platinum, and palladium) for which banks historically set the market.

In addition to these new areas of enforcement activity, government agencies directed their attention to those issues that played a large role in the financial and subprime crisis. Under the auspices of the Financial Fraud Enforcement Task Force and its Residential Mortgage-Backed Securities (RMBS) Working Group, recoveries exceeding $36 billion have been made, with the largest settlement of nearly $17 billion with the Bank of America. There were also investigations related to the packaging, marketing, sale, arrangement, structuring, and issuance of RMBS, collateralized debt obligations (CDOs), and banking practices concerning the underwriting and origination of mortgage loans, all or some believed to be the cause of the financial meltdown of 2008-09. Among the settlements arising from these investigations were ones with Goldman Sachs ($5 billion), Morgan Stanley ($2.6 billion), JPMorgan Chase ($13 billion), and Citigroup ($7 billion).

Not all of the heightened enforcement activity in recent years can be traced to the factors that brought about the financial crisis. Prosecutors and enforcement agencies have also turned their attention to a number of important insider trading cases, perhaps as a way of assuring the public that, regardless of their form, breaches of fiduciary duty in the financial sector would be taken seriously.

In its 2014 and 2015 annual reports, the SEC continued to remind the investment community that insider trading remained a high priority, because illegal tipping or trading undermines "the level playing field that is fundamental to the integrity and fair functioning of the capital markets." Over the past six years, the SEC and DOJ have brought hundreds of insider trading cases against entities and individuals, including financial professionals, corporate insiders, attorneys, and others from all walks of life.

In an effort to address other abuses that led to the financial crisis, and perhaps one of the most significant outgrowths of the crisis, was the creation by Dodd-Frank of the Consumer Financial Protection Bureau (CFPB). Assuming the oversight of consumer compliance from a patchwork of different federal agencies, the CFPB was created as a watchdog empowered to write rules for consumer protection governing all companies offering consumer financial services or products. These companies include most banks, mortgage lenders, and credit card and private student loan companies, as well as payday lenders.

The CFPB was also given the authority to examine and enforce consumer finance regulations for banks and credit unions with assets of more than $10 billion and all mortgage-related businesses, payday lenders, student lenders, and other non-bank financial companies, such as debt collectors and consumer reporting agencies. The CFPB also oversees the enforcement of federal laws intended to ensure the fair, equitable, and nondiscriminatory access to credit for individuals and communities.

Beginning in 2010, the CFPB wasted no time in getting to work. The agency's purview has been sweeping and has targeted debt collectors, credit card issuers, mortgage businesses, student loan issuers, and banks from large to small. In his July 2015 testimony[11] before the Senate Committee on Banking, Housing, and Urban Affairs, CFPB Director Richard Cordray proudly boasted that in the five years since the passage of Dodd-Frank and the four years since the CFTC opened, it had brought enforcement actions that resulted in more than $10 billion in relief for more than 17 million consumers and that its supervisory actions had resulted in financial institutions providing more than $178 million in redress to more than 1.6 million consumers.

Enforcement actions have targeted misconduct and illegal practices in the mortgage industry, deceptive practices in the marketing and enrollment of credit cards, unfair billing, and illegal debt collection. Among other areas, actions have been taken against payday lenders and installment lenders for unlawful lending and collection practices.[12]

Evolving Risks and Shifting Enforcement Priorities

As part of the new initiatives led by SEC Chair White, which she has referred to as the "broken windows" strategy[13]—fashioned after the strategy that was used to reduce crime in New York City in the early to mid-1990s by focusing on low-level crimes as a means to reduce more serious crimes—the SEC filed 135[14] accounting related enforcement actions in the fiscal year ended in September 2015, a 41 percent increase over the 96[15] brought in 2014 and nearly double the accounting related enforcement actions brought in 2013.[16] Concededly, these new cases were smaller in scale and mostly involved less egregious conduct than the accounting scandals of the early 2000s.

As part of this renewed initiative, the SEC has used new technologies, and in 2012 it deployed a computerized system designed to root out accounting fraud. To drive this initiative, the SEC set up a task force in 2013 to identify and prosecute financial reporting misconduct.[17] There can be little doubt that the SEC is putting more resources into pursuing accounting fraud and is looking into an array of potential accounting fraud cases. These range from how companies recognize revenue to how they value assets and other obligations, and whether disclosures properly inform investors.

These new initiatives resulted in sanctions involving the largest pharmacy healthcare provider in the United States, which settled allegations of misconduct including improper acquisition-related accounting adjustments that boosted reported earnings in 2009. Other significant SEC accounting fraud cases in the wake of the mortgage meltdown involved a $20 million settlement with the Bank of America in which the bank admitted failing to disclose uncertainties about potential higher costs related to mortgage repurchase claims, as part of its $16.5 billion mortgage settlement with the government. Diamond Foods paid $5 million as part of its settlement with the government for inflated earnings related to its failed recording of costs.

More recently in 2015, the SEC settled with a bank holding company charged with misrepresenting the value of the bank's loan portfolio to investors by failing to downgrade and impair delinquent loans that would not be repaid in full. Other settlements involved a $15 million fine for an online consumer finance company for manipulating company revenues and a $35 million settlement for a China-based advertising company accused of understating the company's valuation in connection with a management buy-out.

A renewed focus on financial reporting fraud and disclosures in 2014 and 2015 meant that both were record-breaking years for sanctions imposed by the SEC. During SEC Chair White's first full year in charge, the commission filed 755 enforcement actions and obtained orders for $4.1 billion in penalties and disgorgement.[18] In her second year, the SEC filed 807 enforcement actions covering a wide range of misconduct and obtained orders totaling approximately $4.2 billion in disgorgements and penalties.[19] This strongly suggests that financial reporting fraud was part of a much broader expansion of enforcement activity.

Shifts in Public Policy Priorities

Shifts in public policies resulting from changes in administration and shifts in domestic priorities have also played a significant role since 2000 in defining enforcement agendas. Two examples of this are the focus since the financial crisis on rising government spending and debt, and the implications of health-care reform. The most obvious consequences of this focus have been the recent attention to offshore tax evasion as well as fraud, waste, and abuse in government spending, particularly government healthcare reimbursement programs.

The passage and signing into law of the Patient Protection and Affordable Care Act (PPACA) highlighted the provision of healthcare services in the United States. One of the revelations, already well known to providers and consumers of healthcare, was the escalating costs of healthcare, much of it financed by the government. An integral part of the government's efforts to implement health-care reform was its commitment to fight fraud, waste, and abuse in healthcare, even touting that its fight, spearheaded by the Department of Health and Human Services and the DOJ, "will continue to improve with the new tools and resources provided by the Affordable Care Act."[20]

In fiscal year 2014, the U.S. government spent $836 billion on healthcare, nearly two-thirds for Medicare.[21] By 2023, government-financed healthcare expenditure is projected to reach $2.5 trillion and account for 48 percent of national healthcare expenditure. In an attempt to curb these escalating costs, the government has placed a high priority on identifying fraud, waste, and abuse in the provision of healthcare services, with an aggressive regime of enforcement designed not only to recoup misappropriated funds, but also to levy fines and penalties. The government is relying upon an arsenal of laws and regulations, including the False Claims Act (FCA), which allows private citizens to become whistleblowers and bring civil actions on behalf of the government and to share in any recovery; the Anti-Kickback Statute, which prohibits drug and device companies from providing incentives to healthcare professionals and organizations for prescribing their drugs or using their devices; and the Stark Law, which limits certain physician referrals. The government's efforts have led to more than $14 billion in recoveries under the FCA alone.

In recent years, the life sciences industry, like the healthcare sector, has also come under intense government scrutiny for the misuse of taxpayer dollars, particularly in the pricing of life sciences products that are subject to government reimbursement. Other public policy interests, such as the health and safety of patients, and the transparency and accountability for drugs and medical devices sold to the public, and often reimbursed by the government, have also been drivers of enforcement efforts in the life sciences industry.

In 2013, Johnson & Johnson (J&J) agreed to pay $2.2 billion to resolve criminal and civil liability arising from allegations relating to the promotion of prescription drugs for uses not approved as safe and effective by the Food and Drug Administration (FDA) (referred to as off-label promotions). The settlement also covered allegations that J&J paid kickbacks to physicians (e.g., paying for speaker programs for doctors to tout the purported benefits of certain drugs, defraying the cost of outpatient clinics to administer the drugs and with the resources and support to bill Medicare).

In announcing the settlement with J&J, then Attorney General Eric Holder emphasized the public policy considerations underlying the settlement, noting, "The conduct at issue in this case jeopardized the health and safety of patients and damaged the public trust." Assistant Attorney General for the DOJ's Civil Division Stuart F. Delery added, "As patients and consumers, we have a right to rely upon the claims drug companies make about their products. And, as taxpayers, we have a right to ensure that federal healthcare dollars are spent appropriately."[22]

Another way in which the government has attempted to address the growing fiscal deficit has been to recoup tax revenues lost in offshore tax havens. Bank secrecy laws in foreign jurisdictions have long provided safe havens for criminals, money launderers, and tax cheats to hide assets from the tax authorities. The result has been not only the loss of billions of dollars in tax revenues, but also a challenge to the enforcement of criminal laws against drug dealers and criminal organizations, among others, and to the effectiveness of AML efforts.

To address this problem, the Internal Revenue Service (IRS) and the Tax Division of the DOJ, along with U.S. Attorneys' Offices, have focused on foreign financial accounts used to evade U.S. taxes and reporting requirements. The United States has used a variety of tactics to pierce the veil of secrecy and anonymity associated with these accounts. The tactics include reliance on self-reporting requirements of the Bank Secrecy Act; lengthy and complex investigations; agreeing with foreign governments on a range of tax treaties and information exchanges; and enforcement actions against foreign banks.

The passage of the Foreign Account Tax Compliance Act (FATCA) in 2010 closed many of the gaps in prior laws and enforcement efforts. FATCA requires financial institutions outside the United States, including banks, brokerage firms, mutual funds, hedge funds, and certain insurance companies, to report information on financial accounts held by U.S. account holders to the IRS or face 30 percent taxes/penalties on withholdable payments received from U.S. sources.

The results of this focus on cross-border tax evasion have been telling. In the United States, more than 43,000 taxpayers joined a voluntary IRS disclosure program, revealing hidden offshore accounts, and paid $6 billion in back taxes, interest, and penalties.[23] In 2008, as a result of government investigations, UBS entered into a deferred prosecution agreement (DPA) with the DOJ, paid a $780 million fine, and turned over 4,700 accounts with U.S. client names that had not been disclosed to the IRS.

Despite this progress, the Senate Permanent Subcommittee on Investigations, Committee on Homeland Security and Governmental Affairs, in its report on Offshore Tax Evasion in February 2014, criticized the DOJ for not having moved more quickly against other Swiss banks and found that "U.S. law enforcement has failed to prosecute more than a dozen Swiss banks that facilitated U.S. tax evasion, failed to take legal action against thousands of U.S. persons whose names and hidden Swiss accounts were disclosed by UBS, and failed to utilize available U.S. legal means to obtain the names of tens of thousands of additional U.S. persons whose identities are still being concealed by the Swiss."[24] Notwithstanding the criticism, it appears that the DOJ Tax Division has been investigating scores of other Swiss banks regarding accounts held by U.S. citizens and in the second half of 2015, the DOJ entered into 75 NPAs and DPAs associated with the DOJ Tax Swiss Bank Program. More than $1 billion was recovered under the program.[25] Even more recently, Julius Baer announced an additional $547 million agreement in principle with the DOJ.[26]

Offshore tax evasion enforcement took on global dimensions with the release in August 2015 by the Organization for Economic Cooperation and

Development (OECD) of three reports.[27] The documents are intended to help governments and financial institutions implement the global standard for the automatic exchange of financial account information to combat offshore tax evasion.

Globalization

Over the past 20 years, we have witnessed a global shift in political and economic power away from the United States, in a phenomenon Fareed Zakaria has described as "the rise of the rest."[28] Among the drivers of enforcement priorities, the risk of doing business in emerging economies has created a new regime of enforcement that did not exist in the twentieth century. With accelerated globalization has come a growing recognition that corruption is endemic in many countries, especially in emerging markets, and that corruption has had a corrosive impact distorting worldwide competition.

Over the past decade, people have become more aware of the harm of corruption on the legitimacy of governments and international commerce. This has prompted efforts to curb the practice of bribery, particularly in the passage and enforcement of anti-bribery and corruption laws around the globe.

For more than two and a half decades since the passage of the FCPA in 1977, the United States stood virtually alone in criminalizing the bribery of foreign government officials, and there seemed to be little appetite in the United States, and virtually none outside of the United States, to prosecute this activity. But in 2004–05, all of this changed. The DOJ and SEC dusted off the FCPA and, with unprecedented vigor, started prosecuting companies and individuals who violated its provisions.

At the same time, dozens of foreign countries passed similar anti-corruption laws and stepped up their enforcement efforts. Perhaps most significantly, enforcement activities have ramped up as never before in Brazil (Embraer and Petrobras), China (GSK), and the EU (Yara International of Norway and SBM Offshore of the Netherlands). In November 2014, U.S. Assistant Attorney General Leslie Caldwell noted, "The global trend against foreign corruption continues to face many challenges, but the tide has turned." With enforcement actions taking place around the globe, there is strong evidence that an anti-corruption trend has been established, with little indication of it subsiding.

The United States continues to take the lead in its enforcement against corruption. While the number of U.S. enforcement actions has been stable in 2012–14 compared to its peak year in 2010, penalties of more than $1.5 billion in 2014 amounted to more than double the amount collected in 2013 and more than the previous three years combined.[29] Outside the United States, there were more enforcement actions in 2014 regarding the bribery of foreign officials than in any other year of the previous decade, other than in 2011.[30] Other notable recent trends include increased cross-border cooperation with foreign law enforcement; continued emphasis by the DOJ and the SEC on the benefits of self-reporting and cooperation; and a sustained focus on the prosecution of individuals, both U.S. and non-U.S. citizens.

Most notably in the past year, the Brazilian government's investigation of the state-run oil company, Petrobras, has dominated headlines, a firm sign that Brazil's 2013 Anti-Corruption Law will be enforced. In March 2015, the Brazilian Office of the Comptroller General, the chief federal enforcement authority for anti-corruption, announced that it had extended its probe and opened cases against 10 Brazilian construction companies doing business with Petrobras. At the same time, Brazil's Supreme Court approved investigations of 54 politicians allegedly involved in kickback schemes. In all, more than 200 companies and 80 individuals faced possible charges.[31] As of August 2015, there were 117 indictments, five politicians had been arrested, and criminal charges had been brought against 13 companies. It has been estimated that the total of all bribes amounted to nearly $3 billion.[32]

The New Era of Government Enforcement Strategies and Tactics

The new era of regulatory enforcement in the United States has been defined as much or more by government tactics as it has been by the areas that the government has chosen to pursue. These new tactics since 2000 are the result of not only a more aggressive enforcement posture, but also the passage of new laws that have expanded the authority of enforcement agencies and provided them with new tools to achieve their objectives. Also, new technologies, and the willingness and ability to deploy them, have added significantly to the enforcement arsenal.

Whistleblower Laws

The expanded use of whistleblowers has been a game changer in the new era of regulatory enforcement and has become a favored tool of the government.[33] To be sure, whistleblower laws have served as useful means to identify potential wrongdoing by incentivizing those with knowledge of such wrongdoing to report directly to the government. These laws have also served another important policy objective. They have created a strong incentive for corporations to shore up their internal reporting mechanisms so that potential whistleblowers will report potential wrongdoing internally through a company's compliance mechanisms.

As mentioned earlier, Dodd-Frank created strong incentives—10 to 30 percent of fines and penalties were more than $1 million—to encourage persons to report potential violations of the federal securities laws or of the Commodities Exchange Act to the SEC and the CFTC, respectively. Since the whistleblower program began in August 2011, the SEC has received more than 14,000 tips from whistleblowers. In fiscal year 2015, eight whistleblowers received more than $37 million, including an award of $30 million to a single whistleblower, the highest award to date under the program. The number of whistleblower tips has increased each year since the program's implementation, with a 30 percent increase from 2012 to 2015.[34]

A particular challenge for companies today is the effectiveness of their anti-retaliation policies and processes. The SEC has stated on numerous occasions that it is paying special attention to instances of retaliation against whistleblowers, even where the underlying whistleblower reports were later unsubstantiated. The SEC has also focused on confidentiality agreements with employees in severance agreements or other agreements attempting to prevent employees from coming forward to the SEC.[35] In April 2015, the SEC said that it had fined KBR, a Houston-based entity, for violating whistleblower protections by requiring "witnesses in certain internal investigations interviews to sign confidentiality agreements with language warning that they could face discipline and even be fired if they discussed matters with outside parties without the prior approval of KBR's legal department."[36]

Other government agencies have found whistleblower programs to be a valuable tool in their enforcement arsenal. Relying in large measure on the actions of private citizens to identify and report government fraud, the FCA has long been a key enforcement tool for the federal government in matters involving government contracts or other government expenditures. Many states and large cities have also enacted their own false claims laws.

In essence, the FCA provides for private citizens (whistleblowers) to file a qui tam civil complaint with the government. If the government decides to go forward with the qui tam action and is successful, the relator is entitled to receive 15 to 30 percent of the amount recovered by the government. This is an enormous incentive since violators of the FCA are liable for three times the amount that the government is defrauded and for civil penalties of $5,000 to $10,000 for each false claim.

The FCA was enacted in 1863 during the Civil War to address the problem of suppliers defrauding the Union Army and has been amended many times since then, most significantly in 1986 and more recently in 2009 in the aftermath of the financial crisis. In the latter case, FERA was enacted and changes were made in 2010 as part of the PPACA. Since FERA amended the FCA, the government has collected nearly $25 billion under the act, initiating more than

4,000 new FCA matters.[37] Before 2010, there was only one year in the history of the FCA when more than 700 new FCA matters were filed.

In 2014, the Justice Department recovered nearly $6 billion under the FCA,[38] an unprecedented amount. Previously, the most robust FCA enforcement had been in the healthcare and defense/procurement sectors, but in 2014, more than half of the $6 billion ($3.1 billion) was from settlements with financial institutions, most of the rest ($2.3 billion) was from Medicaid and Medicare fraud cases. Also, it is worth noting that nearly half of the $6 billion was recovered through lawsuits (qui tam actions) originally filed by whistleblowers.

In 2015, saw a slight decline in government recoveries under the FCA with over $3.5 billion in settlement or judgments.[39] Nonetheless, the FCA remains a powerful weapon in the government's arsenal against fraud and corruption. FCA enforcement continued to cover any industry that received government funding from healthcare to defense contracting to housing finance, to education, to technology and beyond. Of particular note is that of the $3.5 billion recovered, $2.8 billion related to recoveries from qui tam actions, and interestingly $1.1 billion or 32% of the year's recoveries were from cases filed by whistleblowers in which the government did not intervene.[40]

The IRS also has a whistleblower law[41] that enables private individuals to report on companies' and individuals' underpayments of tax, and persons otherwise guilty of violating the internal revenue laws. The IRS Whistleblower Law, like the FCA, rewards whistleblowers who report allegations of fraud on the government. In general, a whistleblower can receive an award of 15 to 30 percent of the collected proceeds (including penalties, interest, additions to tax, and additional amounts). In fiscal year 2014, the IRS made 101 awards to whistleblowers, totaling $52 million.[42]

With or without the government's intervention, there is little doubt that FCA cases will continue. While the trend of relators bringing actions, even without the government's intervention, will likely rise, no one should question that the government remains strongly committed to the use of this powerful tool. In a September 2014 speech,[43] Assistant Attorney General for the Criminal Division Leslie Caldwell said that the DOJ would "be stepping up (its) use of one tool (to combat crime) . . . (and) investigating and filing cases under the False Claims Act. Through our Fraud Section, we will be committing more resources to this vital area, so that we can move swiftly and effectively to combat major fraud involving government programs."

Use of Data Analytics and Market Surveillance

In the same way that the private sector over the past few years has learned to harness "big data" and use data and analytics tools and techniques to develop business insights and manage risks, so too has the government begun to make use of the same tools and techniques to assist in its identification of potential wrongdoing. It is widely known that agencies such as the SEC, Financial Industry Regulatory Authority (FINRA), and CFTC are using sophisticated data and analytics and trade surveillance techniques to investigate market manipulation and insider trading cases.

An example of this is the SEC's Division of Economic Risk and Analysis (DERA), which has developed a computer program, Accounting Quality Model (AQM), that analyzes large amounts of companies' financial data looking for outliers that would be indicators of financial reporting abuses. In addition to looking at various fraud indicators, it relies on an analysis of financial ratios to identify potential anomalies. More recently, DERA has stated that it is developing text analytics to identify potential deception in SEC filings or other public information.

The CFTC also performs broad types of surveillance including market, financial risk, and business analytics. The CFTC's market surveillance includes the monitoring of trading and positions of market participants on an ongoing basis. Through the acquisition and leveraging of large volumes of information throughout the organization and the development of sophisticated analytics, it seeks to identify trends and/or outlying events that warrant further investigation.[44] Its financial risk and surveillance technology enables it to identify traders whose large open trading positions might pose a financial risk to the industry or a clearing firm. Finally, its business analytics platform allows it to keep pace with the growth in industry data volume and complexity to improve its ability to conduct surveillance, investigations, and economic analysis. Not to be left behind, FINRA has also made known its efforts to develop a suite of "big data" information sources and analytics to improve its regulatory oversight of securities firms.[45]

Increased Global Cooperation Among Enforcement Agencies

In addition to parallel enforcement actions by state and local agencies within the United States, perhaps the most pervasive change over the past few years has been the increased cooperation among global regulators and government enforcers. This is especially so in the areas of anti-bribery and corruption, AML, and market manipulation. Assistant Attorney General Leslie Caldwell emphasized this point when she observed, "[W]e increasingly find ourselves shoulder-to-shoulder with law enforcement and regulatory authorities in other countries . . . and this includes not just our long-time partners, but countries in all corners of the globe."[46]

One example of the pervasiveness of global cooperation that brought together authorities in Europe, the Middle East, and Asia was the investigation and settlement of bribery charges against Alstom S.A., a French power and transportation company.[47] In December 2014, Alstom agreed to pay a $772 million criminal fine, the largest FCPA criminal fine up to that time.[48] Alstom pleaded guilty to resolve charges of corruption around the globe, including in the Bahamas, Egypt, Indonesia, Saudi Arabia, and Taiwan. In its press release announcing the guilty plea and settlement, the DOJ acknowledged the assistance of authorities in Indonesia, Switzerland, Saudi Arabia, Cyprus, and Taiwan. In addition, the United Kingdom and Indonesia have also filed charges related to corruption.

Increased Use of Civil Fraud Complaints and Administrative Courts

In an effort to bring greater efficiency to enforcement and to leverage its limited resources, the DOJ has increasingly turned to the use of civil fraud complaints, while the SEC has made greater use of administrative proceedings. The result has been that in the first half of fiscal year 2015, the SEC levied more civil penalties than in any other comparable six-month period since 2005.[49]

Since the passage of Dodd-Frank, the SEC has chosen to bring an increasing number of enforcement actions to its in-house administrative law judges (ALJs) instead of federal district courts. Dodd-Frank expanded the range of individuals who are subject to SEC administrative proceedings and increased penalties that could be imposed by ALJs in these proceedings. Administrative proceedings versus proceedings in district courts also have the advantage for the SEC of limiting the scope of discovery, not requiring a jury, and not being subject to the federal rules of evidence. Clearly, the SEC is availing itself of the new authority and jurisdiction of its ALJs.

The use of administrative proceedings has come under some criticism, and litigants have challenged the jurisdiction and use of ALJs by the SEC. To address some of this criticism, in May 2015, the Division of Enforcement released written guidelines on the factors (e.g., use of limited SEC resources, types of claims, and legal theories, etc.) that it will consider when determining whether to bring contested enforcement actions in federal court or before its own ALJs.

More recently, in September 2015, the SEC announced that it had voted to propose amendments to rules governing its administrative proceedings.[50] While these changes address some of the criticism by moving closer to what a charged party might receive in federal court by, among other things, expanding the administrative proceeding schedule, making greater discovery available to respondents, and providing for the exclusion of unreliable evidence, critics nonetheless still argue that the amendments do not go far enough and still do not equate with the rights afforded in a federal civil proceeding.[51] Perhaps as a result of this mounting criticism, it appears as though the SEC may have slowed down the number of contested cases that it is sending to administrative law judges. In the full fiscal year ended in September 2015, the SEC sent 28 percent of its contested cases to its administrative judges compared to 43 percent for the previous 12 months.[52] Where the SEC will end up on this issue remains to be seen.

Just as the SEC has made greater use of administrative proceedings, the DOJ has relied more on bringing civil fraud proceedings where it once might have considered bringing a criminal case. The use of civil fraud complaints has its advantages. Civil fraud cases require a lower burden of proof and give the government the advantage of conducting more expansive discovery than would otherwise be the case in a criminal matter. In addition, these quasi-criminal actions are brought by a prosecuting attorney, often require admissions of wrongdoing to settle and offer no guarantee against a subsequent criminal charge for the same conduct.[53] As one legal commentator observed, "[I]n place of grand jury indictments, the Department of Justice has focused more and more on bringing fraud charges against entities and individuals through civil complaints alleging violations of FIRREA [the Financial Institutions Reform, Recovery, and Enforcement Act] or the False Claims Act."[54]

Focus on the Prosecution of Individuals and Gatekeepers

Even though corporations have been the object of extensive fines, penalties, and sanctions, it is individuals within the organization who commit wrongdoing, not the company, and it is individuals who have the responsibility to ensure that the company upholds standards of integrity designed to prevent and detect wrongdoing.

While prosecutions of individual wrongdoing have always been part of the government's enforcement strategy, the DOJ put an exclamation point on its intention to focus on individual wrongdoing in a memorandum (Yates Memo) released in September 2015 and followed by a major policy address[55] the next day by Deputy Attorney General Sally Q. Yates. The memorandum issued new guidelines to government prosecutors regarding individual accountability for corporate wrongdoing. While some of the points in the memo reflect existing practices regarding the investigation and prosecution of corporate wrongdoing, other points, however, are groundbreaking and create new challenges for internal corporate investigations.

In setting out six principles to guide DOJ enforcement actions, the main message was the requirement that a company seeking cooperation credit by self-reporting must make full disclosure of wrongdoing, particularly by identifying culpable individuals within the organization. Deputy Attorney General Yates discussed the rationale for the six principles in saying, "Some are institutional policy shifts that change the way we investigate, charge and resolve cases. Some address the way that DOJ interacts with the targets of an investigation. Some of these policies are new and some are already being practiced at various places within DOJ but now will apply to everyone across the department. Fundamentally, these new policies ensure that all department attorneys—from main justice to the 93 U.S. Attorney's Offices across the country—are consistent in using our best efforts to hold individual wrongdoers accountable."

The six principles are:

- To be eligible for any cooperation credit, corporations must provide to the DOJ all relevant facts about the individuals involved in corporate misconduct.
- Both criminal and civil corporate investigations should focus on individuals from the inception of the investigation.
- Criminal and civil attorneys handling corporate investigation should be in routine communication with each other.
- Absent extraordinary circumstances, no corporate resolution will provide protection from criminal or civil liability for individuals.
- Corporate cases should not be resolved without a clear plan to resolve related individual cases before the statute of limitations expires and declinations as to individuals in such cases must be memorialized.
- Civil attorneys should consistently focus on individuals as well as the company and evaluate whether to bring suit against an individual based on considerations beyond that individual's ability to pay.

To be sure, even prior to the release of the Yates Memo, the government had made clear that it intended to focus its enforcement efforts on individuals within the organization, with a particular emphasis on gatekeepers. In the first six months of fiscal year 2015, median fines levied by the SEC on individuals were the highest in a decade, with half of the fines exceeding $122,500. This represents a 66 percent increase since 2005, when half the fines exceeded $60,000. This comes at a time when median fines paid by firms have declined sharply. In the same period of time, half of the SEC's fines on firms fell below $200,000, a decline from $600,000 in 2005.[56]

An example of the government's focus on gatekeepers can be seen in enforcement actions of the SEC in 2015. The SEC has made a point of charging compliance personnel who fail to identify and call out wrongdoing in their companies.[57] In August 2015, the SEC brought an action against a former compliance consultant in the Retail Control Group of the compliance department at Wells

Fargo and its predecessor entities.[58] However, an SEC administrative law judge, Cameron Elliot, refused to sanction[59] the former compliance consultant for violating securities laws even though he found that the consultant failed to raise any red flags indicating insider trading by a Wells Fargo employee despite evidence to the contrary. In 2015, the SEC charged chief compliance officers (CCOs) from BlackRock and SFX Financial Advisory Management Enterprises for allegedly failing to properly implement compliance procedures at their respective firms. In 2014, the Treasury Department's Financial Crimes Enforcement Network (FinCEN) fined the CCO of MoneyGram $1 million for failing to ensure that his company abided by the AML provisions of the Bank Secrecy Act.

In 2014, Andrew Ceresney, the SEC Director of the Division of Enforcement, provided the standard for the type of conduct that could lead to liability for a compliance or legal officer when he said, "we have brought—and will continue to bring—actions against legal and compliance officers when appropriate. This typically will occur when the Division believes legal or compliance personnel have affirmatively participated in the misconduct, when they have helped mislead regulators, or when they have clear responsibility to implement compliance programs or policies and wholly failed to carry out that responsibility."[60]

Use of Monitorships, Deferred and Non-Prosecution Agreements

Over the past 15 years, prosecutors and enforcement agencies have brought actions intended not only to determine liability and assess fines and penalties, but also to reform industry practices. To this end, the government has frequently used corporate settlements and integrity agreements for settling corporate fraud and misconduct in the form of DPAs and NPAs and the requirement of monitors to police these agreements. Some changes are under discussion, but the DOJ's and the SEC's continued aggressive use of DPAs and NPAs is a clear indication that these resolutions are "a vital part of the federal corporate law enforcement arsenal, affording the U.S. government an avenue both to punish and reform corporations accused of wrongdoing."

In 2015, the DOJ and SEC entered into 100 DPAs and NPAs. This was a substantial increase over 2014 when the DOJ and the SEC entered into a total of 30 DPAs and NPAs, two more than the number issued in 2013. The overwhelming number of DPAs and NPAs have been with the DOJ. Many of these have been related to the FCPA. In 2015, the substantial majority of the 100 corporate DPAs and NPAs were associated with the DOJ Tax Swiss Program.[61]

Assistant Attorney General Caldwell stated that these negotiated resolutions allow the DOJ to "impose reforms, impose compliance controls, and impose all sorts of behavioral change."[62] She went on to describe these settlements as "a more powerful tool than actually going to trial." DPAs and NPAs are likely to continue to be used for the foreseeable future as the DOJ Tax Division settles with approximately 100 Swiss banks related to their participation in a DOJ tax disclosure and non-prosecution program.[63]

In the healthcare and life sciences sectors, the regulators often settle matters with companies alleged to have engaged in fraudulent conduct through the use of corporate integrity agreements (CIAs). These function in a similar way to DPAs and NPAs in that they require the settling party to comply with requirements related to the conduct of its business. As with DPAs and NPAs, settlements under a CIA will frequently require the company to engage an independent review organization (IRO) to monitor, test, and attest to compliance with specific matters in the CIA. The CIA has become an important vehicle used by the government to change industry practice. For example, between 2004 and 2009, settlements were reached with 11 manufacturers to resolve allegations of improper promotion of drugs for unauthorized purposes (off-label promotion). By 2015, the list was more than 30.

One important common component of many settlements with federal and state regulators is the requirement that after a settlement the corporation hire a monitor for a period of time to review and report on the company's compliance efforts. In most cases, the "monitor's primary responsibility should be to assess and monitor a corporation's compliance with those terms of the agreement that are specifically designed to address and reduce the risk of recurrence of the corporation's misconduct, including, in most cases, evaluating (and where appropriate proposing) internal controls and corporate ethics and compliance programs."[64] The use of corporate monitors as a means to verify an organization's compliance with settlement agreements has become an increasingly popular tool of the government. It is estimated that 40 percent of DPAs and NPAs with the DOJ and the SEC from 2004 through 2010 included the requirement of a monitor.[65]

The government will consider a number of factors in determining the need for a monitor, including the severity, duration, and pervasiveness of the offense or misconduct and subsequent remediation efforts. To address the criticism about the cost of monitorships, recent settlements with the DOJ and SEC involving separate matters with Weatherford International and Avon Products Inc. have included a hybrid approach of requiring the company to retain a monitor for 18 months and then self-report for 18 months thereafter.[66]

Importance of Effective Compliance Programs, Voluntary Disclosure, and Cooperation

As a condition of leniency and as a way of affecting corporate behavior, government enforcement agencies make a practice of evaluating the effectiveness of an organization's compliance programs. The government will seek, among other things, to determine whether there is a strong culture of integrity, whether third-party risk has been mitigated, and whether internal controls have been designed and implemented to ensure that the risk of misconduct within the organization has been addressed.

The challenge for many organizations is that there is no universally accepted definition of an effective compliance program. Guidance for what the government will require in a compliance program can be found in a number of different sources. Compliance programs are mandated under numerous laws and regulations, including, but not limited to, the Bank Secrecy Act's anti-money laundering rules, the Dodd-Frank Act's rules on swap dealers and futures commission merchants, SEC rules governing investment advisors and investment companies, bank regulations implementing the Volcker Rule against proprietary trading by banking firms, and rules of self-regulatory organizations such as FINRA and NASDAQ. Agreements to institute or upgrade compliance programs are often found in consent agreements with regulatory agencies, deferred prosecution agreements and non-prosecution agreements, and settlements of shareholders derivative lawsuits and class action litigation.[67]

One of the best examples of the benefit of an effective compliance program was the case of Morgan Stanley where the managing director of their Chinese real estate investment and fund advisory group secretly arranged the payment of nearly $2 million to himself and a Chinese government official, disguised as finder's fees that Morgan Stanley's funds owed to third parties. Even though the managing director pleaded guilty to FCPA violations and the DOJ and SEC could have charged Morgan Stanley with criminal and civil violations of the provisions of the FCPA, the government declined to charge Morgan Stanley. In declining to bring any enforcement actions against Morgan Stanley, the government explicitly pointed to the company's voluntary disclosure of the matter and how it had constructed and maintained a system of internal controls reasonably designed to avoid the conduct that its managing director pleaded guilty to, and a robust compliance program that itself included, among other things, anti-corruption policies, extensive training programs, various reminders of the company's gift-giving and entertainment policies, guidance on the engagement of consultants, requirements for employees to disclose outside business interests, and annual certifications of adherence to Morgan Stanley's code of conduct.

One of the most important developments in recent years is the government's heightened scrutiny of the effectiveness of an organization's compliance program. Assistant Attorney General Caldwell stressed the need for companies to design compliance programs "that don't just look good on paper, but actually work." She described a company's compliance program and its compliance personnel as "the first lines of defense against fraud, abuse and corruption" and made clear that from the perspective of the DOJ "effective compliance programs are those that are tailored to the unique needs, risks and structure of each business or industry."[68]

More specifically, Assistant Attorney General Caldwell listed the hallmarks of what the government would examine to determine if a company's compliance program was effective. These hallmarks included:

- Senior leadership providing "strong, explicit and visible support for its corporate compliance policies . . . and not tacitly encourage or pressure employees to engage in misconduct to achieve business objectives."
- Looking beyond written policies "to other messages otherwise conveyed to employees, including through in-person meetings, emails, telephone calls, incentives/bonuses, etc.; and will make a determination regarding whether the company meaningfully stressed compliance or, when faced with a conflict between compliance and profits, encouraged employees to choose profits."
- Senior leadership taking responsibility "for the implementation and oversight of compliance."
- Clearly written policies that could be "easily understood by employees. But having written policies—even those that appear specific and comprehensive 'on paper'—is not enough."
- The sufficiency of stature within the company and adequacy of "funding and access to necessary resources" for compliance teams.
- Effective processes and adequacy of resources for "investigating and documenting allegations of violation."
- The periodic review of "compliance policies and practices to keep it up to date with evolving risks and circumstances, including when the company merges with or acquires another company."
- "An effective system for confidential, internal reporting of compliance violations."
- "Mechanisms designed to enforce its policies, including incentivizing compliance and disciplining violations."
- Sensitizing third parties with which the company interacts to the company's expectations and "taking action—including termination of a business relationship—if a partner demonstrates a lack of respect for laws and policies."

For practical guidance, Assistant Attorney General Caldwell referred companies and their attorneys to documents released by the DOJ in connection with the resolutions of investigations, including plea agreements, DPAs, and NPAs, to determine whether a compliance program will pass muster. The principal guidance for what constitutes an effective compliance and ethics program can be found in the FS Guidelines that were originally adopted in 1991 and amended in 2004 and 2010. Organizations that can demonstrate good corporate citizenship, including voluntary disclosure of misconduct to the government, full cooperation with government investigations, and an effective compliance and ethics program can mitigate, or even avoid, potential criminal sanctions.

The DOJ and the SEC, in interpreting the FS Guidelines, have made it clear[69] that the effectiveness of a company's compliance program will be a critical factor in determining the outcome of an enforcement proceeding and whether the proceeding will result in criminal charges, the requirement of a monitor, or whether potential penalties and fines will be mitigated. From the perspective of the DOJ, compliance programs must not only have the hallmarks discussed by Assistant Attorney General Caldwell, but they must also have adequate governance, technology infrastructure, software, and record keeping to be able to document the effectiveness of the company's compliance program.

Since the FS Guidelines are very broad, the DOJ, SEC, and other agencies have issued additional guidance over time. One such attempt at clarification can be found in the "Hallmark of Effective Compliance Programs" contained in the Resource Guide to the FCPA.[70] This additional guidance provides companies and their attorneys more detailed direction on how the government will assess a company's efforts at preventing, detecting, and responding to potential misconduct. Other guidance can be found in the "Principles of Federal Prosecution of Business Organizations" in the U.S. Attorneys' Manual.[71] Perhaps the most explicit indicator of the government's seriousness about its evaluation of a company's compliance program was the DOJ Fraud Section's hiring of Hui Chen as compliance counsel to provide expert guidance to prosecutors as they consider the enumerated factors in the U.S. Attorney's Manual and whether a company has taken meaningful remedial actions.[72]

Conclusion

The experiences of the first 15 years of the twenty-first century hold some powerful lessons for business leaders as they seek to avoid the consequences that have plagued corporations that were unprepared for the relentless, often unpredictable, flow of events and circumstances that have been the genesis of the new era of regulatory enforcement that exists today. Effectively managing risk in this new era is not only a challenge for business leaders, it is an imperative. No responsible organization can hope to thrive, let alone survive, in this environment unless it is prepared to devote the effort and resources that are necessary to ensure that it has appropriate and effective governance, risk, and compliance programs and processes in place to foster and support a culture of integrity.

The pace, volume, and complexity of regulatory change, together with the heightened scrutiny, broader authority, and more aggressive tactics of enforcement authorities have raised the bar to new heights for companies. Compliance can no longer be looked at as an isolated or occasional exercise. It must now be part of a continuing alignment and integration of the activities and businesses of an organization. All parts of a company need to be responsible and accountable for fostering a culture of integrity that sets and supports core values, understands its risk profile and tolerance, and embeds ethics and compliance into its business strategies and operations as well as its performance management and compensation framework.

Those organizations that will lead the way in this new era will not only seek to comply with the letter of the law, but will also work tirelessly to create an environment of trust with their employees, customers, regulators, and shareholders that is based on sound ethical principles and behaviors. This is not only a prescription to manage the risks in the new era of regulatory enforcement but also a way forward to strengthen a company's brand and reputation and to ensure its sustainable success.

Chapter 2

Raising the Bar: A Framework for Managing Risk

Timothy P. Hedley
Richard H. Girgenti

Managing Risk and Building a Values-Based Culture

As discussed in Chapter 1, with the bar raised, companies today face unprecedented challenges in managing risk in the new era of regulatory enforcement. To thrive, leading organizations must devote effort and resources into ensuring they have appropriate and effective programs and processes in place to build a framework for managing this risk effectively and to foster and support a culture of integrity. There are regulatory frameworks, discussed in this chapter, that offer general guidance from which organizations can select the specific practices that best support compliance in light of their unique culture and risk profile. When management designs compliance activities within these frameworks, it needs to put into motion a strategic and practical plan that is integrated and aligned with business strategy and operations. Management will then need to position the right resources, implement controls, and develop a strong corporate culture of ethics and integrity, not only to effectively manage risk, but also to foster a high-performing organization.

A culture of ethics and integrity is the intangible that is reflected in the choices and behaviors of an organization's employees as they respond to the

Ori Ben-Chorin was a major contributor to the content of this chapter. Mr. Ben-Chorin is a director in KPMG's Forensic practice in Washington, DC, where he advises clients on the design, implementation, and evaluation of corporate ethics and compliance programs and related antifraud programs and controls.

espoused values, goals, and priorities that management uses to define an entity's success. Building the right culture is certainly, at a minimum, about helping, encouraging and ensuring that members of an organization are committed to and embrace the organization's code of conduct and obey the law and applicable regulations. However, it is this and much more. A corporate culture is the overall professional environment of a company that reflects its values, customs and traditions. A culture of integrity is marked by specific values such as integrity, trust, and respect for the law; fostering an environment that places a premium on the organization's unique purpose; and timely identification, assessment, and mitigation of emerging risks. The right corporate culture provides a basis for decision making in every aspect of a business's activities and dealings and is a foundation for success. The specific programs and control elements that help create the framework for such a culture and that make up an effective compliance program are described in the following pages. The specific programs and control elements that help create the framework for such a culture and that make up an effective compliance program are described in the following pages.

Three Lines of Defense

An effective compliance effort must be embraced by all parts of an organization and operates best in a framework that has strong governance, robust risk identification and mitigation processes, and a properly functioning and resourced compliance function. This governance, risk, and compliance (GRC) framework requires an infrastructure that supports accountabilities, practical oversight, and a compliant culture at all organizational levels. To accomplish the objectives of the GRC framework, leading organizations will most likely operate along three lines of defense that allocate responsibility across the organization for who will own and manage risk, which functions will oversee and provide guidance on how to mitigate the risk, and which will ensure its effectiveness by providing independent assurance that the program is functioning as intended.

The three lines of defense model clarifies the essential roles and duties of key parts of the organization, from the board of directors, to management and operations (first line of defense), to the compliance function (second line of defense), and the internal audit function (third line of defense). This organizational construct requires the first line of defense to identify key risks to the organization; put in place ongoing processes, systems, and programs against defined standards (regulations, guidelines, policies, and procedures); and create an environment that builds a culture of integrity. The second line of defense is responsible for driving the overall design and implementation of the organization's compliance function, advising management and the board, and assessing the effectiveness of the organization's control environment to ensure that the business is designing and implementing effective controls to mitigate risks. The third line of defense (internal audit) conducts audits in key risk areas to assess the effectiveness of key controls to mitigate risk.

Regulatory and Evaluative Frameworks

The challenge for leading organizations is to design the roles and responsibilities of the three lines of defense described above and have them hardwired into both the organization's culture and its strategic planning process. Fortunately, there are a variety of non-prescriptive regulatory and evaluative frameworks that provide high-level guidance on key controls. Leading companies use these models in the context of designing, implementing, and evaluating an overall corporate compliance program and related risk management controls to prevent, detect, and respond to regulatory risk.

For example, the U.S. Federal Sentencing Guidelines for Organizational Defendants (FSG or the Guidelines) establishes minimum compliance and ethics program requirements for organizations seeking to mitigate penalties for corporate crimes. First adopted in 1991 and amended in 2004 and 2010, the FSG make it explicit that organizations are expected to promote a culture of ethical conduct, tailor each compliance program element based on compliance risk, and periodically evaluate program effectiveness. Specifically, the FSG calls upon organizations to:

- Promote a culture that encourages ethical conduct and a commitment to compliance with the law
- Establish standards and procedures to prevent and detect criminal conduct
- Ensure that the board and senior executives are knowledgeable and exercise reasonable oversight over the compliance program
- Assign a high-level individual within the organization to ensure that the organization has an effective compliance program and delegate day-to-day operational responsibility to individuals with adequate resources and authority and direct access to the board
- Ensure that high-level individuals and those with substantial discretionary authority are knowledgeable about the program, exercise due diligence in performing their duties, and promote a culture that encourages ethical conduct and a commitment to compliance with the law
- Use reasonable efforts and exercise due diligence to exclude from positions of substantial authority individuals who have engaged in illegal activities or other conduct inconsistent with an effective compliance program
- Conduct effective training programs for directors, officers, employees, and other agents and provide such individuals with periodic information appropriate to their respective roles and responsibilities relative to the compliance program

- Ensure that the compliance program is followed, including monitoring and auditing to detect criminal conduct
- Publicize a system, which may include mechanisms for anonymity and confidentiality, under which the organization's employees and agents may report or seek guidance regarding potential or actual misconduct without fear of retaliation
- Evaluate periodically the effectiveness of the compliance program
- Promote and enforce the compliance program consistently through incentives and disciplinary measures
- Take reasonable steps to respond appropriately to misconduct, including making necessary modifications to the compliance program

Other regulatory and evaluative frameworks take many of the concepts contained in the Guidelines and refine them for their specific needs. For example, both the New York Stock Exchange and the National Association of Securities Dealers Automated Quotations adopted corporate governance rules for listed companies. While the specific rules for each exchange differ, each includes standards that require listed companies to adopt and disclose codes of conduct for directors, officers, and employees and disclose any code of conduct waivers for directors or executive officers. In addition, the rules of each exchange require listed companies to adopt mechanisms to enforce the codes of conduct.

Moreover, other frameworks aim to provide guidance on many of the same compliance program elements. For example, the Department of Justice (DOJ) has recently amended its guidelines related to the federal prosecution of business organizations in cases involving corporate wrongdoing. While the guidance states that a compliance program does not absolve a corporation from criminal liability, it does provide factors that prosecutors should consider in determining whether or not to charge an organization or only its employees and agents with a crime. These factors include evaluating whether:

- The compliance program is merely a paper program or has been designed and implemented in an effective manner
- Corporate management is enforcing the program or tacitly encouraging or pressuring employees to engage in misconduct to achieve business objectives
- The corporation has provided for a staff sufficient to audit and evaluate the results of the corporation's compliance efforts
- The corporation's employees are informed about the compliance program and are convinced of the corporation's commitment to it

Select legislation also provides guidance in the context of organizational efforts to enhance the control environment—for example, the U.S. Dodd-Frank Wall Street Reform and Consumer Protection Act (Dodd-Frank or the

Act), which affects all U.S. financial institutions, many non-U.S. financial institutions, and many nonfinancial companies, altering practices in banking, securities, derivatives, executive compensation, consumer protection, and corporate governance. Among others, Dodd-Frank establishes a bounty program for whistleblowers who raise concerns with the U.S. Securities and Exchange Commission (SEC). The SEC has adopted a final rule to implement the Act's whistleblower award provisions, permitting individuals who provide the SEC with high-quality tips that lead to successful enforcement actions to receive a portion of the SEC's monetary sanctions while attempting to discourage them from sidestepping their internal reporting systems.

The road map for this chapter is summarized graphically in the compliance transformation wheel shown in Figure 2.1. Each of the elements included in the wheel will be explored, staring with governance and culture and expanding through the three lines of defense. This will provide a clear understanding of how the regulatory and evaluative frameworks come together to help organizations meet the challenges of managing risk in a new era of enforcement.

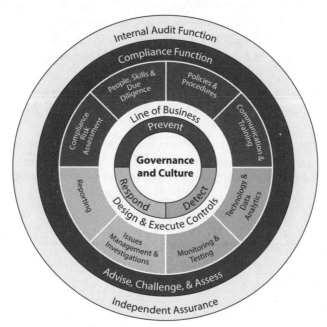

Figure 2.1. The Compliance Function Framework

Governance

The regulatory and evaluative frameworks discussed above provide management with guidance on the building blocks of an effective program to prevent, detect, and respond to fraud, misconduct, and compliance violations. The actual responsibility for putting in place the critical building blocks is given to management, the first line of defense. However, the starting point for setting it all in motion is an organization's governing authority—the board of directors.

Board of Directors

Board members have individual fiduciary obligations for the organizations they serve and are the primary stakeholders of the organization's compliance risk management efforts. To sustain the organization's culture for ethics and integrity, the board provides the oversight to ensure that management sets the core values and expectations for the organization and defines those behaviors that are consistent with the entity's values and expectations. The board is responsible for helping to (1) set the organization's risk appetite, (2) validate management's risk strategy, (3) evaluate strategic risks, and (4) provide checks and balances on management's decisions. The board's role is vitally important because it helps secure organization-wide support for management's compliance initiatives. In fact, enforcement and regulatory authorities often seek evidence of high-level support for organizational risk management, and direct involvement by the board can help fulfill this need. As Deputy Attorney General James Cole explains, the board "cannot simply go through the motions and hope that the company's compliance program works. They must make clear to employees that compliance is important and mandatory."[1]

As a practical matter, the board typically delegates principal oversight for risk management to a committee (e.g., the audit committee), which is then tasked with:[2]

- Reviewing the organization's compliance strategy and risk oversight processes, ensuring that risk management efforts are sufficiently resourced
- Receiving reports and key performance indicators on the effectiveness of the program
- Reviewing the organization's risk profile and process for identifying emerging risks
- Reviewing delegations of oversight responsibility
- Reviewing technology-related risks
- Periodically assessing whether or not the organization's culture and incentive compensation structures are in line with the goals of the compliance program
- Reviewing the organization's emergency response plans
- Discussing with the internal and external auditors their findings on the effectiveness of the organization's risk management programs and controls
- Establishing procedures for the receipt and treatment of questions or concerns regarding questionable accounting or auditing matters[3]

While the board provides general oversight for the organization's compliance program and risk management activities, day-to-day management of such efforts is typically delegated to other individuals, for example to a chief compliance officer (CCO), who serves as part of the organization's second line of defense. Through its oversight responsibility, the board is uniquely positioned to support the CCO, helping to safeguard the independent aspect of the CCO's position and enhance its influence. The board can do so by providing the CCO with unfettered access to the board via a dotted-line reporting relationship, as well as requiring the board's agreement to the hiring or firing of the CCO.

The CCO plays an important role in helping the board exercise its oversight responsibility by providing timely reports on the effectiveness of compliance-related activities. While the level of detail in such reports may vary, the board should typically receive regular updates on the activities of the compliance function in the form of key performance metrics, compliance audits, and risk assessment results and the outcome of efforts to evaluate the effectiveness of the organization's compliance activities.

The Compliance Function

Designating a Chief Compliance Officer.   As stated above, the compliance function is typically led by a chief compliance officer (CCO) who is a high-level individual within the organization. The CCO ensures program effectiveness and functions as the chief coordinator and facilitator for compliance. The CCO can be a full-time position or an added-task position for an existing high-level position. Depending upon the size of an organization, the CCO may be assisted by a deputy and is further guided by subject-matter experts who advise on matters related to program implementation. It is not uncommon for organizations to struggle when determining who would be an appropriate high-level individual that can lead compliance efforts.

Fundamentally, such an individual must be seen as a senior member of management, with unrestricted access to information necessary to pursue compliance goals (e.g., involvement in strategic planning that may include new acquisitions as well as internal audit or investigative findings). The CCO must also be in a position to advise other executives on ethical matters—illustrating the ethical dimensions of business decisions and helping drive integrity into business processes.[4] But more than all such attributes, the thought process about whether or not the CCO is high-level enough should include an assessment of the CCO's upward reporting relationships, as these can be crucial in determining whether the individual truly has the requisite authority to serve as head of a compliance function.

Optimally, a CCO would report directly to the highest levels of management (e.g., to the CEO or another member of the executive team such as the general counsel) and, as discussed above, would have unfettered access to, and a reporting relationship with, the board of directors. A CCO who has no such reporting relationships may not be deemed to have an appropriate level of authority and independence to bring about required organizational change. Nevertheless, the CCO's reporting responsibilities often depends upon the organization's industry norms and its litigious environment. For example, CCOs in financial services organizations may in fact report to a chief risk officer, while organizations that are subject to a corporate integrity agreement with the government may be required to have the CCO report directly to the board of directors rather than within the legal function.

Irrespective of reporting obligations, the CCO is responsible for working together with other compliance staff and designated subject matter experts from relevant functions (e.g., legal, human resources, internal audit) to coordinate the organization's approach to preventing, detecting, and responding to compliance and integrity violations. When misconduct and integrity issues arise, the CCO should draw together the right resources to address the problem and make the necessary operational changes. The CCO, as head of the compliance function, is responsible for driving the overall design and implementation of the organization's compliance function by:

- Developing communications and training materials that explain to employees their compliance-related roles and responsibilities
- Coordinating the organization's risk assessment
- Assisting in auditing and monitoring activities
- Establishing internal reporting mechanisms for employees to seek advice or report potential issues
- Responding appropriately to allegations of misconduct
- Evaluating the effectiveness of controls to mitigate identified risk
- Reporting to the chief executive officer (CEO), the board, and/or the audit committee on risk management activities

The experience and background necessary for the position of CCO vary across industries, and there is no universally agreed-upon background that such an individual should have. While legal and human resources are perhaps the most common background for a CCO, the CCO may also come from internal audit or operations. While some organizations hire their CCO from outside the organization (with the advantage of freeing the individual from possible cultural baggage accumulated after many years with the same organization), other organizations often prefer to add this task to a high-level insider. In any case, the real test of the CCO's effectiveness is the ability to function effectively within the organization's culture and in the context of the regulatory framework(s) for the industry and jurisdiction(s) in which the organization operates.

Note that when the CCO's compliance responsibilities are an added task, rather than a full-time appointment, or in a larger organization, the board may appoint a full-time subordinate to oversee the day-to-day operational administration of the program. Generally, such a deputy compliance officer (DCO) is thought of as a full-fledged stand-in for the CCO in day-to-day matters. In those organizations where the DCO has day-to-day operational responsibility for the program, it is important for him or her to be the one providing the board with data on the implementation and effectiveness of the program. This is because the Guidelines offer an increased potential for a company to receive credit for its compliance program (even when high-level personnel were involved in misconduct) if the individual who is tasked with day-to-day operational responsibility for the program has direct reporting obligations to the governing authority (e.g., board or audit committee).[5]

The commentary to the Guidelines characterizes such a direct reporting obligation as the express authority to communicate personally with the governing authority promptly on any matter involving criminal conduct or potential criminal conduct and no less than annually on the implementation and effectiveness of the program. So, the specific language does not clarify whether the individual with operational responsibility "must" or merely "may" report to the governing authority. But organizations that seek to enhance the potential credibility of their program should consider requiring that the individual with operational responsibility for the program (e.g., the DCO who is a stand-in for the CCO) have at least one annual, mandatory, documented report on program effectiveness presented in person to the board or audit committee.

Evaluating the Compliance Program. It is also the responsibility of the compliance function to evaluate the organization's risk mitigation efforts and provide the board and management with key performance metrics on the effectiveness of risk management activities. While many of these metrics are quantitative and one-dimensional (e.g., number of calls to a hotline) or multidimensional (e.g., number of identified hotline calls versus anonymous calls), organizations should also seek to collect and benchmark qualitative metrics. These may be difficult to gather, but they can provide important effectiveness criteria.

Qualitative performance metrics are best gleaned by conducting employee interviews, focus groups, and workshops, as well as fielding an employee perception survey. A survey can help the organization evaluate subjective data points such as employees' comfort level in using available advice and reporting mechanisms; propensity to use one mechanism over another; perception of the ethical tone-at-the-top from senior leaders, local managers, and supervisors, etc.

A third category of metrics that can be provided to compliance stakeholders is often referred to as forward-looking metrics (Figure 2.2), which can alert the organization to future risks.

An increase in vendor dependency	⇨	May suggest a greater risk of diminished control
An increase in the growth rate of customer interaction channels	⇨	May suggest a greater future risk
An increase in the number of regulatory changes	⇨	May suggest a greater risk resulting from increased complexity
An increasing trend in negative customer survey results	⇨	May suggest increasing risk in the corresponding product or business
Aggressive profitability targets compared to past performance	⇨	May suggest increasing risk from actions needed to meet goals
Missed remediation timelines	⇨	May suggest risk management and resource issues
Declining average years of experience for employees in key business units	⇨	May suggest diminishing risk-specific technical compliance skills

Figure 2.2. Sample of Forward-Looking Metrics

The Corporate Compliance Committee. In order to ensure the smooth operation of the compliance program and related risk management activities, an organization's board and executive management often form a corporate compliance committee, which is chaired by a senior-level member of management (often the CCO). The committee's membership should reflect a mix of functions with an eye toward helping ensure that key skill sets support the CCO's efforts (e.g., legal, audit, human resources). Operational leaders are included as members to help ensure that compliance is informed by a real-world perspective of the organization's operations and to facilitate integration of compliance into those activities. The corporate compliance committee has among its goals the following responsibilities:

- Establishing policies, procedures, and standards of acceptable business practice

- Overseeing the design and implementation of compliance program controls
- Coordinating the organization's risk assessment efforts
- Reporting to the board and/or the audit committee on the results of risk management activities

While the frequency of the committee's meetings depend upon a variety of factors, it is often the case that such a committee meets at least quarterly, and more frequently during the design and implementation of compliance program initiatives.

Designing and Implementing the Compliance Function. As mentioned earlier, management serves as the first line of defense with responsibility for implementing organizational controls. The second line of defense rests with the compliance function, which is tasked with assisting in the design and implementation of risk management controls helping to ensure employee compliance with applicable laws, regulations, and the organization's own standards, policies, procedures, and practices.

As executives design and implement the organization's compliance function and program, they often struggle with how to do so and achieve maximum effectiveness. For example, should the compliance function be managed centrally out of corporate headquarters, or should it be driven geographically in organizations that have dispersed operations? Is there a hybrid option that may make sense for some organizations? The reality is that an effective compliance function structure depends upon the organization's risk profile, culture, operations, and resources. For example, an organization with relatively homogenous operations that are spread across a contiguous geography may choose a centralized approach to compliance and risk management efforts. By contrast, organizations that operate across multiple geographies may choose a decentralized model. In other organizations, a hybrid model might work best.

Moreover, because compliance initiatives should reach all employees, organizations that are geographically dispersed or have business units and functional areas of different sizes and uneven levels of maturity often find it effective to design a compliance function infrastructure that includes not only staffing at the headquarters level but also compliance coordinators (also called "liaisons" or "ambassadors") at various key locations. By designating field compliance personnel with substantive responsibilities, the organization can extend the influence of its compliance initiatives.

Although compliance may not be a full-time role for field-based compliance personnel, they should be empowered to draw on the authority and resources of the CCO and act as the CCO's representative. Moreover, as part of this wide network of compliance personnel, organizations may also find it useful to designate subject matter experts to provide support in specific (and often complex) compliance areas. For instance, if a local manager has expertise in export compliance, he or she may be designated as a point-person to whom others may go when in need of help.

Business Unit, Functional, and Operational Compliance   Because effective risk governance at all levels of the organization is critical to the success of risk management efforts, senior management must actively embrace and promote the program and ensure that it is adopted throughout the enterprise. Senior executives help sustain the organization's culture for ethics and integrity by setting the ethical "tone-at-the-top" of the organization, helping to promote a common view of risk at the operational level by influencing the organization's risk culture, which in turn determines how the entity identifies and mitigates key compliance risks.

Tone at the top begins at the very top with the organization's CEO, who is ideally positioned to influence employee actions through executive leadership, specifically by providing a personal example for the ethical tone of the organization and playing a crucial role in fostering a culture of high ethics and integrity. As Procter & Gamble's CEO Bob McDonald explains, "Tone-from-the top is really critical . . . and it starts with me as the CEO. . . . I hold myself accountable; I hold my leadership team accountable; I hold the leaders of the business accountable."[6]

Moreover, functional senior leaders such as department heads (e.g., product development, marketing, regulatory affairs, human resources) also have important responsibilities in providing tone-at-the-top and implementing the organization's risk management strategy. Such individuals are expected to oversee areas of daily operations in which risks arise and serve as subject matter experts to assist the CCO in their particular areas of expertise or responsibility.

Equally as important, but often overlooked with respect to compliance program implementation, are the organization's middle managers, and especially those who have discretionary authority for compliance activities. Middle managers provide the organization with what has been coined as the "tone-in-the-middle," enforcing the organization's core values, expectations, and standards of conduct; managing workplace behaviors; and taking a role in risk management activities. In fact, management at this level is often where employees will turn to when they are seeking help related to an integrity issue or when they want to report misconduct.

Middle managers are also important contributors to compliance efforts because they help distribute and manage organizational resources, require their direct reports to communicate regularly with their employees on matters related to the organization's compliance program, and hold employees accountable for compliance violations. Further, lower-level operational managers have a special responsibility for identifying and assessing key risks, designing and implementing risk management controls, and taking actions to mitigate risks. In doing so, operational managers monitor (1) processes, systems, products, and services to help ensure that they remain in compliance; and (2) entity and process level controls to help ensure that they are operating effectively through systems testing, management review and approval, self-inspections, etc.

The Internal Audit Function

Working alongside the organization's second line of defense is the third line of defense—internal audit, typically reporting to senior management and independently to a committee of the board. Traditionally, internal audit has served as management's and the board's proxy for evaluating the organization's internal controls—those policies and procedures established to provide reasonable assurance that organizational goals will be achieved. While the historical focus of such efforts has been the organization's ability to report financial data, the role has expanded to performing operational and efficiency reviews and audits of compliance with applicable laws and regulations, as well as communicating the result of such evaluations to senior management and the board. Generally, internal audit's compliance related duties include, among others:

- Assisting in planning and conducting risk-based evaluations of the design and operating effectiveness of compliance programs and controls
- Assisting in conducting internal investigations into allegations of misconduct
- Assisting in the organization's compliance risk assessment and helping draw conclusions as to appropriate mitigation strategies
- Considering the results of the risk assessment when developing the annual internal audit plan
- Reporting to management and the audit committee on internal control assessments, audits, investigations, and related activities

The CCO and director of internal audit should work together to ensure that all employees responsible for conducting audits (including departmental self-audits) have the necessary knowledge and experience to adequately perform an assigned compliance audit. Since internal audit is a key, albeit independent, participant in risk management activities, supporting management's approach to compliance, auditors must understand the organization and have sufficient training and experience to evaluate competently key compliance-related risks and controls.

Often, the entity's own managers can become capable auditors, as they are closely familiar with operations (e.g., technical requirements such as the operating procedures for a particular process), the controls in place to prevent and detect errors, and the laws and regulations that apply to the process at hand. Those managers also typically have good knowledge of how management interacts with employees in the area in question, as well as any irregularities that may exist.

Compliance Program Controls

Effective business-driven compliance risk management controls are designed, implemented, and evaluated with three objectives in mind:

- **Prevention**: controls designed to reduce the risk of misconduct and compliance violations
- **Detection**: controls designed to discover misconduct and compliance violations when they occur
- **Response**: controls designed to take corrective action and remedy the harm caused by the misconduct or compliance failure

Preventative Controls

These controls are designed to reduce the risk of misconduct from occurring in the first place. Here, we cover some of the most important preventative controls.

Compliance Risk Assessment

Like a more conventional operational risk assessment, the organization's compliance function should conduct a compliance risk assessment to help the board and senior executives understand the legal and regulatory risks that are unique to the organization, identify gaps or weaknesses in controls, and develop a practical plan for targeting the right resources and controls to mitigate such risks. Management is often challenged by how a compliance risk assessment should be conducted. All too often, risk assessments are undertaken in an ad hoc manner and using stale risk-assessment data as a starting point for their efforts. Figure 2.3 below provides typical process steps for conducting a risk assessment.

For the risk assessment to be effective, it is imperative for management to view the assessment process as a regular, from the ground up, adaptive exercise that has mileposts and deliverables due each business quarter and that uses fresh input data throughout. The ongoing nature of risk assessments, refreshed periodically (e.g., as new regulations arise, enforcement actions are taken, or there is an understanding of changes in leading practices) is essential to the effectiveness of the process. Moreover, such a risk assessment should be futuristic in character, taking into consideration the future risks of the enterprise (and not merely present day risks).

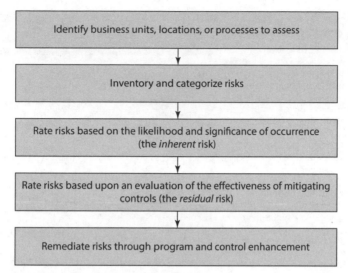

Figure 2.3. Risk Assessment Process Steps

In doing so, management should take into consideration forward-looking key performance indicators (KPIs) that can alert the organization as to future risks. While members of management are typically responsible for performing the risk assessment and considering its results in evaluating control effectiveness, the audit committee, and often the compliance function, typically have an oversight role in this process. The audit committee and the compliance function are responsible for reviewing management's risk assessment and ensuring that it remains an ongoing effort across the entire organization.

Global organizations often conduct the compliance risk assessment on a global scale and, in doing so, find themselves challenged to ensure the quality and consistency of assessments conducted overseas. For example, some international locations may suffer from a lack of risk assessment methodologies, as well as a lack of trained and experienced resources to competently evaluate organizational risks. Companies can mitigate such challenges by enlisting and training appropriate local country resources and providing them with a consistent risk assessment methodology. Additional challenges in conducting a compliance risk assessment are discussed in Figure 2.4.

Codes of Conduct and Risk-Specific Policies and Procedures

An organization's code of conduct is one of the most important communication vehicles that management can use to educate employees about the key standards

Risk Assessment Challenges	Rating Solutions	
Participants in the risk assessment process often struggle with the process of rating the likelihood and significance (i.e., cost) of organizational risks (the inherent risk). For example, how likely is it that employees would attempt to bribe a foreign official in violation of the provisions of the U.S. Foreign Corrupt Practices Act? If such a violation occurred, what would be the penalty for the organization? In assessing the likelihood and significance of a violation, risk managers and their operational counterparts must use sound professional judgment and experience to evaluate a variety of factors individually, and in consideration of one another, as illustrated in the table to the right.	**Significance (Cost) Factors**	**Likelihood Factors**
	High • Potential criminal investigation • A major change to strategy • Unplanned resignations of C-level executives • National media attention • Potential for financial restatement **Medium** • Potential regulatory intervention • Major changes to business unit strategies • Unplanned resignation of business unit heads • Regional or trade media attention **Low** • Potential for isolated litigation • A major change to functional strategies • Unplanned resignation of functional head • The ability to meet performance targets is threatened	• Known instances/allegations • Previous history of the violation occurring within the organization • Pervasiveness of the risk across operations • Complexity of the risk • Results of employee surveys and focus groups • Violations by other companies or industry peers • Industry/competitor litigation trends • Government enforcement priorities • Criticisms by the media or NGOs • Other internal considerations • Volume of transactions/activity • Effectiveness of relevant internal controls

Figure 2.4. Risk Assessment Challenges and Solutions

that define acceptable business conduct. In the words of Leslie R. Caldwell, assistant attorney general for the Criminal Division, "[a] company should have a clearly articulated and visible corporate compliance policy memorialized in a written compliance code . . . [and] employees need to know what to do—or not do—when faced with a tough judgment call involving business ethics."[7]

A well-written and communicated code is typically developed by an organization's compliance and legal functions, in consultation with and with the approval of management. Beyond restating company policies, such a document should set the tone for the organization's culture of strict adherence to the code, raising awareness of management's commitment to integrity and informing employees of the resources available to them to help achieve management's compliance goals.[8]

The organization should also have detailed and risk-based internal policies and operating procedures for each key business process and function. These detailed policies and procedures are typically designed and implemented by management and may or may not incorporate compliance with specific laws and regulations. It is important that the organization revise regularly such policies and procedures to ensure that they are audited, incorporate compliance, reflect current regulations, and are implemented by employees.

Codes historically were distributed in a paper-based format; today organizations typically provide their employees with simple URL links to downloadable electronic copies of the code, which reside in an easy-to-update format on the organization's intranet. Moreover, as a result of the enactment of the U.S. Sarbanes-Oxley Act, organizations that are required to comply with this Act must now make their codes publicly available, such as on their Internet websites or as exhibits to annual reports filed with the SEC.

While some organizations choose to apply the code of conduct only to employees, an increasing number of organizations also choose to develop and distribute a separate code of conduct (which is often smaller than the organization's main code) for agents, suppliers, and relevant third parties or, in lieu of that, provide their codes to such third parties and require them to certify that they agree to abide by the standards contained therein. For example, Google's code of conduct advises that, although the document "is specifically written for Google employees and Board members, we expect Google contractors, consultants and others who may be temporarily assigned to perform work or services for Google to follow the Code in connection with their work for us. Failure of a Google contractor, consultant or other covered service provider to follow the Code can result in termination of their relationship with Google."[9] A well-designed code of conduct typically includes the following attributes:

- High-level leadership endorsement, underscoring a commitment to ethics and integrity
- Guidance on values, principles, or strategies aimed at guiding business decisions and behaviors
- Simple, concise, and positive language that can be readily understood by all employees
- Topical guidance based on each of the company's major policies or compliance risk areas
- Practical guidance on risks based on recognizable scenarios or hypothetical examples
- A visually inviting format that encourages readership, usage, and understanding
- Ethical decision-making tools to assist employees in making the right choices

- Mechanisms that employees can use to report concerns or seek advice without fear of retaliation
- A method for employees to periodically certify that they have received the code, agree to abide by the standards contained therein, and pledge to disclose any known or suspected code violations

Organizations often spend significant resources designing and implementing a code; however, many are challenged in understanding whether the document is actually effective in achieving its purpose. All too often, a code that is rolled out with much fanfare ends up languishing on a dusty workspace shelf. Therefore, it is important for organizations to periodically measure the effect that their code is having on employees in order to obtain critical data that can help enhance its effectiveness.

Such an evaluation can generally be accomplished using a variety of tools, including interviews, focus groups, and employee surveys. And organizations are typically well served by choosing several of these information gathering methods to augment their assessment efforts. Regardless of what method is used, the assessment inquiry should center on determining, among others, the degree to which employees are familiar with and rely upon the code to guide them in their day-to-day activities, as well as their perceptions of whether the code is taken seriously by company managers and employees.

Challenges for Global Organizations

Many organizations with a global footprint are challenged when they attempt to implement a U.S.-centric code of conduct in overseas operations. Increasingly, they are learning that in some jurisdictions their code may need to be translated to be enforced, or that employees may not be compelled to certify that they have read and understood the document. Managers often resolve such challenges by creating a code that can bridge numerous countries' laws, regulations, and customs. Organizations that do a good job in designing and implementing effective global codes, which take into consideration each overseas location's laws, regulations, and enforcement priorities, as well as local values and cultural norms, generally find that their codes engender a higher level of employee acceptance and comprehension.

Due Diligence

Employee Due Diligence.   An important component of an effective risk management strategy is exercising an appropriate level of caution or investigation prior to the hiring, retention, and promotion of employees. Without conducting such due diligence, organizations run the risk of hiring individuals who may otherwise be disposed to commit misconduct. Organizations are often challenged in conducting due diligence, especially when employees reside or operate in higher-risk geographic locations, have discretionary authority over the financial reporting process, or have authority in discreet compliance areas.

While the scope and depth of the due diligence process typically varies from jurisdiction to jurisdiction, it should be tailored to the organization's identified risks, the job function and level of authority, and the specific laws where the organization and/or the employee resides.[10] But how often should the screening of employee backgrounds be performed? While the frequency of background screening will vary by job function or industry, organizations would be well advised to consider performing such screening not only once, at the time of hire, but also upon promotion or transfer into a position that calls for such a background check. For most organizations, it is customary for due diligence to begin at the start of employment and continue periodically thereafter.

While the factors included as part of background checks vary by job function or industry and should be confirmed by the organization's in-house or external counsel, they may include the following:

- Criminal histories
- Regulatory or professional trade disciplinary actions
- Credit or bankruptcy histories
- Civil litigation histories
- Substance abuse screening
- Driving records
- Credential verification
- Previous performance evaluations or disciplinary actions (if with the same employer)
- Reference checks

Third-Party Due Diligence.   Globalization and regulatory pressures require organizations to examine their business relationships in order to assess risk, make informed decisions, and comply with relevant laws and regulations. A growing number of governments globally are tightening regulations or introducing new ones. Many jurisdictions are also demanding high standards of business integrity, and an organization's failure to adequately scrutinize clients, vendors, agents, and business partners, and to know who they are and how they operate, could expose the enterprise to reputational damage, operational risk, government inquiry, monetary penalties, and even criminal liability.

As organizations enter and operate in new markets, they are especially vulnerable because of their reliance on third-party intermediaries (TPI), many of whom operate far from headquarters, in a foreign language, and with different customs and ways of conducting business. Such TPIs can often pose a great risk to operations. For example, a recent survey by KPMG International found that although a very high proportion of illegal bribes are typically paid by such TPIs, many companies reported that they are not monitoring their intermediaries for anti-bribery and corruption risk.[11] Increasingly, regulators both in the United States and elsewhere are making it a high priority to police business relationships with TPIs, and when something goes wrong, the penalties can be significant. As such, organizations would be well served by designing and implementing an effective third-party risk program, which requires the business to undertake the following efforts, among others:

- Identify the universe of TPIs and those that the organization determines to be within scope (i.e., to be included in the risk program)
- Conduct an assessment of the risk posed to the organization by the TPI
- Assign a risk score to each key TPI (e.g., high, medium, and low) and conduct enhanced due diligence on those TPIs with a high risk score
- Conduct ongoing monitoring of certain TPIs, especially those with a high risk score

Organizations are also often aided in screening third parties by technology tools that can offer good solutions to conduct such screening in a robust and cost-effective manner. For example, online due diligence tools that use advanced technology to search an extensive range of online public data sources can help management obtain information and proactively manage the risk associated with customers, agents, brokers, and counterparties. Sample sources to be searched include global sanctions and regulatory enforcement lists, corporate records, court filings, and press/media archives to gather important integrity and reputational information on subjects. Analyzing this data can identify apparent red flags or integrity warning indicators that can help an organization assess significant, high-profile, or high-risk transactions or business relationships.

It is important to note that the ability of the business to conduct third-party due diligence does vary from one country to another, due to differing privacy and data protection laws. Therefore, it is important for the organization to seek legal advice and clarification on local laws and regulations before undertaking due diligence abroad or on foreign-based TPIs.

Challenges for Global Organizations.   Global companies may face challenges in conducting due diligence on employees and third parties residing overseas. In the United States companies are free to practice due diligence in the hiring and retention of employees, agents, and suppliers (such due diligence is stressed in

U.S. governmental compliance models and is typically subject to certain legal restrictions). However, many international jurisdictions restrict or limit the type of background information that may be collected. For instance, collecting criminal records is illegal in some European countries, and EU data privacy laws can impose severe restrictions on the availability of information for background checks. Global companies should seek legal advice and check the laws and regulations for each country in which a background check is to be conducted.

Performance Evaluations and Incentives

Adherence to standards of high ethics, integrity, and compliance with the law should be a criterion for all performance evaluations. Doing so conveys to employees an awareness that their failure to contribute to a high-integrity culture or follow organizational standards will have a significant impact on careers and compensation. Moreover, organizations should seek out creative methods for preventing misconduct, for example by looking to rewards and positive incentives as a means of ensuring the effectiveness of compliance efforts, creating a culture of high ethics and integrity, and fostering an atmosphere where compliance policies and guidelines are followed.

To help build the organization's culture for ethics and integrity, regulatory and evaluative frameworks often advise management to offer financial and nonfinancial incentives to all levels of employees, rewarding behaviors that support the organization's core values and expectations, and using corrective actions to deal with behaviors that do not model the entity's aspirations. There are many types of incentives that management can use to encourage good employee behaviors, and these should be tailored to each organization's specific business, culture, and regulatory environment.

All incentives that reward ethical behavior and compliance with the law should be developed in much the same way that rewards and incentives are developed by the business to encourage operational results. Examples of such employee incentives include:

- A percentage of a human resources manager's performance review or bonus can be tied to his or her success in promoting a particular behavior or cause
- Employees can be evaluated on how well they represent their department in an ethical, informed, and courteous manner
- Management can issue public commendation letters to deserving employees
- Employees can win a small, discretionary cash bonus or gift if their work unit achieves an agreed upon organizational goal for a set period of time

Similarly, if employees fail to follow compliance-related standards or requirements (e.g., failing to complete required compliance training), they should become ineligible to share in the organization's discretionary bonus pool and incentives.

Communication and Training

Communication and training provide all employees with guidance on the organization's core values and expectations, as well as the consequences for failure to uphold them. Because management typically requires compliance to be everyone's responsibility, all employees are required to participate in risk management activities, which require frequent, persistent, and effective training and communication efforts that help align employees with the organization's risk culture and strategy. Having said that, many organizations wrongly assume that publishing a code of conduct and distributing it to all employees constitutes an effective communication strategy. However, studies and experience show that a code, standing alone, is relatively ineffective at influencing employee behavior and buy-in. It is only when surrounded by a wide-ranging communications and training strategy that a code can become a unifying and respected source of compliance guidance.

Making employees aware of their obligations to mitigate organizational risks begins with practical communication and training. Efforts to do so in an ad hoc

---

Potential Communication and Training Methods

Because employees have different learning styles and receptivity patterns, good communication and training should employ creative and engaging methods to help keep the message fresh. Examples of types of communication that can be utilized include the following, among many others:

- Internal and external mail
- Group or town hall meetings
- Articles in newsletters
- Speeches by senior executives
- Bulletin board postings
- Voice mail messages
- Letters or memos
- Videos
- Posters
- Wallet cards with the hotline number and the organization's core values

manner or by using a one-size-fits-all approach may fail to educate employees or provide them with a clear message that their risk management responsibilities are to be taken seriously. Managers should consider developing a wide-ranging strategy and plan that calls for frequent, relevant, and appropriate communication and training for all relevant employees in key risk areas (e.g., discrimination, sexual harassment, environmental health and safety, conducting business with government officials, acceptable sales practices, and accepting gifts and entertainment).

Developing such a detailed strategy and plan often takes careful thought, planning, and coordination; however, when done well, the strategy can help ensure that specific individuals receive communications and training in areas most relevant to their job functions. Also, gaps or overlaps in coverage are minimized, and staff time and other resources are used efficiently. In preparing such a plan, the organization should take into consideration the following:

- Results of a risk assessment that inform on key risks appropriate for communications and training
- Real examples and scenarios from the organization's workforce
- Relevant topics for potential communications and training (e.g., advice and reporting mechanisms, standards of conduct, and related policies and procedures)
- Training needs of specific individuals based upon their job function and risk areas

Because communicating and training individuals identically in all job functions will inevitably result in inefficiency, lack of focus, and poor understanding, organizations must tailor their communication and training efforts to individuals' respective roles and responsibilities. Therefore, organizations should develop a separate topic-specific training plan to determine the training needs for each group of employees based on their specific job function and risk areas. For example, senior members of management have different communication and training needs from frontline supervisors, and these two groups in turn have different needs from employees who work in, for instance, the organization's finance and accounting function.

- **Senior Managers**. An organization's senior managers are expected to set the ethical "tone-at-the-top" for the organization and, as such, should receive communication and training to help them succeed in fostering an organizational culture that values workplace ethics and integrity.
- **Frontline Supervisors**. Supervisors are critical sources of information for employees and important in shaping employee perceptions of the organization's culture. In fact, respondents to KPMG's Integrity Survey of more

than 3,500 employees (spanning all levels of job responsibility, 16 job functions, 12 industries, and 5 thresholds of organizational size) reported that they would feel most comfortable seeking advice and counsel from supervisors and local managers (76 percent and 67 percent, respectively), underscoring the need for organizations to ensure that the latter are well prepared to respond appropriately to employee questions.[12] Training for such individuals should focus on their responsibilities for addressing employee concerns when they seek advice or report misconduct and generally promoting compliance program aims (e.g., by distributing compliance-related guidance and discussing compliance issues at regular staff meetings).

■ **Current Employees**. Existing employees often present a greater hurdle to communication and training as they typically know the organization closely and have usually developed their own perceptions. They also invariably sit in different functional and operational areas of the organization. Accordingly, communication to and training for them should be frequent and regular, as well as directly tailored and linked to their day-to-day job.

■ **New Personnel**. Starting with orientation, an organization has the ability to set the tone of a desired corporate culture, and management should take advantage of this window of opportunity to help new employees understand the specific rules that apply to performing their jobs, as well as the resources available to them to answer questions or report problems.

No matter how effective the training is, some individuals may never fully buy into the compliance program. However, frequent communications, required training, and various control systems that tie commitment to compliance and the carrying out of compliance responsibilities to the performance review and compensation process can help motivate many individuals to support the compliance program aims, helping to ensure that employees receive the right messages. In other words, it is important to foster a strong culture of compliance and adherence to ethical values.

Detective Controls
Advice and Reporting Mechanisms

Employees are more likely to raise concerns and report misconduct when they know where to turn for help, feel comfortable doing so without fear of retaliation, and believe that management will be responsive to their raising the issue. Those organizations that have a better chance of detecting misconduct early are ones that have built a culture where employees believe they have a stake in the company and have an affirmative responsibility to raise their hands and report improper conduct.

An important attribute of an organization's culture of ethics and integrity is the willingness of its employees to report misconduct without fear of retaliation.

Research has shown, in fact, that such employee reports are by far the most common detection method for misconduct, as illustrated by the results of a recent KPMG survey where participants reported that: (1) more than 40 percent of all cases of organizational fraud were detected by an employee's tip—more than twice the rate of any other detection method; and (2) employees accounted for almost half of all tips that organizations used to discover fraud.[13]

Recent enforcement actions and reports by the SEC and other federal and state agencies have made it clear that the government has found whistleblower programs to be a valuable enforcement tool and that enforcement agencies have increasingly paid bounties to employees and others who came forward with information to help identify organizational misconduct.[14] In light of the government's increasing reliance on whistleblowers as a source of information on potential misconduct, organizations would be remiss if they neglected to offer their own whistleblower mechanism to employees (e.g., a telephone hotline or webline) to increase the likelihood that employee whistleblowers voice their complaints internally rather than with government regulators who will seek to trigger a time-consuming and resource-intensive regulatory investigation.

In typical organizations, employees can seek advice or report misconduct in various ways—for example by contacting board members, senior executives, supervisors, local managers, compliance resources, and human resources professionals. While employees should be encouraged to use whichever mechanism is most appropriate given the particular situation at hand, they are typically most comfortable reporting misconduct to their immediate superiors. This is well illustrated by the results of KPMG's survey where respondents opined that they would feel most comfortable reporting misconduct to supervisors and local managers (76 percent and 62 percent, respectively).[15] Importantly, the option that tied for second place for reporting misconduct was the organization's ethics or compliance telephone hotline (62 percent).

Some version of a telephone or Internet (web) hotline is used at most large organizations, typically providing a viable method whereby employees, as well as other key third parties (e.g., agents, customers, vendors, suppliers, etc.), can communicate concerns about potential misconduct and seek advice when the appropriate course of action is unclear. A well-designed hotline typically includes the following features:

- **Organization-wide Availability**. Employees at international locations are able to use the hotline through features such as real-time foreign language translation and toll-free call routing (or alternatively, have access to local hotlines in specific countries or regions).
- **Anonymity**. The organization's policies allow for the anonymous submission and resolution of calls. For instance, callers who wish to remain

anonymous are given a case tracking number that they can later use to provide additional details related to their question or allegation and/or check the status or outcome of their call. Note that Section 301 of the Sarbanes-Oxley Act requires that the audit committee of an organization listed on a U.S. exchange take steps to establish procedures for the receipt, retention, and treatment of employee complaints, as well as a way for employees to submit confidential and anonymous concerns regarding questionable accounting or auditing matters.[16]

■ **Confidentiality**. All matters reported via the hotline are treated confidentially. Hotline operators inform callers that relevant safeguards will protect caller confidentiality—for instance, limiting access to personal information (if volunteered). Hotline operators disclose to callers any limitations the organization may have in preserving caller confidentiality (e.g., callers should have no expectation of confidentiality if the call leads to a government investigation).

■ **Nonretaliation**. The organization's policies prohibit retaliation against employees who in good faith seek advice or report misconduct. Such retaliation may be overt (e.g., terminating the reporting employee) or covert (e.g., failing to provide the employee with a well-deserved promotion, raise, bonus, or even a desirable work assignment). The organization requires a follow-up with employees periodically after the hotline case has been closed (e.g., at one-, three-, and six-month intervals) to ensure that they have not experienced retaliation. The company encourages the employees to report any instances of retaliation and takes swift action against those who do retaliate. In tandem with the development of such mechanisms, management should also design and implement a monitoring program that can continuously monitor employees and other third parties (e.g., witnesses) reporting misconduct, to see if there are significant changes in their organizational success factors that may indicate they are experiencing retaliation (e.g., monitoring of red flags such as productivity, revenue generation, performance ratings, career advancement, compensation awards).

■ **Real Time Assistance**. The hotline is designed to provide an immediate, "live" call response to facilitate thorough and consistent treatment of a caller's report of misconduct or to provide immediate guidance (if the hotline offers such assistance). Thus, hotline operators need to be appropriately qualified, trained, and, in some situations, authorized to provide advice.

■ **Data Management Procedures**. The organization uses consistent protocols to gather relevant facts, manage and analyze hotline calls, and report key performance indicators to management and the board. This is often accomplished, for example, by using a computerized, back-end case management system to store, organize, prioritize, and route employees' reports. Later in the chapter we discuss using technology to better mitigate compliance risks.

- **Classification of Financial Reporting Concerns**. The hotline includes protocols whereby qualified individuals (e.g., internal audit, legal, security) can determine whether the nature of an allegation could trigger a financial reporting risk or a regulator/compliance risk.
- **Audit Committee Notification**. The hotline includes protocols that specify the nature and timing of allegations that are escalated to the audit committee (particularly important for companies that must comply with the requirements of the U.S. Sarbanes-Oxley Act).
- **Prominent Communications**. The organization publicizes its hotline prominently. Such communications may include, among others: (1) describing the hotline within the code of conduct, in key company publications and training, and at management "town hall" type meetings; (2) featuring the hotline telephone number on posters, banners, wallet cards, screen savers, telephone directories, or desk calendars; and (3) communicating illustrative case studies based on hotline calls to employees (e.g., in newsletters, training programs, or intranet sites) to demonstrate that the organization values hotline calls and is able to provide assistance to those who use the hotline.

Multinational organizations are often challenged to design and implement a hotline that can be used in their various international operations. For example, language and cultural barriers may hinder a hotline's effectiveness (e.g., in some paternalistic societies, going around one's supervisor by calling a hotline may be regarded as a demonstration of a lack of respect). Moreover, there may be legal restrictions overseas associated with having employees blow the whistle on misconduct; for example in some international locations a hotline policy cannot be implemented in its entirety due to legal limitations.

The challenge for organizations is to create a borderless culture of compliance that encourages (or at least tolerates) reporting of improper conduct, and this can be achieved by designing and implementing customized hotline policies and procedures for each international jurisdiction, providing effective training and communications in each key native tongue, and generally remaining attuned to the cultural nuances and sensitivities inherent in conducting business overseas.

Auditing and Monitoring

Auditing and monitoring systems that are reasonably designed to detect misconduct are important tools that management can use to determine whether the organization's controls are working as intended. Since it is impossible for the internal audit function to audit every risk, management should develop a comprehensive auditing and monitoring plan that is based on risks identified through a risk assessment process.

To carry out effective auditing and monitoring, organizations should consider following broad design elements. First, an organization should design its auditing and monitoring activities around overall priorities for compliance-related activities, as well as both short- and long-term organizational objectives. Some questions that may be helpful in this regard include the following:

- How is leadership's commitment to compliance integrated into business goals, strategies, decisions, and day-to-day practices?
- What methods does management use to promote, reward, and enforce a culture of high ethics and integrity and commitment to the organization's core values?
- How are specific compliance policies, programs, and controls intended to operate?
- How are authorities and accountabilities delegated to various functions so that they may achieve ethics and compliance objectives?
- How are compliance resources budgeted and allocated?
- How are key performance indicators (KPIs) used to measure the effectiveness of ethics and compliance activities?
- How does the organization ensure that professional standards, industry practices, and regulatory expectations are adhered to?

Second, effective implementation of auditing and monitoring initiatives can help ensure that senior management receives persuasive data regarding the effectiveness of key controls to mitigate risks. Despite the fact that different organizations have different policies, procedures, programs, controls, and risk tolerances, the following key implementation considerations often remain constant:

- Is there clear support from the board of directors and senior management?
- Are there well-established objectives for auditing and monitoring initiatives?
- Are reporting lines well established, with direct access to the board, if applicable?
- Has an assessment been performed to identify any barriers to success, including a remediation plan to overcome identified barriers?
- Have sufficient resources been provided to help ensure that auditing and monitoring efforts are not merely window dressing?
- Are auditing and monitoring activities performed by personnel who have the requisite skills and training?

- Have existing organizational structures been taken into account? (e.g., a highly decentralized structure may make it difficult for centralized auditing and monitoring functions to succeed.)
- Have key stakeholders (e.g., HR, legal, compliance, security, accounting, operations) been consulted in planning auditing and monitoring activities?
- Is there an established timeline for the implementation of auditing and monitoring activities?
- Is there a process for evaluating the success of such implementation efforts?

Third, reports on the results of auditing and monitoring activities should be designed such that they ensure effective communication to relevant corporate stakeholders. Such reports should include not only sufficient detail on observed findings, but also guidance on how to evaluate the severity of deficiencies and the effectiveness of subsequent remediation efforts. Three key elements for an effective communication process include prioritizing findings, reporting findings to the appropriate oversight level, and detailing subsequent remediation actions.

While the process for auditing and monitoring focuses on both the likelihood and impact of potential fraud and misconduct, the scope for such activities should include the entire organization, including its significant business units, operational divisions, and accounts. Those controls that are not periodically assessed for relevance and practicality may deteriorate over time. Consequently, regular auditing and monitoring of controls often leads to organizational efficiencies and reduced costs associated with public reporting on internal control. Accordingly, identification of control deficiencies should be addressed proactively, rather than reactively, to help ensure efficient resolution.

Technology and Compliance Innovation

Despite the growing maturity of the compliance profession, most CCOs and their teams still find themselves with precious little time and/or resources to conduct a thorough and meaningful analysis of the millions of data points their companies collect or have at their disposal. Instead of letters, journals, or newspapers, or even word-of-mouth rumors, most of our information now travels at the speed of light in simple binary code of 0s and 1s, and yet they hold potentially critical insights into an organization's compliance profile.

The problem companies struggle with is the explosion of data creation in the past several years; consider the following evolution—kilobyte to megabyte to gigabyte. One estimate by IBM is that 2.5 quintillion bytes of data are being created every day; and it's commonly accepted that 90 percent of the data in the world today has been created in the past two years alone.[17]

The reality, unfortunately, is that many companies have critical data in multiple formats or files and in multiple company silos—human resources, audit, compliance, security, operations, sales, and finance, to name but a few, all have their own sets of data, which often overlap as each function does its part to prevent and detect possible misconduct. Gaining access to such information is often difficult, and some compliance teams encounter classic internal turf battles and turf mindsets. Even if given access, as mentioned above, many functions lack the staff to assess the data thoroughly.

Many companies in the compliance field offer clients configurable dashboards that aggregate and highlight key data generally derived from helpline allegations, investigations, and enterprise compliance training. While these are extremely important areas to track and monitor, such dashboards tend to be backward-looking assessments—events that have been concluded, or soon will be—and fall short of what is now possible with emerging software applications.

In the past several years, technology has transformed the way many compliance functions have executed communications and training strategies. Mobile devices and phones have created new avenues for short burst communications messages, or even training refreshers. Training in particular has become more technology based and segmented, directing the right message in the right dose to the right target audience. In many ways, compliance and human resource teams are the beneficiary of the advances in technology and the developing science around adult learning. The time has come for compliance professionals to avail themselves of similarly new technologies and software applications to open doors for program measurement and assessment, as well as potentially provide an early warning to an unhealthy culture or potential misconduct.

Data and Analytics   In many ways we are just at the start of a new wave of technology advancements, data analytics, and connectivity, forces that will help manage data from across the globe virtually instantaneously. The world of big data will become infinitely more challenging and complex, whether we are ready for it or not. And this includes tying in social media outlets to one's internal data to more proactively manage potential risk. Fortunately, the growing capabilities of the data and analytics (D&A) discipline, currently used by many sales, marketing, supply chain, and finance functions, can now be applied to compliance data. These business functions have pioneered, and thus tested the capabilities of D&A, and have ultimately paved the way for ethics and compliance (E&C) functions to follow.

Simply put, D&A provides insights that enable executives to see quickly the interrelationships between disparate parts of the business. Recent survey research shows that experts in the analytics space believe that the companywide benefits of a robust D&A initiative include enhanced corporate performance, improved risk management, and a better customer experience—all of which can, and do, apply to the scope of the compliance function, particularly if one considers employees to be "customers."

In order for compliance teams to get the most out of their available data, it helps to understand and use the language of the evolving D&A profession. Think of D&A along a maturity continuum comprising four different stages:

1. Descriptive: simply understanding current conditions (where many compliance functions may find themselves trapped)
2. Diagnostic: retrospective analysis to understand drivers of an outcome that occurred (many current compliance metrics fall into this category, such as investigations and outcomes, training completed)
3. Predictive: the use of current and historical data and drivers analysis, combined with advanced analytical modeling, to understand potential ranges of outcomes
4. Prescriptive: development of models incorporating predictive analytics to optimize solutions

Moving from descriptive to diagnostic involves data integration and is a critical first step, one that many compliance teams regrettably still struggle with today. To move from diagnostic to predictive begins to engage true analytics capabilities, the 1.0 version of D&A for compliance functions today. The last step in the chain, moving from predictive to prescriptive, draws on true culture change as it relates to the use and analysis of a company's data; this may in fact be version 2.0 for compliance in the not-too-distant future.

Companies who self-identified as "market leaders" in a recent KPMG survey were more likely (59 percent) to apply D&A to the management of enterprise risk and performance than companies who self-identified as "non–market leaders" (47 percent). While the percentage gap in application is significant, D&A experts believe it will quickly shrink once the early adopters share their successes, helping the later adopters to make more compelling business cases for following that same path. While it is too early to present similar research focused on compliance leaders, many believe that day is coming soon.

What are the current barriers to the expansion of early adoption of D&A by companies and/or functions like compliance? Here, compliance leaders have the benefit of learning from the challenges facing other business leaders in their D&A efforts. Research indicates there are two main challenges: (1) too many D&A initiatives and/or opportunities creating difficulty in focusing on the priority initiatives; and (2) an apparent lack of support from executive management for the suggested D&A proposals, which may stem from a basic lack of understanding of the way to use D&A. Clearly these barriers are connected and require business leaders to make better links to overall business strategies and to better explain the full benefits of a D&A application.

Today several software providers offer configurable platforms that allow the compliance function to develop a multilayered data environment that for the first time brings together diverse data sets in a way that is tailored for trend analysis. These software systems generally sit inside a company's firewall, lowering cost and easing implementation barriers. Of critical importance, the software systems can also manage sensitive data via encryption, and various levels of access permissions can be configured for eventual users.

How does it all come together? First and most important, the compliance team must gain the trust and support of sister functions, particularly information technology, legal, human resources, and audit, early in the process, otherwise the initiative is likely to fail. Convincing them of the functional and enterprise benefit of consolidating data into a single analytics repository in many cases will take considerable time, and compliance officers need to factor this into their development plans. Certainly if the company has engaged D&A in other disciplines, the E&C business plan ought to maximize that experience for enhanced insights and cost/time savings when advocating for a similar innovation for the compliance function.

After securing the support of senior management and functional leadership, corporate compliance teams often work with third-party advisory firms to guide the software providers in the planning and development stage of the project. These collaborative teams establish the working framework for the D&A application, scope the available data sets, define security and access protocols, design the dashboard interface, create implementation plans, and ultimately test the systems before going live.

While not quite artificial intelligence, predictive systems can be configured to allow for manual data selection/sorting fields; once the comparative data sets are selected, the D&A trend analysis can be run (and create management reports and/or PowerPoint slides for internal reporting purposes). Compliance staff can benefit from the dynamic reporting powered by a D&A engine. Staff time and attention shifts from trying to capture, collate, and understand the data to incorporating the data analysis into active response strategies, either to reinforce processes and procedures and training, or to proactively launch a targeted mitigation strategy.

As the software platforms become more sophisticated, machine learning will be implemented, allowing for the continual review of data sets, with alerts and notifications going out to prepopulated internal subject matter experts. Imagine a simple data set with appropriate feeds into the D&A application, such as corporate offices/locations, business units, employee headcount and personnel numbers, functional assignment, helpline allegations, investigations, outcomes, and disciplinary actions that can be quickly and easily sorted by a compliance leader who conducts historical trend analysis (for six months, one year, or multiple years, depending on the available data) on a particular data point, and then quickly exports the data analysis into a presentation template.

In the case of a recent acquisition, these same data points can be fed into the D&A tool and see problematic areas of the newly acquired business, matched against the existing company profile. Tracking these outlier data points against mitigation strategies helps assure that the right resources are applied against real potential risk. Thus far, these examples are relatively straightforward tasks for the underlying software, yet they can save compliance staff countless hours of heretofore manual data gathering and analysis.

The real power of these D&A applications is how simple it is to add additional layers of complexity and context simply by linking new data feeds—say, the results of the last several employee surveys or employee tenure. Matching the previous results with positive and/or negative survey results begins to shed new light on the actual culture that may exist across a given enterprise, and the profile of persons who report potential wrongdoing and the profile of those who may be found in violation of company policy or the law.

Prevent, Detect, and Respond   D&A is about more than connecting the obvious dots; it's about finding additional insights from themes sometimes beyond the conventional wingspan of the compliance office. First, let's look at the cultural component from the FSG's Section 8(a)(2), which states that "[an organization shall] otherwise promote an organizational culture that encourages ethical conduct and a commitment to compliance with the law."

A compliance team might consider running a trend analysis of near misses and/or notices of violations from a company's facility and operations team, a sign of a potentially growing culture problem. Or, if there are no factories, a CCO might consider filtering employee turnover and exit interview data; unusually high turnover in a given function or office may align with the high number of helpline calls, low employee satisfaction and/or fear of retaliation, and low management trust. Indeed, the D&A platform is flexible enough to accept data feeds from social media monitoring software, again, adding a layer of input and insight into corporate risk exposure. Triangulating these multiple data points could lead to a mitigation or intervention strategy.

For example, the compliance team could commit, with local human resources, to conduct employee focus groups and/or interviews that may help further identify underlying issues and potentially lead directly to a local management improvement plan. Ultimately, such initiatives might reverse the employee exodus trend, prevent injuries, improve morale, and either rehabilitate or terminate an underperforming leader.

Let's take another example—compliance officers and management must take care in the hiring and promoting of key staff per the FSG's statement in Section 8(b)(3), which states that "[t]he organization shall use reasonable efforts not to include within the substantial authority personnel of the organization any individual whom the organization knew, or should have known through the exercise of due diligence, has engaged in illegal activities or other conduct inconsistent with an effective compliance and ethics program." A compliance officer, utilizing the power of D&A and in partnership with human resources, can easily run the list of employees in line for potential promotions against the helpline allegation database, starting with current cases and going back one or more years. Such a data sort can easily be done with unique employee identification numbers and an agreed definition of positions within the company that constitute "substantial authority personnel."

Consider the outcome: Certainly if a senior leader is working under a performance improvement plan for a policy violation via the compliance or HR group, management may think twice about the timing of a promotion. In large, decentralized organizations such a potential disconnect on promotions between compliance, line management, and human resources is unfortunately quite probable. A disciplined approach supported by processes, procedures, and management and an underlying D&A application will help reduce the likelihood of such an occurrence. Moreover, for key positions, the organization may consider an additional step by running an external criminal background check.

And to the point raised above on social media and how D&A can incorporate external data feeds, it is possible for the D&A application to reach out externally and proactively to search certain databases, such as state and federal criminal convictions in the United States, thereby providing a constant mitigation strategy. This is particularly important in industries like transportation and logistics where a DUI violation can, in fact, disqualify a driver from continued active driving. As in most cases of regulatory violation, ignorance is not a defense for the corporation; rather it's likely a violation if that driver is found to be behind the wheel following a DUI conviction.

Consider when there is a reduction in force where human resources generally partners with the affected business units and designs a legally appropriate list of employees scheduled for separation. In most cases, because of the confidential nature of investigations, employees involved are unknown to the business leaders and HR team looking at candidates for separation. Compliance teams utilizing the capabilities of a D&A application could run that separation list against current and historical cases or investigations. Employees who raised issues or participated in investigations as a witness could be among those slated for separation, and potentially raise a retaliation concern (more on this below). Such a discovery would lead to informed discussions with HR, legal, compliance, and management about the timing of separation at the very least. Similarly, what if the case is under active investigation? Would it be prudent to terminate a reporter or potential key witness to a matter that could result in litigation or increased loss to the company?

Next, consider a company's obligation to employees to create a retaliation-free workplace, certainly the most important commitments compliance teams and senior management can make to employees after their physical safety and well-being. D&A can again help compliance teams monitor for potential retaliation by tracking all reporters and investigation witnesses (again utilizing their unique employee ID numbers) for a period of years. The timing may vary according to company policy, leading industry practice, regulatory requirements, and regulator expectations. They can cross-check this list for potential terminations, transfers, reassignment, performance improvement plans, and of course annual performance reviews. This process requires disciplined coordination between human resources and compliance, but in the interest of protecting employees from retaliation and to ensure the integrity of the corporate compliance commitment to all employees, a coordinated effort is simply the right thing to do.

Responsive Controls
Conducting Internal Investigations

When information relating to actual or potential misconduct is uncovered, a second line of defense functions (e.g., compliance, in association with legal and HR) should be prepared to conduct a comprehensive and objective internal investigation. The purpose of such an investigation is to gather facts leading to an objective and credible assessment of the suspected violation and allow management to decide on a sound course of action. By conducting an effective internal investigation, management can address a potentially troublesome situation and have an opportunity to avert a potentially intrusive government investigation. A well-designed investigative process will typically include the following considerations, among others:

- Oversight by the audit committee, or a special committee of the board, either of which must comprise independent directors who are able to ward off undue pressure or interference from management
- Direction by outside counsel, selected by the audit committee, with little or no ties to the entity's management team, and that can perform an unbiased, independent, and qualified investigation
- Activities undertaken by investigators who understand the legal dimensions of the matter at hand, as well as the necessary investigatory skills

- Briefing the organization's external auditor so that the latter can consider the proposed scope of work in the audit of the organization's financial statements
- As an expectation of cooperation with investigators, allowing no employee or member of management to obscure the facts that gave rise to the investigation
- Reporting protocols that provide management, the board, external auditors, regulators, and, where appropriate, the public with information relevant to the investigation's findings in the spirit of full cooperation, self-disclosure, and transparency

Challenges for Global Organizations

The challenge for global organizations in conducting investigations is that as rapid advances in global trade increase the risk of cross-border misconduct, they face mounting pressures to develop or enhance their cross-border investigative capabilities. For instance, international subsidiaries may not follow effective investigatory protocols, or even have access to internal or external resources with the requisite experience and training to follow multiple international regulatory directives, requirements, and laws.

At the same time, enforcement authorities, such as the Criminal Division of the DOJ, are busy reaching out to their international counterparts, as explained by Marshall L. Miller, principal deputy assistant attorney general: "Today, in the Criminal Division, we are capitalizing on the cooperative relationships we have developed with foreign prosecutors, law enforcement, and regulatory agencies to better access evidence and individuals located overseas. Even more significantly, we have dramatically increased our coordination with foreign partners when they are looking at similar or overlapping criminal conduct—so that when we engage in parallel investigations, they complement, rather than compete with, each other."[18] Although global organizations should enhance their ability to conduct a global investigation, they must also take care that their investigations do not violate local law. For example, in some international jurisdictions, government and enforcement authorities may consider an organization's internal investigation to be an obstruction of justice if it is undertaken contemporaneously with an ongoing government investigation.

Enforcement and Accountability Protocols

A consistent and credible disciplinary system is a key control that can be effective in deterring misconduct. Appropriate discipline is also a requirement under leading regulatory and evaluative frameworks. By mandating meaningful sanctions, first line of defense managers can send a signal to both internal and external stake-holders that the organization considers managing misconduct risk a top priority. As such, organizations do well to establish and communicate to employees a well-designed disciplinary process that includes company wide guidelines that promote:

- Progressive sanctions consistent with the nature and seriousness of the offense (e.g., verbal warning, written warning, suspension, pay reduction, location transfer, demotion, or termination)
- Uniform and consistent application of discipline regardless of job level, tenure, or job function

Holding managers accountable for the misconduct of their subordinates is another important consideration. Managers should be disciplined in those instances where they knew, or should have known, that misconduct might be occurring, or when they:

- Directed or pressured others to violate company standards to meet business objectives or set unrealistic goals that had the same effect
- Failed to ensure employees received adequate training or resources
- Failed to set a positive example of acting with integrity or had a prior history of missing or permitting violations
- Enforced company standards inconsistently or retaliated against others for reporting concerns

Disclosure Protocols

Voluntary self-disclosure to the government of criminal misconduct, followed up by cooperation with law enforcement investigations, has long been considered favorably by the government in reducing criminal penalties for convicted corporations. In a recent speech, a top DOJ enforcement official reinforced this practice by opining that "if there is no cooperation, we will continue to investigate and prosecute the old-fashioned way. And companies will face the consequences. . . . [I]f a corporation wants credit for cooperation, it must engage in comprehensive and timely cooperation; lip service simply will not do."[19] The policy of receiving credit for cooperation is also illustrated by various governmental compliance models, including the False Claims Act, where the government's maximum claim is reduced if the organization makes a full disclosure about the false claims, and the FSG, which leave the potential for a reduction in sanctions for those organizations that disclose violations and cooperate with enforcement authorities.

Because of the potential importance of self-reporting, senior management executives and the board, in consultation with second line of defense functions (e.g., compliance and legal) should consider designing formal, principles-based protocols for voluntary and prompt disclosure of violations of law to the government, as appropriate. When misconduct surfaces and the question of whether to report arises, existence of self-disclosure mechanisms will suggest what the right answer is and foster an environment of openness and cooperation. Note, however, that the existence of self-disclosure is never a guarantee against indictment. Self-disclosing criminal misconduct may still result in an enforcement action and eventual collateral litigation by private parties.

Moreover, in certain situations, investigations uncover activities that may trigger financial statement disclosures. For example, illegal acts may have an effect on the amounts presented by management in the entity's financial statements. In this regard, loss contingencies resulting from illegal acts that may be required to be disclosed should be evaluated. Likewise, a disclosure in the financial statements may be triggered by an investigation uncovering an illegal act that may have an effect on the entity's operations. If material review or earnings are derived from transactions involving illegal acts, or if illegal acts create significant unusual risks associated with material revenue or earnings, such as the loss of a significant business relationship, such information should be considered for disclosure. If such cases arise, management must discuss potential disclosures with counsel and the entity's public auditors.

Remedial Action Protocols

Once misconduct has occurred, senior executives and the board, in consultation with second line of defense functions (e.g., compliance and legal) should consider taking action to remedy the harm caused. For example, the organization may wish to consider taking the following steps where appropriate:

- Voluntarily disclosing the results of the investigation to the government or other relevant body (e.g., to law enforcement or regulatory authorities)
- Remedying the harm caused (e.g., initiate legal proceedings to recover monies or other property, compensate those injured by the misconduct, etc.)
- Examining the root causes of the relevant control breakdowns, ensuring that risk is mitigated and that controls are strengthened
- Administering discipline to those involved in the inappropriate actions as well as to those in management positions who failed to prevent or detect such events
- Communicating to the wider employee population that management took appropriate, responsive action

Although public disclosure of misconduct may be embarrassing to an organization, management may nonetheless wish to consider such an action in order to combat or preempt negative publicity, demonstrate good faith, and assist in putting the matter to rest. Moreover, when an organization experiences a substantial integrity breakdown and agrees to cooperate with government enforcement authorities,[20] the latter may allow the organization to enter into a government settlement agreement (GSA) and postpone, or avert entirely, prosecution for the alleged misconduct.[21] Under the terms of a typical GSA, the organization agrees to a list of substantial government demands as an alternative to trial. Such demands may include the requirement for the organization to agree to some or all of the following conditions: conduct an internal investigation or cooperate fully with the government's own investigation; accept full responsibility for the underlying misconduct; agree to pay a fine; undertake substantial changes to the organization's internal controls to help ensure the misconduct is not repeated in the future.

As part of its remediation efforts, the offending organization may also be required to host (and pay for) a corporate monitor to oversee the implementation of the GSA's terms. Such a monitorship may last for a period of years (e.g., a three- to five-year term), overseeing and providing annual reports on the organization's efforts to design and implement a variety of internal controls. Such controls may include drafting an organizational code of conduct; creating a compliance officer position or compliance function; implementing policies to prevent the misconduct from occurring again; conducting compliance training related to the particular risk area in question; establishing anonymous advice and reporting mechanisms (e.g., a hotline or webline). It is important to note that while the incentives to entering a GSA are substantial, so are the organizational resources typically expended to meet the agreement's conditions.

Conclusion

In this chapter we outlined a path that started with understanding the criticality of having the right governance, risk, and compliance framework and an organizational culture that guides decision making at all levels, reflects the company's core values and encourages a commitment to ethical conduct and compliance with the law. We moved out from there and explained how the first line of defense designs and implements the critical policies, programs, and controls needed to support accountability, practical oversight, and a compliant culture at all organizational levels. From there we moved out to establishing a compliance function that is tasked with assisting in the design and implementation of risk management controls to help ensure employee compliance with applicable laws, regulations, and the organization's own policies.

Finally, the path takes you to internal audit and the third line of defense. Internal audit provides assurance on the effectiveness of governance, risk management and internal controls.[22] These activities also provide assurance on the way in which the first and second lines of defense achieve their compliance objectives.[23]

It is important to note that managing organizational compliance is not something that is done once, nor is the effort complete once the compliance program and its attendant internal controls have been designed and implemented, as discussed above. Rather, the real work begins once the program becomes fully operational. At that point, management and the board must provide oversight and leadership for others to follow, the organization should allow internal controls to operate under a watchful monitoring eye, employees must be engaged with meaningful training and communications, and adjustments to the program should be made based upon realities in the field.

All these endeavors (and others) are essential and must be undertaken if the organization's compliance efforts are to be successful. While it will always be impossible to control the behavior of every employee or to entirely eliminate all forms of misconduct, making sure that compliance efforts are constantly renewed and failures are viewed as part of the learning process will allow organizations to reap the rewards of a good record for compliance and a sustainable culture of ethics and integrity.

Chapter 3

Bribery and Corruption

Pamela J. Parizek

The U.S. Department of Justice (DOJ) and the U.S. Securities and Exchange Commission (SEC) have vigorously enforced the U.S. Foreign Corrupt Practices Act (FCPA) since 2005, in contrast to the quiescence of the previous two-and-a-half decades. With public reports indicating that there were more than 100 active corruption investigations in 2015, nearly $2 billion in fines and penalties over the past two years,[1] and an increase of 10 DOJ prosecutors and additional FBI agents focused on FCPA, there can be little doubt that FCPA remains a top priority of the DOJ and SEC, with the DOJ predominantly focused on holding individuals culpable and the SEC the predominant corporate enforcer.

It is equally clear that multijurisdictional enforcement and global cooperation are on the rise. Five of the major FCPA cases in 2014 (Alstom S.A., Alcoa Inc., Smith & Wesson Holding Corp., Hewlett-Packard Co., and Marubeni Corp.) involved cross-border investigative efforts, including not only the United Kingdom's Serious Fraud Office (SFO) but also enforcement agencies in Bahrain, Indonesia, Mexico, Pakistan, Poland, and Russia.[1] According to

Einar B. Gitterman was a major contributor to the content of this chapter. Ms. Gitterman is a senior associate in KPMG's Forensic practice in Washington, DC. Additional contributions were made by **Brian J. McCann, Karen A. Lynch, Nicholas D'Ambrosio** and **Jonathan Meyer**. Mr. McCann is a managing director based in Philadelphia specializing in Investigations. Ms. Lynch, based in Philadelphia, and Mr. D'Ambrosio, based in Houston, are both directors specializing in Investigations. Mr. Meyer, based in Chicago, specializes in Forensic Technology.

TRACE International, non-U.S. enforcement actions concerning alleged bribery of foreign officials more than doubled between 2012 and 2014.[2]

In 2015, that number continued to rise. Over the past decade, the fines levied for corruption have also continued to rise, as governments around the world in this new era of global anti-corruption enforcement have tightened their regulations and increased their enforcement activity and cross-border cooperation. In addition to the general cost in lost output and inefficiency (estimated by the World Bank at $1 trillion a year[3]), companies found to have bribed officials have paid billions of dollars in fines and penalties to the DOJ, the SEC, and foreign regulators.

The surge in regulatory enforcement around the world and the continued expansion of companies into new geographical areas have created a challenging environment in which to conduct anti-bribery and corruption (ABC) compliance. A global survey in 2015 by KPMG International found that the most difficult aspect in managing ABC programs is auditing third-party intermediaries for compliance and conducting due diligence over them.[4] Third parties and due diligence are dealt with later in the chapter.

A corollary to this vigorous enforcement gleaned from a review of U.S. criminal and civil enforcement actions over the past five years shows a marked trend toward leniency for companies with effective compliance programs. As a result, bribery investigations and remediation efforts tend to go hand in hand. These remediation efforts are not limited to policies and procedures at U.S. corporate headquarters; they tend to span worldwide operations and to include training, risk assessments, due diligence, and compliance audits.

As the U.S. government has become more sophisticated in evaluating corporate compliance and governance, regulators are imposing higher standards on companies for implementing effective compliance programs Significantly, more than half of the top FCPA cases against corporate entities in 2014 resulted in the identification of a need to improve FCPA compliance controls (Alstom, Avon, Bio-Rad, Bruker, Marubeni, Layne Christensen Co., and Smith & Wesson). With the DOJ's appointment of a Chief Compliance Officer in 2015, compliance programs will undergo rigorous scrutiny.

The trend toward FCPA enforcement and effective ABC compliance started in the United States and has spread to other countries. The Organization for Economic Co-operation and Development (OECD) established the Convention on Combating Bribery of Foreign Public Officials in International Business Transactions in 1997,[5] and the United Nations (UN) approved a Convention against Corruption in 2003.[6] The United Kingdom was one of the first countries to follow the U.S. lead and, in certain respects, the U.K. Bribery Act[7] goes further than the FCPA, by imposing strict liability for failure to implement "adequate procedures" designed to prevent bribery. Developed countries such as Germany,[8] France,[9] Canada,[10] and Australia[11] have tightened their anti-corruption regulations.

Enforcement by OECD member countries is by no means uniform. In its 2015 progress report,[12] Transparency International, a global anti-corruption watchdog, said that there was little or no enforcement of the OECD's anti-bribery convention in 20 of the 41 member countries, including Japan and Mexico. Overall, though, evidence among more developed countries shows a strengthening in enforcement in 2014–15.

Emerging markets, such as Brazil, Russia, India, and China (the so-called BRICs), have not only stepped up their own ABC enforcement recently but also enacted compliance mandates in some cases that, at least on paper, go beyond the FCPA and the U.K. Bribery Act.

U.S. authorities have made it clear that anti-corruption enforcement is taking on an international dimension. Marshall Miller, principal deputy attorney general for the Criminal Division of the DOJ, has said that the DOJ's recent prosecutions of multinational corporations reflect failures "in global enforcement of compliance programs" and "of any 'culture of compliance' to extend beyond U.S. borders," and the rise of a culture favoring profits over compliance.[13] As a result, anti-corruption agencies around the world are cooperating to investigate wrongdoing that crosses borders. The former U.S. Attorney General, Eric Holder, has said that companies should expect further cooperation among governments, because the United States "must harmonize our domestic regulatory scheme with its global counterparts" in order to "pursue even more criminal cases against bad-actor institutions in the future—no matter their size."[14]

With the United States taking the lead over the past few years, there has been an increased focus on the prosecution of individuals. In 2013 and 2014, more than 20 individuals were prosecuted by the DOJ and SEC. In 2015, U.S. Deputy Attorney General Sally Yates issued a mandate (the "Yates Memorandum") to all federal prosecutors to hold individual corporate officers accountable for corporate misconduct, and 8 of the 10 FCPA cases brought by the DOJ were against individual defendants. In all of the cases brought against a corporation, officers associated with that corporation were also prosecuted.[15] A similar focus on individual prosecutions can be found in actions by the U.K. SFO, as well as prosecutions in Brazil, China, and other countries.[16]

This chapter will analyze the applicable regulations in four jurisdictions (the United States, United Kingdom, Brazil, and China), with a view toward identifying a common approach to global ABC compliance. Through a review and analysis of ABC law and compliance regimes in these countries, the chapter will identify common principles that may be more simple and more effective than customizing compliance for each country. The chapter will also consider the key aspects of an organization's program to prevent, detect, and respond to misconduct involving bribery and corruption.

United States

The United States was the first major economy to criminalize bribery and corruption of foreign officials, enacting the FCPA in 1977 in response to the Watergate scandal, which exposed the use of slush funds to make illegal political contributions. During the SEC's investigation of these political contributions, it learned that companies also used these slush funds to bribe foreign officials. In response to an amnesty program devised to evaluate the extent of the practice, about 400 U.S. companies admitted to paying more than $300 million in bribes to foreign officials. In an effort to restore confidence in the integrity of U.S. business practices, Congress enacted the FCPA.

The FCPA has three principal objectives:

- To prevent and deter the payment of bribes to non-U.S. government officials
- To foster greater transparency in financial reporting
- To create a level playing field for companies operating overseas

Over time, these objectives have evolved through the FCPA enforcement apparatus to include greater responsibility for corporate compliance, more accountability for subsidiaries operating overseas, and enhanced collaboration with foreign regulatory authorities.

The FCPA prohibits the bribery of foreign government officials by U.S. persons and prescribes accounting, record-keeping practices, and implementation of internal controls. The FCPA is codified in two provisions of the 1934 Securities Exchange Act (the Exchange Act): Section 30A contains the anti-bribery provisions and Section 13 contains the accounting provisions.

Anti-Bribery Provisions (Section 30A)

The anti-bribery provisions of the FCPA contain a general rule prohibiting U.S. persons, entities, and issuers from giving anything of value to any "foreign official" in order to obtain or retain business, to influence the official, or to induce the official to act in violation of his lawful duties. The term "foreign official" is defined as any foreign government or employee of any such government or department, agency, or instrumentality; any political party, official, or candidate; any public international organization; or "any person acting in an official capacity for, or on behalf of, any such government or department, agency, or instrumentality, or . . . public international organization."

By definition, this includes third-party agents and intermediaries who act on behalf of foreign officials. The prohibition against payments of "anything of value" is broadly construed by the U.S. government, and there is no materiality threshold. The sweeping nature of the law makes it particularly challenging for multinational enterprises with decentralized global operations to identify who may be covered and what constitutes "anything of value." As a result, most companies have adopted a zero-tolerance policy for payments to any foreign official or intermediary.

Despite the expansive interpretation of the FCPA by U.S. government officials, there is one exception to this general rule and two affirmative defenses to an alleged FCPA violation. The exception applies to routine governmental action and appears in Section 30A (b) of the Exchange Act, which provides that Section 30A (a) shall not apply to "any facilitating or expediting payment" to a foreign official "to expedite or to secure the performance of a routine governmental action." Routine governmental action is defined as an action that is ordinarily and commonly performed by a government official, such as: (1) obtaining licenses or permits to do business; (2) processing government papers such as visas or work orders; (3) providing police protection, mail, or cargo pickup or delivery; (4) providing telephone service; or (5) "actions of a similar nature."

While the latter category is not clearly defined, enforcement activity has established that the action must be clearly ministerial in nature and specifically does not include any decision to award new business or to continue existing business or "to secure any improper advantage." Accordingly, a key question is whether the foreign official or entity to which the payment is made has discretionary authority over the matter at hand.

One of the greatest challenges in qualifying for the facilitation exception is that it is often difficult to make the case that payments made to expedite routine government action really fits within the exception if the payments continue to be made over time. The government has taken the position that routine payments to expedite government action, over time, may create an improper advantage. Another complicating factor is that even where payments are truly made for facilitation purposes, they are not always described as such in the company's books and records. As a result, a company may technically qualify for the facilitation exception but still run afoul of the books and records and internal control provisions of the FCPA. (Notable examples include IBM and Delta Pine, where very small facilitation payments were deemed to violate the books and records and internal controls provisions.)

Aside from the facilitation exception, there are two affirmative defenses to an alleged FCPA violation. To avoid liability under the FCPA, a U.S. company can show that (1) the payment was lawful under the laws of the foreign official's country; or (2) that the payment was a reasonable expenditure for promotional activities. For the payment to be lawful, there must be something in writing to support its legality.

Arguments that the activity is "traditional" or "customary" or that violations are "not enforced," even if confirmed by local counsel, are insufficient. There must be written local authority carrying the force of law. Promotional expenses must be reasonable, bona fide, and clearly connected to the business of the company.

Accounting Provisions (Section 13)

The accounting provisions of the FCPA apply to the books and records and internal controls of corporate issuers. Section 13(b)(2)(A) of the Exchange Act requires issuers to maintain books and records and accounts, which, in reasonable detail, accurately reflect the transactions and dispositions of the issuer. Section 13(b)(2)(B) requires issuers to devise and maintain a system of internal accounting controls sufficient to provide reasonable assurance that transactions are authorized by management and are recorded as necessary to account for assets and to permit the preparation of financial statements in conformity with GAAP. When read in conjunction with Section 30A, this means that permissible payments to foreign officials must be accurately recorded in the issuer's financial statements. The accounting provisions of the FCPA are principally enforced by the SEC.

One of the most instructive cases on the books and records and internal control provisions of the FCPA is a case in 2007 involving Lucent Technology. While the conduct was egregious (thousands of trips for the entertainment of senior Chinese executives to Las Vegas, Disney theme parks, and Niagara Falls), the case was not brought as a bribery case. Instead, it was brought as a textbook violation of the books and records and internal control provisions, because the payments were improperly booked to accounts classified as "factory expense" and "employee lodging." The lapse of internal controls occurred because the company did not have controls in place to prevent those violations and lacked procedures to determine whether the guests they entertained were foreign officials.

An Official Guide

In November 2012, the DOJ and SEC jointly released a guide to FCPA entitled "A Resource Guide to the U.S. Foreign Corrupt Practices Act"[17] (referred to in this chapter as the Guide). The Guide was created to provide businesses and individuals with more details concerning the FCPA, its provisions, and enforcement. The stated objective of the DOJ and SEC was for the Guide to assist businesses and individuals to "abide by the law, detect and prevent FCPA violations, and implement effective compliance programs."

The Guide is 120 pages long and provides the history of the act, the antibribery provisions, accounting provisions, other related U.S. laws, guiding principles of enforcement, FCPA penalties, sanctions and remedies, resolutions, whistleblower provisions and protections, and DOJ opinion procedure. While the Guide goes a long way to clarify some of the ambiguity in the statute, critics have argued the Guide is too broad and does not provide a strict enough interpretation of the law. In June 2015, the DOJ and SEC revised the Guide to provide further clarity on the accounting provisions and criminal penalties, and to bring those chapters into conformity with the language of the statute.

Penalties

The FCPA has both civil and criminal penalties for companies and individuals. The DOJ uses the U.S. Federal Sentencing Guidelines for Organizational Defendants (Guidelines) in order to establish a consistent pattern of criminal penalty assessment. The Guidelines are used to analyze the penalties for all DOJ resolutions including guilty pleas, deferred prosecution agreements (DPAs), non-prosecution agreements (NPAs), and declinations.

The DOJ reviews the facts and the severity of a case in order to determine the "offense level." The offense level can be reduced, depending on such factors as the degree of cooperation with authorities during the investigation, acceptance of responsibility, voluntary disclosure, and preexisting compliance programs, as well as the remediation that has occurred. Liability may extend to the parent company for the misconduct of its subsidiaries. Under the Guide, the DOJ assigns "points," depending on the severity of the violation, and grants credits against those points to reduce the overall penalty. The well-publicized NPAs of Morgan Stanley (2012) and Ralph Lauren (2013) were earned in this way, through self-disclosure, extraordinary cooperation, and timely remediation.

Figure 3.1 summarizes the monetary penalties that may be imposed per violation and the possible imprisonment periods.

	Anti-Bribery	Financial Reporting
Criminal		
Individual	Fines up to $250,000 5 years' imprisonment	Fines up to $5 million 20 years' imprisonment
Corporate	Fines up to $2 million or twice the pecuniary gain	Fines up to $25 million or twice the pecuniary gain
Civil		
Individual	$16,000 per violation	$7,500 to $150,00 per violation or the amount of the pecuniary gain
Corporate	$16,000 per violation	$75,000 to $725,000 or amount of the pecuniary gain

Figure 3.1. Penalties
Source: http://www.sec.gov/spotlight/fcpa/fcpa-resource-guide.pdf

Collateral Consequences

In addition to the criminal and civil penalties detailed above, individuals and companies may face collateral consequences. These include suspension or debarment from contracting with the federal government; cross-debarment from receiving loans from multilateral development banks; the suspension or revocation of export privileges; and/or the appointment of a compliance monitor, defined in the Guide as "an independent third party who assesses and monitors a company's adherence to the compliance requirements of an agreement."[18]

The goal of the monitor is to ensure the implementation of the enhanced compliance requirements placed on the company by the sentence, or by the DPA or NPA. The monitor's aim is also to reduce the likelihood of a future violation. The Guide outlines the following factors the DOJ and SEC consider when determining whether to appoint a monitor: the seriousness of the offense; the duration of the misconduct; the pervasiveness of the misconduct (including whether the conduct cuts across geographic and/or product lines); the nature and size of the company; the quality of the company's compliance program at the time of the misconduct; and subsequent remediation efforts.

Resolutions

Depending upon the facts of the case and how the investigation transpired, there are various considerations the DOJ or SEC may use when determining a final resolution. According to the Guide, when prosecutors assess the existence of federal interest, they weigh all relevant considerations, including:

- What is the nature and seriousness of the offense?
- What is the pervasiveness of wrongdoing within the corporation?
- What is the corporation's history of similar misconduct, including prior criminal, civil, and regulatory enforcement actions against it?
- Was there timely and voluntary disclosure of the wrongdoing?
- Was there willingness to cooperate?
- Did the company have a preexisting compliance program?
- Did the corporation take any remedial actions, such as efforts to implement or improve upon an effective corporate compliance program?
- Did it replace the management responsible, discipline or terminate wrongdoers, pay restitution, and so on?
- Were there any collateral consequences such as disproportionate harm to shareholders?

Possible DOJ and SEC resolutions

DOJ

Plea Agreement. The defendant admits guilt to the charges presented and is generally convicted of the charges when the court accepts the plea agreement.

Deferred Prosecution Agreement (DPA). The DOJ files a charging document in the courts, but simultaneously defers the prosecution. Generally, the defendant will admit to the facts alleged, pay a fine, and undertake additional compliance measures associated with the resolution. In order to obtain a DPA or NPA, the company has to provide evidence of a well-constructed, efficient, well-implemented and enforced ethics program as well as evidence that the company self-policed prior to the discovery of the misconduct. DPAs are posted on the DOJ's website.

Non-Prosecution Agreement (NPA). The DOJ does not formally file charges but retains the right to do so. NPAs differs from DPAs in that the former is not filed in court, but is similar in admission of relevant facts and ongoing compliance measures. NPAs are also posted on the DOJ's website.

Declination. The DOJ declines to bring enforcement under the FCPA. The DOJ will not present nonpublic information on the company or individual.

SEC

Civil Injunction. The SEC seeks a court order to compel the defendant to obey the law in the future. Generally the civil injunction has two main goals: forcing compliance or compensating the injured party as a result of the violation.

Civil Administrative Actions. The SEC brings this type of action when it believes a law has been violated. It is litigated before an SEC administrative law judge. There are various sanctions that can occur as a result of this resolution such as censure, limitation on activities, suspension of up to 12 months, and/or bar from association with the Commission.

Deferred Prosecution Agreement (DPA). The SEC agrees to forgo enforcement action if the company or individual agrees to cooperate

(continued)

fully, waives the right to claim the litigation should be dismissed, complies with the prohibitions and other requirements, and lastly, admits to the charges presented.

Non-Prosecution Agreement (NPA). The SEC will not pursue enforcement action as long as the company or individual agrees to cooperate fully and comply with the terms of the agreement.

Declinations. Declinations and termination letters provide evidence of the SEC's decision not to pursue enforcement action under the FCPA.

Enforcement Trends

Over the past decade, the number of FCPA matters brought by the DOJ and SEC has vastly outnumbered the handful of actions brought in the prior two decades. These statistics represent aggressive cross-border prosecution of individuals and corporate entities (Figures 3.2 and 3.3), and record penalties of more than $1.5 billion in 2014 (Figure 3.4).

Among the lessons learned, corporations with inadequate compliance programs were heavily penalized, whereas those with effective programs received NPAs and declinations. This disparity may be explained by the fact that

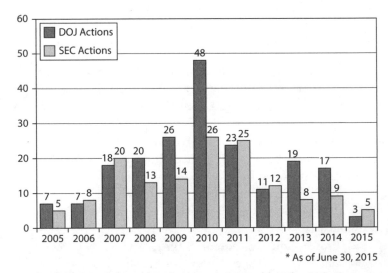

* As of June 30, 2015

Figure 3.2. FCPA Enforcement Actions Initiated by the U.S. Department of Justice (DOJ) and U.S. Securities and Exchange Commission (SEC)
Source: Gibson, Dunn & Crutcher, 2015 Mid-Year FCPA Update, July 6, 2015

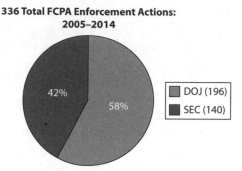

336 Total FCPA Enforcement Actions:
2005–2014

42%
58%

DOJ (196)
SEC (140)

Figure 3.3. FCPA Enforcement actions 2005–2014 (Total 336)
Source: Gibson, Dunn & Crutcher, 2014 Year-End FCPA Update, January 5, 2015

aggressive enforcement by U.S. authorities, coupled with credit for good corporate citizenship, is shifting the burden from the government to corporations to prevent, detect, and respond to ABC risk.

Organizations have responded to this regulatory trend by enhancing their FCPA programs and controls. On the prevention side, companies with global operations have stepped up their FCPA policies, procedures, and training in the

Company	Total Resolution	DOJ Component	SEC Component	Date
Siemens AG*	$800,000,000	$450,000,000	$350,000,000	12/15/2008
Alstom S.A.	$772,290,000	$772,290,000	--	12/22/2014
KBR/Halliburton	$579,000,000	$402,000,000	$177,000,000	02/11/2009
BAE Systems**	$400,000,000	$400,000,000	--	02/04/2010
Total S.A.	$398,200,000	$245,200,000	$153,000,000	05/29/2013
Alcoa	$384,000,000	$223,000,000	$161,000,000	01/09/2014
Snamprogetti/ENI	$365,000,000	$240,000,000	$125,000,000	07/07/2010
Technip S.A.	$338,000,000	$240,000,000	$98,000,000	06/28/2010
JGC Corp.	$218,800,000	$218,800,000	--	04/06/2011
Daimler AG	$185,000,000	$93,600,000	$91,400,000	04/01/2010

* Siemens's U.S. FCPA resolutions were coordinated with a €395 million ($569 million) anti-corruption settlement with the Munich Public Prosecutor.
** BAE pleaded guilty to non-FCPA conspiracy charges of making false statements and filing false export licenses, but the alleged false statements concerned the existence of the company's FCPA compliance program, and the publicly reported conduct concerned alleged corrupt payments to foreign officials.

Figure 3.4. Corporate FCPA Top 10 List
Source: Gibson, Dunn & Crutcher, 2014 Year-End FCPA Update, January 5, 2015

United States and abroad. With respect to detection, the whistleblower bounty program adopted by the SEC as part of its Dodd-Frank reforms has had a significant impact. As a result, on the response side, more companies are inclined either to self-report or to conduct an investigation as rigorous as it would have been had the company elected to self-report (for example, if a whistleblower comes forward and the company has to rationalize, explain, and document its decision not to self-report).

After 10 years of stepped-up enforcement by the DOJ and the SEC, there has been a clear shift from "reactive" FCPA investigations to "proactive" FCPA compliance, through enhanced policies and procedures, redesigned internal controls, pre- and postacquisition FCPA due diligence, more thorough scrutiny of third-party agents, and continuous monitoring and auditing of FCPA compliance. And, as anti-corruption enforcement has spread across the globe, countries are looking to the U.S. FCPA enforcement model for leading practices. To be sure, the U.S. paradigm has been replicated by other regulators, most notably the United Kingdom.

United Kingdom

Enacted in July 2011, 34 years after the FCPA, the U.K. Bribery Act is considered one of the strictest anti-bribery laws internationally.[19] The act creates a modern, single piece of legislation criminalizing, for the first time, a corporation's failure to prevent bribery in the United Kingdom or abroad by an "associated person," which it broadly defines as a person who performs services for, or on behalf of, the corporation. This allows U.K. law enforcement to combat bribery whether committed in the United Kingdom or abroad.[20]

The United Kingdom passed legislation in April 2013 authorizing the use of DPAs in bribery, fraud, and money laundering cases. Some of the factors the prosecutors may consider when deciding whether to enter into DPAs include the existence of a proactive corporate compliance program; the timing of self-reporting; the existence of an isolated incident; and the risk of collateral effects on the public. Organizations under DPAs are required to admit to certain facts publicly, specify the wrongdoing, and agree to comply with strict requirements such as the payment of financial penalties, implementation or enhancement of a compliance program, or disgorgement of profits in return for suspension of the criminal charges.

In June 2013, the City of London Police announced the creation of an international foreign bribery task force to enable countries with similar anti-bribery standards (including the United States, the United Kingdom, Canada, and Australia) to share knowledge, skills, and experience, and to support the OECD and UN anti-bribery conventions.

Key Provisions and "Adequate Procedures" Defense

The U.K. Bribery Act covers the offering, promising, or giving of a bribe (active bribery) and the requesting, agreeing to receive, or accepting of a bribe (passive bribery). The act also sets forth two commercial bribery offenses, including a provision regarding the bribery of foreign public officials in order to obtain or retain business or gain an advantage in the normal course of business. The legislation introduces a new strict liability offense[21] pursuant to which companies and partnerships could be charged criminally if they fail to prevent bribery. An organization could be held criminally liable for bribery in connection with its business, by those working for it or performing services on its behalf ("associated persons").

There is a statutory defense if the organization can demonstrate it had "adequate procedures" in place to prevent bribery. The determination of the level of adequate procedures will depend on the bribery risks the organization faces, as determined during the risk assessment stage, as well as the nature, size, and complexity of the business.

The act applies to U.K. citizens and residents, as well as commercial organizations and entities headquartered, organized, or operating all or part of a business in the United Kingdom, together with any "associated persons" defined as an employee, agent, or subsidiary. Consequences of violations include unlimited corporate fines, a maximum of 10 years' imprisonment, and disqualification from public sector work in the EU and in the United States.

Enforcement to Date

In December 2014, the SFO secured its first conviction under the U.K. Bribery Act (and its predecessor, the Prevention Against Corruption Act) against two officers and two directors of Sustainable AgroEnergy PLC, Sustainable Wealth Investments UK Ltd, and associated companies in connection with sales of biofuel investment products in Southeast Asia.[22] In 2015, the SFO entered into its first-ever DPA with Standard Bank PLC for "failure to prevent bribery" under Section 7 of the Act, pursuant to which a company may be prosecuted for failing to have "adequate procedures" to prevent active bribery by "associated persons." Standard Bank also settled with the SEC. The SFO brought a second Section 7 case against Sweett Group plc for its failure to prevent its Dubai subsidiary from paying bribes to win a hotel construction contract.

Outside the United Kingdom, the SFO has been collaborating with law enforcement agencies in other countries. In late 2013, the SFO[23] and DOJ opened two formal criminal investigations for allegations of bribery and corruption at U.K. aircraft engine maker Rolls-Royce in Indonesia and China.[24] In 2014, the SFO has been working alongside Chinese authorities in the first

Anglo-Chinese investigation of alleged corruption and bribery case at the drug maker GlaxoSmithKline.[25] The company was accused by Chinese authorities of funnelling up to 3 billion yuan (approximately $480 million) in bribes to encourage doctors to use its medicines. And in late 2015, UK authorities arrested five Nigerians for alleged bribery and money laundering. Examples of cross-border cooperation among anti-bribery agencies are likely to grow. "The global nature of financial markets provides enormous business opportunities, but also creates opportunity for economic crime. The criminal justice response can only be effective if it is able to respond on a global level, untrammeled by physical and jurisdictional barriers," said Dominic Grieve, the U.K. attorney general in January 2014.[26]

Future Trends

Although it is too soon to identify a pattern of enforcement in the United Kingdom, it is safe to assume that there will be greater enforcement activity as the United Kingdom gains experience in the field. While the number of enforcement actions has been low, given that the Bribery Act applies only to conduct that occurred after July 1, 2011, this number is rising as the SFO builds its capability and commitment to bring successful large-scale prosecutions of complex cases of economic crime. In response, companies will need to develop and implement an effective compliance program to mitigate legal, reputational, and financial risk.

Bribery Act Guidance

As in the United States, the United Kingdom provides guidance to help manage compliance. The act sets forth six principles[27] that are intended to assist organizations in determining what anti-bribery procedures, if any, need to be implemented. The principles include:

- **Proportionality**. The actions the organization takes are proportionate to its size and assessed risk.
- **Top-Level Commitment**. The leaders of the organization demonstrate a commitment to countering bribery and to set an example for transparency and integrity, establishing a culture where bribery is never acceptable. The leadership also assigns responsibility and authority for implementing the anti-bribery program.
- **Risk Assessment**. Conduct regular and comprehensive risk assessment to determine the nature and extent of risks relating to bribery.
- **Due Diligence**. Ask the right questions and perform background checks before doing business with third parties, agents, contractors, or suppliers.

- **Communication and Training**. Communicate policies and procedures, and provide training to all employees and high-risk third parties including agents, intermediaries, contractors, and suppliers.
- **Monitoring and Review**. Internal controls are subject to regular internal review and audit, with periodic reporting to the audit committee, the board of directors, or an equivalent body. Obtain external assurance or verification of the organization's anti-bribery program.

Brazil

Brazil has long been viewed as having a significant problem with corruption and bribery. In 2015, Brazil was ranked seventy-sixth out of 175 countries on Transparency International's Corruption Perception Index.[28] In recent years, there have been some efforts to address this issue. In 2005, Brazil became a party to the UN Convention against Corruption. Then, following widespread public protests against corruption, lawmakers passed the Clean Companies Act[29] (the Brazilian Act), which became effective as of January 2014. The passage of the Act was timely. Two months later, the Brazilian authorities learned of a kickback schemein which senior executives in Petrobras, the government-controlled oil company, colluded with a cartel of enterprises to overcharge it for construction and service work. As of August 2015, the Brazilian authorities had issued 117 indictments, arrested five politicians, and brought criminal cases against 13 companies in its ongoing investigation, dubbed "Operation Lava Jato" (car wash). Petrobras officials estimate that the amount of bribes totaled $3 billion.[30]

Scope and Key Provisions

The Brazilian Act establishes strict civil and administrative liability for companies found guilty of foreign or domestic bribery. Previously, there was no specific law that enabled Brazilian authorities to prosecute corporations for corrupt acts committed by their employees or agents, as the law only imposed liability on the individuals who committed the acts. The Brazilian Act covers areas broader than just corruption. The Brazilian Act includes provisions that deal with bribery, fraud in public procurement, bid rigging, and fraud in contracts signed with public bodies, impairing public officers' investigative activities, and influencing or financing others to engage in illegal acts against the government.

The law defines bribery as "promoting, offering or giving, directly or indirectly, an improper benefit to a public agent or a third person related to him (or her)." Specifically, the Brazilian Act prohibits the following "wrongful acts":

- Promising, offering, or giving an undue advantage, directly or indirectly, to a public official, or a third person related to the official

- Financing, sponsoring, or in any way subsidizing the performance of a wrongful act under the law
- Using another person or entity as an intermediary in order to conceal the company's real interests or the identity of the beneficiaries of the illegal act
- Obstructing or interfering with the investigations, audits, and the general work of public agencies, entities, or officials

Furthermore, the Brazilian Act contains provisions that specifically address government tenders and contracts. The Brazilian Act prohibits defrauding the competitive nature of a public tender process; preventing, hindering, or defrauding the performance of any act of a public tender process; creating a fraudulent entity to secure a government contract; and illegally benefiting from modifications or extensions of government contracts.

The Brazilian Act applies to all Brazilian companies and entities operating in Brazil, which essentially means that any company with offices, branches, or agents in Brazil could be held liable under the Brazilian Act for corruption against public authorities in Brazil or abroad. Additionally, the Brazilian Act imposes successor liability in the event of mergers and acquisitions. As in the United Kingdom, sanctions imposed are not dependent on proof of criminal liability on the part of officers, directors, employees, or agents of the company. Of special note is that prosecutors are not required to establish intent on behalf of the parties involved.

Penalties

The Brazilian Act imposes severe penalties for violations that include administrative and judicial sanctions. Violations could result in fines of up to 20 percent of the company's total gross revenue for the prior year or a maximum of 60 million reais (approximately $27 million). Additionally, the law allows government authorities to suspend the company's operations, seize its assets, force dissolution, or prevent the company from being able to compete for government contracts. The law also gives the government the authority to ban a company from receiving any form of public lending for up to five years.

Enforcement Trends

According to Transparency International,[31] prior to the act, Brazil had pursued only one case and two investigations of bribery in the 12 years since ratifying the OECD convention. Since the act became effective in 2014, there have been some notable developments. Soon after its enactment, there was an indictment by the Brazilian regulatory authorities against Brazilian aircraft manufacturer

Embraer in connection with alleged bribes to secure a $92 million military procurement contract in the Dominican Republic. The indictment was based upon information provided in a parallel proceeding by the DOJ and SEC. More recently, Brazilian officials opened corruption investigations into Petrobras (discussed above) and Eletrobras, the state-owned electric utility company.

Compliance Credit

Similar to the U.S. and U.K. anti-bribery laws, the Brazilian Act provides less stringent treatment for companies that have an adequate anti-bribery compliance program and for companies that self-report misconduct. The Brazilian Act generally outlines compliance efforts that would enable companies to negotiate reduced penalties or be eligible for a leniency agreement. Those efforts include the existence of an effective internal compliance program, audit capabilities, reporting policies and mechanisms, and the existence and effectiveness of internal codes of ethics and conduct. Article 7 of the Brazilian Act states that "the existence of internal mechanisms, procedures of integrity . . . as well as the effective enforcement of codes of ethics will be taken into account when applying sanctions." Other factors listed are the seriousness of the offenses, the company's level of cooperation, and the degree of damages.

Additionally, the Brazilian Act permits local enforcement authorities to sign leniency agreements under certain conditions, such as under circumstances where companies self-report, end the alleged misconduct, and fully cooperate with the investigation. Companies who fulfill the above may be able to negotiate an agreement in which their penalties are reduced by up to two-thirds of the total potential fines (except forfeiture or restitution), and protection against the withholding of benefits as well as the confidentiality of some parts of the agreement.

Brazilian companies and foreign companies operating in Brazil that have yet to take any measures to prevent bribery and corruption should promptly consider implementing such measures. Foreign companies operating in Brazil should examine their existing policies and procedures to assure that they are in compliance with Brazilian law. Anti-corruption mechanisms, such as a code of conduct, internal controls, and compliance training, should be examined and enhanced where necessary to assure that all directors, employees, and agents are aware of the new requirements.

China

Most U.S. companies operating internationally have established systems to comply with the requirements of the FCPA. Additionally, many companies have established systems to comply with the anti-bribery laws of their host countries, such as the U.K. Bribery Act. Fewer companies have developed compliance systems designed specifically to ensure compliance with the anti-corruption laws in China, where the government, as part of its "Five-Year Anti-Corruption Plan" announced by President Xi Jinping, has been emphasizing the importance of combatting bribery since the 18th National Congress in November 2012.[32] The Chinese government has stepped enforcement as a result. According to China's Supreme People's Procuratorate (SPP), prosecutors in 2014 probed 3,664 cases of graft, bribery, and embezzlement of public funds involving more than 1 million yuan (approximately $164,000). In addition, 7,827 bribers were prosecuted for criminal offenses in 2014, 38 percent more than the previous year.[33]

2015 was a landmark year for China with respect to its focus on eradicating bribery. On May 1, 2015, the PRC enacted a new law, the Ninth Criminal Law Amendment of the PRC (effective November 1, 2015) criminalizing bribery of non-PRC government officials, officials of public international institutions, and close relatives of such officials. It also provides for monetary penalties against individual defendants. Conspicuously absent are any exceptions or affirmative defenses, as in the United States and the U.K. The new PRC legislation, coupled with an uptick in whistleblower reports and aggressive enforcement action marks a new anti-corruption regime in China.

The new criminal law supplements two existing statutes that pertain to corruption and bribery:

- The Criminal Law of the People's Republic of China, effective 1979 (Criminal Law)[34]
- The Anti-Unfair Competition Law (AUCL) of the People's Republic of China, effective 1993[35]

There are additional anti-corruption related regulations, interpretations, and other supplements to these statutes, including the Provisional Measures on the Prohibition of Commercial Bribery issued by the State Administration for Industry and Commerce. Additionally, China has been a party to the UN Convention against Corruption since 2006.

While the AUCL mainly focuses on commercial bribery, the Criminal Law covers both official bribery and commercial bribery, depending on the identity of the recipient of a bribe.

Official Bribery

Under the Criminal Law, official bribery is an offer to bribe a "state functionary." The law defines a "state functionary" to include (1) a person who performs public services in a state-owned company or enterprise, institution, or organization; (2) a person who is assigned by a state or a state-owned company, enterprise, or institution to a company, enterprise, or institution that is not owned by the state to perform public services; and (3) any other person who performs public services. Official bribery is considered a criminal offense and is covered under the following articles:

- Acceptance of a bribe by a public official (Article 385)
- Acceptance of a bribe by a public entity, including state-owned enterprises and other public entities (Article 387)
- Active bribery of a public official by an individual (Article 389)
- Active bribery of an entity by an individual or an entity (Article 391)
- Active bribery of a public official by an entity (Article 393)
- Serving as an intermediary in the commission of an illegal bribe (Article 392)

In August 2015, China's National People's Congress adopted amendments to the Criminal Law that added the crime of providing bribes to state functionaries' close relatives. They also added further monetary penalties and raise the bar for bribe-givers to be exempted from punishment.[36]

In general, state functionaries are not allowed to receive bribes, small or large. However, Bribery Prosecution Standards issued by the Supreme People's Procuratorate in 2000[37] stated that cases will be prosecuted only if the amount at stake exceeds 100,000 yuan. In cases where the amount is less than 100,000 yuan, the individual giving the bribe is likely to be prosecuted for the following reasons: if the bribe was to seek an illegal interest or given to a communist party official or government leader; if more than three individuals were bribed at the same time; and/or if the bribe negatively affected social or national interests.

Commercial Bribery

Under the Criminal Law, commercial bribery refers to unfair anticompetition acts committed by private individuals or companies. The AUCL definition for a commercial bribe is broader than the Criminal Law, and Article 8 of the AUCL defines commercial bribery as an offer of property or use of "other means" to purchase or sell products or services in a manner that excludes fair competition. The term "property" is defined as cash, assets, or kickbacks, and the term "other means" is referred to as travel or entertainment. Since the definition of commercial bribery under the AUCL is very broad, the act of giving gifts or other benefits in a commercial setting could be considered commercial bribery. Commercial bribery could result in either a criminal or a noncriminal offense, depending on the value of the bribe.

In civil actions, Chinese authorities have jurisdiction to investigate in cases where:

■ The contract was entered into or executed in China
■ The property under dispute is located in China
■ The defendant has an office in China

In criminal actions, Chinese authorities have jurisdiction to investigate the following crimes:

■ The crime is committed in China, or on Chinese ships or aircrafts
■ The result of the criminal act occurs in China
■ The act is committed by Chinese citizens outside China
■ The act is committed by foreigners against China or its citizens outside China
■ The act is committed under international treaties, where China is obligated to exercise its jurisdiction

Penalties

The official bribery offenses under the Chinese Criminal Law could trigger severe criminal liability and could result in criminal detention, life imprisonment, and confiscation of property. The penalties for commercial bribery include up to 10 years' imprisonment and criminal fines. Management personnel could be held liable if found directly responsible for the matter. Chinese companies and companies operating in China should consider existing policies and procedures in place when dealing with representatives of state-owned enterprises.

Under the AUCL, penalties are less severe than under the Criminal Law and the violations do not amount to a criminal offense. Potential penalties include up to 200,000 yuan and up to 10 years' imprisonment. Additionally, competitors are allowed to bring a civil claim for damages if they believe they were negatively affected by the commercial bribery.

Whistleblower Legislation

China has established a 24-hour corruption hotline with various Chinese authorities such as the Public Security Bureau, the Bureau of Administration for Industry and Commerce, and various court and prosecution departments.[38] The goal of the hotline is for the government to receive reports of corrupt practices of government officials who receive bribes. Unlike the incentives that exist for whistleblowers in the United States, in China, the financial incentives are limited, depending on the province, and are capped at 200,000 yuan.

Defenses and Mitigation Measures

Currently, there are only two defenses for noncriminal commercial bribery in China:

1. Discounts or commissions are permitted if they are properly accounted for in the company's books and records
2. Promotional goods of small value are permitted, if they are a common practice in the particular industry

There are no specific provisions in the current Chinese anti-bribery regulation stating that the implementation of anti-bribery measures such as a compliance program would provide a defense against prosecution by the Chinese government. Nevertheless, in 2009, Chinese authorities initiated a new anti-corruption campaign targeting public officials, state-owned enterprises, and domestic and international companies operating in China. As part of the campaign, all businesses were expected to have taken measures such as establishing or modifying their code of conduct, policies and procedures, and training programs. Businesses that failed to do so are viewed unfavorably by local authorities from both a legal and political standpoint.

Although not specified in the law, companies may present their anti-bribery prevention methods as evidence that the acts under investigation were in fact contrary to the company's policies and procedures and could potentially prevent the company from being prosecuted.

Enforcement Trends

In the past year, there has been a significant shift in regulatory enforcement activity in China. Before, enforcement activity was directed primarily at domestic organizations and individuals. But recently, multinational corporations and non-Chinese nationals have found themselves targets of Chinese investigations and enforcement actions in connection with China's well-publicized anti-corruption campaign.[39] The local authorities in charge of enforcing the majority of the anti-bribery regulation in China are the police and the People's Courts. However, given the fact that the fight against corruption has a political dimension, other agencies also have begun to play significant roles in the enforcement of anti-corruption laws.

The current climate of enforcement has shown that Chinese authorities are now taking a more active role in the fight against bribery. This has included increased cooperation with neighboring countries, the United States and United Kingdom. According to China's Ministry of Justice,[40] China has signed more than 50 mutual legal assistance agreements for criminal matters and more than 35 bilateral extradition treaties in the past few years. In September 2014, the provincial court in Hunan ruled that the Chinese subsidiary of pharmaceutical company GlaxoSmithKline (GSK) had offered money or property to nongovernment personnel in order to obtain improper commercial gains, and was found guilty of bribing nongovernment personnel.[41] The company was fined 3 billion yuan (approximately $480 million) following investigations by China's Ministry of Public Security.

In 2013, Chinese authorities investigated several other China-based multinational pharmaceutical companies. China's National Health and Family Planning Commission issued the Regulations on Establishment of Commercial Bribery Records for the Purchase and Sale of Medicines that blacklist healthcare companies engaging in commercial bribery.[42] The rule took effect in March 2014 and poses significant commercial and reputational risks for companies operating in the healthcare sector in China.

Compliance Program Controls

Given all the different compliance requirements and regimes, how can organizations effectively prevent ABC risk? By all accounts, the most effective weapon is a strong compliance program. As articulated by the DOJ and SEC in the Guide, there is no "one-size-fits-all" compliance program.[43] Each compliance program should be tailored to the companies' specific needs. According to the Guide, when the DOJ and SEC evaluate the effectiveness of a compliance program they rely on three questions:

- Is the company's compliance program well designed?
- Is it being applied in good faith?
- Does it work?

To answer these questions, the Guide published 10 "Hallmarks of an Effective Compliance Program"[44] to help companies identify the necessary measures:

- Commitment from senior management against corruption and a clearly articulated policy
- Code of conduct and compliance policies and procedures
- Oversight, autonomy, and resources
- Risk assessments
- Training and continuing advice
- Incentives and disciplinary measures
- Third-party due diligence and payments

- Confidential reporting and internal investigation
- Periodic testing and review for continuous improvement
- Mergers and acquisitions: preacquisition due diligence and postacquisition integration

The Guide is similar to the Internal Control—Integrated Framework of the Committee of Sponsoring Organizations of the Treadway Commission[45] (known as the COSO Framework) and lists three main components of an effective compliance program: prevention, detection and response. When these components are implemented correctly and work in tandem, they assist in mitigating the risk of corruption. In Chapter 2, a comprehensive framework for compliance was presented. Figure 3.5 highlights the key attributes of an effective ABC compliance structure focused on the three components of prevention, detection, and response that need to be part of the larger, more comprehensive compliance framework discussed earlier.

Within the compliance program, all components and subcomponents are interrelated. The aggregate is referred to as anti-bribery "programs and controls." To ascertain whether an ABC compliance program is effective, it is necessary to establish, as with all compliance programs, that it is well-designed, implemented, and operating effectively. In other words, it must be well designed, it must be applied in good faith, and it must work.

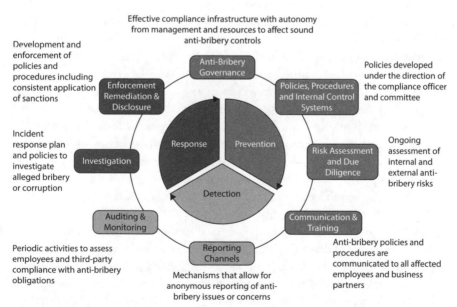

Figure 3.5. Anti-Bribery and Corruption Compliance Framework

Preventative Controls

An organization's board of directors and the audit or compliance committee are ultimately responsible for providing oversight of antifraud programs and controls regarding FCPA/ABC laws and regulations. The day-to-day responsibility for these controls, however, resides with management, typically the chief compliance officer, who is also expected to ensure that an appropriate tone at the top and culture of compliance exists and is supported with appropriate resources based upon the company's size, complexity, geographical scope, and business risk. According to the Guide, the DOJ and SEC will specifically consider the company's staffing and resources relative to the size, structure, and risk profile of the business.[46]

For companies with global operations, governance should be evaluated at the country level or, at a minimum, at the regional level. To this end, many companies have established a compliance function in each region, with direct reporting responsibility and accountability to headquarters.

Risk Assessment.   To develop an effective compliance program to detect, prevent, and respond to ABC risk, an organization must understand the types of risks it faces. All organizations face a variety of corruption risks. However, particular focus needs to be placed on the risks that third parties present. The 2014 OECD Foreign Bribery report noted that 75 percent of the cases in 2014 involved improper payments to third parties.

In conducting a risk assessment, the most critical risk factor is the extent to which the organization interacts with foreign government officials. Additional risk factors to be considered include country risk, industry risk, corporate structure, compliance maturity, and track record. An ABC risk assessment may be performed as part of an entity-wide risk assessment or it can be performed separately. An effective ABC risk assessment will consider the entity level, the business cycle, all business units or operational divisions, including international operations, and all significant accounts or classes of transactions. Additionally, ABC risk assessments should be performed annually or as circumstances warrant. Changes in operations, implementation of new technology, corporate restructurings, mergers or acquisitions, or the allegation or instance of fraud or misconduct may warrant a new corruption risk assessment.

As with any such assessment, it is critical to assess both the likelihood that a risk might occur and the significance of its occurrence. In assessing the risk of corruption, it is critical to understand the touch points with foreign governments and the reliance on third parties such as agents, brokers, vendors, attorneys, or consultants. Among other things, the Guide specifically cautions that risk assessments focusing on entertainment and gifts rather than large government bids, questionable payments to consultants, or excessive discounts to resellers and distributors "may indicate that a company's compliance program is ineffective."[47]

The risk assessment process is critical to the development of policies, procedures, and internal controls. The Guide specifically requires compliance programs to address issues identified during the risk assessment process. Further, as an organization's risk increases, the Guide prescribes increased compliance procedures, including due diligence and periodic audits based on country and industry sector, prospective business partners, level of government interaction, and exposure to customs and immigration officials, to name a few.

Policies and Procedures. An effective system of internal controls is a cornerstone of an organization's ABC compliance program. In April 2014, Kara Brockmeyer, the chief of the SEC Enforcement Division's FCPA Unit, emphasized the importance of internal controls when she said that "companies have a fundamental obligation to ensure that their internal controls are both reasonably designed and appropriately implemented across their entire business operations."[48] However, even the most well-designed policies and procedures will fail to prevent misconduct if they are not implemented or operating effectively. Accordingly, it is critical to assess whether the policies, procedures, and associated internal controls are working.

The COSO framework provides guidance on establishing reasonable assurance that internal controls are operating effectively. The framework defines internal control as a process, effected by an entity's board of directors, management, and other personnel, designed to provide reasonable assurance regarding the achievement of objectives relating to operations, reporting, and compliance.

In practice, an organization's internal controls will include ABC-related policies, procedures, and other control activities to address relevant ABC risks. ABC-related policies are statements by management or the board to guide compliance with applicable laws and regulations. Policies are effectuated through procedures. Control activities are actions established by policies and procedures and undertaken by an organization's personnel to mitigate risks of noncompliance. ABC-related policies, procedures, and control activities commonly include all processes that relate to interactions with government officials or "government touch points."

Examples of typical ABC-related processes include controls governing payments for gifts and entertainment, licensing and permits, fines and penalties, trade and customs as well as the selection of, due diligence on, and payments to third-party intermediaries (TPIs) and business partners. As risky processes become more circumscribed, personnel predisposed to obtaining unfair advantage by paying bribes and making other corrupt payments are incentivized to devise ways to work around more loosely controlled processes to achieve their ends. For this and other reasons, internal control systems must constantly evolve through periodic iterations of risk assessment, gap analysis, control redesign, implementation, and monitoring to maintain their effectiveness.

According to global guidance issued by the Institute of Internal Auditors (IIA), the organization's ABC standards should be clearly defined and should include protocols for third-party dealings, payment processing, expense reporting, and training. The IIA also advocates the use of the internal audit function to test whether policies and procedures are appropriately documented, approved by management, compliant with applicable laws and regulations, and implemented effectively.[49]

With respect to implementation, it is essential for ABC standards of conduct to be rolled out to all company employees, third-party agents, and intermediaries where applicable, and to include mechanisms to grant waivers, document approvals, retain records, and respond to inquiries. Operating effectiveness requires periodic review by the board and executive management to address changes in the legal or operating environment. Finally, ABC policies and procedures should be updated periodically and translated into local languages for all geographic locations. They should also be provided to new employees and any third-party agents and intermediaries at the time of issuance, upon hire, and upon contract execution and/or renewal.

Contracts with TPIs should include clauses requiring compliance with ABC laws and specifically prohibiting third parties from making any illegal payments to government officials as part of their business relationship. Contracts should also include language requiring compliance with all local laws and company policy, prior approval of subagents, a right to audit clause, and a termination clause for failure to abide by the terms of the contract.

Due Diligence.   In addition to general policies and procedures, many companies will risk-score all third parties and conduct FCPA-specific enhanced due diligence on those with the highest risk score; these often include agents and TPIs. Typically this is achieved via questionnaires completed by the third parties during the onboarding process and may be supplemented with background checks. It is important to note that third-party due diligence processes may vary dramatically from country to country due to privacy and data protection laws. As such, it is important to consult with local laws before undertaking due diligence in new jurisdictions. In the context of mergers and acquisitions, preacquisition due diligence alone will not suffice. U.S. regulators will also expect postacquisition integration of the acquired entity including, but not limited to, translation of, and training on, ABC policies and procedures, as well as implementation of ABC compliance controls at the acquired entity.

The Guide issued by the DOJ and SEC provides information on enhanced monitoring of TPI relationships. It recommends that "companies should undertake some form of ongoing monitoring of third-party relationships. Where appropriate, this may include updating due diligence periodically, exercising audit rights, providing periodic training, and requesting annual compliance certifications by the third party." This level of suggested oversight increases corporate responsibility to ensure TPI relationships are operating in a compliant manner. As such, setting up a formal program to enforce audit rights and to assess and monitor the activities of TPIs is pivotal to demonstrating that a compliance program is adequate. A robust TPI assessment program should include:

- Precontract negotiations
- Pre- and postacquisition due diligence
- Continuous TPI reporting
- FCPA/ABC compliance audits

Communication and Training. Good communications and training are essential components of any compliance program, including ABC compliance. The SEC and DOJ expect that policies and procedures will be communicated throughout the organization and include training and certification to all officers, directors, employees, and as appropriate, agents and business partners. As a practical matter, training should be conducted in local business units in native language, with real-life scenarios and case studies. Training should also include information on resources available to seek advice or report potential improper payments.[50]

In evaluating the design, implementation, and operating effectiveness of ABC communication and training, it is important to verify that a formal communication plan exists and includes communications by senior managers setting the correct tone, as well as ABC standards of conduct that apply to employees, third-party agents, and intermediaries. In addition, channels should be available to employees and outside parties to seek advice or report suspected misconduct.

Training should be based on the organization's risk assessment process, and it should be periodically reassessed in response to changes in assessed FCPA/ABC risk. The IIA recommends general ABC training for all employees and customized training by function or job responsibility to address specific ABC risks. Attendance at training events should be tracked where permitted under local law, and noncompliance with training requirements should be sanctioned and reflected in performance evaluations. Finally, per the Guide, a company should establish mechanisms to provide guidance on complying with the company's ethics and compliance program.

Detective Controls

The best-designed ABC compliance programs, even if implemented and operating effectively, will not eliminate ABC risk. The question then becomes, how can organizations most effectively detect potential violations? The two most common methods for detecting potential corruption issues are reporting channels and ongoing auditing and monitoring.

Hotlines and Whistleblower Mechanisms.   Reporting channels include hotlines and whistleblower mechanisms for employees or third parties to seek guidance and report concerns or violations of ABC laws, regulations, or organizational standards. Local law may govern protocols for reporting potential misconduct and should be carefully considered in each jurisdiction where the company does business. Germany and France, for example, have very strict laws that govern the reporting of potential misconduct.

Where hotlines exist, it is important that they be manned by qualified operators, trained in identifying potential issues relating to ABC policies and able to provide real-time guidance on those policies. Training should also be provided for appropriate company personnel to identify and classify ABC concerns that may trigger financial reporting risk, as well as protocols to escalate ABC allegations to the audit committee. Finally, reporting channels should be prominently publicized, and include communications with not only employees, but also external and third-party entities such as agents, vendors, and consultants. Implementation audits should be performed to ensure that these reporting channels are operational.

Auditing and Monitoring.   Auditing and monitoring in the ABC context are the responsibility of internal audit and management, respectively. According to the International Professional Practices Framework Practice Guide published by the IIA, the role of internal audit is to establish auditing and monitoring activities to provide management and the board adequate and timely information, and to test ABC controls to ensure that those controls are operating effectively. This retrospective testing is distinct from the real-time monitoring responsibilities expected of management. However, both activities are expected to be conducted in accordance with the company's risk assessment, with attention to any specific concerns identified in the risk-assessment process.

Data Analytics.   The use of data analytics is important for ongoing auditing and monitoring activities, including monitoring transactions with third parties for indications of potentially problematic payments. Many companies have developed a suite of ABC tests that assess all transactions against known characteristics of bribery to develop a risk score for each transaction. The advantages are twofold. While individual tests can highlight specific instances of bribery on a continuous or near-real-time basis, the risk scores form the foundation of the sample methodology for periodic audits and controls testing. The development of these tests is often closely linked to the risk assessment performed in earlier stages, and the tests may vary from country to country, depending on the particular risk factor.

A well-functioning data analytics component often includes dynamic dashboards and interactive visualizations to permit individualized access to the underlying data sets. Additionally, incorporating text analysis capabilities to evaluate payment description fields against a library of suspicious terms and phrases is particularly helpful in identifying novel bribery schemes. By proactively analyzing the vast quantities of transactional and other data, a company can not only detect possible bribery in near real time, but also demonstrate a good-faith effort to implement an effective compliance program.

To illustrate, technology can help to demonstrate an effective compliance program by providing ongoing monitoring of three key process-specific antifraud controls: authorization controls, segregation of duties, and automated exception reporting. By way of example, one significant authorization control pertaining to FCPA/ABC compliance relates to facilitation payments. Specifically, approval of facilitation payments should be made in accordance with management's general or specific ABC policies and procedures. For instance, facilitation payments should be reviewed by a senior manager, as well as individuals in the compliance and/or legal function, to ensure that the proposed disbursement does not constitute an improper payment.

By leveraging technology, it is possible to monitor authorizations, or to reject reimbursement requests that lack such authorizations. Similar programs may be used to monitor "preapproval" of gifts, hospitality, and entertainment expenses of sales and marketing personnel and any other individuals that interact with foreign officials. Other examples include the review and approval of political and charitable contributions, payments to third parties, and payments to offshore accounts for services performed locally, payments inconsistent with vendor authorization or contract terms, and payments processed without proper segregation of duties.

Responsive Controls

A review of DOJ prosecutions and SEC enforcement proceedings over the past decade reveals a willingness to exercise leniency toward companies with effective response protocols. Response protocols include internal investigations, remediation, accountability, and disclosure protocols. In recent years, there has been a tendency to conduct internal investigations and remedial measures simultaneously. Those companies that have done so effectively, in accordance with the Guide, have been recognized for their efforts. With that background, how can organizations effectively respond to ABC risk?

Internal Investigations.   Once an organization has knowledge of a potential ABC violation, it must conduct a comprehensive, objective, and professional internal investigation. The purpose of the investigation is to gather facts leading to a credible assessment of suspected violations. If ABC policies, guidelines, or procedures have been violated, an effective investigation will help the organization to ascertain the reason for the violation and design appropriate remedial measures. Whenever there are investigations conducted in connection with DOJ and SEC proceedings, it is often necessary to retain independent external counsel.

Enforcement, Disclosure, and Remediation.   The reality today is that investigations and remediation are often conducted simultaneously. Disclosure may occur at the same time or subsequent to the conclusion of the investigation or regulatory matter. Those companies that determine to self-report a potential ABC violation to the government tend to make a public disclosure at the same time.

Enforcement and accountability protocols, which are as important as investigation and remediation protocols, are designed to enforce disciplinary actions within the organization and to hold both management and employees accountable for their actions and the actions of their subordinates. Disclosure protocols govern the extent to which communications are made inside and outside the company. In most cases, management's voluntary and public disclosure of misconduct can preempt negative publicity, demonstrate good faith, and help an organization avoid or mitigate the consequences of a government enforcement action when ABC violations occur.

Conclusion

The compliance framework outlined in the preceding pages is largely U.S.-centric, given the prominence of U.S. regulation in the ABC enforcement arena. The compliance paradigm reflects a predominantly principles-based approach to ABC prevention, detection, and response that arguably has universal application. Certainly the ABC compliance requirements in the United States and the United Kingdom have much in common, while ABC compliance in the BRICs is in its infancy.

Yet all jurisdictions provide some form of credit for establishing an ABC compliance program. In the United Kingdom, an adequate compliance program is recognized as a defense to an allegation of ABC noncompliance. Although it is not a defense in the United States, Brazil, and China, an adequate compliance program may reduce penalties for ABC noncompliance.

The conclusion is that, as a general rule, it is possible to adopt a principles-based approach to the design, implementation, and operating effectiveness of ABC compliance programs on a global basis. The adoption of different standards in different jurisdictions is generally unnecessary except where there are anomalies in the law, in the compliance culture, or in the economy that require a deviation from the general rule (Figure 3.6) and implementation of rule-based controls. As companies expand their ABC compliance regimes around the world, these common principles will promote consistency and transparency.

	United States	United Kingdom	Brazil	Russia	India	China
Source of Law	Foreign Corrupt Practices Act	The Bribery Act 2010 (in force from 1 July 2011)	Anti-Corruption Law on the Liability of Legal Entities (Clean Companies Act) The Criminal Code	Criminal Code Code on Administrative Offences Federal Law on Anti-Corruption Federal Law on Counteraction Against Laundering of Income Received by Illegal Means and Financing of Terrorism Federal Law on State Civic Service	Companies Act of 2013 The Prevention of Corruption Act 1988 ("PCA") The Foreign Contribution (Regulation) Act 2010 ("FCRA") The Indian Penal Code 1860 ("IPC")	The PRC Criminal Law The PRC Anti Unfair Competition Law The Interim Rules of the State Administration for Industry and Commerce on Prohibition of Commercial Bribery
Is an adequate compliance program a defense?	No, but an adequate compliance program could reduce potential penalties.	Yes.	No, but an adequate compliance program and self-reporting of misconduct could reduce penalties.	No.	Yes.	No, but companies can present ABC prevention programs as evidence that an act violated company policy and protect the company from prosecution.
Compliance Requirements	Commitment from senior management and clearly articulated policy against corruption Code of conduct and compliance policies and procedures Oversight, autonomy, and resources Risk assessments Training and continued advice Incentives and disciplinary measures	Proportionality: Organization's actions are proportionate to risks and size top-level commitment by leadership Risk assessments Due diligence with third parties Communication of policies and procedures as well as	Effective internal compliance program Audit capabilities Reporting policies and mechanisms Existence and effectiveness of internal codes of ethics and conduct	Clear ABC compliance policies Appropriate tone at the top Ensuring sufficient autonomy and resources for compliance personnel Involving employees in ABC communications and training and providing reporting mechanisms Tailoring measures to organization's risks	No current, official compliance framework	No current, official compliance framework. Companies are encouraged to establish a code of conduct and appropriate policies, trainings, and procedures.

Figure 3.6. Comparison of Country Anti-Bribery and Corruption Laws

Compliance Requirements	third-party due diligence and payments Confidential reporting and internal investigation Continuous improvement, periodic testing, and review Preacquisition due diligence and postacquisition integration during mergers and acquisitions	training of employees and high-risk third parties Monitoring and review: internal controls subject to both internal and external audit and review		Risk assessments Monitoring effectiveness of ABC prevention programs Ensuring consistent discipline of employees for misconduct Promoting transparency of business with external compliance communication and third-party due diligence Establishing policies to detect and report conflicts of interest Cooperation with law enforcement agencies Engaging in collective action initiatives		Only for non-criminal commercial bribery Discounts and commissions were property accounted for in the company's books and records Promotional goods are small in value and common practice in the industry
Possible Defenses	Local Law Defense: prove that the action was lawful under the written laws of the foreign country at the time it was taken. "Lawful" does not mean normal, common, or customary. Reasonable and Bona Fide Promotional Expense: prove that the payment promotes a business or a product.	Ability to demonstrate that adequate procedures designed to prevent bribery were in place	None.	Individuals: actively contribute to solving or preventing the bribery offence and report it to authorities	Ability to demonstrate that adequate procedures to prevent persons associated with the organization from undertaking corrupt conduct.	
Includes both public and private bribery?	Yes.	Yes.	Only public.	Only public, but also bribery of management of commercial companies	PCA: Only public FCRA: Public and private	Yes.

Figure 3.6. Comparison of Country Anti-Bribery and Corruption Laws

	United States	United Kingdom	Brazil	Russia	India	China
Fines and penalties: Individuals	**Anti-Bribery** **Criminal** Fines up to $250,000 5 years imprisonment Civil Fine of $16,000 per violation **Financial Reporting** **Criminal** Fines up to $5 million 20 years imprisonment Civil Fines of $7,500-$150,000 per violation or amount of pecuniary gain	Unlimited fine Imprisonment for up to 10 years	Fines 12 years imprisonment	Fines up to 100 times amount of bribe 15 years imprisonment Ineligible to hold certain job positions	Unlimited fines Seizure and disposal of article/currency/security received in violation of FCRA 5 years imprisonment	Fines Confiscation of property Fixed-term/life imprisonment

Figure 3.6. Comparison of Country Anti-Bribery and Corruption Laws (*continued*)

Chapter 4

Money Laundering

Teresa A. Pesce
John F. Caruso

ew industries are more heavily regulated and scrutinized than financial services, particularly in the area of anti–money laundering (AML) and financial crime. In their effort to keep the financial system safe, the authorities have taken enforcement activity to unprecedented heights, in terms of both the level of scrutiny applied to a firm's AML/Bank Secrecy Act (BSA) Program and the severity of regulatory responses if and when programmatic weaknesses are identified.

The sources of the underlying legal and regulatory obligations are not new. For many years, the BSA was the primary source of AML regulation in the United States. Enacted in 1970, the BSA initially established requirements to report cash transactions to the U.S. Treasury. It evolved over the years to establish, for example, requirements for designated financial institutions, such as banks, to report suspicious activity. In the wake of the September 11, 2001, terrorist attacks, Congress enacted the USA PATRIOT Act (Uniting and Strengthening America by Providing Appropriate Tools Required to Intercept and Obstruct Terrorism Act—the Patriot Act), which amended and enhanced the BSA.[1] The Patriot Act and the regulations enacted pursuant to it not only codified certain AML program requirements, but also broadened them to cover other financial institutions, such as broker-dealers, money service businesses, insurance companies, casinos, and dealers in jewels and precious metals.

These regulations continue to evolve and apply to additional types of entities. In fact, in August 2015, the Financial Crimes Enforcement Network of the U.S. Treasury Department (FinCEN) issued a Notice of Proposed Rulemaking (NPRM) to extend certain of the Patriot Act's requirements to SEC-registered investment advisors (IAs).[2] By being added to the BSA definition of "financial institutions," IAs will be subject to many of the same requirements as banks and broker-dealers. For example, they must establish AML programs as defined in the Patriot Act, implement controls to detect suspicious activity and file Suspicious Activity Reports, and comply with several other BSA requirements around record keeping and reporting, such as Currency Transaction Report filing, the funds transfer and travel rules, and the information sharing provisions of Patriot Act section 314. By virtue of Dodd-Frank's requirements expanding the types of entities that now must register as IAs, the new rules will cover not only the traditional large IAs, but many hedge funds, private equity firms, and other pooled investment entities. Thus, many of the components of a sound AML program described below will need to be addressed by these additional institutions, many of which have not, to this point, focused as much on AML compliance as their banking counterparts.[3]

Closely related to these BSA/AML regulations are a range of laws and regulations related to economic sanctions and enforced by the U.S. Treasury's Office of Foreign Assets Control (OFAC). OFAC administers a number of sanctions programs against both individuals and entities, as well as others directed at specific countries. We mention the sanctions laws here because many, if not most, financial institutions manage sanctions compliance as part of their AML compliance or financial crimes compliance organization, and regulators will typically assess sanctions compliance as a component of the AML examination process. We devote Chapter 5 to sanctions compliance.

Despite the increased codification of laws and regulations covering AML and sanctions, the regulatory landscape is more difficult to navigate than one can master solely by understanding the text of these written requirements. Enforcement activity, while grounded in law, is often based on regulatory interpretation and an expectation of what is actually required as part of a sound AML and sanctions compliance program. Firms must pay close attention to other sources to understand regulatory expectations. These include published guidance from regulators (e.g., the Federal Financial Institution Examination Council's BSA/AML exam manual); releases from FinCEN; informal guidance obtained during regulatory meetings, conferences, and so on; reports of public enforcement actions against similar institutions; even anecdotal descriptions of peer best practices. All of these must be in a compliance officer's toolbox to maintain a compliant program.

Regulatory Landscape

Recent years have seen an increasing number of high-value monetary penalties imposed by regulators for sanctions violations or for AML program gaps that may have facilitated money laundering, financial crimes, or possible terrorist financing. This is in contrast to a decade ago. In the early years of the Patriot Act, there was a steady flow of enforcement actions from various federal and state regulators, but many of these involved more discrete programmatic deficiencies. For example, early enforcement actions focused primarily on failures to adequately monitor and report suspicious activity, requiring firms to undertake transaction reviews.

While one should not oversimplify these actions, they addressed basic program elements and appeared more targeted than some of the more recent enforcement actions. Recent actions seem to hit at virtually every aspect of firms' AML programs, from governance and oversight to customer due diligence, monitoring and detection systems, reporting, staffing, training, and independent testing. While banks have borne the brunt of these penalties, enforcement activity is increasing against other financial institutions as well, such as broker-dealers and money service businesses. Figure 4.1 provides a sample of the more prominent, publicly announced cases.

Consistent with the focus of enforcement efforts in other areas such as anti-bribery and corruption, another trend in this industry is a stated intent to hold individuals accountable for the compliance failures of their institutions. In public addresses, representatives from financial regulators have made it plain that they intend to pursue individuals for the shortcomings of the institutions they work for. "[I]n my opinion, if in any particular instance we cannot find someone, some person, to hold accountable, that just means we have stopped looking. . . . [R]eal deterrence, in our opinion, means a focus not just on corporate accountability, but on individual accountability," said Benjamin M. Lawsky, former superintendent of financial services for the State of New York, in February 2015.[4]

The intended targets appear to be personnel in charge of compliance, presumably for causing the institution to fail to have an adequate AML program. Within the past year, in fact, we have seen instances where compliance officers have been subject to enforcement proceedings in their personal capacities, and specifically to individual monetary fines, in one case a fine of $1 million and potentially a bar from working in the industry. This move to penalize individuals seemingly echoes political calls to find criminal culpability on the part of firms and their employees, as politicians argue that no bank and no bank employee is too important to punish.

Institution	Penalty	Primary Authorities	Year	Summary
Commerzbank	$1.45 billion and deferred prosecution	Federal Reserve; New York State Department of Financial Services; U.S. Department of Justice; New York County District Attorney	2015	OFAC/Sanctions Failure to detect and report fraud and money laundering Monitor installed
BNP Paribas	$9 billion	New York County District Attorney; U.S. Department of Justice; Federal Reserve; New York State Department of Financial Services; U.S. Treasury	2014	OFAC/Sanctions
Standard Chartered	$640 million total, $300 million of which was a subsequent fine based on monitor findings	New York State Department of Financial Services	2012/2014	OFAC/Sanctions Monitor installed; found additional transaction monitoring weaknesses
MoneyGram International Inc.	$100 million and deferred prosecution; Chief compliance officer individually named	U.S. Treasury; U.S. Department of Justice	2012/2014	Failure to maintain an adequate AML Program Failure to detect and report fraud and money laundering
Brown Brothers Harriman	$8 million; Global AML compliance officer individually named	Financial Industry Regulatory Authority	2014	Low-priced securities monitoring deficiencies AML officer found individually liable
Bank of Tokyo Mitsubishi-UFJ	$250 million	New York State Department of Financial Services	2013	OFAC/Sanctions
HSBC	$1.9 billion and deferred prosecution	U.S. Department of Justice; U.S. Treasury; Office of Comptroller of the Currency; Federal Reserve	2012	BSA program deficiencies OFAC/Sanctions

Figure 4.1. Banks Penalized Under AML Regulations
Source: Author; compiled from official sources and news accounts

A final trend of note is the increasing use of court- or regulator-appointed monitors to oversee a firm's compliance with enforcement actions. Monitorships have been imposed in a small number of cases to date, and there is speculation that this tool will be used more widely going forward, including in a capacity to increase a regulator's examination resources.[5] While courts have appointed monitors in different industries for different reasons, their increased use in AML matters raises additional challenges. First, having a monitor oversee enhancements to an AML program is likely to make the program more difficult to manage from day to day. A compliance department will need to address the often strict demands of the monitor on top of implementing program enhancements and running a complex AML program. Second is the simple matter of cost. In the standard arrangement, the monitor is appointed by, and operates under the direction of, the court or regulator. Yet the costs are covered by the institution. Such costs are considerable: the typical monitorship is a multiyear engagement, and the monitor will be an experienced, highly skilled attorney, consultant, or other professional who may employ others to assist.

External threats of financial crime and terrorism may not be the sole cause of increased expectations on financial institutions. As external threats and missteps by financial institutions grab headlines, the pressure on the agencies themselves has increased. Recently the legislative branch has become more actively involved in the regulatory process; in one case a congressional inquiry into HSBC's program deficiencies included a focus on whether a federal regulatory agency effectively oversaw the AML program at the bank.[6] As a result, regulators are likely to turn up the heat on the banks they examine.

We could not fully convey the impact of the issues described above without discussing the growing costs of AML compliance. Experts see little likelihood that they will stabilize anytime soon. In a survey[7] of global AML practitioners conducted by KPMG and released in 2014, KPMG asked participating firms to compare their 2014 AML compliance costs to those of 2011. Some 27 percent of respondents reported increased spending of 50 percent or more. Seventy-four percent of respondents said they expected costs to increase further in the following three years.

The KPMG survey identified three main causes of rising costs: transaction monitoring systems; the collection of customer due diligence information or "know your customer" (KYC) information; and recruitment of compliance staff. The first two factors will be discussed later in this chapter; recruitment requires special mention here, due to its impact on the financial services industry, where companies have been scrambling to hire professionals with the relevant experience. This has pushed up costs and made it difficult for financial institutions, both large and small, to build a sustainable program, when employees frequently leave for higher-paid jobs elsewhere. Faced with these challenges, financial firms are advised to design and implement a sound AML program that is tailored to the specific risks inherent in their businesses, to prevent, detect, and respond to illicit activity. Such a program should be based on the foundation of a well-defined risk assessment.

Compliance Program Controls

Considering the high level of regulatory attention and risks to financial institutions, the fundamental elements of a BSA/AML compliance program should be familiar to all professionals in the industry. Given the maturity of the Patriot

Act, regulated institutions should have in place the so-called "four pillars" of an AML program as mandated in Section 352 of the Act. These include:

- A competent BSA/AML compliance officer and support staff
- Robust policies, procedures, and controls
- AML training modules of adequate depth
- An annual independent review of the program

If any of these elements is lacking or falls short of expectations, the institution will face significant challenges during regulatory examinations.

Preventive Controls

Risk Assessment.   A successful program that will withstand regulatory scrutiny in this harsh environment must be tailored to the institution's specific clients and products, lines of business, and risk profile. This is best achieved by starting with the BSA/AML risk assessment. When properly designed, a risk assessment can identify all the compliance obligations applicable to a firm's business. It can determine which of the firm's business lines face a measurable degree of risk associated with these obligations and whether the firm's existing control structure is designed to address these risks. Based on this information, the firm can then develop a sound AML compliance program. It can undertake remedial measures to address any gaps, and it can help drive a "business as usual" program that is fit for that purpose. The risk assessment outcomes should also provide guidance for other control areas (audit, quality assurance, compliance desk reviews, and training) as they set their agendas.

The first step in the risk assessment process is to understand the laws, regulations, and other forms of regulatory guidance that will inform a thorough compilation of all of the legal obligations a firm must meet in order to be compliant in BSA/AML. BSA/AML compliance is unique and challenging, as the landscape does not present a set of documented precise, rule-based requirements. Rather, the key obligations of AML/BSA come in broad strokes. Written regulatory requirements require banks and certain other financial institutions to collect and verify customer identification information (known as CIP for customer identification program). Regulators, however, expect banks not only to identify but also to know their customers, by performing sufficient risk-based due diligence prior to the opening of an account. The purpose is to understand who the client is and what risk the client and his or her activity may pose. Banks must then monitor accounts and transactions for unusual or suspicious activity. The requirement to monitor for and report on suspicious activity is a critical mandate, but the regulations do not offer definitive guidance on which transactions to monitor, which rule typologies to measure against, or what makes a transaction suspicious enough to warrant reporting. Thus, it is critical for the legal and compliance staff to have a high level of understanding of money laundering and financial crimes to assist the bank in meeting the expectations of regulators.

This depends on building a solid risk assessment framework involving key persons in all business areas of the firm. All business divisions must be brought into the assessment process as stakeholders. It is they who best understand the products they offer and clients they serve. They can explain where and how they solicit clients, what client types they serve, and the value and volume of transactions that their divisions handle. These points will determine the levels of risk of certain activities and whether mitigating controls are needed. Furthermore, it is the business divisions that must understand they are the true owners of this risk. By aligning the legal obligations to the activities of the particular business area, the risk assessor will be able to identify the legal requirements applicable to the business line and determine which products, clients, and business divisions entail the most risk.

The next step is to assess the controls that are in place to mitigate the risks. Controls take many forms, from broader concepts such as written policies and training, to more specific controls such as transaction monitoring, data analysis, supervisory review protocols, and the schedule for reviewing client data.

A disciplined process of (1) identifying your legal requirements and inherent risks and (2) determining whether the controls properly address any risk is the key to identifying whether there are gaps in the program. Many institutions have faced formal enforcement actions or private regulatory findings related to inadequate monitoring of correspondent banking, which is considered to be a high-risk line of business. But the risk assessment should reveal, for example, if the rules used for automated transaction monitoring cover suspicious types of activity. It should also determine whether the institution is capturing sufficiently detailed information about its correspondent banking customers to understand what kinds of activity are normal. Indeed, if the analysis is comprehensive, it is bound to find gaps in coverage of its risks. Identifying these improvement opportunities and tracking them to full remediation is a primary objective of the risk assessment.

The main output, which should inform the list of improvement opportunities, consists of a series of residual risk ratings for the many components of this exercise. The expectation on the part of examiners is that each risk element for each line of business be measured both qualitatively and quantitatively, that the controls be viewed in light of that risk, and that a residual risk score is arrived at. Thus a risk score should be set for each geographical region, business activity, product, or client category that is being assessed. Most firms have done this by assigning quantitative values[8] to a number of items: the inherent risk of a given activity/product/client; the strength of the targeted controls; and the residual risk (i.e., the risk that remains even after the controls are factored in).[9] The residual risk ratings should drive a number of aspects of the AML program, including:

- *Staffing.* Business areas that pose the highest residual risks should have relatively significant levels of staffing. This is not satisfied by numbers alone, but by trained and knowledgeable resources.
- *Technology.* If the risk assessment exposes the need for new or improved technology solutions, these upgrades are not only costly, but time consuming. In fact, the increasing importance of data analytics for monitoring transactions means that this should be a primary focus of the risk assessment.[10]
- *Compliance testing.* The compliance department should have its own team to review the results of the risk assessment in setting the risk-based testing approach.
- *Internal audit.* This function should review its testing approach and, in part, rely on this information when developing its annual testing plan. But regulators now expect internal audit to review the risk assessment and conduct its own risk assessment to inform its testing plan.

A sound risk assessment should inform the development of the overall AML program. If done correctly, it will show the compliance officer what is needed in terms of policies, procedures, and targeted training programs. It will help determine where resources should be deployed. It will drive the design of the KYC program by identifying the unique client risks of the various business areas, and it will make clear where transaction monitoring needs to be deployed and at what levels of complexity. All of these components are required to prevent, detect, and respond to money laundering risks.

Due Diligence.   One of the broad concepts inherent in a risk assessment is customer risk—that is, lines of business that serve a larger number of high-risk customers will be considered to present a higher risk to the institution. The collection of this information is facilitated by a firm's KYC program, or the customer due diligence (CDD) program, which has seen the development of a substantial amount of guidance for the practitioner. The idea of knowing one's customer forms the basis for preventing a financial institution from being used for illicit activities. In theory, the institution should learn enough about potential customers to turn them away if they present a foreseeable risk.

As mentioned above, the Patriot Act is specific in some areas, including delineating the required elements of customer identification information and verification in the CIP provisions.[11] These include the collection of basic elements such as name, physical address, date of birth for an individual, and a government-issued identification number. Similarly, the law is more prescriptive when discussing special due diligence requirements for correspondent bank accounts or private bank accounts.[12] FinCEN issued a notice of a proposed rulemaking for obtaining beneficial ownership information for those natural persons that are behind legal entity accounts. The notice, if ultimately adopted as proposed, will require firms to verify the identity of all natural persons with beneficial ownership of at least 25 percent of an entity, but sets a process whereby the firm need only obtain certification from the client in order to identify those owners.

That said, there are many facets of the KYC process that remain subject to interpretation and customization at each firm. At the outset, the firm must decide which third parties will be viewed as "customers," so that the CIP and KYC procedures apply. In any jurisdiction, a client who wishes to open an account relationship is subject to KYC procedures. In the United States, what constitutes a "customer" and an "account" is defined in the CIP regulation. Expectations for KYC may not be so clear-cut, however. In certain jurisdictions, such as those in the European Union,[13] counterparties to certain transactions, entities with which the institution enters into a business contract, or mergers-and-acquisitions advisory clients are generally treated in the same way as customers and are required to be placed in the KYC process. In the United States, entities with which business is regularly conducted may be considered customers even if they do not meet the technical definition.

Once the "customer" is defined for KYC purposes, risk-based and customer-segment-specific KYC information should be collected. While the information collected will initially be determined based on customer type and initial risk ranking, additional facts can be learned during the course of due diligence that increase the risk rating of the customer, such as relevant negative media information. This should drive the process of enhanced due diligence review, and in some cases may cause a firm to decline to do business with the prospect. Key baseline KYC questions include: (1) What accounts or relationships should be deemed high risk? (2) What is the effect of the high-risk (or medium- or low-risk) designation? and (3) How does the firm's AML transaction monitoring platform incorporate both this risk designation and customer-specific information to drive true risk-based monitoring of customer activity?

The approach to each of these variables must be defined by the institution itself. While there are some well-established approaches from which no firms would deviate (e.g., correspondent bank accounts and private wealth accounts for foreign government officials are deemed high risk), ultimately the parameters established should be tailored to the particular institution based on a number of factors, such as the characteristics of its client base, operational locations, products offered, and size of institution.

Regulators have focused on some key aspects of an acceptable KYC program. These include the documentary requirements for all information collected and a well-defined audit trail for all due diligence processes. The Patriot Act provides that CIP and other records be collected, retained, and readily available for internal purposes or if requested by a regulator or a representative of law enforcement. Requirements for documentary verification must be articulated and followed. Negative media searches, OFAC searches, and searches to determine if a customer is, or is affiliated with, a politically exposed person (PEP) should be executed for potential clients and the results retained. The entire work flow, and the documentation collected, must follow strict procedures.

Collecting KYC information on a customer or counterparty is not a one-time exercise. Frequency of reviews of customer files must be dictated by the risk category. Such reviews will inform the firm whether relevant information about the customer has changed and whether a risk profile has increased. In such a case, additional due diligence should be collected and the new risks should be evaluated by both compliance and the unit doing business with the customer. Any increased risk should be documented and accepted, and transaction monitoring may need to be adjusted. Even the most comprehensive KYC programs are vulnerable to gaps, however. Compliance departments should develop a plan to test the work and performance of the KYC teams to ensure that they are working as intended and, if necessary, develop a plan to address deficiencies.

Detective Controls

Once customer and product risks are defined, a critical element of any AML program is transaction monitoring and the detection, investigation, and reporting of potentially suspicious activity. Detection of potential money laundering within the wide range of transactions conducted by today's financial institutions can be a daunting task. Finding those transactions that may be unusual, or potentially suspicious, requires complete, accurate, and relevant data, a strong methodology, sound transaction processing systems, a robust transaction monitoring and case management system, and a validation process that ensures the transaction monitoring system and related models are functioning as intended.

Auditing and Monitoring.   Regulators' expectations have increased sharply in the area of transaction monitoring. Regulatory agencies have deployed quantitative analysts to conduct exams of firms' transaction monitoring systems and capacities. The expectation is that firms will conduct model validation exercises with respect to their monitoring capabilities to ensure that systems are working as intended and capturing suspicious activity. Firms falling short will be subject to criticism or worse.

A fundamental issue for financial institutions is the quality of the data available to identify potential money laundering issues. Transaction monitoring is only effective if the data inputs into any system are complete and accurate. This includes the customer information collected in the KYC process, as firms must understand who or what a customer is before they can determine if related activity is unusual. In many cases, transaction records are incomplete with critical data elements missing. Or the data is spread across multiple transaction processing systems and there is incomplete data in each system, or the data is inconsistent across systems. Without a sound foundation of data, decisions regarding the validity of transactions may be compromised. Thus any transaction monitoring program should begin with a validation of data inputs. This entails ensuring that the data is collected in a uniform format and/or is normalized to be in such a format and that all relevant data is being properly fed into the systems used for monitoring.

Working with sound data, financial institutions need a sound methodology to identify transactions that may present a risk. This methodology should address the risks inherent in the portfolio of customers, products and services, and geographies, and how those risks translate into the transactions conducted. For example, a system may incorporate certain behavioral typologies that indicate red flags for risks in a certain product line, or a system may profile the ordinary activity of a customer base to detect when anomalies occur. A sound risk assessment, as discussed above, provides the foundation necessary to build effective processes for detecting unusual, potentially suspicious activity. Data around customers and the expected usage of products and services maintained in customer databases should be analyzed to aid in the assessment of risk at the customer and institutional level. This methodology is the foundation for the transaction monitoring system engine.

It is essential that transaction monitoring systems are robust and flexible. Even with good quality data, ineffective transaction monitoring systems may not identify those transactions that present a risk to the institution. The transaction monitoring systems and the underlying rules or profiles need to be tied to the institution's inherent risks both overall and at the customer level. And these transaction monitoring systems must link to a comprehensive case management system. Case management systems or tools allow a firm to keep track of alerts, cases, and investigations conducted on individual or related clients. Thus if subsequent activity gives rise to suspicion or concern it can be tied to earlier activity and either cleared as normal or alerted for further review and investigation. Such a system will allow for the timely tracking of investigations, a complete and accurate assessment of all relevant documentation, and an audit trail. It should additionally link related cases and parties to enable a firm to view customer and activity risk over time and across related entities.

The information gleaned from risk assessments can and should provide the framework for the transaction monitoring system. The overall risk assessment may be useful in setting up initial rules and/or thresholds for transactions. Customer-specific risk assessments could then be used to target specific customers and activity types for further review. For example, the overall risk assessment may be useful for establishing rules (transaction types) and thresholds (dollar values) used to generate alerts for more homogenous customer segments and for individual retail transactions. Customer-specific profiling rules might be very difficult to manage in such an area and may not yield more effective results.

Customer-specific rules, however, are more effective for less homogenous groups such as commercial banking, trade finance, or correspondent banking. In these areas, a clear understanding of the risks associated with the customer and the customer's anticipated normal activity is critical to setting rules, thresholds, or behavioral patterns that can help to highlight anomalies for further review.

The ultimate goal of any transaction monitoring system is to provide a firm with a mechanism to detect potentially suspicious activity, then to investigate that activity, and to report that activity to regulatory and law enforcement authorities. Moreover, detecting suspicious activity on the part of a customer should trigger a review of the customer relationship and an evaluation of whether the risk presented by keeping the customer exceeds the firm's risk appetite or its ability to control the risk.

Regardless of the method for identifying transactions for further review, a robust transaction monitoring system must also have, or tie to, a robust case management system. Such a case management system should fully document the transaction or transactions and all relevant parties to the transactions. This will allow for supporting documentation to be maintained both for cases where suspicious activity reports (SARs) are filed and for those cases where a determination has been made that the activity does not warrant the filing of an SAR.

Data Analytics.   Regulatory expectations regarding data quality continue to rise. The integrity of the data feeding AML transaction monitoring systems is critical to a system's success. A financial institution's collection and use of data must be fully defined and understood by those who are responsible for the AML transaction monitoring system. For those who oversee AML compliance, and in particular the AML transaction monitoring systems, a series of questions require answers:

- What relevant data is available?
- Who provides, collects, and records the data?
- When is it collected?
- Where does it reside?
- Is the data accurate?
- How is the quality determined?

Data relevant to each customer, each product and service used by that customer, and each transaction conducted by, through, or to that customer needs to be identified. While all data may be important, each data element that affects or measures AML risk needs to be further identified. For example, jurisdictions where the customer is resident or conducts business as well as the location of the counterparties to the transactions should be identified and documented.

For these AML data elements, a financial institution needs to understand who provides, collects, and records the data, as a means to assess the integrity of the data. Data provided by a customer should be subject to independent verification. Data collected and recorded by the financial institution should be subject to standard controls to ensure completeness and accuracy such as segregation of duties and input/output verification controls.

Understanding when data is collected is important when assessing the timeliness of detection afforded by AML transaction monitoring systems. While all data collected is important, data collected at the time a transaction is conducted will be more relevant in the timely detection of potential money laundering than data collected at, say, the opening of an account.

Perhaps the greatest challenge for a financial institution is gaining an understanding of where data is resident. There may be multiple data sources that contain relevant data for a single transaction or for a single customer. Wire transfer data may be housed in a wire transaction or correspondent banking database, while related SWIFT messages are housed in a separate database. Additionally, once found, a question arises as to whether the data is consistent across the various sources, and whether it is source data or data that has been manipulated in some manner as it migrates from a source system to a data repository.

Finally, a firm must determine how to assess the overall quality of the data. The use of standard controls, such as the segregation of duties and input/output verification controls, has already been mentioned. In addition, data analytics can be helpful in assessing data quality. For example, are customer relationships connected throughout the firm? Are naming conventions uniform? Are related accounts linked? With the abundance of data that may be available to a financial institution, data quality cannot be effectively assessed in a manual environment alone. No doubt, manual intervention will be necessary to make a final determination on specific data quality issues, but data analytics is a powerful tool in this effort.

As noted, a risk assessment is critical to identifying and controlling risk in a program, as it pertains to both overall risk and customer risk. There are simply too many customers and transactions to review each and every one. Nor should time be wasted reviewing customers and transactions that present minimal risk and where information would be of little value to law enforcement.

Data analytics should be used as a means to support overall and customer risk assessments, and its complexity will vary. Simply identifying the number of customers by type and number of transactions to and from certain jurisdictions has long been an expectation of regulators. Nowadays, however, a more robust analysis is expected. This may include analyzing the frequency of transactions and patterns or linkages among parties to the transactions. Such an analysis helps in forming a baseline from which anomalies can be more easily detected and analyzed.

Data analytics is not the only area that requires robust testing. It is vitally important that regulatory expectations be met in the area of model validation and that a robust process is used to ensure an effective means for detecting unusual, potentially suspicious activity. Models should be validated on a regular basis to ensure that they are functioning as intended.

Guidance issued by financial regulators defines a model as "a quantitative method, system, or approach that applies statistical, economic, financial, or mathematical theories, techniques, and assumptions to process input data into quantitative estimates."[14] Regulators apply this definition to a broad range of models from the more simplistic, rules-based models to more complex, algorithmic models. In AML compliance, this is most often applied to technologies such as transaction monitoring and automated customer risk rating.

The simplest model validation involves all manner of system testing to ensure that the right data is being reviewed and measured, that it is being measured against the proper criteria, and that the model applies appropriate parameters to achieve optimal results. Thus, model validation of a transaction monitoring system will look at such things as whether all relevant and correct data is being fed into the systems, whether it is being run against all proper rules, scenarios, or profiles, and whether these rules, scenarios, or profiles are sensitive enough to achieve optimal results without being so broad as to generate an unmanageably large number of alerts.

Responsive Controls

Financial institutions must be continuously alert to the risks posed by financial crimes and be aware that regulators' expectations are rising. However, despite best efforts, firms often find themselves responding to the findings of regulators. Such findings can be informal, as in a report of examination or nonpublic memorandum of understanding, or in the form of a public formal agreement, regulatory order, court-ordered settlement, or worse. In each case, a firm must respond efficiently and effectively.

When regulatory findings are in the form of a report of examination, they are generally framed in the form of "Matters Requiring Attention" or "Matters

Requiring Immediate Attention." These require a written response and action plan to address the deficiencies. Firms are advised, however, not just to remediate the problems identified, but also to determine the root cause of the deficiency and put in place program enhancements to ensure that the problems will not recur. If a regulator identifies deficiencies in client due diligence, for example, companies should not just remediate existing customer files, but ensure that their customer due diligence program is enhanced appropriately to ensure that customers are properly risk ranked.

Firms subject to formal regulatory or law enforcement orders often do not have the ability to set the time frame for a responsive action plan. Such orders generally impose strict timelines and stringent remediation and/or investigation requirements, often requiring the firm to bring in the assistance of an independent third party. More recently, firms under regulatory orders have been subject to the oversight of a court or a monitor appointed by the regulator, which was discussed above.

In almost all cases, remedial measures can be time-consuming and costly. They detract from business as usual and may distract compliance officers from proactively addressing risk. Firms are advised to understand risks and the resources needed to address such risks and to anticipate issues before they become the subject of intense scrutiny. Overall, maintenance of a functional AML program requires vigilance.

Conclusion

With regulatory expectations rising, financial institutions must move to meet them. It is no longer feasible to wait for the regulator to find issues in the firm's BSA/AML/sanctions programs or to view the programs in silos. What is required is constant diligence and the effective use of data analytics and other tools to assess and mitigate the BSA/AML/sanctions risks. The new regulatory paradigm is to identify and mitigate risks across all program areas and to correct potential weaknesses.

Chapter 5

Economic and Trade Sanctions

Charles M. Steele

The U.S. government is using economic and trade sanctions more expansively and aggressively than ever before. The government increasingly looks to sanctions as a primary tool of foreign policy and national security, as demonstrated by its actions over the past several years relating to Iran and, beginning in March 2014, to Russia's activities in Ukraine. And the government is also enforcing sanctions violations more aggressively than ever, bringing civil monetary penalty actions—and, in some cases, parallel criminal cases—against companies that do business with sanctioned persons and entities.

Over the past few years the U.S. Department of the Treasury's Office of Foreign Assets Control (OFAC) has brought some of the largest enforcement actions in the agency's history against a wide variety of businesses for violating a broad range of sanctions programs. Between 2012 and 2014, OFAC resolutions of enforcement cases included settlements of $91 million with Weatherford International, a U.S. oilfield manufacturing and services company; $51 million with Fokker Services B.V., a Dutch aerospace services company; and $5.2 million with American Express Travel Related Services Company.

There have also been a number of large settlements with U.S. and foreign banks, including $963 million (BNP Paribas), $619 million (ING Bank), $375 million (HSBC Holdings), $152 million (Clearstream Banking), $33 million

Mr. Steele, a former managing director at KPMG, is now of counsel at Davis Polk & Wardwell LLP.

(Royal Bank of Scotland), and $16.5 million (Bank of America).[1] Sanctions violators also suffer serious reputational harm, over and above their monetary losses. And, in addition to the United States, many other countries are increasingly implementing sanctions as well, as are the United Nations and the European Union, adding to the complexity of the challenges facing companies that operate internationally.

Sanctions are intended to inflict economic pain on designated persons and entities by cutting them off from the U.S. financial system and markets, and by causing the blocking (or freezing) of their assets that are, or that come within, the possession or control of U.S. persons.[2] Sanctions can succeed only if the private sector complies with them by refusing to deal with designated targets. When U.S. persons engage in prohibited dealings with sanctioned parties, the coercive effect of the sanctions is lost, undermining U.S. policies.

The government has therefore implemented broad enforcement authority to bring punitive actions, both civil and criminal, against U.S. persons who engage in prohibited dealings with designated targets. OFAC has the authority to bring civil monetary penalty actions against sanctions violators.[3] There is strict liability for sanctions violations; that is, prohibited dealings constitute violations without regard to whether the violator acted intentionally, recklessly, or negligently, or even where the violation results from a mere mistake.

Some violations are, however, willful, meaning the violator knows that it is committing a violation and intentionally does so anyway. When this is the case, the U.S. Department of Justice (DOJ) can also bring a criminal action for the same acts, parallel to and in coordination with OFAC's civil action.[4] Moreover, in recent years state and local authorities have brought actions when violations of federal sanctions regulations also implicated their own authorities. Examples include the New York State Department of Financial Services and the Manhattan District Attorney's Office, both of which in recent years have brought actions under New York State law against financial institutions for violating OFAC sanctions requirements.[5] And the Bureau of Industry and Security (BIS) in the U.S. Department of Commerce, which implements and enforces export controls, often joins OFAC in parallel enforcement actions where their authorities overlap.[6]

Because sanctions are a tool of foreign policy and national security, they change often, adding to the compliance challenges that companies face. The government chooses its targets, and the timing of imposition of the sanctions, to suit its policy goals, without regard to the impact of the sanctions on the private sector. Targets are selected through nonpublic government deliberations, and sanctions are then imposed with no prior notice or warning. Once a person or entity is designated, it is added to OFAC's public Specially Designated Nationals and Blocked Persons (SDN) list,[7] putting the public on notice that all business dealings with the particular person or entity are prohibited unless licensed by OFAC.

The prohibition takes effect immediately upon designation; there is no grace period or wind-down period, unless OFAC expressly provides one. Even accepting past-due payments under a contract with a payor who is subsequently designated and added to OFAC's list would, for example, be prohibited, unless first licensed. And the SDN list changes on at least a weekly basis, with parties added to or removed from the list.[8]

An important example of the changing nature of OFAC sanctions is the implementation of Ukraine-related sanctions. In response to Russia's actions in Ukraine, President Obama issued a series of executive orders (EOs) authorizing sanctions against persons and entities responsible for those actions. In one of those EOs he took unprecedented action. Departing significantly from decades of practice, he authorized, pursuant to EO 13662, a new type of sanction, called sectoral sanctions. These new sanctions did not apply across Russia's economy but were limited to certain specific sectors (financial services, energy, and defense). And the new sanctions did not prohibit all business dealings with sanctioned parties; rather, OFAC issued two directives (a new tool) that imposed specific and limited prohibitions on U.S. persons.[9]

In July 2014, OFAC imposed the first round of sectoral sanctions. It created a new list, called the Sectoral Sanctions Identifications (SSI) List,[10] to distinguish parties subject to the new sanctions from parties on its more familiar SDN list. Later, OFAC took further action to refine the sectoral sanctions, issuing amended versions of the two directives and two other directives that imposed new prohibitions with respect to the energy and defense sectors. OFAC also continued to add new names to both the SSI list and the SDN list.

Another example of the dynamic nature of sanctions can be seen with regard to trade with Iran. For years, Iran had been subject to comprehensive sanctions by the United States. In November 2013, the "P5+1," made up of China, France, Germany, Russia, the United Kingdom, and the United States, reached an agreement with Iran, called the Joint Plan of Action (JPOA), in return for Iran's agreement to limit its nuclear program in certain respects. In return for Iran's commitments, the P5+1 agreed to provide Iran with limited, temporary, and targeted sanctions relief[11] for a period of six months, starting on January 20, 2014, and concluding on July 20, 2014 (the JPOA period). As of February 2015, the JPOA period had subsequently been extended twice, to June 30, 2015, to give the parties time to continue negotiations.

OFAC's creation of the sectoral sanctions, and the changes arising from the JPOA efforts, illustrate the unpredictability and complexity of sanctions. This presents significant compliance challenges for companies that need to stay alert to sanctions developments as they unfold, and to be able effectively to account for the changes in the design and execution of their compliance programs. In particular, companies engaged in international business need to screen current and prospective business partners (buyers, suppliers, vendors, joint venture partners, and so on) against the SDN list and, if appropriate in light of their risk profile, the SSI list as well.[12] How frequently a company should screen will depend on its particular risk profile, but all companies should screen frequently enough to avoid violations.

Moreover, sanctions prohibitions tend to be very broad, applying to all types of business activity and all sectors. Sanctions issues can therefore arise suddenly, in a wide variety of contexts that often overlap with other regulations, such as anti–money laundering (AML) rules. Indeed, federal regulators examine financial institutions for both AML and sanctions compliance; sanctions examination provisions are included in the Federal Financial Institutions Examination Council's (FFIEC's) Bank Secrecy Act/AML Examination Manual.

Similarly, sanctions issues can overlap with anti-bribery and corruption (ABC) issues, when U.S. companies' business dealings involve foreign parties who are both corrupt government officials and on the SDN list. A recent example of this involved multiple U.S. government enforcement actions against Weatherford International in late 2013. The government brought civil and criminal actions against Weatherford for violations of both the Foreign Corrupt Practices Act (FCPA) and sanctions prohibitions. The actions included a $91 million settlement with OFAC for the violation of sanctions related to Iran, Sudan, and Cuba.[13]

In light of this overlap between the very broad sanctions rules and other civil regulatory and criminal prohibitions, companies would be wise to integrate sanctions principles into their broader compliance programs. In this chapter we will discuss sanctions implementation and enforcement in the United States. It begins with a background of the history of sanctions in the United States. It then moves to a discussion of how a company can prevent violations and position itself to promptly detect violations. It then addresses how a company should respond in the event that violations occur. It concludes with some perspectives on what the future holds for sanctions, in both the short term and the longer term.

Background

In the United States, economic sanctions have been used since the early years of the nineteenth century.[14] In the period leading up to the War of 1812, the United States imposed sanctions on Great Britain for harassment of American ships. In the Civil War, the Union imposed sanctions on the Confederacy and authorized the forfeiture of goods involved in any prohibited transactions. The Civil War sanctions also created a licensing regime that permitted otherwise prohibited dealings under certain circumstances when approved by the Treasury Department.

After Germany invaded Norway in 1940, the Treasury Department formed the Office of Foreign Funds Control (FFC). The FFC's mission was to prevent the Nazis' use of the occupied countries' holdings of foreign exchange and other assets. The program was subsequently extended to cover other invaded countries. After the United States entered World War II in December 1941, the FFC played a leading role in economic warfare against the Axis powers through the imposition of sanctions, prohibiting trade and financial transactions and blocking assets in the possession or custody of U.S. persons.

OFAC, the successor to the FFC, was created in December 1950, after China entered the Korean War. President Truman declared a national emergency and blocked all Chinese and North Korean assets subject to U.S. jurisdiction. Since then, OFAC has been the principal agency in the U.S. government with authority and responsibility for implementing, administering, and enforcing sanctions.

In 2004 there was an important development in the evolution of the use of sanctions when the Treasury Department created the Office of Terrorism and Financial Intelligence (TFI). TFI was formed to consolidate, under an under secretary of the Treasury, the department's financial enforcement and intelligence functions, with the "twin aims of safeguarding the financial system against illicit use and combating rogue nations, terrorist facilitators, weapons of mass destruction (WMD) proliferators, money launderers, drug kingpins, and other national security threats."[15]

OFAC, the Financial Crimes Enforcement Network (the department's agency engaged in AML and countering the financing of terrorism), and the Treasury Executive Office of Asset Forfeiture (TEOAF) were moved into TFI.[16] In addition, the department created two new entities to enhance TFI's ability to execute its mission. The Office of Terrorist Financing and Financial Crime (TFFC) is "the policy and outreach apparatus for TFI." The Office of Intelligence and Analysis (OIA) executes TFI's intelligence functions. It is a member of the U.S. intelligence community and provides analysis services to TFI and Treasury Department leaders and to the community.[17] TFFC and OIA are headed by assistant secretaries who, like the under secretary, are appointed by the president and confirmed by the Senate.

With the creation of TFI, the Treasury Department now plans and executes its national security functions in a more disciplined, extensive, and effective manner than before. All of the department's national security functions now fall within a unified chain of command dedicated exclusively to bringing Treasury's tools to bear in support of the government's efforts against terrorist financing, WMD proliferation, money laundering and other financial crimes, and other threats to U.S. foreign policy and national security policy.

OFAC's sanctions are, in many ways, the principal weapon in TFI's arsenal. TFI made some fundamental changes in the way in which sanctions are implemented and executed, which has contributed to the increasing visibility, role, and impact of the tool.[18] In particular, TFI began to focus sanctions more on bad conduct by targets (e.g., providing support to terrorists, WMD proliferation, and drug trafficking) as opposed to relying solely on country-based programs. Among other things, the Treasury found it easier to build multilateral coalitions around such sanctions than around country-based programs, which sometimes tend to be viewed as more politically motivated.

TFI also increased the focus on private sector entities as sanctions targets, as opposed to focusing exclusively or predominantly on government entities as targets. TFI found this to be effective because private sector actors tend to be sensitive to the need to follow rules and regulations, and are also highly motivated to avoid reputational harm. The idea is that they will therefore be quicker to change their behavior in order to avoid being sanctioned, or to obtain their deletion from the SDN list. And with the creation of OIA, Treasury significantly increased the use of intelligence information in sanctions programs. This enhanced the Department's targeting abilities by providing a broader base of data and information with which to identify potential targets and to confirm that the targets are, in fact, engaging in sanctionable behavior.

Implementation and enforcement of economic sanctions, at least in the United States, have a number of particular characteristics of which companies should be aware, in order to avoid violations and to put themselves in the best compliance posture. One critically important aspect of U.S. economic sanctions is that violations are assessed on a strict liability standard. Unlike other enforcement regimes (civil and criminal), all that is necessary for an OFAC (civil) sanctions violation is that the prohibited transaction or dealing occurred. It will be a violation whether the violator acted intentionally, recklessly, negligently, or through a good-faith mistake. (OFAC will generally treat an intentional or reckless violation more harshly than a negligent or good-faith violation, but they are all violations, nonetheless.) This creates a higher level of risk for violations than companies face in many other regulatory spheres.

OFAC's 50 percent rule, first announced in 2008, is another example of a particular nuance of sanctions authorities that poses unusual challenges to companies. Under this rule, if a blocked party owns, directly or indirectly, 50 percent or more of another entity, then that other entity is also blocked by operation of law, even if it does not itself appear on OFAC's list. Any dealings with that entity are therefore prohibited in the same manner and to the same extent as if that party were on the list itself.

To further complicate matters, in August 2014 OFAC issued "revised" guidance on the 50 percent rule.[19] The revised guidance stated that ownership, for purposes of the rule, includes aggregate ownership. In other words, ownership interests held by blocked parties will be aggregated (whether or not the blocked parties are business partners, or know of each other's interests) for purposes of the rule. Thus, if two blocked persons each own 26 percent of Company A, or if three blocked persons each own 17 percent of Company A, then Company A is also blocked as a matter of law, even if Company A does not appear on OFAC's list. So, while screening prospective business partners against OFAC's lists is necessary, it will not always be sufficient; in some circumstances, companies will need to do further third-party due diligence, in order to account for, and mitigate, their level of risk for sanctions violations.

Another unusual aspect of OFAC's authorities is their sheer breadth. OFAC's blocking sanctions generally prohibit having any kind of business dealing, directly or indirectly, with sanctioned parties. Even entering into preliminary contract negotiations, and making business referrals to persons or companies in other countries, can constitute violations. Some of these scenarios can be counter-intuitive, and companies may often be surprised to learn that what seems like an innocuous, de minimis, or trivial interaction can in fact constitute a violation, with a significant and, in some cases, very harsh penalty.

These unusual characteristics of U.S. sanctions, together with the government's increasing use of them as a foreign policy tool, have given sanctions an increasingly prominent role in international commerce. This enhanced role is likely to remain the norm for the foreseeable future.

Compliance Program Controls

Preventative Controls

Policies and Procedures.   Sanctions compliance programs should have effective procedures in place for prompt escalation of possible violations, especially where there is any uncertainty as to whether or not there is a hit against the SDN list, or that a violation has been discovered. In criminal matters, the government bears the burden of proving its allegations beyond a reasonable doubt. In certain civil contexts, the government must prove its allegations by a preponderance of the evidence, or by clear and convincing evidence. But not OFAC; its regulations impose strict liability.

This makes it important to act promptly. If a company engages in a regular, high volume of a particular type of transaction—bank processing wire transfers, for example, or a company selling and servicing oil drilling parts and equipment—and takes too long to explore a possible violation, then it may end up committing tens, dozens, or even hundreds more violations before it realizes it has committed any. Given the severity of OFAC's maximum monetary penalties,[20] companies cannot afford to take the risk. Compliance policies should therefore include provisions and mechanisms to ensure prompt identification, escalation, and resolution of possible violations. Among other things, there should be clear escalation policies and practices for employees to follow, to make sure that apparent hits quickly come to the attention of all appropriate personnel for follow-up. The company should not proceed with any dealings with the prospective partner until it is satisfied, after sufficient due diligence, that the party is not, in fact, blocked.

Due Diligence.   Ongoing due diligence is important in the sanctions arena, particularly in light of the fact that the OFAC list is updated frequently. Ongoing third-party due diligence is therefore particularly important. Companies with substantial international business should consider not only screening of prospective business partners at the initiation of the relationship, but also ongoing screening of existing partners. The frequency of the screening should be risk-based—the higher the risk level for sanctions violations, based on the company's areas of operation, customer base, types of products and/or services, and so on, the more frequently the company should screen. This will increase the company's chances of learning as early as possible if important circumstances have changed. For example, if a current business partner has been added to OFAC's list, this immediately makes it unlawful to do business with that entity. A similar situation arises if a company is contemplating moving into a new geographic region or expanding its product or service offerings.

The best way to prevent violations is to have a well-conceived, risk-based, effective compliance program in place. Economic sanctions are more about "who" than "what." Sanctions focus principally on the parties with whom you do business, rather than on the type of business you do, the types of products you export, and so on. OFAC's enforcers certainly take the type of business into account (prohibited exports of oil-drilling equipment and dual-use items will likely be treated more harshly, for example, than will prohibited exports of medical products or cosmetics), but the key question is "who"—if you engage in any dealings with a sanctioned party, then you are violating the sanctions, no matter the nature of those dealings. Since the purpose of sanctions is to cut the designated party off from U.S. markets entirely, sanctions prohibit all transactions and dealings with listed parties, unless the dealings are licensed by OFAC.

Therefore, the most important component of an OFAC compliance program is proper screening. Companies should screen all prospective business partners—suppliers, vendors, customers, joint venture partners, and so on—against OFAC's SDN and SSI lists. In order to prevent violations, the screening must be conducted prior to any transactions or dealings. And because the list changes frequently, companies must screen frequently. The decision on how often to screen should be risk-based—a company should screen frequently enough to reasonably head off the possibility of violations, in light of the company's geographic regions of operation, customer base, and so on. If a prospective partner seems to be on the list, the company should assess it thoroughly before engaging in dealings with the party.

It is necessary, but not always sufficient, to screen against the OFAC list. As noted above, OFAC's 50 percent rule means that companies must also be concerned about doing business with entities that have certain relationships with listed entities, even if the former are not themselves named on the list. It is easy to see how this rule presents considerable challenges to U.S. companies engaged in international commerce and puts a premium on thorough third-party due diligence. As a threshold matter it is necessary to screen customers, vendors, distributors, contractors, and other prospective business partners against OFAC's SDN list. But in light of the 50 percent rule, and depending on its risk profile, a company may also need to do further third-party due diligence in order to effectively address its level of sanctions risk.

It should obtain and review data from multiple sources to assess the possibility that a prospective partner, while not itself on OFAC's list, may be owned 50 percent or more, individually or in the aggregate, directly or indirectly, by blocked parties that are on the list. The risk that this might be the case will be greater in some geographic regions and industries than in others; these are among the considerations companies need to take into account in making risk-based judgments about how much due diligence to undertake beyond merely screening against the SDN list.

While the 50 percent rule is triggered only by ownership, OFAC's revised guidance further states: "U.S. persons are advised to act with caution when considering a transaction with a non-blocked entity in which one or more blocked persons has a significant ownership interest that is less than 50 percent or which one or more blocked persons may control by means other than a majority ownership interest. Such entities may be the subject of future designation or enforcement action by OFAC." So while ownership is the most important element that companies should explore, they should also be alert and sensitive to issues of control, for example, membership on the board of directors, or senior management positions. Such relationships will not automatically trigger blocking under the 50 percent rule, but they carry risk nonetheless.

Communications and Training.   Proper and effective training is a key component of any regulatory compliance program. Sanctions training programs should include all of the elements and meet the standards of compliance programs generally, as discussed elsewhere in this book. But they should also be tailored to address the matters and issues particular to OFAC's authorities, especially where those authorities might be counterintuitive. For example, it is important for employees to understand the broad scope and strict liability nature of OFAC's regulations. The regulations do not merely prohibit exports of goods or processing of financial transactions; they are much broader, and training programs must make that concept clear.

Training must also thoroughly cover the critical concept of facilitation. OFAC's regulations prohibit not only direct dealings with blocked parties, but also any acts by U.S. persons that facilitate dealings by non-U.S. persons that would be prohibited if engaged in directly by a U.S. person. The term is not formally defined in OFAC's regulations, but the agency has provided some guidance as to what it means. The Iranian Transactions and Sanctions Regulations, for example, include an interpretative provision that gives examples of conduct that would constitute prohibited facilitation, including altering operating policies or procedures to remove requirements for U.S. person approval of transactions (when done to facilitate prohibited transactions), or referring to a non-U.S. person a business opportunity to which a U.S. person could not directly respond.[21]

The Sudanese Sanctions Regulations contain a similar interpretation provision that states more generally that facilitation includes any act that "assists or supports" trading activity with Sudan by any person.[22] Companies would do well to assume that whatever "facilitation" means, it means the same thing when used in any of OFAC's regulations. It should not be difficult to see how counterintuitive OFAC's application of this concept might be; therefore, training programs should make employees sufficiently familiar with the concept that they are able, at a minimum, to quickly spot and escalate possible instances of prohibited facilitation.

Training programs present an important opportunity to enable early detection. Employees should be educated to be alert to indicators of possible violations. For example, employees should be aware that if they see terms in documents that refer to persons, companies, places, addresses, and so on in countries that are subject to sanctions (e.g., Iran, Sudan, Cuba), that the document may reflect a possible violation. Employees should therefore also be made aware of company policies and procedures for initial response and assessment, and the proper protocols for escalating possible matches with the OFAC list, to ensure prompt attention by the appropriate personnel.

Detective Controls

Even after good faith efforts to prevent violations, companies sometimes end up running afoul of the regulations by dealing with blocked parties. The extensive scope and rapid pace of modern international commerce and the complex nature and structure of transactions and corporate relationships can make it very difficult completely to avoid violations, even for companies with well-conceived and mature compliance programs.

Given all that, and in light of OFAC's strict liability standard and heavy penalties for violations, it is important for companies to be positioned to detect violations right away, as soon as possible after the violations occur. A large company with extensive international operations, engaged in large numbers of recurring transactions with overseas partners, can commit several, or dozens, or even a few hundred violations before it learns it has committed any. This can mean big trouble. For example, the maximum penalty for 10 violations under the International Emergency Economic Powers Act (IEEPA) is at least $2.5 million, and for 100 violations, it is at least $25 million.[23] A company positioned to detect violations quickly will be better able to respond quickly, thereby reducing the possible exposure and putting itself in a much better compliance posture.

Data analytics can not only assist in the prevention of violations, but also help detect violations. Properly planned and executed analytics can uncover indicators of possible sanctions violations. This enables early discovery of violations, which puts the company in the best position to halt the violative conduct and to remediate deficiencies in the compliance program. It also puts the company in the best possible light in the event that OFAC decides to take enforcement action. For example, data analytics can help the company determine which of its business activities carry the highest sanctions risk, based on its customer and business partner profiles, types of products and/or services, geographic areas of operation, and so on.

By identifying areas of particularly high risk, the company can deploy its limited resources more efficiently and maximize its chances of uncovering unacceptably risky activities, or even violations. Analytics can also enable a company to determine if controls have been overridden, which can be an indicator of intentional attempts to commit or conceal prohibited conduct. In short, data analytics can be a cost-efficient way of detecting violations early on and therefore of preventing future violations by exposing specific vulnerabilities in compliance mechanisms.

It is always important to periodically test and assess compliance programs. It is particularly important to do so with respect to sanctions compliance programs, in light of both the changing nature of the government's implementation of sanctions and the fact that OFAC changes its list so frequently. Proper periodic assessments of, and enhancements to, the sanctions compliance program can help a company maximize its chances of prevention and early detection.

Responsive Controls

Suppose a company discovers there is an apparent sanctions violation. What should it do? If the apparent violations arise from ongoing business activity, it is important to consider suspending that activity until such time as the company can determine whether or not violations are, in fact, occurring. This can be challenging and costly, especially if the activity is central to the company's business (e.g., delivering products or fulfilling service contracts to a high-volume customer, or a bank processing financial transactions). But the costs of continuing the activity can be painfully high. OFAC may eventually conclude not only that further violations occurred, but that the company showed reckless disregard for sanctions requirements by proceeding with business as usual in the face of known apparent violations.

This may be OFAC's view even if the company begins considering, or even taking, remedial measures right away, while the business activity is continuing. A recklessness finding will almost certainly lead to a significantly higher penalty than OFAC would otherwise impose. So the decision whether to suspend the activity, like most decisions relating to regulatory compliance, should be risk-based—the more likely it appears that violations have in fact occurred and the greater the possible penalty exposure, the more the company should err on the side of suspending the activity.

Internal Investigations

Whether or not the company decides to suspend the activity, it should promptly undertake an internal investigation, for which the scope is determined in proportion to the risk and possible penalty exposure, to evaluate as quickly as possible whether there are, in fact, violations.

The investigation should gather and assess all relevant facts with reference to OFAC's Enforcement Guidelines and, in particular, the 11 General Factors Affecting Administrative Action (the General Factors).[24] OFAC considers the General Factors in determining whether to impose a monetary penalty and, where a penalty is imposed, in determining the appropriate amount of any such penalty. The General Factors address, for example, whether the violations were the result of willfulness or recklessness, as opposed to a good-faith mistake; who within an organization was aware of the conduct constituting the violations, and what were their roles and levels of seniority; the nature and severity of harm to sanctions program objectives resulting from the violations; the individual characteristics of the violator (e.g., size, commercial sophistication, and so on); the existence, nature, and adequacy of any compliance program in place at the time of the violations; the violator's remedial response, if any, to the violations; and any cooperation the violator provided to OFAC's investigation.

The scope, nature, and details of the investigation, as is the case with internal investigations generally, should be commensurate with the nature and apparent severity of the possible violations and the enforcement consequences that are likely to follow. In any case, however, the investigation should be geared toward: (1) identifying all apparent violations; (2) determining the monetary value to be assigned to each violation; and (3) identifying all facts relevant to the nature and commission of the violations, and to application of the General Factors. This is the information that OFAC will use to decide on its enforcement response and on the amount of the penalty, if it chooses to impose one. Of course, the company should also be promptly responsive to any questions or guidance OFAC might give during the course of the investigation, to ensure that the final investigative report is sufficiently thorough and addresses any issues or questions that OFAC has raised or might raise.

Enforcement Protocols

Understanding how OFAC decides whether to impose a monetary penalty and what the amount of any such penalty should be will help companies to design and execute effective investigative plans when they discover that there have been violations. OFAC's methodology is laid out in its Economic Sanctions Enforcement Guidelines (the Enforcement Guidelines).[25] These make clear that OFAC employs a thorough, fact-intensive process to assess the nature and severity of apparent violations. It first gathers as much information as it can about the violations, including not only transactional data, but also internal company e-mails, memos, and other communications that can shed light on who within the company knew about, or participated in the violations. It then analyzes the facts against the General Factors and other criteria set forth in the Enforcement Guidelines.

If OFAC determines that the violations merit a penalty, it then makes two threshold determinations: (1) whether the violator made a "voluntary self-disclosure" of the violations to OFAC and (2) whether the violations were "egregious." "Voluntary self-disclosure" and "egregiousness" are terms of art, defined in the Enforcement Guidelines.[26] The yes or no answers to those two questions place the case in one of four boxes in the Base Penalty Matrix (Figure 5.1); each box will have a specific dollar amount, with reference to the statutory maximum penalty for the violations, the monetary amount of the transactions constituting the violations, and/or a schedule of dollar amounts set forth in the Enforcement Guidelines. The difference in amounts between the four boxes can vary greatly, and the penalties for egregious cases can be very large.

Here is a simple example that illustrates how OFAC determines the base penalty, with reference to the Base Penalty Matrix. Assume a hypothetical case involving a single violation, for example, a prohibited export of an item, valued at $6,000, to a sanctioned party in Iran. The base penalty in Box 1 will be one-half of the transaction value, or $3,000. The number for Box 2 is determined by reference to

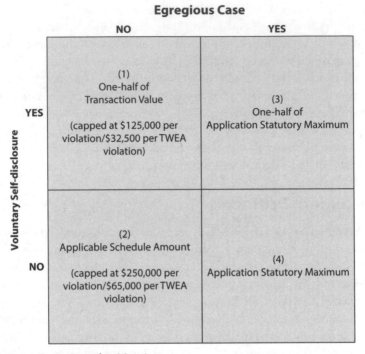

Figure 5.1. Base Penalty Matrix
Source: http://www.treasury.gov/resource-center/sanctions/Documents/fr74_57593.pdf

the schedule on the first page of OFAC's Enforcement Guidelines. For a violation valued at $3,000, the schedule yields a Box 2 base penalty of $10,000. The base penalty for Box 3 is one-half of the statutory maximum penalty for the violation; for Box 4, the base penalty is the full statutory maximum. For violations involving Iran, the statutory maximum is the greater of (1) twice the value of the violation or (2) $250,000. So in this case, the base penalty will be for Box 3 $125,000 and $250,000 for Box 4. Note the wide disparity between these four figures.

If the violator voluntarily self-disclosed to OFAC and the violation was not egregious, then Box 1 applies and the base penalty will be $3,000. If, however, there was no voluntary self-disclosure and the violation was egregious, then Box 4 applies, and the base penalty will be $250,000. Or, the base penalty could end up being the Box 2 ($10,000) or Box 3 ($125,000) penalty, depending on the answers to the two threshold questions. It is easy to see how the base penalty will vary significantly, depending on which of the four boxes applies, and how quickly the base penalty can grow to a large number.

Once OFAC has determined the base penalty, it applies the 11 General Factors set forth in the Guidelines[27] to the facts of the case and determines whether the base penalty amount should be mitigated, aggravated, or left unchanged on the basis of each General Factor. The cumulative results of this analysis yield the final penalty amount. So, when a company discovers violations, it should tailor its investigation to these General Factors and OFAC's definition of egregiousness. This will enable the company to get an idea of the likelihood that OFAC will decide to pursue a penalty and the likely amount of the penalty. It will also help to inform the company's decision on whether or not to self-disclose the violation to OFAC.

Here again, a company can benefit from using data analytics, particularly in large-scale matters involving, for example, large numbers of transactions or where company personnel are dispersed across a number of geographic locations. Effective use of data analytics will enable the company to more quickly retrieve data about the transactions constituting the possible violations; among other things, this will enable the company to identify and determine the monetary value of the violations, which will in turn enable the company to begin to assess the amount of the penalty it may be facing. In addition, the company will be able to gather and assess other data relevant to OFAC's enforcement decisions and penalty calculations—for example, internal e-mails and other communications among company personnel, and between company personnel and outsiders.

This type of data can be critical evidence in an OFAC enforcement action, as it can form part of the basis for OFAC's determinations on how to apply the General Factors. For example, OFAC will look to see if the evidence shows that the violations were intentional and willful, or the result of recklessness, or the result of program failure. Such data can also show at what level within an organization there was knowledge of the acts constituting the violations—did senior officials and managers know of the conduct, or was knowledge limited, instead, to mid- and low-level personnel? In short, effective use of data analytics will enable a company to put itself in the best possible enforcement posture by quickly gathering, analyzing, and interpreting all relevant information.

Disclosure Protocols

If the company develops facts that make it reasonably likely that there has, in fact, been a violation, then it immediately faces another important decision—whether or not to self-disclose the possible violation to OFAC. There is no legal duty to self-disclose, but there are considerable benefits to doing so. OFAC encourages the practice and substantially rewards self-disclosures, both in deciding whether to take an enforcement action in response to the violations and in determining the amount of the penalty it will impose when it does decide to take action. For example, in cases involving egregious violations, where the violator self-discloses, OFAC cuts the base penalty in half in recognition of the self-disclosure. This is before it applies the General Factors to adjust the base penalty, where further reduction through mitigation is possible.

For OFAC's purposes, voluntary self-disclosure (VSD) is a term of art, defined in OFAC's Enforcement Guidelines.[28] To qualify as a VSD, the disclosure to OFAC must, among other things, be made "prior to, or at the same time that, OFAC, or any other federal, state, or local government agency or official, discovers the apparent violation or another substantially similar apparent violation." So there is a premium on disclosing promptly, as soon as the company has reasonable indications that violations have occurred.

If OFAC receives information about the apparent violations from any source other than the company (e.g., notice from a bank of the blocking or rejection of a transaction relating to the violations, a tip from a whistleblower, notice from another government agency, and so on), then the company cannot receive the benefits of submitting a VSD. For the same reason, a company that is required to, or is otherwise going to, make a disclosure of sanctions violations to another regulator (e.g., a bank making a disclosure to its prudential regulator) then it should make the same disclosure to OFAC at the same time.

In non-regulated or lightly regulated sectors, whether or not to self-disclose to OFAC can be a more difficult decision. This is because OFAC has traditionally taken a long time to resolve enforcement matters. OFAC is a single, small agency, unlike the DOJ, which has several thousand prosecutors in 93 U.S. Attorney's Offices across the country and in the department's headquarters in Washington. A review of the web posts announcing OFAC's enforcement actions will show how common it has been for resolutions to be announced at least a few years after the most recent violations were committed.[29]

The same web posts show how frequently OFAC seeks agreements to toll the five-year statute of limitations. In fact, OFAC expressly includes a target's entering into a statute of limitations tolling agreement as a mitigating factor under the guidelines it uses to calculate penalties for violations. In short, if a company self-discloses and OFAC opens an investigation, the company can safely assume that it will probably take at least a few years until the matter is resolved. This can disrupt business and generate increased legal and other costs.

Therefore, an alternative to self-disclosure in such a situation might be (1) to not self-disclose and hope that OFAC does not learn of the violation some other way, and instead (2) to promptly investigate the apparent violations, and then (3) fix the problem by enhancing the compliance program as necessary and taking other appropriate remedial actions. Then, if OFAC does learn of the violations, the company will be able to show that it recognized and proactively fixed the problem. And even though the company will not be able to reap the benefits of a VSD, it will have the opportunity to gain substantial mitigation of the penalty by cooperating with OFAC in its investigation.[30]

If the company decides to disclose a matter to OFAC, it should also prepare an effective presentation to advocate for the best possible resolution under the facts and circumstances of the particular matter. It is important to keep in mind that OFAC is different in this respect from criminal enforcers and even most other civil enforcers. In the criminal context and many civil contexts, the government must present evidence to a neutral third party—a judge and jury, or an administrative law judge (ALJ), for example—and bears the burden of proving that there is a sufficient factual and legal basis for its action. OFAC is different. With the exception of the Cuba program, OFAC does not, in the first instance, have to go through any judicial or other third-party process to bring an enforcement action.[31] Instead, it has authority unilaterally to issue a self-executing Penalty Notice when it decides that violations have been committed and that a particular penalty is the appropriate response. Under OFAC's regulations, imposition of a Penalty Notice creates a debt due the U.S. government; if the violator does not pay, then OFAC refers the matter to the Treasury Department's Financial Management Division, which will take action to collect the penalty. Such action may include referral to the DOJ for appropriate action to collect the penalty.

Violators, therefore, have less leverage with OFAC than they do with most other enforcers, making it difficult in most cases to negotiate in the ordinary fashion. Many of the most persuasive arguments for government concessions that a violator can make to other criminal and civil enforcers are inapplicable to OFAC. If the violator rejects OFAC's terms, then OFAC can simply issue a Penalty Notice and move on to its next case. Companies should keep these dynamics in mind if and when they reach the advocacy stage.

Conclusion

The trend toward the more expansive and aggressive use of economic and trade sanctions, particularly by the U.S. government, appears to be with us for the foreseeable future. Events over the past several years relating to Iran, Sudan, and Russia and Ukraine, among others, clearly demonstrate that governments have growing confidence in sanctions as a means to advance their policy goals. The U.S. Treasury Department's strategies of using "secondary" sanctions against private-sector entities as a means to pressure and isolate targeted governments and bad actors (e.g., terrorist financiers and drug traffickers), and of bringing aggressive enforcement actions against violators, likewise appear to have become fixtures in the landscape of international business. Companies can assume that sanctions will remain dynamic, with new programs and individual designations arising frequently and without prior notice. And sanctions issues and risks often overlap with other risk areas such as AML and ABC.

Those engaged in cross-border business therefore need to include economic sanctions in their business plans and overall compliance efforts. Whatever changes arise with respect to particular sanctions and prohibitions, a strong compliance program will always be the best way to prevent and detect violations. And, since sanctions are more about "who" than "what," effective screening and other third-party due diligence efforts will remain particularly important elements of sanctions compliance programs.

Companies also need to be able to promptly detect violations and then to respond quickly and effectively. Strong training programs and effective use of data analytics will enable companies to quickly identify, gather, analyze, and interpret information relating to violations. This will in turn allow the company both to terminate the violative conduct and to promptly begin to develop its response. This will require a thorough, risk-based internal investigation, tied to OFAC's 11 General Factors. The investigation will point the company toward whatever remedial steps it needs to take to shore up its compliance program, and will also equip it to make its presentation to OFAC and/or other relevant government agencies, if necessary, and to advocate effectively for the best possible outcome under the particular facts and circumstances of the matter.

Chapter 6

Market Manipulation and Insider Trading

Richard J. Bergin
Nathan B. Ploener
Timothy P. Hedley

Securities and Exchange Commission (SEC) Chair Mary Jo White said in September 2013 that a "robust enforcement program is critical to fulfilling the SEC's mission to instill confidence in those who invest in our markets and to make our markets fair and honest."[1] Passed in the wake of the most recent financial crisis, the Dodd-Frank Wall Street Reform and Consumer Protection Act (Dodd-Frank) represented the most comprehensive financial regulatory reform since the Great Depression.

The passage of Dodd-Frank ushered in an era of increased regulatory scrutiny, particularly in the financial services sector and on potential market abuses. This has resulted in heavy enforcement activity by a variety of U.S. and foreign agencies including the U.S. Securities and Exchange Commission (SEC), the

Howard A. Scheck was a major contributor to the content of this chapter. Mr. Scheck is a partner in KPMG's Forensic practice in Washington, DC. He specializes in assisting counsel in conducting accounting-related investigations and in defending companies and individuals involved in SEC enforcement inquiries.

Sean P. Macdonald and Gurhan Uslubas were major contributors to the content of this chapter. Mr. Uslubas, based in New York City, and Mr. Macdonald, based in Boston, are both senior associates in KPMG's Forensic practice specializing in dispute advisory services.

U.S. Department of Justice (DOJ), the U.S. Commodity Futures Trading Commission (CFTC), and the United Kingdom's Financial Conduct Authority (FCA). These enforcement efforts have focused on market abuse cases, including market manipulation and insider trading.

Market Manipulation

We define market manipulation as the attempt to interfere with the legitimate forces of supply and demand in a market in order to improperly influence the price or the price-setting mechanism. Successful market manipulation can be costly, as it introduces economic inefficiencies to and undermines the integrity of the market in which the manipulation occurs.

A wide range of markets have been manipulated, from interest rates to commodities to equities to foreign exchange. In fact, market manipulation can touch upon firms in financial services, energy, transportation, metals and mining, and agribusiness, among others. Among these markets, the majority of manipulative instances belong to one of three distinct types of market manipulation: abuse of market power, fraud, and uneconomic trading/bidding.

Abuse of Market Power

In the strictest economic sense, market power refers to the ability of an individual or firm to raise or influence the price of a service, security, commodity, etc., above its marginal cost. In markets that are perfectly competitive, market power does not exist. Every firm takes the price set by the market forces of supply and demand.

By contrast, in markets where imperfect competition is present, a market participant may have market power. If a firm has market power, it is a "price maker" rather than being a "price taker" and is able to shape the price. The extent to which a firm can shape the price determines the extent of its market power. Manipulation of the market involves the exercise of this ability to shape prices. Traditionally, this is achieved through the use of the firm's high overall market share and/or concentration to create a price movement that is beneficial to the positioning of the trader with market power.[2]

Because few markets are perfectly competitive, the mere possession of market power may not be illegal. It is the abuse of market power, or the excessive exercise of this market power (as defined by the relevant regulation), that may be illegal.

Certain financial markets may be more prone to the traditional exercise of market power than others. Commodity futures markets, which are standardized contractual agreements to buy or sell a particular commodity, of a particular grade/quality, in a specific quantity, at a designated delivery location, and at a predetermined price in the future, may be at a greater risk of falling prey to the exercise of market power than traditional equity markets are.

This stems, in part, from the fact that, at the time that a particular futures contract expires, the supply of the specific grade of the commodity called for in the futures contract, for delivery at the specified location, is essentially fixed. Contracts (or the physical commodity itself) in other grades, or for other delivery locations or dates in the future, do not meet the specific criteria of the particular futures contract in question and thus cannot satisfy the demands of those individuals who own that contract. As a result, market power for the particular contract in question can be achieved by controlling a sufficient concentration of the futures contracts and/or the underlying physical commodity.

Types of Manipulation Using Market Power. Two common manipulative schemes using market power are a "squeeze" and a "corner." A squeeze is a situation in which, due to a lack of adequate supply, a futures contract's open interest, the total number of futures contracts long or short in a delivery month that have been entered into and not yet settled,[3] exceeds the supply that can be delivered. A corner refers to a situation in which a trader has established a large position in the physical commodity, as well as ownership of long futures contracts for that commodity. The trader then withholds some of his physical commodity from the market. As a result, the open interest of the futures contract is greater than the deliverable supply of the physical commodity.

In order to cover their positions upon expiration of the contract, traders who have sold futures or who are committed to sell the commodity, and who are thus considered to have a short position ("the shorts," who benefit from price decreases), must agree to a cash settlement with their counterparties. The counterparties are those who have purchased futures or whose position commits them to buy or take delivery of the commodity, and who thus have a long position ("the longs," who benefit from price increases).

Alternatively, those traders who are short can purchase the commodity in the spot market, and then physically deliver the commodity to the longs in order to settle their obligation. However, in both a squeeze and a corner, because the longs outnumber the deliverable supply, the longs have market power and can influence the price. As a result, in order to satisfy their obligation to the longs, the shorts are forced to pay a higher price than they otherwise would have, either to settle in cash with the longs or to purchase the underlying physical commodity and then deliver it to the longs.[4]

Fraud

In the context of market manipulation, fraud refers to the distortion of the legitimate forces of supply and demand, or perception thereof, by disseminating false or misleading information. Fraud often manifests itself in the form of a rumor or report that induces market participants to act a certain way, but which later turns out to be false. However, fraud can take other forms, such as orders or executed trades that are fraudulent in nature. The purpose of such orders or trades is typically to insert false information into the market. For the fraud to be successful, the false information that enters the market must be believed by other market participants long enough for the fraudster to capitalize on the actions of others and adjust his or her positions accordingly.

Types of Manipulation Using Fraud.   There are several common types of manipulation that rely upon fraud.[5] One of the best known of these manipulative schemes is the false rumor. For example, in the commodity markets, a trader with a sizeable long futures position may spread a rumor that, due to an impending drought that he just learned about, there will be a market shortage of the physical commodity. As a result, prices for futures will subsequently increase, allowing the trader who started the rumor to exit his futures position at an elevated price. False rumors are also found in equity markets and form the basis of both "pump and dump" and "short and distort" schemes.

In typical "pump and dump" schemes, the fraudster purchases the stock of a company, and then proceeds to tout the company's stock as false and/or misleading statements enter the marketplace. The "pump and dump" initiator's hope is that by hyping up the stock and the company's prospects, other investors will be persuaded to buy the stock, allowing the fraudster to liquidate shares at a premium. Conversely, in "short and distort" schemes, the fraudster first short sells the company's stock, and then spreads negative false or misleading information about the company in the marketplace. Here, the hope is that other investors will be prompted to sell, decreasing the stock's price and enabling the fraudster to cover the short position at a depressed price.

Another type of manipulation via fraud is the act of "painting the tape" or "painting the screen." In "painting the tape," certain market participants attempt to create the illusion of significant trading activity (liquidity) in the market for a particular asset by repeatedly buying and selling the asset among themselves. In so doing, the traders who are "painting the tape" typically aim to generate outside interest in the asset that is being traded. The fraudsters' hope is that other investors will enter the market for that asset. Once outside investors enter the market, those traders who were "painting the tape" offload their holdings to a third party, often at an inflated price.[6]

Uneconomic Trading/Bidding

It is typically assumed that individuals act as rational agents and seek to maximize the total satisfaction they receive from consuming a good or service. In the context of financial markets, rational economic agents participating in the financial markets seek to maximize their profits for each transaction in which they participate. By contrast, uneconomic trading or bidding refers to a transaction or bid submission in which the individual fails to act in accordance with the principle of profit maximization. Specifically, this means that the individual either buys or offers to buy at a price that exceeds an asset's true value, or sells or offers to sell at a price below its true value. As a result, in that transaction or submission, the individual fails to maximize his potential profit (and could actually be losing money).

When this uneconomic trading or bidding is performed in an effort to create an artificial market price, it can be classified as a form of market manipulation. The manipulator may lose money on the individual uneconomic transactions, but ultimately aspires to reap the greatest potential profit by directionally affecting the price in a way that benefits other positions within his portfolio. By seizing upon certain moments when market liquidity is low, a trader may be able to have an outsized impact on the market price by flooding the market with what is then a large number of buys and/or sells relative to the depth and breadth of existing bids and/or offers at that exact moment.

Types of Market Manipulation Using Uneconomic Bidding.[7]   There are a handful of market manipulation schemes that make use of uneconomic trading or bidding. One of the most common examples is known as "banging the close." Generally, "banging the close" refers to a trading practice in which a trader buys or sells an asset in large volumes during the closing or price-setting period (the period of time during which the settlement or benchmark reference price is determined) in an attempt to influence the resulting closing or benchmark reference price. "Banging the close" is often performed either to make one's position in the security where "banging the close" occurs appear more favorable than it otherwise would have, or to benefit an even larger position in another security that is tied to the settlement or closing price of the security where the "banging" occurred.

Manipulation via uneconomic trading can occur at virtually any point throughout the trading day. In situations where uneconomic trading occurs during the day rather than during the closing or price-setting period, the manipulator often aims to induce the market to believe that his trading is motivated by valuable private information. In other words, the manipulator suddenly engages in trades that may appear uneconomic to other market participants, given all public information and other market participants' private information at that time. However, the manipulator hopes to signal to the market that he possesses valuable private information that will affect the legitimate forces of supply and demand, and that renders his trading rational.

Therefore, the manipulator's aim is to generate a cascade effect. The hope is that other market participants see the manipulator's trades, become convinced that he knows something valuable that they do not, and subsequently initiate their own trades in the same direction. The typical manipulator hopes that this cascade effect lasts long enough, and carries the price far enough in the desired direction, that he is able to, before a price reversal, either successfully close his position in the manipulated security at an advantageous price or successfully use the price action to take offsetting positions in a related security at an artificially advantageous price.

In addition, market manipulation via uneconomic trading or bidding can also occur in markets where there may be only a handful of market participants, or where the market lacks a centralized exchange and consists of primarily private, bilateral transactions. In such instances, the lack of many market participants or a centralized exchange may render price discovery more difficult, as there may be no generally accepted market price at all points in time. In such markets, in order to ease price discovery, an index may be used as a proxy for the benchmark market price. In these cases, uneconomic trading or bidding behavior can be used to influence the price of the index and therefore manipulate the market price. Such instances may be referred to as "index-based manipulation."

For example, in a market where the reference price is determined via index, and where the index is calculated as the average price of all executed trades by a predetermined group of traders over a certain period of time, one trader in the group may conduct a handful of sales at prices below the asset's value. As a result, the final calculated index price is lower than it would have been had the trader executed only profit-maximizing sales. This, in turn, potentially enables the trader to subsequently purchase an even larger volume of the asset at prices tied to the index price, which is thus cheaper than it would have been otherwise.

A recent example of market manipulation accomplished (at least in part) by uneconomic bidding through the manipulation of an index, according to settlements with the CFTC, was the attempted manipulation of the London Interbank Offered Rate (LIBOR).[8] LIBOR is an interest rate used as a benchmark for unsecured loans made between banks in the London interbank market and serves as a key benchmark for many interest rates around the world and is used as reference rate for both debt products (e.g., corporate bonds, college loans, and credit cards) and financial instruments (e.g., currency swaps and interest rate swaps). As of May 2015, more than $2.6 billion of penalties had been imposed for manipulative conduct related to LIBOR and other interest rate benchmark abuses by the CFTC alone.[9]

Regulatory Landscape

Since the financial recession of 2008–09, lawmakers and regulators have focused on ensuring the integrity of the financial markets, such as the alleged manipulation of the foreign exchange market, where average currency trading activity exceeds $5 trillion a day.[10] According to Bloomberg, the U.K.'s FCA was the first regulatory agency to reveal that it was looking into allegations that foreign exchange dealers timed certain trades in an effort to influence prices and shared information with dealers at other banks.[11] Since then, authorities on three continents have initiated their own investigations into allegations of market manipulation, collusion, and other forms of misbehavior in the foreign exchange market. As of mid-May 2015, more than 20 separate probes had been initiated and $9.9 billion in fines assessed in connection with the alleged manipulation in the foreign exchange market.[12]

Market manipulation is a complex area; not only does it involve a multiplicity of government regulators around the world, but it is also potentially governed by a wide range of laws and regulations within each geographical jurisdiction. For example, market manipulation actions in the United States can be initiated by several regulatory agencies, including the DOJ, SEC, CFTC, and Federal Energy Regulatory Commission (FERC). The involvement of a particular agency depends not only on the market in question, but also on the manipulative schemes allegedly employed.

The DOJ may become involved in cases of alleged market manipulation where antitrust concerns have been raised regarding the potential violation of laws governing the organization, behavior, and actions of businesses aimed at promoting fair competition to the benefit of consumers. In particular, the DOJ may become involved in instances where collusion (an agreement, usually secretive in nature, made between firms or individuals to limit or prevent open competition via deceptive or fraudulent means in order to gain a market advantage), a cartel (a group of firms or individuals that explicitly agree to coordinate their activities in a market), and/or the abuse of market power are alleged to have been used to manipulate the market.

The SEC, by contrast, tends to use a broad, fraud-based rule to deal with manipulation in connection with the purchase or sale of securities—chiefly, any note, stock, bond, or debenture.[13] The SEC has typically brought actions related to alleged manipulation under Rule 10b-5[14] even though it is a general antifraud rule rather than a rule intended to curb manipulation.[15] Rule 10b5 maintains that it is illegal for any person, directly or indirectly, in connection with the purchase or sale of any security to (1) employ any device, scheme, or artifice to defraud; (2) make any false statements of material fact or omit to state a material fact necessary in order to make the statements made, in light of the circumstances in which they were made, not misleading; or (3) engage in any act that would operate as a fraud or deceit upon any person.[16]

The anti-manipulation rules of FERC, FTC, and CFTC are all based on this antifraud provision of the SEC. As a result, their language is similar to that of the above. However, it is important to note that the areas to which each of these antifraud rules applies are distinct. For example, the FERC's anti-manipulation rule is specific to the energy markets.[17] The FTC's market manipulation rule applies "in connection with the purchase or sale of crude oil, gasoline, or petroleum distillates at wholesale."[18] The CFTC's focus, by contrast, is on conduct in connection with the purchase, sale, or termination of any swap (an agreement between two parties to exchange a series of future cash flows) or contract of sale of any commodity in interstate commerce, or for future delivery.[19, 20]

Given the litany of market manipulation rules administered by several distinct regulatory agencies, fines stemming from manipulative activities have been substantial and increasing. As illustrated in Figure 6.1, fines for market manipulation in the United States have increased from $163 million in 2009 to $2.8 billion in 2015.[21]

One agency that has been especially active in the area of market manipulation has been the CFTC, whose enforcement capabilities changed with regard to market manipulation following the passage of the Dodd-Frank Act. Historically, there has been little written, explicit evidence of manipulative intent in matters alleging market manipulation. As a result, the CFTC has had to rely almost exclusively on trading or market data to draw an inference of manipulative intent. Additionally, demonstrating that prices were affected by a factor inconsistent with the legitimate forces of supply and demand can be a complex task requiring economic and statistical analyses. As a result, the CFTC faced a difficult task proving cases of market manipulation and so had limited success prosecuting perfected market manipulation cases prior to the passage of Dodd-Frank.

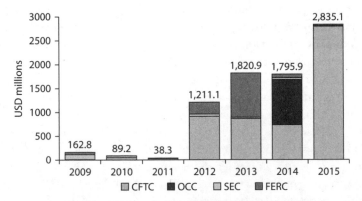

Figure 6.1. U.S. Market Manipulation Penalties, 2009–2015
Source: Author; compiled using data available in press releases issued by four government entities: CFTC, OCC, SEC, and FERC and available on their websites

As a result of the Dodd-Frank amendments to the Commodity Exchange Act (CEA), which became effective in August 2011, the CFTC has more powerful enforcement tools. This, coupled with the CFTC's increased focus on manipulative actions, has caused a substantial growth in the number of enforcement actions and monetary penalties assessed by the CFTC in market manipulation cases.

Among the changes ushered in by Dodd-Frank that grant the CFTC new and enhanced enforcement tools, the CEA now has an antifraud provision as well as an updated artificial price provision; these changes are codified in Regulations 180.1 and 180.2. Rule 180.1, the antifraud provision, prohibits "the employment, or attempted employment, of manipulative and deceptive practices," making it unlawful for any registered entity to intentionally or recklessly:[22] (1) use manipulative devices or schemes to defraud; (2) make misleading or false statements and material omissions; (3) employ practices that operate or would operate as a fraud; and (4) deliver any misleading or inaccurate reports concerning conditions that tend to affect the price of any commodity.[23] As such, it is important to note that violation of Rule 180.1 does not require proof of an artificial price, nor does it require proof of actual knowledge; it merely requires that an entity is shown to have intentionally or recklessly engaged in, or attempted to engage in, the fraudulent behavior.

At the same time, Rule 180.2, the CEA's updated artificial price provision, states that it is unlawful for a person "directly or indirectly, to manipulate or attempt to manipulate the price" of any swap, commodity, or futures contract.[24] In contrast to Rule 180.1, Rule 180.2 does require a specific showing of intent; mere recklessness does not suffice. Rule 180.2 extends its application to include swaps (in addition to commodities and futures contracts) and to include direct, indirect, attempted, or actual manipulation.

In order to prove actual manipulation by applying Rule 180.2, the CFTC may bring charges of attempted manipulation. In such cases, the CFTC is required to show that (1) there was intent to affect the market price; and (2) there was some overt act in furtherance of that intent.

Dodd-Frank also amended section 4c(a) of the CEA, which addresses "Prohibited Transactions," by adding a new section (section 5) titled "Disruptive Practices." New CEA section 4c(a)(5) prohibits any person from engaging in any trading, practice, or conduct, subject to the rules of a registered entity, that (1) violates bids or offers; (2) demonstrates intentional or reckless disregard for the orderly execution of transactions during the closing period; or (3) constitutes "spoofing,"[25] the practice of bidding or offering with the intent to cancel the bid or offer before execution.

Violating bids (offers) refers to the practice of buying a contract on a registered entity that is higher than the lowest available offer price (or selling a contract on a registered entity at a price that is lower than the highest available bid price). Regarding CEA section 4c(a)(5)(B), the CFTC interprets this prohibition as applying to any trading, conduct, or practice during the closing period, as well as any trading outside of the closing period that would disrupt orderly transactional execution during the closing period.[26]

Compliance Program Controls

The increased enforcement powers of the CFTC, coupled with its intent to aggressively pursue investigations, has increased the need for businesses that engage in trading to reevaluate the compliance training of all employees; this is particularly relevant for a firm's traders, compliance personnel, executives, and risk managers. At the same time, it has also increased the need for such firms to augment internal monitoring of their traders' communications, trading strategies, and trading behavior. Both the level of economic risk (due to increasing fines and penalties imposed around the globe) and the accompanying reputational risk require a compliance culture capable of reducing the risk of regulatory violations.

Preventative Controls   The primary tools for prevention in the area of market manipulation are education and compliance training, particularly for a firm's traders, compliance personnel, executives, and risk managers. Education and compliance training should focus on the applicable laws and regulations so that the traders are made aware of dos and don'ts and what trading activity is likely to draw regulatory attention. The training should be broad enough in scope to cover the various markets and regulations applicable across all relevant jurisdictions. Training should also focus on communications, both internal and external. Adequate supervision of trading strategy and traders is also critical. Finally, a reasonable value-at-risk (the potential loss in value, over a defined period of time, for a given portfolio and statistical confidence interval) limit, consistent with the business needs of an enterprise, can help reduce and prevent a business from attracting regulatory scrutiny.

Detective Controls

Trader Surveillance.   As part of a robust compliance program, it is important to monitor traders' communications. The lessons of the benchmark manipulation cases illustrate how revealing chats, instant messages, and e-mails can be used as key evidence in the investigations. Internal monitoring of such communications enables a firm to stay on top of any potential regulatory violations by catching questionable discussions or practices before they are scrutinized by regulatory agencies and the financial media. As part of an automated monitoring system, a glossary of key search terms can be developed, and regular searches of traders' communications can be performed continuously on an automated platform.

In addition to communications monitoring, it is important to monitor trading activity closely. This too can be done on an automated basis, and it ideally should include all positions (both on- and off-exchange) to ensure that the enterprise is within all applicable position limits; a comparison of a trader's activity to what has previously been defined as his "normal" or baseline trading behavior and patterns; an analysis of anomalous price movements in any relevant financial markets; and an inquiry as to what the intended purpose was of the observed trading. It may therefore be necessary for compliance personnel to periodically hold discussions with the firm's traders about their trading strategies. A review of trading authority (i.e., what transactional actions can be performed, by whom, and under what parameters) can also be a useful way to keep tighter control over the amount of risk that traders can maintain in their respective books.

Examples of Detection Methods.   Although we will discuss several potential methods for detecting the main types of market manipulation, it is crucial to recognize that there is no single statistical test or indicator that can be used to detect all possible forms of market manipulation. This is due to the fact that the detection of market manipulation often relies upon the use of statistical tests that are designed to identify behaviors in markets that are anomalous or are potentially indicative of manipulation. Since no two markets are alike, a test may detect a type of manipulation in one market but not in others. Thus, any screen for manipulation should be carefully tailored to the specific market (and, if applicable, to the particular manipulative method) by well-qualified individuals to ensure its robustness and utility.

Signs of Market Manipulation via Exercise of Market Power.   There are several market phenomena that may indicate market manipulation via the exercise of market power. Specifically, abnormally high market concentration or market share may suggest attempts to manipulate a market. Also, if one has access to trading data of the purportedly manipulating party, a strong correlation between the manipulator's trading activity and subsequent market price movements could indicate market power. If every time the alleged manipulator purchased a security, the security then quickly increased in price, it might be due to the alleged manipulator's buying activity caused the price increase. This would indicate that the alleged manipulator likely possessed market power, which could then be abused.

In addition, the existence of anomalous prices that cannot be explained by underlying fundamental factors could be caused by market manipulation. For instance, if the price of a commodity futures contract cannot feasibly be reconciled with the cost to purchase the commodity in the spot market, store it, and then ship it for delivery upon expiration of the futures contract, this decoupling of the spot and future markets could point to a manipulated market.

Signs of Market Manipulation via Fraud.   Several items may point to the existence of market manipulation via fraud in certain forms. For instance, a sudden and marked uptick in press releases, Twitter traffic, and/or Internet forum posts pertaining to a stock with a small capitalization, coupled with an initial increase of the stock's price on low buying volume, may be indicative of an effort to "pump" up the stock's price. In equity markets, such stocks are generally more susceptible to "pump and dump" schemes, as there is usually a dearth of reliable information about them.

Additionally, the thinly traded nature of many microcap stocks makes it easier to disrupt the normal forces of supply and demand. In circumstances where "painting the tape" is alleged to have occurred, trading data can be instrumental in determining whether this is the case. For bilateral transactions conducted over the counter (rather than on an exchange), a pattern of repeated buys and sells, for the same asset and with the same counterparty or group of counterparties, could indicate an attempt to "paint the tape."

Signs of Market Manipulation Using Uneconomic Bidding.   There are several clues that may point to the existence of market manipulation via uneconomic trading or bidding. Possibly the most telling sign of attempted manipulation via uneconomic trading can be a litany of trades that appear to be losing money or that are not profit maximizing on an individual basis. Another indication of potential manipulation using uneconomic trading is a pattern of a noticeable surge in trading, by the same particular party, during the closing period or at times when the market is known to be relatively illiquid. A pattern of such behavior may be indicative of a concerted effort by the party to influence the closing reference price by "banging the close," or an attempt to temporarily overwhelm the legitimate forces of supply and demand at times when the structure of bids and asks is likely to be most vulnerable to such behavior.

Responsive Controls   If potential market manipulation is identified, there should be an internal investigation, preferably under the advice of counsel. All documents, trading records, and electronic records must be identified and preserved. A company should consider whether to self-report, depending on the outcome of the internal investigation. If the internal investigation indicates likely violative conduct, the company must evaluate how to mitigate. Should it suspend or terminate the responsible employees? Were red flags missed by supervisors or other personnel? Do there need to be stronger controls and monitoring? Dealing with these issues before the regulatory inquiry will likely mitigate regulatory and financial risk arising from manipulative conduct.

Summary and Future Trends

It is clear that market manipulation is an increasingly important area of focus for regulators. In recent years, billions of dollars of fines have been assessed in connection with market manipulation, predominantly touching upon the financial services, energy, and agribusiness. To further complicate matters, instances of alleged market manipulation may be targeted by several regulatory agencies, depending on the market in which the alleged manipulation took place and the alleged schemes employed to execute the manipulation. Given the substantial fines and myriad regulatory investigations that can befall a firm for engaging in manipulative behavior, legal counsel, executives, and managers should familiarize themselves with the three main types of market manipulation—market power, fraud, and uneconomic trading/bidding—as well as potential methods for preventing, detecting, and responding to alleged instances of manipulation.

It seems likely that there will be an increased number of examinations of potential instances of market manipulation, and, in turn, increased fines and regulatory oversight. Given the recent revelations of the LIBOR and foreign exchange investigations, renewed attention is being paid to benchmarks used in financial markets around the world.

Another important trend is regulators' focus on traders' discussion of their strategies and trades in chat rooms, instant messages, and e-mails as evidence of their purportedly manipulative intent. In three recent market manipulation cases—LIBOR, foreign exchange, and Athena Capital—these forms of written electronic communication were relied upon extensively by regulators. In the regulatory agencies' settlements with the perpetrators, these forms of communication were excerpted and cited frequently, making it much easier for regulators to presume that the perpetrators were indeed acting with manipulative intent. This trend is likely to continue.

Insider Trading

The SEC defines illegal insider trading as "buying or selling a security, in breach of a fiduciary duty or other relationship of trust and confidence, while in possession of material, nonpublic information about the security. Insider trading violations may also include 'tipping' such information, securities trading by the person 'tipped,' and securities trading by those who misappropriate such information."[27] There is also a legal form of insider trading, which takes place when corporate insiders—officers, directors, and employees—buy and sell stock in their own companies. Such trades must be reported to the SEC.

U.S. insider trading law is not proscribed by a specific "insider trading" statute or rule.[28] Rather, the parameters of illegal insider trading have largely been based on court interpretations of the antifraud provisions of Securities Exchange Act Section 10(b) and Exchange Act Rule 10b-5. These provisions prohibit "manipulative or deceptive devices" in connection with securities transactions; insider trading is simply one manifestation of this deception.[29]

Illegal insider trading while in possession of material nonpublic information means that the individual was aware, at the time of his transaction in the security, of the information in question.[30] The trader does not necessarily have to use or rely on the nonpublic material information as the impetus for buying or selling; rather, the individual merely has to trade while having such information.

Material information is information that a reasonable investor would consider important in making an investment or trading decision.[31] It should be pointed out that the material information in question does not necessarily have to be the most important piece of information at the time; examples of information that has been considered "material" in prior insider trading cases include news regarding mergers or acquisitions, changes in company leadership, quarterly/annual earnings, and accounting restatements.

"Nonpublic information" refers to information that is not available to the general public. Generally, information is considered to be in the public domain if it has been disseminated via company press releases, publicly filed financial statements, financial publications, research reports, or by other means. An example of nonpublic information is information received under a confidentiality agreement or nondisclosure agreement.

Types of Insider Trading

While numerous insider trading cases have been filed that cover a variety of situations, there are generally considered to be two main types of insider trading—"classical" and "misappropriation." Under the classical type of insider trading, corporate insiders (such as a company's officers, directors, or employees) are prohibited from trading on material nonpublic information. This trading restriction on corporate insiders stems from their fiduciary duty to the security's issuer (i.e., the corporation) and its shareholders to use company information (including material, nonpublic information) solely for the company's benefit.

Note that in addition to these corporate insiders, there are individuals known as "constructive insiders," "temporary insiders," or "quasi-insiders" to which the prohibition on insider trading also extends. Temporary insiders are individuals such as external auditors, investment bankers, outside legal counsel, brokers, and other personnel external to a firm who, while providing services to the firm, receive confidential corporate information that may be material. These individuals, by the nature of their work, acquire the fiduciary duties of the traditional insider, provided the corporation expects these temporary insiders to keep the information confidential.[32]

As a result, both corporate insiders and temporary insiders are subject to what is known as the "disclose or abstain" doctrine. The "disclose or abstain" doctrine holds that corporate and temporary insiders in possession of material nonpublic information must either publicly disclose the information prior to trading or else abstain from trading altogether until the information is made public.

The misappropriation type of insider trading pertains to certain parties that would not fall under the classical definition. Specifically, it posits that an individual is prohibited from trading when he misappropriates confidential information in a breach of a duty of trust or confidence owed to the source of the information.[33] In this case, misappropriation insider trading does not require a corporate insider to breach his fiduciary duty. Instead, the misappropriation theory is applicable in circumstances where a mutual expectation of trust and confidence exists between the source of the information and the alleged wrongdoer.[34] In the case of U.S. v. O'Hagan, "a fiduciary's undisclosed, self-serving use of a principal's information to purchase or sell securities, in breach of a duty of loyalty and confidentiality, defrauds the principal of the exclusive use of the information."[35]

A well-known example of misappropriation insider trading is the 1986 criminal insider trading case *U.S. v. Winans, et al.* R. Foster Winans was a reporter at the *Wall Street Journal* who contributed to a column called "Heard on the Street." He was charged with operating a scheme in which he would trade stocks that were the subject of upcoming *Wall Street Journal* articles in a way that was likely to affect the prices of the stocks in which he traded.[36] The district court held that while Mr. Winans did not owe a duty to the shareholders of the companies in whose stock he had traded, he did owe a duty to his employer, the *Wall Street Journal*. Since Mr. Winans took confidential information about the timing and content of articles from his employer, the court ruled that the trading was a fraud on his employer.[37]

Thus, in either classical or misappropriation insider trading, it may be considered illegal if a person trades a security while in possession of material nonpublic information that was inappropriately obtained. A person may also be found culpable of insider trading if, rather than trading on his own behalf, that person shares the information with another individual, who then uses that information to transact in the relevant company's securities. In such a scenario, known as "tipping," the individual who shares the material nonpublic information is referred to as the "tipper," and the individual who receives and trades on the information is known as the "tippee." In this situation, both the tipper and the tippee can be held liable for insider trading.[38]

Recent Enforcement Trends

As Figure 6.2 shows, insider trading prosecutions continue to be a major emphasis for the SEC and its Enforcement Division. The SEC brought 87 insider trading enforcement actions in fiscal year 2015; this represents a marked uptick compared to prior years, where the SEC brought roughly 50 separate cases every year, as shown in Figure 6.2.

The SEC's vigor in pursuing insider trading cases has been closely matched by that of the DOJ, and particularly by the Southern District of New York (SDNY). From October 2009 through July 2015, the SDNY charged 56 individuals with insider trading, securing 51 convictions.[39] These insider trading actions initiated by the SDNY have charged a variety of individuals, including those employed at hedge funds, consulting companies, law firms, government agencies, technology firms, and pharmaceutical companies, among others.

As noted earlier, much of the existing insider trading law in the United States stems from the evolution of case law, based on Section 10(b) of the Securities Exchange Act of 1934, and for tender offers under Section 14(e)[40]

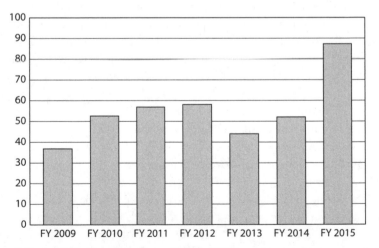

Figure 6.2. Insider Trading Cases 2009–2015
Source: Author; compiled using data available from the SEC's website

of the Securities Exchange Act of 1934. Criminal insider trading actions, by contrast, are initiated by the DOJ, but are also predominantly brought under Sections 10(b) and 14(e) of the Securities Exchange Act of 1934.

Section 10(b) of the Securities Exchange Act of 1934 is an antifraud provision, stating that it is unlawful for any person "to use or employ, in connection with the purchase or sale of any security registered on a national securities exchange or any security not so registered, or any securities-based swap agreement, any manipulative or deceptive device or contrivance in contravention of such rules and regulations as the Commission may prescribe as necessary or appropriate in the public interest or for the protection of investors."[41]

Rule 10b-5, which was advanced by the SEC in 1942 in order to implement Section 10(b), states that it is unlawful for any person to: "(a) employ any device, scheme, or artifice to defraud; or (b) make any untrue statement of a material fact or omit to state a material fact necessary in order to make the statements made, in light of the circumstances under which they were made, not misleading; or (c) engage in any act, practice, or course of business which operates or would operate as a fraud or deceit upon any person, in connection with the purchase or sale of a security."[42]

While Section 10(b) and Rule 10b-5 do not directly and explicitly prohibit insider trading, the antifraud provisions have been interpreted to address a broad range of fraudulent behaviors, including insider trading. In 2000, the SEC promulgated Rules 10b5-1 and 10b5-2 to provide clarity on certain issues pertaining to illegal insider trading. Rule 10b5-1 addressed the issue of whether a trader had to trade on the basis of the material nonpublic information—i.e., use the information, to be liable for insider trading, or only had to be in possession of such information.[43] Rule 10b5-2 was designed to provide clarity on misappropriation insider trading and prescribes when personal and other nonbusiness relationships may create "duties of trust or confidence."[44, 45]

Government Investigations of Insider Trading

The SEC's investigation teams across the country have the ability to open and conduct investigations, which are typically staffed by one or two attorneys, along with trade surveillance specialists and possibly accountants. The SEC's Market Abuse Unit drives the Division's innovations, identifying insider trading schemes and investigating insider trading rings and expert networks using data analytics and other tools. Potential red flags include unusual price spikes before major corporate announcements such as mergers and acquisitions, price rises before earnings releases, unusually large trades, use of margin accounts, and options trading in accounts that have not historically traded them.

It is rare that insider trading targets admit wrongdoing to prosecutors. As a result, many cases are largely based on circumstantial evidence showing that the persons had access to and possession of the information in light of their employment and nature of their job, had communications at relevant times with others possessing material nonpublic information, and then traded and/or tipped at opportune times. In criminal investigations, prosecutors use additional tools, including undercover agents, wiretaps, search warrants, and flipping witnesses in an effort to make their cases. Communication between civil and criminal prosecutors should be expected, as they commonly work together.

Responding to an SEC or DOJ Insider Trading Investigation

The response to any government investigation involving insider trading depends on the facts and circumstances of the case, as well as where persons or entities fit within any alleged scheme. For public companies and regulated entities, cooperation and provision of relevant trading data may be the best course of action; however, such an approach has to be determined and coordinated through counsel. In the M&A context, for example, investigators need to establish a timeline of events to understand which persons (from the acquirer, target, or legal or consulting firm advising on such transactions or otherwise) knew about the transaction, when they knew, and the communications such persons had with colleagues, friends, and family. Prosecutors routinely request that companies provide "chronologies" so that they can piece together the timeline and understand the facts.

The government will also likely want access to corporate communications including e-mail, voice mail, and any recorded conversations (broker-dealers). Providing quick access to such data, including searching various locations, backups, and possibly translating or transcribing conversations, are among the things that prosecutors may request.

Illegal insider trading can affect many types of companies and can have significant consequences for employees and corporations alike. For individuals, consequences include termination of employment, exclusion from the industry, reputational damage, hefty fines, and even jail time. For companies, accusations of insider trading can be highly damaging, even if ultimately shown to be untrue. Consequences include severe reputational harm, impaired ability to seek out new deals, an outflow of assets, substantial fines, and debilitated ability to conduct business moving forward. As a result, it is of vital importance that firms have programs in place to prevent insider trading, the ability to detect its potential occurrence, and the capability to respond swiftly and appropriately should insider trading transpire.

Prevention, Detection, and Response

From a company's perspective, deterring insider trading through a variety of measures is likely to be the most desirable approach, as it may prevent allegations of improper trading in the first place. However, an effective compliance program may also need to include monitoring and detection capabilities so that anomalies can be followed up and allegations can be investigated.

In November 1988, Congress passed the Insider Trading and Securities Fraud Enforcement Act (ITSFEA), which amended the securities laws by requiring financial services firms and investment advisers to create and enforce written policies aimed at the prevention of insider trading. Section 15(f) of the Exchange Act requires broker-dealers to establish, maintain, and enforce policies and procedures designed to prevent the misuse of material nonpublic information.[46] Section 204A of the Advisers Act states that every investment advisor shall establish, maintain, and enforce policies and procedures devised to prevent the misuse of material nonpublic information.[47] Based upon these provisions, brokerage firms and investment advisers have an obligation to prevent, deter, and detect insider trading. In fact, the SEC has previously initiated actions against firms for failure to establish and maintain policies aimed at preventing insider trading, even in instances where no insider trading may have actually occurred. As such,

---

Best practices for prevention, detection, and response include:

- Insider trading policies in place that are tailored to the organization's business
- Training of company personnel, as well as training for, or communication with, temporary insiders that may be working with an entity
- Supervision
- Trading windows and blackout dates when persons cannot trade
- Preclearance procedures in which persons can consult with someone in the compliance or OGC to determine whether there are any issues
- Periodic monitoring of brokerage accounts and trades made
- Monitoring that relevant personnel are filing SEC forms 3, 4, and 5, which are required for certain securities purchases and sales
- Investigations when allegations arise
- Appropriate disciplinary actions

there is both an expectation and a requirement that financial services firms have robust policies and controls in place to curtail such behavior.

Preventative Controls   Insider trading may harm a variety of companies, but there is no single prevention program or set of procedures that works across all corporations in every instance. Rather, it is important that the policies and procedures are specifically tailored to the industry and operations of the firm. We will briefly touch upon insider trading compliance measures for three main groups of firms: publicly traded companies, financial services firms, and companies acting as temporary insiders.

Publicly Traded Companies.   For those who work at a publicly traded company, education and training regarding the obligations of corporate insiders are paramount in order to avoid violating securities laws. It is critical that all employees (especially officers, directors, and others in possession of sensitive corporate information) have a strong understanding of the relevant regulations regarding their knowledge and handling of material nonpublic information, as well as their trading activities.

To supplement this, publicly traded companies should have their own explicit policies that prohibit insider trading and tipping; these policies should be often updated and circulated so as to keep employees abreast of their relevant responsibilities. Also, it is key that publicly traded companies try (to the greatest extent possible) to keep confidential, nonpublic information secure and on a need-to-know basis. In this way, there is decreased risk that someone who might be tempted to misuse the information ever comes into contact with it; doing so also narrows the pool of potential suspects should the company later discover that insider trading on the information did in fact occur.

Further, the adoption of "quiet periods" or "blackout" periods—periods when transactions in the company's stock are prohibited (such as before the end of a fiscal period but prior to public release of financial results)—may be useful to prevent insider trading. It may also be beneficial to have company officers and directors adopt Rule 10b5-1 plans. These plans, which allow publicly traded companies' insiders to transact in a predetermined number of shares at a predetermined time, can provide an affirmative defense to insider trading charges under Rule 10b5-1(c).[48] Potential risk areas for publicly traded companies include nonpublic information regarding potential M&A transactions, share repurchase plans, quarterly or annual financial results, any major new product developments, and key personnel departures.

Financial Services Companies.   In light of the obligations of registered broker-dealers and investment advisors to establish, maintain, and enforce policies and procedures devised to prevent the misuse of material nonpublic information, there other policies and programs these firms can implement to hinder insider training. For example, broker-dealers and investment advisors can hold periodic, mandatory trainings related to all pertinent insider trading regulations; in this way, employees can be taught and reminded about what is and is not permissible. Also, the offering of multiple services by a single firm (such as an investment bank) can precipitate potential conflicts of interest and therefore necessitate strict control over confidential information. In such firms, the establishment of informational barriers between those groups that have access to material nonpublic information and those groups that engage in trading is essential.

Financial services firms should also develop and maintain an updated watch list (a list of companies for which the firm has, or is likely to soon be in the possession of, nonpublic inside information as a result of some relationship) and a restricted list (a list of companies whose securities the firm and its personnel are typically prohibited from trading in as a result of the firm's access to material nonpublic information for the companies in question). Select members of the legal and/or compliance department should closely monitor any transactions in the securities of entities on these lists to ensure that employees are adhering to company policy and not transacting in the securities, on behalf of the company or otherwise, for which the firm possesses material nonpublic information.

Further, broker-dealers and investment advisors should require all employees, if they have personal trading accounts, to either maintain such accounts with the firm only or submit all transaction confirmations to the firm's compliance department for review. In this way, the firm can monitor all personal trading activity and raise questions if necessary. Finally, these firms should consider a system for continually reviewing all outgoing and incoming electronic communications, looking specifically for the transmission of any confidential or inside information. Notable risk areas for financial services firms include when research analysts change buy/sell/hold recommendations; when new macroeconomic research pieces are issued; and when firm personnel get advance notice of pending client trade orders.

Temporary Insiders. For firms with employees acting as temporary insiders due to the nature of their work, such as external auditors, it is important that such individuals understand the fiduciary duty that is created via their access to privileged, nonpublic information. As such, these firms should maintain written policies prohibiting insider trading and tipping, and ensure that all employees are clear on exactly what is and is not allowable. To this end, periodic training on insider trading issues and the handling of sensitive information can be very instructive. In addition, firms acting as temporary insiders should maintain a restricted list of companies that employees are expressly barred from transacting in until the firm no longer possesses any material nonpublic information. Also, these firms should periodically have all employees certify that they have not transacted in the securities of any restricted entities; here, annual questionnaires inquiring into the trading activities of employees, as well as intermittent audits of financial assets and brokerage accounts, may prove helpful.

For firms acting as temporary insiders, it is crucial that all privileged and confidential information is treated with the utmost care. Only those employees directly working on the relevant project, and who absolutely need to have access, should come into contact with material nonpublic information. This information, if in physical form, should be secured at the end of each day so that nonessential personnel cannot access, review, or otherwise see the information. If in electronic form, the information should be stored on a secure, encrypted device or in a protected server environment so that it is accessible only to authorized personnel. Potential risk areas for temporary insiders can include information related to an internal investigation concerning wrongdoing by company personnel, discovery of material accounting errors or misstatements, and analyses concerning potential damages amounts for those embroiled in litigation.

Detective Controls   While a set of robust policies and procedures can go a long way toward the prevention of insider trading, it is also necessary to have systems and programs in place to detect insider trading, should it occur. As mentioned above, one way of potentially detecting insider trading in real time is the implementation of an automated trade surveillance system. At the level of the company, an automated trade surveillance system would automatically monitor all trading activity, using a bevy of screens and flags to highlight seemingly anomalous trading behavior potentially consistent with insider trading. Parameters around which potential flags could be crafted include the size of a particular trade; the frequency of transactions; the length of time positions are held; the time at which orders are submitted; the profitability of a trade; the industry sector in which a transaction is initiated; the type of financial instrument bought or sold; and a variety of other criteria.

In doing so, it is important to develop a baseline trading pattern or decision rule(s) against which the transactions of traders and portfolio managers will be evaluated. After this baseline or threshold has been established, each subsequent transaction can be compared to the appropriate point of reference. It is important to keep in mind, however, that the calibration of this baseline scenario or decision rule(s) will have a significant impact on which trades are ultimately flagged as potentially anomalous. Miscalibration of the relevant screens and screening specifications can result in flags that produce a large number of false positives, or conversely, that fail to catch truly problematic behavior.

Another way of potentially detecting insider trading is an automated review of electronic communications at the firm. This review would include all available communications, with a likely emphasis on communications between disparate groups within the company that would have no reason to share information; communications between firm personnel and third parties; and communications between investor relations, executives, directors, and all other parties. While such an automated review would clearly not catch all possible attempts to share material nonpublic information, it would focus on key words and phrases. Further, this review could provide additional scrutiny during sensitive periods, such as during any quiet periods or immediately after the close of a quarter or fiscal year.

Responsive Controls   The response to any government investigation involving insider trading depends on the facts and circumstances of the case, as well as where persons or entities fit within any alleged scheme. For public companies and regulated entities, cooperation with the authorities and the provision to them of relevant trading data may be the best course of action; however, such an approach has to be determined and coordinated through counsel.

In the M&A context, investigators need to establish a timeline of events to understand which persons (from the acquirer, target, or legal or consulting firm advising on such transactions or otherwise) knew about the transaction, when they knew, and the communications such persons had with colleagues, friends, and family. Prosecutors routinely request that companies provide "chronologies" so that they can piece together the timeline and understand the facts. The government will also likely want to have access to corporate communications including e-mail, voice mail, and any recorded conversations that may be relevant.

Should potential illegal insider trading or tipping have occurred at a firm, the best path forward is a rapid response. Investigation scope and strategy will depend on the facts and circumstances; to this end, the firm should conduct an investigation aimed at determining the exact extent of any illicit activity. Such an investigation can be performed internally, although an inquiry assisted by, or conducted independently by, an outside third party may prove more beneficial.

The initial thrust of an insider trading investigation should determine whether the issue was an isolated incident or a symptom of a larger, systematic deficiency; in the former case, individual punishment may be appropriate, while in the latter case, there may be the need for more drastic reforms on a group-level or firm-wide basis.[49] As part of this investigation, a forensic review of files, including communications, trading confirmations, and other relevant records, should likely be performed by lawyers or external consultants. Such a review allows for an accurate re-creation and piecing together of information that existed at the time of the trading, providing greater insight into the situation.

A company should also consider whether to self-report to regulatory agencies, depending on the outcome of internal investigation.

During the investigation, or in the event that insider trading allegations for an entity or an individual proceed all the way to trial, it may be necessary to retain a statistician, economist, or financial expert to study the instance(s) of alleged insider trading. In particular, these individuals can study the informational releases in question, assessing both the materiality and magnitude of the information at issue. These professionals may also assess whether the purported insider information was truly nonpublic at the time, as well as gauge whether there was other, material public information that may have motivated the observed trading behavior.

Conclusion

It is clear that insider trading will continue to be an important area of focus for regulatory agencies. The SEC's increasing reliance upon administrative proceedings for insider trading matters is something that bears watching. In 2014, of the 77 civil insider trading penalties that were imposed by the SEC, 13 were imposed via administrative proceedings, or nearly 17%; this represents an increase from the 14% seen in 2013.[50] Administrative proceedings offer the SEC several advantages over federal district courts, including a streamlined discovery process and the ability to introduce hearsay evidence.[51]

Chapter 7

Financial Reporting Fraud

Howard A. Scheck
Timothy P. Hedley

In the early 2000s, the financial reporting scandals involving companies such as Enron, WorldCom, and HealthSouth captured the news headlines. In an effort to curb similar abuses, the U.S. Sarbanes-Oxley Act was passed in 2002, which led to a wave of enforcement surrounding financial reporting fraud. Much of the action targeted such wrongdoing as improper revenue and expense recognition, earnings management, stock options backdating, and misstated loan losses. Since then, the wave of enforcement actions has receded. While there had been an uptick in SEC accounting-related enforcement actions in 2014 and 2015, the number of such cases had declined from 31 percent in 2007 to 10 percent in 2013. Practitioners attribute much of the decline to improvements in financial reporting and corporate governance spurred by Sarbanes-Oxley, which has led to fewer (and less severe) restatements.[1]

Statements made since 2013 by Mary Jo White, the SEC chair, and Andrew Ceresney, the SEC's director of enforcement, however, have indicated a desire to refocus enforcement efforts on financial reporting. In a speech in 2014, for example, Chair White said, "Good financial reporting and vigilant auditing obviously go to the heart of the integrity of our markets and strong investor protection, which is why we have again intensified our focus on this area."[2] Ceresney warned about the potential loss of investor confidence, saying,

"The importance of pursuing financial fraud cannot be overstated. Comprehensive, accurate and reliable financial reporting is the bedrock upon which our markets are based because false financial information saps investor confidence and erodes the integrity of the markets."[3]

It is true that most public companies disseminate accurate and transparent financial statements. However, when allegations of financial reporting fraud surface, investors tend to suffer losses and other serious market repercussions may occur. Even if allegations are later found to be immaterial or unfounded, companies face significant reputational, legal, monetary, and collateral consequences. The effects include delayed SEC filings, class action lawsuits, and significant investigation costs. When restatements are required, other consequences may follow, such as changes in management, significant remediation costs, and possible civil and/or criminal actions.

Financial Statements

Understanding financial reporting fraud requires an understanding of the way financial statements are used and how they are falsified. Financial statements are intended to provide users with information about a company's financial condition. There are four main financial statements to analyze when making judgments about a company's current financial condition and future prospects:

- Balance Sheet—a snapshot of assets/liabilities and equity on a particular date
- Income Statement—revenues, expenses, gains, losses, and net income for a given period
- Statement of Cash Flows—a summary of inflows and outflows of cash from operating, investing, and financing activities for the period
- Statement of Changes in Equity—dividends, stock issuances, and other items causing assets and liabilities to change due to transactions with owners during the period

These financial statements are interrelated, and all are necessary to provide users with the relevant information.[4] A complete set of financial statements also includes footnotes that disclose quantitative and qualitative information not reflected in the financial statements themselves. Misstatements occur when transactions are not accounted for in conformity with U.S. Generally Accepted Accounting Principles (GAAP), International Financial Reporting Standards (IFRS), or other relevant accounting standards.[5] By contrast, misleading disclosures omit or misrepresent material information, typically to mask poor performance or declining trends.

Chair White has stressed the importance of financial reporting: "At its core, financial reporting, using accounting standards adopted by the FASB, is a critical component of communication between a company and its investors. Financial reporting can and should provide investors with a clear picture of a company's financial condition to help them make an informed investment or voting decision."[6] These benefits are lost when public companies disseminate false financial information.

Channels of Distributing Financial Information

Public companies distribute financial information in many ways, including SEC filings, earnings press releases, calls with securities analysts, materials published on their websites, and communications by the investor relations department.[7] The primary avenue for distributing financial statements is by means of annual and quarterly reports filed with the SEC on Forms 10-K and 10-Q.[8] Form 10-K is an annual report containing audited full-year financial statements, and Form 10-Q is a quarterly report containing unaudited financial statements.[9]

These SEC filings also contain important disclosures that are not technically part of the financial statements, such as Management's Discussion and Analysis of Financial Condition and Results of Operations (MD&A), which highlights significant events, trends, uncertainties, and so on. The MD&A is necessary because while financial statement footnotes provide useful information, they do not explain the business activities underlying the numbers. The MD&A helps to bridge this gap by providing insights to investors as if they were "seeing the company through the eyes of management."[10]

Management Stewardship of Financial Statements

As the MD&A suggests, management is responsible for preparing financial statements. It sets accounting policies and establishes internal controls over financial reporting (ICFR) and disclosure controls and procedures (DC&P) to ensure that transactions are accounted for according to GAAP and that reliable financial statements are prepared and disseminated in SEC filings. Key management personnel include the chief financial officer (CFO) and chief accounting officer (CAO). Both of them certify the accuracy of a company's financial statements by signing SEC filings and providing certifications in accordance with Section 302 of Sarbanes-Oxley. Management is also responsible for maintaining effective ICFR and DC&P and for reporting conclusions concerning ICFR effectiveness (and material changes thereto), pursuant to Section 404 of Sarbanes-Oxley.

Section 302 requires signing officers to certify that they reviewed the filing, that it contains no omissions or misleading or "untrue statements," and that the financial statements and other information "fairly present" in all material respects the issuer's financial condition, results of operations, and cash flows. They also certify that they reported any significant ICFR changes or other factors that could significantly affect ICFR subsequent to the date of their evaluation. Additionally, they certify that all significant internal control deficiencies and material weaknesses have been disclosed to the company's audit committee and auditors. For DC&P, signing officers certify that they are responsible for establishing and maintaining controls designed to ensure that material information is made known to them and that such controls are effective.

Many companies have developed a system of obtaining subcertifications ("subcerts") from other employees involved in financial reporting. For example, controllers of subsidiaries and other members of the company's accounting department may provide subcerts, designed to further ensure the accuracy and reliability of the information. Subcerts also provide a mechanism for communicating any potential financial reporting issues up the chain of management so they can be addressed at a senior level.

Role of Public Company Independent Auditors

Independent auditors conduct quarterly reviews of public companies and opine on year-end financial statements after annual audits. Unqualified audit reports state that financial statements present fairly, in all material respects, the financial position of the company and the results of operations and its cash flows in accordance with GAAP. For larger public companies, auditors also render a year-end opinion that the company has maintained effective internal controls over financial reporting.

Audit reports emphasize that management is responsible for the financial statements and that the auditor's responsibility is to express an opinion on them based on the audit. Auditors do not examine all transactions and company records. Instead, they review materials on a test basis in accordance with the Public Company Accounting Oversight Board (PCAOB) auditing standards that require a reasonable assurance about whether the financial statements are free of material misstatement.

Regarding fraud, PCAOB auditing standards require auditors to perform certain procedures. These include conducting fraud brainstorming sessions that are designed to assess fraud risks and risk factors, as well as to develop audit responses to such risks. Audit responses may change the nature, timing, and extent of audit procedures and may include steps such as journal entry testing, performing surprise procedures, making targeted oral inquiries of customers or suppliers, disaggregating data to perform analytic procedures, and interviewing personnel involved in risky areas. If auditors uncover or become aware of potential accounting fraud, or other illegal acts, they must comply with Section 10A of the Securities Exchange Act requiring them to assess whether the errors are material and if so whether the audit committee has been advised and has taken appropriate remedial measures. In circumstances where the company fails to take appropriate remediation, the auditor is required to report the matter to the SEC. In 10A situations, audit firms typically monitor or "shadow" the investigative procedures done by the company and its legal and forensic advisors to determine the impact on the financial statements and the ability to accept management representations. Depending on the circumstances, restatements may occur, and the auditor, if deemed appropriate, will issue an audit report on the corrected financial statements. In some instances, the auditor may resign and be replaced by a new audit firm that will be responsible for the audit report.

Definition of Financial Reporting Fraud

Financial reporting fraud under the federal securities laws means intentionally or recklessly disseminating materially false or misleading information in financial statements or other disclosures. As both materiality and intent are required for financial reporting misstatements to be fraudulent, it is important to understand these concepts.

Materiality

Under case law, errors are generally "material" when investors would have considered the information important enough to influence their investment decisions.[11] Accountants generally consider an error to be material based upon the magnitude of the inaccuracy—that is, a quantitative measure of its significance. Quantitative materiality factors are assessed by calculating percentages of important GAAP and non-GAAP financial measurements, such as net income, revenue, and EBITDA (earnings before interest, taxes, depreciation, and amortization).

Auditors must also consider qualitative factors that could render small errors important to investors. Examples of qualitative factors include an error that enables a company to meet or exceed analysts' revenue or earnings expectations, comply with debt covenant agreements, or meet regulatory requirements. Other qualitative factors include errors that have converted a loss to a profit or enabled a favorable trend to continue.[12]

SEC guidance, including Staff Accounting Bulletin 99[13] addressing materiality, indicates that there is no rule of thumb regarding the magnitude necessary for an error to be material (or to be presumed immaterial), as both quantitative and qualitative factors must be taken into account. Case law suggests that materiality determinations will involve "delicate assessments of the inferences that a 'reasonable shareholder' would draw from a given set of facts."[14] Whenever errors are discovered or allegations arise, materiality will be assessed by the company, its auditors, and regulators investigating the matter, as well as class action plaintiff that have sued the company.

Fraudulent Intent

Under the federal securities laws, fraudulent intent—referred to as "scienter"—includes both intentional and reckless conduct.[15] The clearest indication of intentional fraud comes from personal admissions. Admissions are sometimes made when perpetrators confess after the fact during an internal investigation interview or SEC enforcement testimony. In some cases, the intent to evade known accounting principles or disclosure requirements is reflected in contemporaneous communications (e.g., e-mails and accounting memoranda) drafted at the time when the financial statements were being prepared or underlying transactions done. At Satyam Computer Services,[16] for example, the SEC alleged a fraud in 2011 in which the chairman of the India-based company admitted that he intentionally inflated revenue and profits because promoters held a small percentage of the equity and because he feared that public knowledge of the company's poor performance would result in a takeover. The SEC's complaint quotes the chairman as stating that "it was like riding a tiger, not knowing how to get off without being eaten."[17]

Without admissions or other direct evidence showing actual intent, prosecutors may allege "recklessness," which means that the person recklessly disregarded accounting or disclosures rules.[18] Recklessness is inferred by showing that the persons acted with "conscious disregard" for the inaccuracy of the information and is established through evidence that a person was aware of red flags. This means that the person understood the proper way to account for the relevant issues, but through irresponsible actions, permitted or enabled the incorrect accounting or misleading disclosure to be disseminated.

Distinguishing Fraud from Non-fraud

It may be difficult, in practice, for prosecutors to determine whether financial reporting decisions resulting in material errors were made in good faith, were unreasonable, or were reckless. Aggravating factors suggesting "bad faith" (rather than lack of prudence) include participation in circumventing controls, fabricating documents, or concealing information from auditors. Those accused of financial reporting fraud often put forth "defenses" that may affect the ability of prosecutors to conclude that fraud occurred (or may add significantly to their litigation risks). Typical arguments made by potential defendants include that they were unaware of material facts and/or that they relied on advice from accountants and lawyers about the relevant accounting and disclosures. They might also argue the applicable accounting standards were unclear or permitted substantial interpretive leeway.[19] Additionally they may argue that the errors were quantitatively immaterial and that market reaction to a restatement was negligible.

The ultimate determination as to fraudulent intent will depend on all the facts, circumstances, and available evidence. However, fairness dictates that the unintentional accumulation of errors made while compiling financial statements[20] (and "good-faith" mistakes made when exercising well-documented accounting judgments), even if later found not to conform with GAAP, should be distinguished from fraud. And while there may be legal consequences for

---

Common Motives for Engaging in Financial Reporting Fraud

- Masking declining trends or poor financial performance. Perpetrators disseminate misleading disclosures or "engineer" accounting results to disguise deteriorating financial health.[21]
- Meeting or exceeding Wall Street analysts' revenue or EPS expectations—this is usually done to maintain trends and to avoid a significant decline in the share price if expectations are not met.[22]
- Income "smoothing" to even out volatile or inconsistent earnings results. While certain earnings management may be legitimate (e.g., reducing costs), other conduct (e.g., arbitrary reserve releases and unreasonable assumptions) may be abusive.
- Maintaining required financial ratios or credit ratings—e.g., leverage or capital ratios—to avoid defaults, regulatory responses, or otherwise.[23]
- Meeting internal financial performance measures needed for employees to earn monetary compensation (e.g., stock options or bonuses tied to net income, revenue, EBITDA).[24]
- Self-dealing and misappropriation of funds.[25]

nonfraudulent accounting errors (e.g., books and records, internal controls), this is different from persons evading GAAP with fraudulent intent.

In SEC enforcement matters, conclusions about intent are made after investigations are completed, at which time the SEC either drops its case or initiates the process for filing an enforcement action. The SEC may settle financial reporting actions on a nonfraud basis, due to a lack of scienter or other factors such as litigation risks and resource constraints. If not settled, both the SEC and defendant "roll the dice" on the level of intent that will be established in litigation.

Representative SEC Financial Reporting Enforcement Actions[26]

Having explained what financial reporting fraud entails, it is useful to understand the wide range of schemes that public companies have used to mislead investors. There are many "recipes" that can be used to "cook the books."

Fictitious transactions involve frauds where the financial statement amounts are simply made up. The "transactions" have no basis in reality and do not require any interpretation of accounting rules because they never occurred. Thus, fictitious revenue would not involve real transactions with real customers and fictitious assets would not be observable or legitimately confirmed. The methods for recording such amounts involve false accounting entries, fabricating documents to support the sales, and possibly orchestrating fake shipments to company-owned warehouses.[27]

Transactions with no economic substance are done with third parties and have little or no legitimate business purpose other than to artificially engineer accounting results. Examples include "round-trip transactions," which are simultaneous, prearranged sales transactions often of the same product in order to create a false impression of business activity.[28]

Improper revenue recognition involves techniques to accelerate or defer revenue from legitimate business transactions into accounting periods before or after it is permitted to be recognized under accounting rules.[29] Accelerated revenue involves actual transactions with real customers, but the associated revenue recognition is improper because "strings attached" to the transactions make revenue recognition inappropriate. These schemes may involve customer participation through a false confirmation to the company's independent auditors. Improperly deferred revenue involves schemes to delay recognition to future accounting periods, possibly because the deferred revenue might be needed in subsequent periods to achieve objectives.

Improper bill and hold involves recognizing revenue on sales even though the company has not shipped the goods to the customer. Bill-and-hold transactions may be legitimate, but there are numerous criteria that have to be met to ensure that such transactions comply with GAAP.[30]

Holding the books open involves artificially extending the length of a 90-day quarter to 91 days or longer. The practice pulls revenue that should be recorded in the next quarter into the current quarter.[31]

Side agreements with customers involve undisclosed verbal or written agreements that reflect unaccounted for contingencies relating to the sale, such as rights of return or extended payment terms until the customer can resell.[32]

Multiple element arrangements create opportunities for accelerating revenue when companies improperly frontload revenue from certain elements into earlier quarters.[33]

Improper expense recognition involves a variety of schemes that may understate or overstate expenses and that typically involve the improper capitalization or deferral of expenses.[34]

Improper capitalization and deferral of expenses prevents expenses from appearing in the income statement in the current period and therefore from decreasing net income during the present quarter. The costs related to the expenditures, however, must be recorded somewhere in the company's accounts; fraudulent schemes typically involve making false entries to improperly "capitalize" costs, which means increasing an asset account instead of an expense account. This was the basis for WorldCom's accounting fraud.[35] Improper deferral of expenses involves the failure to allocate legitimately recorded asset costs to "expenses" over a period of time. For example, fixed assets (such as plant, property, and equipment) and intangible assets (such as patents, trademarks, or copyrights) must be depreciated or amortized over the life of the asset. Companies may intentionally overstate the useful lives of such assets in order to stretch out the period of time over which the assets are depreciated or amortized.[36]

Failing to accrue or underaccruing occurs when certain expenses that need to be recorded are not done so properly. Schemes may include putting invoices for expenditures "in the drawer" and simply not recording them at all (or deferring recordation to a later quarter). Other situations may involve manipulating accounting interpretations relating to accruals for contingencies. These require accrual when it is probable that a liability has been incurred and the amount can be reasonably estimated, such as liabilities for litigation damages or environmental remediation. Other examples involve understating bad debt expenses in connection with notes receivable from borrowers or accounts receivable from customers when collectability is not assured. This overstates the asset and understates expenses.[37]

Improper earnings management refers to creating reserves or "rainy day" accruals that are excess liabilities booked when times are good and then "released" into earnings later when times are bad. It involves both the overstatement and understatement of expenses in different accounting periods to smooth income. This violates accounting principles when the buildup and releases have no basis other than to meet targets.[38]

Overstating assets involves schemes to overvalue assets, which also results in understatements of expenses. For example, overstating accounts receivable understates bad debt expense; overstating inventory understates the cost of goods sold.[39] Overstated valuations can also inflate values of marketable securities owned, or they can support a company's decision not to take certain impairment charges.

Understating liabilities involves improperly keeping liabilities off the balance sheet.[40]

Misappropriations involves assets stolen from the company via a variety of methods. Schemes may include fake vendors, loans, and business expenses. When they involve self-dealing by a high-ranking executive, the amounts may become qualitatively material.[41]

Improper disclosure arises when there are false or misleading disclosures in the financial statement footnotes or MD&A. Disclosure violations could occur when the accounting has technically complied with GAAP, but the disclosures failed to fairly present the financial condition of the company.[42] Examples of issues with footnotes include failing to adequately disclose information about business segments or related-party transactions.[43]

Misleading MD&A disclosures[44] involve a failure to disclose known demands, commitments, events, or uncertainties.

Investigations of Financial Reporting Matters

The SEC is the primary government regulator that investigates and prosecutes financial reporting fraud. The U.S. Department of Justice (DOJ) also investigates allegations of fraudulent financial reporting, but it tends to do so only in the most egregious cases involving willful violations, obstruction, self-dealing, and embezzlement.[45] When matters involve interpretations of accounting or auditing standards, which may be highly judgmental, or when violations involve deficient books and records and internal controls (putting Foreign Corrupt Practices [FCPA] cases aside), the DOJ is less likely to investigate or take the lead. If the criminal authorities are involved in accounting cases, the SEC often conducts its own parallel investigation and may provide technical accounting and auditing expertise to the criminal investigation team.

The Division of Enforcement (Enforcement), the largest of the SEC's divisions, has about 1,200 professionals, including approximately 100 accountants whose main role is to investigate financial reporting matters. The accountants work with Enforcement's attorneys in conducting all fact-finding aspects of the investigation and also provide technical expertise on the application of GAAP and PCAOB auditing standards.[46] The Division's chief accountant oversees accounting investigations and provides advice on strategies and technical matters and views on the charging and settlement recommendations.

Most financial reporting investigations are carried out by teams of two or three lawyers and accountants, excluding supervisory and technical support personnel from other SEC divisions.[47] These investigations may take several years to complete due to the complexities of the accounting, disclosure, and legal issues involved. Many persons from the public company's accounting and finance departments may need to be interviewed, from lower-level accountants all the way up to the controller, the CFO, and the chief executive officer (CEO), and may include persons at subsidiaries and offices overseas. Additionally, transaction and business personnel may be interviewed as well as representatives from counterparties.

Accounting Enforcement Metrics

Figure 7.1 shows the number of Issuer Reporting and Disclosure enforcement actions filed each fiscal year from 2002 to 2015 and the percentage of total SEC enforcement actions each fiscal year. As Figure 7.1 reflects, between 2002 and 2015, the SEC filed as many as 205 Issuer Reporting and Disclosure actions (in 2007) and as few as 68 of such actions (in 2013), with an average

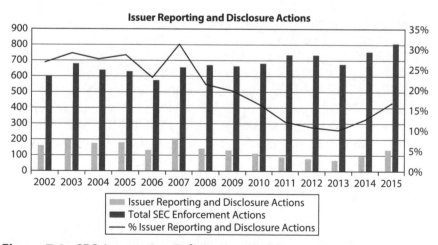

Figure 7.1. SEC Accounting Enforcement Actions
Source: Author; compiled using data available from the Select SEC and Market Data available at http://www.sec.gov/about/secreports.shtml

of 136 Issuer Reporting and Disclosure actions a year.[48] The number of Issuer Reporting and Disclosure actions had declined steadily from just over 31 percent of total actions in 2007 to 10% of total actions in 2013. In 2014 and 2015 the downtrend reversed with 96 actions (12.7%) filed in 2014 and 135 actions (16.7%) filed in 2015.

These statistics might suggest that Sarbanes-Oxley has led to fewer violations, due to improvements in internal/disclosure controls, better corporate governance, and audit quality. The possibility of criminal prosecution may also have changed the cost/benefit calculus for those preparing financial statements and certifying SEC filings. Despite the improvements since the enactment of Sarbanes-Oxley, it is possible that some financial reporting fraud remains undetected. Michael Maloney, the Enforcement chief accountant, said in January 2015 that financial fraud now "in many cases, is harder to detect than those earlier scandals, but we do get there."[49] For his part, the director of Enforcement said in a speech in September 2013 that "I find it hard to believe that we have so radically reduced the instances of accounting fraud simply due to reforms such as governance changes and certifications and other Sarbanes-Oxley innovations. The incentives are still there to manipulate financial statements and the methods for doing so are still available."[50]

Initiation of Cases

Financial reporting investigations are initiated when information comes to the attention of the SEC about potential accounting improprieties. The reasons vary, but include when the company files a restatement or self-reports an issue to the authorities. The SEC may receive tips by whistleblowers, or information may appear in the news media. Enforcement may also receive referrals from the Division of Corporation Finance, which reviews the financial statements and disclosures of public companies. The Division may also conduct risk-based investigations to identify potential wrongdoing before it is reported to the SEC. Enforcement will consider a number of factors when deciding whether to proceed with a full investigation of a financial reporting matter. These include:

- **Size of the issuer** and market capitalization
- **Nature of the accounting issues**—such as fictitious transactions, accelerated revenue, application of GAAP, and accounting estimates
- **Materiality**—including both quantitative and qualitative factors
- **Seriousness of the allegations**—high-ranking officers or directors implicated, multiple schemes or accounting periods, prior violations, failures to remediate

- **Availability of evidence**—the likelihood that the allegations can be proven; for example, whether there is a credible whistleblower who can corroborate the allegations or whether evidence can be obtained from overseas

Restatements arise when a company determines that a material error existed in previously issued financial statements upon which third parties are relying. This could come about because a company identifies material errors in the course of preparing its financial statements, assessing internal controls, or conducting an internal audit. The independent auditors may identify an error during their interim or year-end procedures, or an internal whistleblower might raise allegations that are investigated and found to be credible.

Depending on the materiality and timing of the errors, companies may need to amend previous SEC filings and file a Form 8-K, notifying the public not to rely on its previously reported financial statements. In some cases, a company may correct its financial statements by revising the numbers in new SEC filings. The SEC has raised concerns about so-called "revision restatements," and companies run the risk of receiving an enforcement inquiry as to the reason for the revision.

Self-reporting occurs when a company reports a potential violation to the authorities. The SEC encourages companies to self-report potential financial reporting violations early on in the process of evaluating whether a restatement is necessary. Companies typically hire attorneys and forensic accountants to investigate allegations that could lead to a restatement. When a restatement is likely and/or when a whistleblower may be present, companies may opt to self-report in order to demonstrate good faith and seek to avoid prosecution or reduce the charges based upon their cooperation with regulators. Companies and their attorneys often struggle to determine whether to self-report in situations where it is unclear whether errors exist at all or are likely to be immaterial.

Whistleblowers make complaints directly to the SEC or to a company's internal hotline and sometimes to both. The SEC's website provides a mechanism for sending in tips, complaints, and referrals. If certain criteria are met, a whistleblower may receive between 10 and 30 percent of monies recovered by the SEC. According to the SEC's 2015 whistleblower report, it received nearly 4,000 whistleblower tips of which 17.5% related to Corporate Disclosures and Financials.[51]

Tips related to financial reporting are evaluated by Enforcement's Office of Market Intelligence (OMI), which rejects many due to the lack of specificity, evidence, or credibility. Tips that appear to have a high probability of material errors are sent to an investigation team right away. Complaints that are less clear-cut may be referred to Enforcement's chief accountant and/or the Fraud and Audit Task Force for "incubation." Incubation can take various forms, such as gathering additional data from the company, counterparties, auditors, or whistleblowers to determine whether a full investigation is warranted.

News organizations and other public sources of information sometimes trigger an SEC investigation. For example, a newspaper may publish an article about an abrupt departure of a CFO or controller, prompting questions about foul play. SEC investigators almost always read and assess articles about suspected financial reporting fraud. Occasionally, academic studies may raise questions about financial statements. Enforcement personnel may also read reports by financial analysts, short sellers, or others who allude to potential accounting improprieties.[52]

The SEC's Division of Corporation Finance refers matters to Enforcement if, after commenting on SEC filings, its concerns are not adequately addressed by an issuer, or when an issuer appears to be obstructing it.

Proactive measures are used by Enforcement to identify financial reporting areas to investigate. These measures include risk-based inquiries and data analytics.[53] Risk-based inquiries (RBIs) are initiated when Enforcement has concerns that there may be financial statement errors regarding a certain issue, but few or no restatements have occurred. An RBI is used to search for evidence of financial reporting fraud. The SEC conducts RBIs sparingly, due to the resources required and the sensitivities of subjecting a public company to an enforcement inquiry without specific evidence of a material misstatement.

An example of a risk-based inquiry involved a China-based reverse merger of companies in 2010. A risk-based inquiry was initiated by the Enforcement Accounting Group in light of a number of indicators suggesting that certain China-based companies might have financial reporting issues.[54] Due to the potential risk for investors, Enforcement took the initiative to obtain information from the accounting firms that audited certain China-based companies and later from certain companies directly.[55] Upon pressing the auditors and companies, the SEC began receiving notifications through 8-K forms and 10A letters indicating that previously issued financial statements could no longer be relied upon.

Further investigations by Enforcement's Cross-border Working Group resulted in the SEC filing fraud cases against more than 65 foreign (primarily China-based) public companies and their executives, and the deregistration of more than 50 entities.[56] Many of the companies recorded fictitious sales and lied about their cash and accounts receivable. Other cases involved misappropriations via undisclosed related-party transactions.

Data Analytics

The SEC is using data analytics to identify insider trading, market manipulation, and other irregularities. For financial reporting abuses, the Division of Economic Risk and Analysis (DERA) has publicly discussed its Accounting Quality Model

(AQM), a computer program that analyzes large amounts of companies' financial data looking for outliers. As initially designed, the model was geared toward identifying discretionary accounting accruals to improperly manipulate financial results. The model looked at various fraud risk indicators and fraud inducers while layering on traditional analysis of financial ratios to identify potential anomalies.

DERA has also stated that it is developing text analytic tools to identify potential deception in SEC filings or other public information. These new methods appear so far to need further enhancements to minimize false positives and differentiate fraudulent accounting/disclosure from outlying results arising from poor business performance. SEC officials indicated that since AQM was announced in 2012, it has been extensively revised.[57] They say the model was "always envisioned as a tool to identify companies we might focus on," rather than a form of automated enforcement. David Woodcock, the former head of the SEC's Financial Reporting and Audit Task Force, said that while "these kinds of tools are only going to get better," human judgment is ultimately needed to bring actual cases.[58]

Given the difficulty in identifying financial reporting fraud from the outside, Enforcement is likely to continue to rely on restatements, self-reporting, and whistleblowers as primary sources for initiating accounting investigations. Restatements are the most logical source because the company has already admitted that the accounting was incorrect. The Division will likely scrutinize more restatements in order to try to increase the number of accounting-related enforcement actions.[59]

Fraud and Audit Task Force

In mid-2013, SEC Enforcement created a Fraud and Audit Task Force to enhance the Division's proactive capabilities relating to financial reporting fraud. With the deployment of additional staff to focus on identifying such conduct and the ability to "incubate" specific situations until they are ripe for full investigation, the Task Force has enhanced efforts that the Division's accountants and lawyers have traditionally undertaken (e.g., risk-based inquiries, assessing restatements, class action complaints, news, and so on). The Task Force has focused on whether "revision" restatements (those without amending previous SEC filings) were appropriate, identifying and monitoring emerging issues, and continuing to work with other SEC offices to develop data analytics tools designed to detect red flags of potential reporting fraud.

Conducting the Investigation

Once an investigation team decides to commence a full financial reporting investigation, there are generally five primary objectives:

- Determine the extent of any misstatements or misrepresentations
- Figure out who was responsible

- Assess their intent[60]
- Determine whether violations occurred, and if so, which ones
- Evaluate what remedies should be sought

The approach to reaching these objectives is to focus on understanding the relevant business transactions and how the company accounted for and disclosed them. It also aims to evaluate any deviations from GAAP or SEC reporting requirements and assess the nature and effectiveness of relevant internal controls over financial reporting and disclosure controls.

Evidence

Investigators obtain evidence by gathering information from the company, its independent auditors, counterparties, and others. This includes transaction documentation, accounting records and memoranda, correspondence (including e-mail and other electronic media), and audit working papers. Testimony will normally include interviewing under oath transaction personnel and financial reporting personnel to understand the nature of the transactions and the basis for the accounting positions taken. The objective is to develop a chronology of who knew what and when about each relevant accounting issue.

The investigators try to piece together possible gaps in knowledge, the level of GAAP research and analysis, and any input that came from the controller, CFO, and others signing or certifying the SEC filings. Other issues include whether employees circumvented or overrode internal controls over financial reporting or disclosure controls, or fabricated documents. They may have changed assumptions without adequate support or lied to others within the company or to independent auditors.

Wells and Settlement Process

Once the evidence is gathered and analyzed, Enforcement will make preliminary conclusions regarding securities laws violations, including whether material financial reporting errors occurred. Enforcement staff will also determine the intent, and may issue a "Wells Notice" to the company and any individual potential defendants/respondents about its intended recommendations. In response, counsel for such persons and entities typically will make a Wells submission to the SEC, explaining why the charges should be dropped or reduced. Enforcement will often grant meetings attended by Enforcement and persons from other divisions.

Sometimes this process occurs before an official Wells notice is issued, whereby the company or individuals may submit white papers supporting their positions. They may also have meetings with the SEC to discuss the issues or a potential settlement. Whether an official Wells notice is issued or not, a large proportion of companies and individuals resolve the issue through settlement, but some matters are litigated in federal district court or before an SEC administrative law judge.[61] In recent years, the number of settlements with only non-fraud charges has increased, as has the number of defendants choosing to litigate.

Prevention, Detection, and Response

Misstatements may arise in companies with the best controls and where boards, management, and employees are generally acting in good faith due to honest mistakes. Alternatively, they may be the result of rogue employees or senior management circumventing or overriding controls. Whatever the case, the best way to avoid or mitigate a potential financial reporting fraud is to develop an effective system of financial control.

Preventative Controls

Tone from the Top. Although audit committees are not immune from ethical lapses themselves, they may be in the best position to set the proper tone to help prevent financial reporting frauds. They can affect and assess the tone across an organization, monitor the activities of high-ranking officers, and interact with independent auditors. They can have robust discussions about critical accounting policies, judgments, estimates, disclosures (including non-GAAP information), internal controls, key transactions, and areas of SEC focus. And they can investigate allegations if they arise.

Internal audit, legal, and compliance personnel are also instrumental in deterring financial reporting fraud and in potentially discovering issues through their daily activities, examinations, or reviews. Due to their potential culpability for false Sarbanes-Oxley Section 302 certifications, certifying officers may be more inclined to create a positive culture to protect themselves from liability. It is clearly important for public companies to hire competent financial reporting personnel to handle the complexities of SEC financial reporting requirements and to provide sufficient resources for preparing accurate and reliable quarterly and annual financial statements and SEC periodic reports.

Risk Assessment. In preparing to participate in a fraud risk assessment, it is useful to peruse relevant internal and external information about the company's business and operations to identify issues. For example, have there been any published reports that have alleged accounting or disclosure issues relating to the company? Have any officers, directors, or employees sold large amounts of stock or unexpectedly left the company?

Risk assessment should consider any fraud risk factors that are present (such as incentives, pressures, and rationalizations) and how improper revenue recognition (or other schemes) may come about, how they may be attempted, and what controls might be easiest to evade. Incentives that may increase the risk of fraud include bonuses and performance-based compensation for meeting financial targets. Pressures may include the desire to meet analyst expectations, maintain earnings trends or debt covenant ratios, or raise capital. Rationalizations may involve minimizing qualitative materiality factors or concluding that the independent auditors do not need to know about certain facts and circumstances.

Risk areas for the particular industry sectors should also be taken into consideration. For example, risk areas for financial institutions include loan loss reserves and the valuation of securities; for manufacturers, inventory and cost of goods sold; for large government contractors, the percentage of completion estimates.[62] Additionally, certain behavioral risk factors should be considered that may signal that something is amiss with a particular employee, such as an overly lavish lifestyle or a reluctance to take vacations.

Participants in assessing fraud risks should include every person within a company that is responsible for, or interested in, financial reporting accuracy, including accounting, compliance, internal audit, legal, and members of the board of directors. Leading the effort should be the controller or CFO and members of the financial reporting process who can best understand the risks of financial reporting misstatements. A fraud risk assessment is done at least annually in connection with a public company's evaluation and report on the effectiveness of their ICFR with their filing of the SEC Form 10-K as required by Section 404 of Sarbanes-Oxley. Companies should consider whether facts and circumstances exist to conduct such risk assessments on a quarterly basis in connection with the filing of the SEC Form 10-Q. Most important, company personnel should be aware of the specific types of financial reporting schemes that can be used to commit fraud within their organizations and understand the red flags associated with them.

Detective Controls

Detecting fraud could come about in a variety of ways including internal whistle-blowers that may have observed improper conduct, internal audit examinations, independent auditors' testing, or anomalies that arise from well-designed ICFR or DC&P. Federal securities laws require public companies to maintain accurate books and records and have internal controls designed to enable companies to disseminate accurate financial statements. But Section 404 of Sarbanes-Oxley (Regulation 308) does not require a specific framework to be used, only that it be disclosed. Many public companies use the *Internal Control—Integrated Framework*, issued by the Committee of Sponsoring Organizations (COSO) of the Treadway Commission.[63]

The COSO framework has five components and 17 principles to ensure accurate and reliable financial reporting, with principle 8 focusing on the fraud risk assessment as an aid in detecting fraud. Whether COSO or otherwise, assessing fraud risks is an important way to prevent fraud, and public companies must tailor their approach and design programs and controls that are calibrated to the organization and the level of risk.

Ongoing Activities and Monitoring. When management cannot provide adequate explanations or cannot otherwise address the audit committee's concerns, then further follow-up may be needed. Audit committees should be particularly sensitive to cases where management is:

- Ignoring a lack of manpower in the financial reporting department
- Pressuring internal audit to change the scope of an examination
- Failing to give key financial reporting matters robust consideration
- Reluctant to implement recommendations by independent auditors
- Reluctant to investigate irregularities
- Downplaying materiality factors relating to accounting errors
- Reluctant to delay an SEC filing while there is an investigation taking place

Responsive Controls

Initial Assessment and Investigation Approach. When allegations of fraudulent financial reporting arise, companies must be in a position to demonstrate to independent auditors and potentially to regulators that they handled the issues appropriately. This involves making an initial assessment of the issues to determine the best way to investigate the matter and reach conclusions. Depending on the circumstances, it may be appropriate for a company's internal legal department, along with assistance from internal audit (or uninvolved financial reporting personnel) to investigate. In other instances it is better for the audit committee to hire independent counsel and forensic accountants to conduct an investigation, which is the method preferred by regulators. In some instances the independent auditors may insist that an independent investigation be conducted.

If the company learns of the issue from an SEC Enforcement request letter or an internal whistleblower or others allege material errors by high-ranking company officials, it may be best for the audit committee to hire independent counsel. If the allegations involve lower-level employees and seemingly immaterial errors, then the internal Office of General Counsel (OGC) approach may suffice. Some companies take a middle-ground approach whereby the company, rather than the audit committee, hires outside counsel to conduct an investigation and also potentially serve as defense counsel if the regulators become involved. Ultimately, the participants in the investigation, including who will direct the investigation, will depend on the facts and circumstances.

Document Preservation

Regardless of the investigation approach, companies must take immediate steps to preserve the relevant evidence, including computer files, e-mail, and other electronic media. This normally involves a preservation request or document hold to be disseminated internally and using company personnel or outside forensic experts to capture the relevant data. Government investigators will want to understand the company's document preservation policies prior to the allegations and how they were followed once an allegation surfaced. Internal or external counsel should be involved in this process to ensure compliance with company policies and potentially respond to government document requests.

Work Plan and Investigation Activities

Investigators must develop a work plan designed to determine whether there were financial statement errors, the materiality of such errors, who was responsible, and why the errors occurred. This will entail determining which accounting records, memoranda, and spreadsheets need to be reviewed and where the information is located. Investigators must also determine which transactions and accounting personnel need to be interviewed to understand why the transactions occurred and the accounting and disclosures related to them. IT professionals and forensic experts will likely need to search company records, e-mail, and other media for relevant information, using search terms and other techniques (e.g., predictive coding).

During investigations, assessments must be made as to whether accounting complied with GAAP, whether amounts of money or information was material, and what SEC filings are involved. It is useful to understand what interactions the company and the auditors had about the specific issues under investigation before and after allegations arose. It is also useful to keep the auditors apprised of developments, and the auditors may "shadow" the work of the company or audit committee.

Decision Points

Depending on when the investigation is initiated and how long it is expected to take, the company may need to decide about disclosing the matter to the public. It may also need to consider whether it will be able to meet the upcoming SEC filing deadline for the next quarterly or annual report and whether it is necessary to file a Form 8-K regarding nonreliance on previously issued financial statements.

As a result, during the investigation process, companies will also need to assess whether to self-report to the SEC or other regulators. If illegal conduct is suspected, some companies inform the SEC very early on, while others wait until its internal investigation is more developed or a restatement is imminent. Others may not self-report at all if errors are found to be immaterial and controls are remediated. Some companies submit amended SEC filings and others file revision restatements in the hope that the SEC does not contact them. When companies do self-report early on, they may have a better chance of receiving cooperation credit from regulators.

The decision whether to self-report depends on many factors, including whether a whistleblower may have contacted the SEC, and it should be made in consultation with legal counsel. At the end of the investigation, companies must determine how to correct errors found, including whether a restatement is required and whether previous SEC filings need to be amended.[64]

Investigation Pitfalls and How to Avoid Them

Among the pitfalls to avoid when conducting internal investigations related to financial reporting are the following:

- Failure to preserve and/or review relevant electronic information (e.g., e-mail)
- Delay in deciding whether to bring in independent counsel
- Delay in hiring forensic accounting assistance
- Failure to keep the independent auditor abreast of the investigation status
- Unrealistic expectations concerning whether the investigation can be completed without delaying an SEC filing or earnings release
- Failure to remove implicated personnel from the financial reporting process through firings, suspensions, or administrative leave
- Failure to communicate with SEC Enforcement personnel

Many of these pitfalls can be avoided by having frequent and frank communications among all those involved in the financial reporting investigation, including the audit committee, management, internal counsel, external counsel, independent auditors, forensic accountants, and lawyers tasked to defend or investigate the matter. Hiring competent forensic technology experts and forensic accountants that have experience conducting accounting investigations is important, as the investigation will go more smoothly when data is captured and preserved correctly. Forensic accountants can help to assess the technical accounting issues, review accounting documents, interview financial reporting personnel, analyze potential accounting errors, and facilitate discussion with the independent auditors and regulators.

The company will not be well served if the investigation has started, only to find that the scope did not meet the expectations of the independent auditors or regulators, potentially requiring additional documents to be analyzed, witnesses interviewed, or additional custodian e-mails captured and searched. Auditors will ultimately need to know that the persons conducting the investigation were competent, the scope of the investigation was adequate, all accounting issues were addressed, all errors were corrected, and all appropriate remedies were taken.

Regulators will have similar concerns but will also focus on determining which persons were responsible and whether they intentionally or recklessly evaded accounting requirements so that charging decisions can be made. Companies and counsel must be in a position to explain to auditors and regulators that the scope of their investigation was reasonable, that all material errors have been identified and corrected, that internal controls have been (or will be) remediated, that all culpable employees have been fired or adequately disciplined, and that relevant disclosures have been made. They will also need to explain how such material errors could have arisen, having previously opined that the company had effective internal controls.

Conclusion

Given the fact the SEC has renewed its focus on financial reporting fraud, there are a number of possible ways in which it may step up its enforcement actions in the future. These may include risk-based inquiries of companies and a focus on gatekeepers who have a responsibility for the integrity of the financial reporting system.[65] Enforcement has also expressed concern about an increase in the number of revision restatements, possibly to avoid Sarbanes-Oxley Section 304 clawbacks,[66] and in 2013 it began making inquiries about these.

Financial institutions may remain under close scrutiny regarding valuation issues and their level of impairment charges during and after the financial crisis. Another area of risk may include situations where a public company may be able to exert pressure on counterparties in order to achieve a desired accounting result. The SEC will continue to investigate "fair presentation" issues, even when it may not be able to prove that GAAP has been violated. As a result, it would be wise for companies to consider what investors would consider important to the total mix of information when crafting disclosures. The SEC may also target deficiencies in internal controls that may not have actually caused a material error and restatement to occur.

Chapter 8

Unfair, Deceptive, and Abusive Consumer Finance Practices

Amy S. Matsuo

Amid the 2007–2008 financial crisis, rising mortgage foreclosures and consumer debt levels in the United States created a public outcry in favor of more protection for consumers. Investigations and supervisory and enforcement actions uncovered a variety of unfair, deceptive, abusive, and/or unethical practices that were deemed to be harmful to consumers.

Leading up to the crisis, federal oversight of consumer finance was a patchwork of regulations administered by multiple federal agencies. None of these agencies had sufficient jurisdiction to ensure that consumer financial markets as a whole functioned fairly for consumers. The fragmentation of regulatory authority made it difficult to coordinate policies. In addition, large parts of the consumer financial markets, such as the mortgage markets, operated without any significant federal oversight, though such distinctions were not readily apparent to consumers. When dramatic increases in consumer lending activity began in the early 2000s, this multifaceted oversight structure proved ineffective at highlighting or containing a variety of growing problems that were later found to put consumers at risk of financial harm.

Karen S. Staines was a major contributor to the content of this chapter. Ms. Staines is a Director in KPMG's Americas Financial Services Regulatory Center of Excellence in Washington, DC.

In response, the Consumer Financial Protection Bureau (CFPB or the Bureau) was established in 2011 by the Dodd-Frank Wall Street Reform and Consumer Protection Act (Dodd-Frank). It was created to serve as an independent bureau in the Federal Reserve System dedicated to protecting consumers of credit, savings, payment, and other consumer financial products and services. It assumed oversight of consumer compliance functions from seven different federal agencies[1] and was designed to level the playing field of consumer financial products and services. It did so by being the single, primary federal regulator of providers of consumer financial products and services, including depository institutions (banks, thrifts, and credit unions—collectively, banks), as well as nonbank companies offering these types of products and services. Many of the nonbank companies had not previously been subject to federal oversight. As the single regulator, the goal of the CFPB is to "reduce gaps in federal supervision and enforcement; improve coordination with the states; set higher standards for financial intermediaries; and promote consistent regulation of similar products."[2]

The CFPB is mandated to exercise its authority under federal consumer financial law for the purposes of ensuring that, with respect to consumer financial products and services: (1) consumers are provided with timely and understandable information to make responsible decisions about financial transactions; (2) consumers are protected from unfair, deceptive, or abusive acts or practices (UDAAP) and from discrimination; (3) outdated, unnecessary, or unduly burdensome regulations are regularly identified and addressed in order to reduce unwarranted regulatory burdens; (4) federal consumer financial law is enforced consistently, without regard to the status of an organization as a depository institution, in order to promote fair competition; and (5) markets for consumer financial products and services operate transparently and efficiently to facilitate access and innovation.[3]

The primary functions of the CFPB are to: (1) conduct financial education programs; (2) collect, investigate, and respond to consumer complaints; (3) collect, research, monitor, and publish "information relevant to the functioning of markets for consumer financial products and services to identify risks to consumers and the proper functioning of such markets"; (4) supervise "covered persons (anyone who engages in offering or providing a consumer financial product or service) for compliance with federal consumer financial law" and take "appropriate enforcement action to address violations of federal consumer financial law"; (5) issue rules, orders, and guidance "implementing federal consumer financial law"; and (6) perform "such support activities as may be necessary or useful to facilitate the other functions of the Bureau."[4]

Since its inception, the CFPB has pursued its mandate to protect consumers from financial harm, initiating enforcement actions that have required both the payment of civil money penalties and restitution to harmed consumers. The breadth and significance of the CFPB's actions have prompted many companies under its jurisdiction to reserve for the possibility of future consumer protection-related penalties. The establishment of the CFPB marks a new era in risk management and consumer protection.

The CFPB uses its authority to regulate against unfair, deceptive, or abusive acts or practices to target many of the products and services offered to consumers primarily for personal, family, or household purposes for which it has received many consumer complaints. These include, among other areas, mortgage servicing, debt collection, debt relief services, credit reporting, and student lending. It is also looking at those product and service areas where it perceives particular risks, such as third-party service provider oversight, add-on products, and payday lending.

The CFPB is not focused exclusively on the largest bank and nonbank providers or cases where large numbers of consumers were harmed. Rather, it is committed to pursuing all entities that violate UDAAP and place consumers at risk of financial harm, even when there are no funds available to pay restitution or penalties (some cases have resulted in $1 of civil money penalties). The aim is to send a message to the industry about the kinds of acts and practices that could be prohibited under the UDAAP provisions. Further, where violations have been identified, the CFPB has required all consumers associated with the product or service to receive restitution independent of whether they have benefited from the product or service at issue.

The CFPB coordinates its activities with other federal and state regulatory agencies, which greatly expands its ability to identify and take action against UDAAP violations. Violations of UDAAP may occur even if an entity is in technical compliance with other federal consumer financial laws. The CFPB has imposed restitution obligations, monetary penalties, and multiyear compliance requirements on entities subject to UDAAP enforcement action.

CFPB Director Richard Cordray sees UDAAP compliance as a straightforward exercise, where placing the needs of the consumer first and protecting the consumer from harm should guide a company's business practices. In April 2014, he said, "Central to our mission here at the Consumer Bureau is the duty to identify and root out unfair, deceptive, and abusive practices in financial markets."[5] The creation of the CFPB, and the legislation that supports it, have changed the complexion of the regulatory compliance review from an assessment of technical compliance to an assessment of a company's principles-based risk management.

The first enforcement action announced by the CFPB a year after inception was a UDAAP-related case against Capital One Bank that concluded with nearly $140 million in restitution payments to roughly two million consumers and the payment of an additional $25 million civil money penalty.[6] The action was quickly followed by two additional UDAAP cases of similar scale and scope. Since then, the CFPB has used its UDAAP authority to open investigations, initiate proceedings, and enter into a variety of consent orders that are focused on both large and small entities. It holds bank and nonbank companies and their third-party service providers to the same standards of compliance. Notably, however, the CFPB has not defined the scope of UDAAP, preferring to rely on the facts and circumstances of each enforcement action to serve as a guide to the industry.

Background

The establishment of the CFPB is a significant milestone in the regulation of business practices aimed at individual consumers. In 1914, Congress passed the Federal Trade Commission Act[7] (FTC Act) to establish a standard making it unlawful to engage in "unfair methods of competition in or affecting commerce" and to form the FTC to define and enforce this standard. The law is a significant antitrust statute intended to protect consumers through the prohibition of anti-competitive business practices. In 1938, Congress passed the Wheeler-Lea Act[8] to add prohibitions on "unfair or deceptive acts or practices," commonly referred to as UDAP, to the FTC Act's Section 5 prohibition against "unfair methods or competition." The Wheeler-Lea Act also gave the FTC authority to impose civil money penalties for violations of these Section 5 standards.

Neither "unfair" nor "deceptive" was defined in the statute, and the types of acts and practices that came to be identified as "unfair" or "deceptive" evolved over time through FTC enforcement actions and court rulings. The terms were eventually defined by the FTC through policy statements issued in 1980[9] and 1983,[10] based on parameters set by criteria refined through regulatory and judicial processes. The definitions, however, remain broad and general, which facilitates their application to a range of facts and circumstances.

The Policy Statement on Unfairness was codified into the FTC Act in 1994[11] and defines an act or practice as "unfair" if it satisfies all of the following three tests:

- The act or practice causes, or is likely to cause, substantial injury to consumers;
- The injury is not reasonably avoidable by consumers themselves; and
- The injury is not outweighed by countervailing benefits to consumers or to competition.[12]

The Policy Statement on Deception was never codified, but the standards remain in use.[13] It defines an act or practice as a "deception" if it meets all of the following three tests:

- The omission or misrepresentation is misleading or likely to mislead;
- The consumer is acting reasonably in the circumstances; and
- The omission or misrepresentation is material (i.e., the consumer would have chosen differently but for the deception).

Most of the FTC's early enforcement activity was limited to sales and marketing practices, primarily related to advertising.[14]

Application to Financial Institutions

Banks,[15] thrifts, and credit unions were specifically exempted from the Section 5 prohibitions until 1975, when the federal prudential regulators—the Federal Reserve Board (Federal Reserve), Office of the Comptroller of the Currency (OCC), Federal Deposit Insurance Corporation (FDIC), Office of Thrift Supervision (OTS), and the National Credit Union Administration (NCUA)[16]—were extended the authority to enforce the UDAP provisions for those institutions under their respective jurisdictions. Each of the prudential regulators was required to institute procedures for handling consumer complaints involving UDAP, and the Federal Reserve was given authority to write UDAP-related regulations.[17]

The Federal Reserve's Regulation AA, Unfair or Deceptive Acts or Practices, was issued in 1985 and contained two subparts covering consumer complaints and credit practices.[18] The bank regulatory agencies (Federal Reserve, OCC, and FDIC) subsequently released a variety of joint and institution-specific guidance covering UDAP risks generally as well as risks specific to certain products, such as debt cancellation and debt suspension contracts, title loans and payday loans, direct lending and loan purchases, overdraft protection, and mortgage lending, all of which continue to pose significant UDAP risks.

After gaining their authorities, the prudential regulators did not begin to enforce UDAP violations for nearly two decades. In the early 2000s, new products and new delivery and payment systems began to change the financial services markets. At that time, the consumer complaints process served as a way for the regulators to initially identify many of the potential problems and UDAP violations inherent in these market changes.[19]

Consumer Financial Protection Bureau and the Dodd-Frank Act

The Dodd-Frank Act was enacted in 2010 to address weaknesses in the financial markets highlighted by the financial crisis. Title X of the Dodd-Frank Act, also referred to as the Consumer Financial Protection Act (CFPA),[20] established the CFPB with a mandate to "regulate the offering and provision of consumer financial products or services under the federal consumer financial laws"[21] and to make the markets for those products and services work for consumers. In particular, the CFPB is tasked with protecting consumers from harm by ensuring "that all consumers have access to markets for consumer financial products and services . . . [that] are fair, transparent, and competitive."[22]

Nonbanks supervised by the Bureau include:

Regardless of size:

- Mortgage companies (originators, brokers, and servicers including loan modification or foreclosure relief services)
- Payday lenders
- Private student loan providers

Larger participants of a market identified and defined by the CFPB:

- Consumer reporting agencies (receiving more than $7 million in annual receipts from consumer reporting activities)
- Debt collectors (receiving more than $10 million in annual receipts from debt collection activities)
- Student loan servicers (handling more than one million borrower accounts, including both federal and private student loans)
- International money transfer companies (conducting at least one million international money transfers annually)
- Automobile finance companies (completing at least 10,000 aggregate annual loan and lease originations)

Other nonbanks in which the CFPB has shown interest include:

- Credit card companies
- Leasing companies
- Tax refund anticipation loan providers
- Check cashers
- Prepaid card companies
- Debt relief service companies

The Dodd-Frank Act gives the CFPB the authority to supervise banks (traditional depository institutions—banks, thrifts, and credit unions) with more than $10 billion in assets and the affiliates of those banks.[23] The CPFB also has the authority to supervise certain nonbanks (nondepository companies) that offer consumer financial products and services. Many of these nonbanks were not previously subject to federal regulatory oversight.

The CFPB has the authority to supervise certain nonbanks regardless of their size, as well as certain other "larger participants" of consumer financial markets as identified and defined by the CFPB.[24] In addition, the CFPB has the authority to supervise any nonbank not otherwise under its supervisory authority when it has reasonable cause, based on consumer complaints or information from other sources, to determine that the nonbank is engaging, or has engaged, in conduct that poses risks to consumers.[25]

Banks with total assets of $10 billion or less remain subject to the supervisory oversight of their primary federal banking regulator (Federal Reserve, OCC, FDIC, NCUA) for purposes of compliance with the federal consumer financial laws. However, the CFPB has rule-writing authority for these laws, as they apply to all providers of consumer financial products and services. What we see today, then, is that although the CFPB supervises the largest of the banks (in addition to the nonbanks), its reach is much broader because the laws for which it has authority apply to banks of all sizes, independent of the primary federal regulator, and its expectations for "best practices" to implement those laws are reflected across the full (bank and nonbank) financial services industry.

The CFPB UDAAP Framework

The CFPA specifically prohibits "any provider of consumer financial products or services or a service provider to engage in any unfair, deceptive, or abusive act or practice"[26] and provides the CFPB with rulemaking authority and enforcement authority (for those entities under its jurisdiction) to prevent UDAAP in connection with any transaction with a consumer for a consumer financial product or service, or the offering of a consumer financial product or service. (Note that the federal bank regulatory agencies retain their UDAP enforcement authority under the FTC Act, while the CFPB alone can enforce UDAAP under Dodd-Frank.)

For the CFPB, the CFPA defines an act or practice as "unfair" if the CFPB has a reasonable basis to conclude that: (1) it causes or is likely to cause substantial injury to consumers; (2) the injury is not reasonably avoidable by consumers; and (3) the injury is not outweighed by countervailing benefits to consumers or competition. This is the same three-part test that is in the FTC's standard for unfairness as codified in Section 5 of the FTC Act.

The statute does not separately define a "deceptive" act or practice, though in its Supervision and Examination Manual the CFPB outlines a definition of "deceptive" that is consistent with, and refers to, the FTC's Policy Statement on Deception. For the CFPB, a representation, omission, act, or practice is deceptive if: (1) it is material; (2) it is likely to mislead a consumer; and (3) the consumer's interpretation is reasonable.[27] The CFPB states that the enforcement actions taken by the other federal regulators may serve to inform the CFPB's determinations of acts or practices that meet the "unfair" or "deceptive" standards, with the caveat that the facts in a particular case are crucial to each determination.

The addition of a third standard, the "abusive" standard, expands the FTC's UDAP analysis beyond complete and accurate disclosures. The CFPA gives the CFPB the authority to declare an act or practice "abusive" if the act or practice meets any one of the following tests:

- It materially interferes with the ability of a consumer to understand a term or condition of a consumer financial product or service;
- It takes unreasonable advantage of:
  - A lack of understanding on the part of the consumer of the material risks, costs, or conditions of the product or service;
  - The inability of the consumer to protect his interests when selecting or using a consumer financial product or service;
  - The reasonable reliance by the consumer on a covered person to act in the interests of the consumer.

Much industry analysis and speculation has surrounded this definition, centering on what many have called the "subjectiveness" of the criteria, including reliance on a particular consumer's understanding of a transaction. To some, the criteria appear to introduce a "suitability" standard, such as a fiduciary responsibility or a duty-of-care requirement, where a bank or nonbank providing or offering consumer financial products and services might be expected to bear the burden of demonstrating what the consumer actually understood at the time of the transaction. To others, the criteria would suggest the need to protect groups of people that, due to their circumstances, may not be able to protect themselves in financial transactions, such as older people, students, service members, and the financially distressed.[28]

To date, the CFPB has cited "abusive" practices in few cases, though in each instance where it has, the Bureau appears to be acting to protect consumers that are "vulnerable" or unable to understand the products. The CFPB may prescribe rules to identify unfair, deceptive, or abusive acts or practices, but is not required to do so. And CFPB Director Richard Cordray has said he does not intend for the Bureau to write such rules but will allow the definitions to take shape through the CFPB's enforcement actions. He has said, "We have given some exam guidance around these concepts, and I think maybe we'll have more to say over time. I don't anticipate us writing a rule around UDAAP. Again, I think a lot of the law is really clear in that area, and what is maybe not clear to people, because they haven't had experience with it, has been specifically defined by Congress, so that is what it is. We'll continue to develop as we go."[29]

This approach is consistent with how the FTC and the federal bank regulatory agencies have continued to interpret and apply UDAP under the FTC Act, which allows the provisions to adapt to changes in the financial markets. Notably, CFPB guidance states that enforcement actions taken by other regulators to address acts or practices alleged to be unfair or deceptive pursuant to the FTC Act "may inform the CFPB's determination."[30] The CFPB has, on occasion, released guidance to coincide with the announcement of an enforcement action to highlight the Bureau's supervisory expectations as well as the kinds of considerations it will entertain when evaluating potential violations of UDAAP.[31]

"Suitability" and Consumer Protection

In the financial services industry, *suitability* is a term generally associated with retail investment in securities and relates to the intersection of an investment strategy with an investor's means and objectives. The Financial Industry Regulatory Authority (FINRA), a self-regulatory organization in the U.S. securities industry, has a mission to protect investors and keep markets fair. FINRA Rule 2111 (Suitability)[32] requires brokerage firms and their associated persons to "have a reasonable basis to believe" that a transaction or investment strategy involving securities that they recommend is suitable for the customer. Such reasonable belief must be based on the information obtained through the "reasonable diligence" of the firm or associated persons to ascertain the customer's investment profile. This is to be derived from information obtained by firms and associated persons about, among other things, the customer's age, financial situation and needs, tax status, investment objectives, investment experience, investment time horizon, liquidity needs, and risk tolerance.[33]

A broker is expected to have a firm understanding of both the product and the customer; the lack of such an understanding violates the Suitability Rule. Taken together with FINRA's Rule 2090 (Know Your Customer), Rule 2111 is considered to be critical to ensuring investor protection and promoting fair dealing with customers, ethical sales practices, and high standards of professional conduct.

In the years following the financial crisis, suitability cases have been among the top enforcement actions taken by FINRA. Cases completed have involved situations where retail consumers were sold products, such as real estate investment trusts, unit investment trusts, and collateralized mortgage obligations, considered to be too complex and risky to be consistent with the investor's investment profile, for example, they were unsophisticated investors, or elderly.

Current UDAAP Environment

The CFPB has exercised its UDAAP authority more broadly than either the FTC or the federal bank regulatory agencies. In fulfilment of its consumer protection mandate, the CFPB has introduced the concept that "fairness" must be employed across the spectrum of an institution's processes. And it has applied UDAAP provisions to issues occurring over the life cycle of a product or service (from development to marketing, sales, and servicing) as well as across the operations of a company (considering the input from board of directors and senior management, corporate culture and "tone from the top," compensation structures, and coordination across business lines). In doing so, it has effectively changed the complexion of the regulatory compliance review from an assessment of technical compliance to an assessment of a company's principles-based risk management.

The enforcement actions the CFPB has taken under its UDAAP authority have been driven mostly by consumer complaints, which, for the Bureau, highlight issues across multiple products and services where large numbers of consumers are experiencing problems and serve to provide insight into the operations of the many nonbanks that were not previously subject to federal supervision but now fall within its jurisdiction.

Since its inception in July 2011, the CFPB has used consumer complaints as one of the cornerstones of its efforts to carry out the consumer protection mandate. More specifically, the Bureau has used consumer complaints to gain an understanding of risks in the consumer marketplace and to drive its regulatory investigations and exams. The CFPB first began accepting consumer complaints related to credit card products in July 2011, followed by mortgages in December 2011. Many other categories have been added since. (Refer to Figure 8.1.)

Once received, the CFPB's Consumer Response group screens the complaints, forwards them to the appropriate company, and monitors the company's response to the consumer as well as the consumer's response to the company's handling of the complaint. The CFPB uses this information to prioritize complaints or areas of complaint for investigation.

The CFPB's Consumer Complaint portal has experienced an increasing number of consumer complaints on a monthly basis since its launch. As shown

Types of Complaints Handled Over Time

Figure 8.1. Types of Complaints Handled Over Time

A variety of consumer products and services have been added to the Bureau's complaints portal, and the array of products and services now includes:

- Credit cards
- Mortgages
- Bank accounts and services
- Payday loans
- Student loans
- Auto loans and other consumer loans
- Credit reporting
- Debt collection
- Prepaid cards
- Additional nonbank products (including debt settlement services, credit repair services, pawn and title loans)
- Money transfers
- Digital currency

Consumers may also register comments on all consumer experiences through the CFPB's *Tell Your Story* web page.

in Figures 8.2 and 8.3, the Bureau has received, in total, more than 770,000 complaints as of December 1, 2015, with the highest percentage of total complaints received as of that date related to mortgage, debt collection, and credit card products and services.

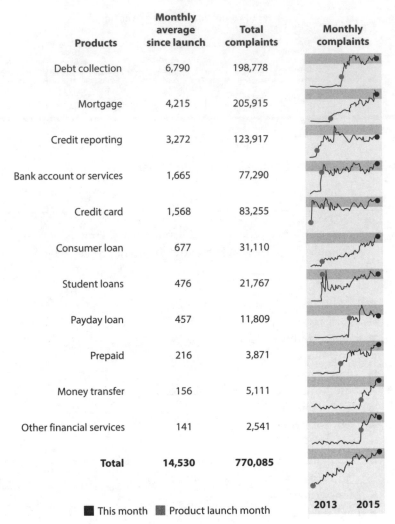

Products	Monthly average since launch	Total complaints	Monthly complaints
Debt collection	6,790	198,778	
Mortgage	4,215	205,915	
Credit reporting	3,272	123,917	
Bank account or services	1,665	77,290	
Credit card	1,568	83,255	
Consumer loan	677	31,110	
Student loans	476	21,767	
Payday loan	457	11,809	
Prepaid	216	3,871	
Money transfer	156	5,111	
Other financial services	141	2,541	
Total	**14,530**	**770,085**	

■ This month ■ Product launch month

2013   2015

Figure 8.2. Monthly Tends by Product Category

The CFPB reports that through December 31, 2014, approximately 62 percent of all consumer complaints were referred to the companies named in the complaint. The companies have responded to approximately 94 percent of those complaints and have closed approximately 90 percent of them. The companies have 15 days to respond and 60 days to provide a final response, where applicable.[34] Consumer narratives related to a complaint are available in the database, and the CFPB currently produces a monthly report that identifies the companies most frequently named in consumer complaints.

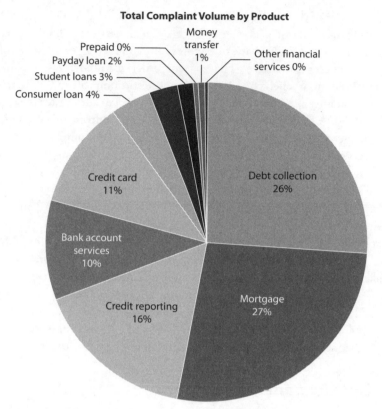

Figure 8.3. Total Complaint Volume by Product

The CFPB has been able to use its database of consumer complaints to identify issues, direct investigations and reviews, focus examinations, and inform its rulemaking. And the broadly defined terms (unfair, deceptive, and abusive) combined with the ability to interpret those definitions on a case-by-case basis make the UDAAP authority a flexible tool to adapt to the emerging supervisory focus that goes beyond strict technical compliance to consumer protection and related risk management.

The first five of the CFPB's publicly announced enforcement actions addressed UDAAP violations. Two of these cases did not cite compliance violations of any federal consumer financial laws other than UDAAP. Three of these cases were joint actions with federal prudential regulators.[35] The role of third parties is a critical feature in each of these cases, serving to set the tone that bank and nonbank providers of consumer financial products and services are expected to hold their third-party service providers to the same compliance standards that they themselves are required to meet.

The largest of the CFPB's UDAAP actions, announced in December 2013, involved charges against a nonbank mortgage loan servicer, Ocwen Financial Corporation, and its subsidiary to "address misconduct at every stage of the mortgage servicing process."[36] The consent order required the companies to provide $2 billion in relief, pay $125 million in restitution to 185,000 borrowers that had been foreclosed upon, plus spend $2.3 million to administer the process.

Other UDAAP actions taken by the CFPB have addressed the activities of payday lenders, student lenders, auto lenders, debt relief companies, and debt collectors. In addition to addressing violations of UDAAP, some of these cases have also sought to protect certain groups for which the CFPB has heightened responsibility, such as service members, older consumers, and students.[37]

A number of cases highlight that the CFPB is using its UDAAP authorities to address unfair, deceptive, or abusive acts or practices engaged in by entities that are not what consumers might think of as traditional bank or nonbank providers of consumer financial products or services. In particular, the CFPB has taken UDAAP actions against a retailer of consumer goods that provides financing for customer purchases; a telecommunications company that provides credit and payment processing for third parties in association with the consumer billings prepared for its own goods and services; and a number of for-profit post-secondary educational institutions that extend credit to their students.

The CFPB Examination

Supervision and Examination.   The CFPB monitors and examines supervised entities' operations and markets for compliance with the federal consumer financial laws and their implementing regulations along with risks to consumers in key regulatory areas. Bank and nonbank financial institutions under the CFPB's supervisory authority that offer the same types of consumer financial products or services or that conduct similar activities will be held to the same standards and supervised using the same procedures. The Bureau has acknowledged that large, complex entities have different compliance oversight and management systems than smaller entities or those offering fewer products or services.[38]

Monitoring and examination will include questioning, data collection from transaction records, and observation of operations to assess institutional compliance with applicable law and the quality of the internal processes for ensuring compliance with federal consumer financial laws and promoting consumer protection. Challenges for financial institutions include noncompliance risks that derive from unique proprietary processes, the scope of CFPB responsibilities (such as information requests and consumer complaint processing), an evolving CFPB examination manual, and penalties for noncompliance.

The Bureau has established multiple examination modules that it may apply to key areas to ensure that financial institutions are meeting CFPB objectives.[39] These modules are organized into three main sections covering the compliance management system, product-based procedures, and statutory- and regulation-based procedures.

Compliance Management System.   The CFPB expects every regulated entity under its supervision and enforcement authority to have an effective compliance management system (CMS) adapted to its business strategy and operations.[40] Each CFPB examination will include the review and testing of components of the supervised entity's CMS. Each provider of consumer financial products or services is expected to comply with federal consumer financial laws and "address and prevent violations of law and associated harms to consumers through its compliance management process."[41]

The CFPB expects that serious and systemic violations of federal consumer financial law are likely to occur without such a system, and that a deficient CMS may make a financial institution unable to detect its own violations. This may render it unaware of resulting harm to consumers and unable to adequately address consumer complaints.[42]

The common control elements of an effective CMS are identified as:

- Board of directors and management oversight
- The compliance program (policies and procedures, training, monitoring and corrective action)
- Response to consumer complaints
- Audit coverage of compliance matters (testing and reporting)[43]

The examination objectives are:

- To assess whether the board of directors and management have developed and communicated clear expectations regarding compliance throughout the financial institutions as well as to its third-party vendors and service providers.
- To assess whether the institution has an effective compliance program (policies and procedures, training, oversight, and monitoring and corrective action) that is consistent with policies approved by the board of directors. Each of these program elements must be relevant, clear, timely, and effectively communicated.
- To test and assess whether the financial institution's consumer complaint processes are responsive to consumers, properly escalate potential legal

issues related to consumer harm, and result in corrective actions to consumers and within the operations of the financial institution.

■ To test, consistent with the financial institution's size and its consumer
products and services offerings, that the financial institution is in compliance with federal consumer financial laws, and that such testing is communicated to the board of directors and management.

Product-Based Procedures.   The Product-Based Procedures in the CFPB's
Supervision and Examination Manual contain examination procedures that
are specifically designed to address those nonbank entities under the CFPB's
supervisory authority, including those that it can examine regardless of size and
those that are larger participants of a consumer market defined by the Bureau.
Some examination procedures also focus on certain specific products or lines of
business that can be applied, as appropriate, to banks or nonbanks. The procedures outline risks and supervisory considerations related to the specific product
or service as they relate to the relevant statutes and implementing regulations,
which are separately covered in detail under the Statutory- and Regulation-Based
Procedures.

Most nonbank providers of consumer financial products and services had
generally not been subject to federal regulatory oversight until the CFPB began
its nonbank supervision program in January 2012, following the appointment
of its first director. The Bureau stated at that time that nonbanks will be subject
to individual examinations, the frequency and depth of which will depend on
the CFPB's analysis of risks posed to consumers based on factors such as the
nonbank's volume of business, types of products or services, and the extent of
government oversight.

Presently, the Product-Based Procedures address:

■ Consumer reporting (larger participants)
■ Mortgage servicing
■ Mortgage origination
■ Short-term, small Dollar lending (payday lending)
■ Debt collection (larger participants)
■ Education loans
■ Automobile finance

Statutory- and Regulation-Based Procedures.   The CFPB Supervision and
Examination Manual incorporates procedures developed under the support of
the Federal Financial Institutions Examination Council (FFEIC) for many of
the federal consumer financial laws now enforced by the CFPB. In addition, it

provides CFPB examiners with guidance to determine whether financial institutions are complying with the federal consumer financial laws, as well as whether their policies and procedures adequately detect, prevent, and correct practices that increase the risk of violating those laws or causing harm to consumers.

In general, the examination objectives for each of the individual statutory- and regulation-based procedures are:

- To determine compliance with the federal consumer financial law and its implementing regulations;
- To assess the quality of the compliance risk management systems;
- To assess the reliability of internal controls and policies and procedures intended to ensure compliance with federal consumer financial law and its implementing regulations;
- To determine the accuracy and timeliness of required reporting; and
- To determine whether corrective actions, including supervisory or enforcement actions as well as restitution to consumer accounts, are appropriate when violations of law or regulation are detected.

The CFPB evaluates compliance with these statutes as part of a financial institution's relevant products and services, such as deposit accounts, and lending and servicing activities. The CFPB's consumer protection focus, especially with regard to UDAAP, has highlighted consumer protection concerns in consumer financial products and services not directly under the CFPB's authority, such as retail retirement savings and pension-related products. In this regard, the CFPB has expressed UDAAP and related consumer protection concerns for certain consumer groups, including seniors (consumers who are 62 or older) and service members, working with other federal regulators to develop an understanding of the consumer protection issues. The CFPB is able to evaluate these products through its consumer complaint websites (reinforcing the need for strong consumer complaint intake and resolution processes) as well as its financial education outreach efforts.

Consequences of Noncompliance.   Financial institutions that do not comply with the federal consumer financial laws and their implementing regulations will be subject to civil actions or administrative enforcement proceedings. Under Section 1055 of the Dodd-Frank Act, these may include:

- Rescission or reformation of contracts;
- Refunds of money or return of real property;
- Restitution;

- Disgorgement or compensation for unjust enrichment;
- Payment of damages or other monetary relief;
- Public notification regarding the violation, including the costs of notification;
- Limits on the activities or functions of the person; and
- Civil money penalties.

Violations are subject to fines ranging from $5,000 for first-tier violations and up to $1 million per day for third-tier violations for knowingly violating a federal consumer financial law. Penalties may vary based on the gravity of the violation, the severity of the loss to the consumers, the organization's financial resources, and whether there is a history of previous violations.

The CFPB considers many factors in the exercise of its enforcement discretion, including:

- The nature, extent, and severity of the violations identified;
- The actual or potential harm from those violations;
- Whether there is a history of past violations;
- A party's effectiveness in addressing violations.[44]

Relationship with State Laws

Each of the states has enacted UDAP-type laws that prohibit unfair and deceptive acts or practices. These laws are similar to those of the FTC Act but may differ in some respects, such as enforcement authorities (e.g., the authorities granted to regulators or State Attorneys General), the rights afforded consumers, or the basis for interpretation of unfairness.

In a unique turn, Section 1042 of the CFPA permits state Attorneys General (AGs) and state regulatory authorities to bring civil actions to enforce the provisions of the CFPA and implementing regulations, including the UDAAP provisions, against state-chartered entities under their respective supervisory authorities. This provision effectively extends the reach of the CFPB's UDAAP authorities, including the breadth and depth of its enforcement remedies, to state-chartered banks and state-supervised nonbanks that might otherwise fall outside of the CFPB's authorities. In 2014, five state AGs and one state regulator initiated actions alleging UDAAP violations under this part of the statute. Director Cordray has said it is not important whether the regulator is federal or statewide: "We frankly do not care what color uniform the prosecutor is wearing, as long as the bottom line is that we enforce the law vigorously and make things right for consumers."[45]

Prevention

The concepts of fairness and suitability are currently evolving beyond compliance to the broader concept of ethics. Spurred in large part by recent scandals in the trading markets[46] and the mortgage servicing industry,[47] financial services regulators and practitioners in the United States and around the world have begun to ask whether something should be done just because it can be done (i.e., because it is legal) or because it always has been done (i.e., standard procedures not flagged through internal or supervisory reviews). They are only just beginning to develop expectations about the way business should be conducted, including the types of products and services that should be offered and the types of customer relationships that should be maintained, and embedding those requirements into their codes of conduct and policies and procedures. The evolution has led to the creation of a new risk category called conduct risk.

Conduct risk assesses how institutions treat customers and investors, which is sometimes termed *culture*. This focus on culture takes a broader perspective to risk management that includes key aspects of compliance, strategic, organizational, and reputational risk. A strong risk culture will be multifaceted and vary by institution, but will, on the whole, indicate if an institution is conducting its business in a fair manner. Features of a strong risk culture include the presence of a focus on the customer; tone from the top; the promotion of "effective challenge"; accountability at all levels; and a properly aligned incentives structure.

Compliance models are generally built to align the delivery of consumer financial products and services with the technical and disclosure requirements of the federal consumer financial laws and their implementing regulations. Consumer financial laws are basically prescriptive in nature, and compliance reviews have generally been designed to assess an institution's technical compliance with the required rules and statements through a "check-the-box" approach.

In contrast, UDAAP (and also the FTC's UDAP) is principles-based and is defined broadly using subjective terms (such as "reasonably avoidable," "substantial injury," and "unreasonable advantage"), making technical compliance indeterminate. And, as noted earlier, no guidelines have been, or will be, forthcoming to offer additional clarity. Similarly, UDAAP is intended, by its nature, to ensure that institutions treat consumers "fairly," and "fairness" varies, depending on the context of specific facts and circumstances, and so is not readily measurable through traditional compliance metrics.

It is this subjectivity and uncertainty that make UDAAP violations very difficult to detect. Considering the increasing regulatory focus on UDAAP and the significant costs associated with related violations, prevention becomes the optimal tack. Compliance models, therefore, must be modified to incorporate an expectation that consumers are to be treated fairly and that their interests are a business priority. An assessment of "fair" treatment should embrace compliance with the spirit, as well as the letter, of the law. It should also be integrated with all aspects of the product life cycle, including product development, marketing, sales, servicing, and complaints management. The potential for UDAAP violations exists at every point of the cycle.

CFPB guidance states[48] that to remain competitive and responsive to consumer needs in the dynamic financial services environment, supervised entities must continuously assess their business strategies and modify product and service offerings and delivery channels. Ultimately, compliance should be part of the day-to-day responsibilities of management and the employees of a supervised entity; issues should be self-identified; and corrective actions should be initiated by the entity. Supervised entities are also expected to manage relationships with service providers to ensure that these third parties effectively comply with the federal consumer financial laws applicable to the product or service provided. Supervised entities are expected to incorporate into their compliance management systems adequate measures to prevent the violation of federal consumer financial laws, including the Dodd-Frank Act's prohibitions on unfair, deceptive, or abusive acts or practices.

A preventive stance toward UDAAP requires entities to define the principles of "fairness" to be used enterprise-wide and to guide a UDAAP compliance program.[49] They should convey the principles to all employees, management, and board members through recurring training and reinforce the message through policies, procedures, and processes, including recourse for failure to comply with the principles. Fairness principles should be understandable to the consumer as well as predictable, valuable, and appropriate.

The development of a culture of compliance across the enterprise requires the CEO, executive management, and board of directors to set the "tone from the top," ensuring the integration of compliance with business line functions and assigning direct responsibility for UDAAP compliance with those officers reporting to executive management. Senior management should support credible challenges of business line practices and decisions, with stated and direct support from the board. Compensation and incentives to achieve "fairness" outcomes should also be established.

These steps require regular enterprise-wide training on the principles of fairness, UDAAP requirements and current developments, and consumer protection and the related rules (such as the laws and implementing regulations for the Truth in Lending Act, Fair Debt Collection Practices Act, and Equal Credit Opportunity Act). Areas of particular regulatory concern should be highlighted in the training, including selected products and services (e.g., debt collection, payday lending) and "vulnerable" groups (e.g., students, elderly, service members). Third-party service providers are to be held to the same standard of compliance.

The management of consumer complaints will need to be reviewed and strengthened, starting by tracking the intake of complaints and their resolution, ensuring that all complaints are addressed and closed. All complaints lodged against the entity, its subsidiaries, affiliates, and third-party service providers should be included, as well as all those received directly, referred through a regulatory agency, or posted on social media sources. Care must be taken to define what complaints should be reviewed for UDAAP issues, such as complaints related to certain products or services, or complaints received by certain consumer groups.

In addition, the entity must define what constitutes a possible UDAAP complaint, such as complaints where consumers indicate they "don't understand," or say their experience is inconsistent with what they were told or read, or when they say they were treated unfairly. Products, services, or practices that can be linked to UDAAP complaints need to be identified and analyzed for trends and root causes to develop risk metrics. "Emerging risks" need to be identified, based on new business plans (e.g., products, vendors, and acquisitions), new regulatory guidance or enforcement actions, and complaints identified in the industry.

When entities conduct a periodic UDAAP review to identify potential risks and conduct remediation as needed, particular attention should be given to the mix of products or services as well as the end users. Emphasis should be placed on any products or services that have the potential to trigger UDAAP challenges, such as those that contain complex terms or features that might be difficult to understand, or that are targeted to "vulnerable" groups. All promotional, marketing, and advertising materials should be evaluated for potential misrepresentations, omissions, or errors. The entity should proactively address any potential violations and, if necessary, curtail activities, instituting monitoring and internal controls, fully remediating any identified harm to consumers, and notifying regulatory agencies, as appropriate. In addition, the compliance risk management system should be strengthened through testing and gap analyses.

Detection

Without specific rules to define "unfair," "deceptive," or "abusive" acts or practices, it is challenging to develop methods to detect and measure potential UDAAP violations using a traditional compliance model designed to measure technical compliance with the federal consumer financial laws. In addition, the standards by which acts or practices are measured as potentially unfair, deceptive, or abusive are complex, steeped in legal adjudications and enforcement actions, and ultimately unique to a given set of facts and circumstances.

Entities should, however, look to consumer complaints activity to identify possible UDAAP-type issues (e.g., the misrepresentation of terms in advertising or a failure to acknowledge affiliate relationships or to obtain consumer consent for billed products) and trends in complaints related to specific products or services. The analysis should include all consumer complaints activity, including complaints received directly, posted on social media, received by a third-party provider, and referred by the CFPB.

In addition, some entities might want to consider developing data analytics that can predict potential compliance violations, including UDAAP violations, based on established performance "standards." For example, to predict possible "robo-signing" of foreclosure documents (an employee of a mortgage servicing company who signs foreclosure documents without reviewing them), volume metrics could be used to detect instances when the number of foreclosures completed in a given day is significantly higher than would be reasonably possible.

Internal Audit.   The role of internal audit should be to assess the processes by which an entity manages the compliance risks associated with UDAAP and to identify potential risks that management should address to prevent such acts or practices. Recognizing that an unfair, deceptive, or abusive act or practice can occur anywhere in an organization, internal audit should evaluate the strength of an entity's compliance risk management program. It should also assess the degree of integration of UDAAP considerations into the evaluation of new product and services development as well as certain marketing, origination, servicing, and vendor management activities.

Response

Entities subject to a CFPB enforcement investigation should consult with their counsel to develop a course of action and response. Entities will want to consider whether they may be able to favorably affect the ultimate resolution of the investigation by "meaningfully" engaging in what the Bureau refers to as "responsible conduct." As outlined in CFPB Bulletin 2013-06, "responsible conduct" is the combination of the four categories. The first category is proactively self-policing for potential violations of consumer financial laws. An entity should consider the nature, pervasiveness, and duration of the violation and its significance to profitability or the business model. It should ask what compliance procedures or mechanisms were in place to prevent, identify, or limit the violation as well as whether senior management participated or knew of the conduct at issue.

The second category of conduct is promptly self-reporting to the Bureau when potential violations are identified. The entity should provide complete and effective disclosure to the Bureau and other regulators and explain whether affected consumers received appropriate and timely information. The Bureau's consideration of the reporting will weigh whether the reporting was proactive or prompted by another impending disclosure (such as supervisory activity, public reporting, or consumer complaints or actions).

The third category is quickly and completely remediating the harm resulting from the violations (even if it is a potential rather than actual violation). The Bureau will want to know how long after identification of the matter did the violations cease and what consequences, if any, were imposed on the responsible individuals. The entity should promptly determine the extent of harm to consumers and make an appropriate recompense, providing a detailed assurance to the Bureau that the misconduct is unlikely to recur.

Fourth, the entity should cooperate with any Bureau investigation, substantially and materially, above and beyond what is required by law. Cooperation should be provided to the Bureau and other regulatory enforcement bodies throughout the course of the investigation. The entity should share fully all findings, including a review of the nature, extent, origins, and consequences of the misconduct and related behavior. And the information should be provided promptly with supporting documentation.

To date, CFPB enforcement activities have focused primarily on the mortgage industry, credit cards, auto loans, and debt collection/relief organizations.[50] The CFPB will generally commence an enforcement action by issuing a Civil Investigative Demand (CID) to the company targeted for documents or testimony. The CID can require a company to respond within certain specified deadlines, even within days of service.

As a result, it is essential that companies quickly develop a response plan, identifying deadlines, implementing a legal hold, and ensuring effective management and oversight of the company's response. CFPB regulations require the recipient of a CID to meet with CFPB staff to discuss and resolve all issues. Companies will need to determine within a specified time period whether they will seek to set aside the CID[51] and what other response strategies they will need to develop.

Given the CFPB's broad mandate, companies under the authority of the Bureau need to ensure that they have the ability to react in a prompt and responsive manner to a CID. They will have to manage the cost of a potentially expensive investigation and effectively mitigate the risks associated with potential enforcement actions.

Conclusion

By its nature, the prohibitions against UDAAP—unfair, deceptive, or abusive acts or practices—are intended to ensure that consumers are treated fairly by all bank and nonbank participants in the market for consumer financial products and services. However, a principles-based approach is needed to adequately address the management of UDAAP risk because the UDAAP terms are broadly defined and may vary depending on specific facts and circumstances.

The optimal approach to preventing UDAAP violations is to establish a strong UDAAP program that follows the key elements of a rigorous compliance program and places governance and culture at the core. Such a program should reflect the expectation that consumers are to be treated fairly at all points along the product life cycle. At a minimum, the program should incorporate identification of the regulatory requirements for UDAAP compliance, related consumer protection requirements, and current and emerging industry issues; identification of product and service areas with potentially heightened UDAAP risk and assessment of the design and effectiveness of controls to mitigate that risk; policies, procedures, and processes that reinforce fair treatment of consumers; required ongoing and enterprise-wide training on UDAAP risk at every level of the entity; and analyses and reporting of consumer complaints intake, resolution, and trends.

The strength of the UDAAP program will rest on strong governance and culture, which together can foster an environment conducive to timely recognition, escalation, and control of emerging risks and risk-taking activities. The board of directors and senior management must champion serving the needs and interests of consumers as a core value of the entity and as a strategic business priority, as well as mirror that focus in their own behavior and in their expectations for the behavior of each individual working on behalf of the entity. Similarly, incentives structures should be designed to support the consumer-focused values, and accountability for failure to uphold those values should be clearly and conspicuously enforced.

The CFPB's UDAAP authority is central to its mission and will continue to be a primary investigative and enforcement tool for the regulator long into the future. It has also invigorated the efforts of other regulatory authorities, such as the FTC and the Federal Communications Commission (FCC), to heighten their attention on the fair treatment of consumers. Fundamentally, it has changed the complexion of the regulatory compliance review from an assessment of technical compliance to an assessment of a company's principles-based risk management.

Chapter 9

Offshore Tax Evasion

Laurence Birnbaum-Sarcy

I t has been a common practice for many years for certain wealthy individuals to transfer assets to offshore entities and deposit funds with offshore financial institutions that provided protection under their jurisdictions' bank secrecy laws. In 2012, it was estimated that more than $21 trillion in worldwide assets were held in offshore bank secrecy jurisdictions.[1] While there are many legitimate reasons for individuals to have foreign accounts, some individuals have used their accounts to hide their assets and avoid paying taxes.[2] Others did it to conceal funds derived from criminal activity. As a result, the United States has been losing billions of dollars in tax revenue a year, as well as limiting the effectiveness of its anti–money laundering (AML) efforts.[3] Starting in 2008, the U.S. government learned, through whistleblowers, the extensive and deceptive methods offshore financial institutions were employing to assist U.S. taxpayers in avoiding their tax obligations. These factors led to a new regime in the battle

Kelly A. Dynes was a major contributor to the content of this chapter. Ms. Dynes is a manager in KPMG's Forensic practice based in New York City. She specializes in providing anti-money laundering and other regulatory compliance services to financial institutions.

Additional contributions were made by **Adam C. Susser**. Mr. Susser is a director in KPMG's Forensic practice based in Boston. He specializes in FATCA and other regulatory advisory compliance services to financial institutions.

against tax evasion, as the U.S. government became more aggressive in recovering its lost revenues and punishing the financial institutions that were supporting abusive tax schemes.

The U.S. Internal Revenue Service (IRS) and Tax Division of the U.S. Department of Justice (DOJ) have joined forces with U.S. Attorneys' offices to focus on foreign financial accounts used to evade U.S. taxes and reporting requirements. This initiative paved the way for the Foreign Account Tax Compliance Act (FATCA) that imposes a new regime for reporting and withholding tax. To highlight the importance of FATCA, the IRS-Criminal Investigation's acting special agent-in-charge, Shantelle P. Kitchen, stated in September 2014, "The investigation of offshore tax evasion and money laundering are top priorities for IRS-Criminal Investigation, and we are committed to using all of our enforcement tools to stop this abuse. The enactment of FATCA is yet another example of how it is becoming more and more risky for U.S. taxpayers to hide their money globally."[4]

The impact of FATCA is broad. Globally, bank secrecy laws are changing as jurisdictions agree to implement common reporting standards to facilitate the Automatic Exchange of Information (AEOI) promulgated by the Organization for Economic Co-operation and Development (OECD). Further, the focus on tax evasion has also drawn attention to the relationship between tax evasion and money laundering, possibly affecting the AML regime in the future.

Regulatory Landscape

The U.S. government's fight against tax evasion has been difficult. As long ago as 1983, the Tax Division of the DOJ reported that the complexity of offshore tax schemes was making it difficult to investigate money laundering and tax evasion.[5] The IRS faces similar challenges today.[6] This is because certain offshore jurisdictions have strict privacy laws that protect foreigners' assets.[7] Some countries make it a crime for financial institutions to disclose customer information, unless the information is released through stringent protocols.[8] As a result, the U.S. government has to go through a lengthy process to obtain account information of U.S. taxpayers subject to investigations.[9]

Some U.S. taxpayers take advantage of these opportunities and move their funds to non-U.S., multilayered, multijurisdictional organizations, such as trusts, foundations, and limited liability partnerships, to conceal their assets from the U.S. government.[10] It can be inexpensive to establish such organizations in these offshore jurisdictions.[11] Further, some foreign governments do not even require proof of an organization's ownership, enabling customers to have complete anonymity.[12] Despite the fact that the funds are held in offshore entities, U.S. taxpayers are able to withdraw funds from their offshore accounts using credit and debit cards.[13]

To detect offshore tax evasion, the IRS would often have to conduct in-depth investigations focusing on promoters[14] who organize such multi-layered schemes.[15] Sometimes these investigations would require a John Doe summons[16] from the DOJ, resulting in lengthy procedures,[17] making it hard to develop an offshore case that could be escalated to the examination stage.[18]

Once in the examination phase, an investigation could be lengthy. The U.S. Government Accountability Office (GAO) calculated that from 2002 to 2005, the median offshore field examination took 70 days more than nonoffshore field examinations.[19] This made it challenging for the IRS to complete examinations before the three-year civil statute expired.[20]

The U.S. government entered into tax treaties to facilitate the exchange of information and established self-reporting programs for financial institutions and U.S. taxpayers to identify their offshore assets. But foreign banks were not properly enforcing the U.S. government's tax policies. Financial institutions were accepting inaccurate or incomplete tax forms to certify that entities were foreign to the United States. Firms were also not properly applying existing withholding requirements established by the Internal Revenue Code (IRC).[21]

In 2008, the U.S. government obtained inside information from former employees of foreign banks who revealed the inner workings of banks' cross-border banking businesses. One of the most notable whistleblowers was Bradley Birkenfeld, who worked for UBS of Switzerland in the private bank from 2001 to 2005.[22] He offered testimony to the U.S. government about the ways in which UBS helped U.S. taxpayers to evade their tax obligations.[23] Soon, the U.S. government learned about similar practices at other Swiss banks and opened a number of investigations. By 2014, U.S. enforcement actions against three Swiss financial institutions resulted in fines totaling more than $3.4 billion.[24] These actions led to a number of investigations into bank executives' practices and criminal penalties and fines were imposed on U.S. taxpayers. Most important, the U.S. government learned that it could no longer rely on self-reporting to combat tax evasion.

The U.S. investigation of UBS ended in February 2009. The bank entered into a deferred prosecution agreement (DPA) with the DOJ and was fined $780 million.[25] In May 2014, Credit Suisse pleaded guilty to conspiracy to aiding and assisting thousands of U.S. taxpayers in falsifying tax returns submitted to the IRS.[26] Credit Suisse paid fines and restitutions totaling $2.6 billion, which was the highest monetary penalty in a criminal tax case.[27] Even financial institutions without a U.S. presence could not avoid enforcement action. In January 2013, Wegelin & Co., Switzerland's oldest bank, pleaded guilty to conspiring with U.S. taxpayers to hide more than $1.2 billion of assets.[28] Wegelin paid $74 million to the U.S. government and closed its operations after 272 years of existence.[29]

Through these investigations, the United States discovered that foreign banks and their cross-border banking businesses employed similar deceptive practices. Despite not being registered as investment advisors or brokers with the SEC, Swiss private bankers traveled to the United States to meet and advise their clients.[30] The banks opened, serviced, and sometimes helped U.S. taxpayers to establish offshore organizations and knowingly accepted falsified W-8 Forms[31] that masked U.S. ownership of offshore entities.[32] Bankers took steps to avoid being detected by the U.S. government, such as opening coded accounts, communicating with clients via personal e-mails, and structuring transactions to avoid reporting requirements.[33] The U.S. government also learned that these actions were done despite the fact that some financial institutions entered into a Qualified Intermediary (QI) agreement with the United States to report income and information from any U.S. client who held an interest in U.S.-based securities.[34] Swiss bankers at financial institutions, participating in the QI Program, assisted in transferring assets to sham offshore accounts or referred outside lawyers and consultants to assist U.S. clients to set up offshore accounts so that they could continue to hold undeclared U.S.-based assets.[35]

The U.S. government's investigations did not stop with Switzerland, however. The Tax Division of the DOJ opened investigations into banks located in India, Israel, and the Caribbean, discovering that these institutions were also supporting U.S. taxpayers' abusive tax schemes.[36]

The U.S. government has armed itself heavily in its battle against tax evasion. The United States has agreements with foreign jurisdictions to obtain information regarding U.S. taxpayers' offshore accounts. These agreements are in the form of tax treaties, Tax Information Exchange Agreements (TIEA), and Mutual Legal Assistance Treaties (MLAT).[37] In 2011, the U.S. Senate Permanent Subcommittee on Investigations reported that the United States had "more than 140 tax treaties protocols, TIEAs, MLATs, or similar tax information exchange agreements with 90 foreign jurisdictions."[38] These agreements have their limitations, however. Depending on the agreement, there can be a number of procedural steps involved before a request can be officially submitted to an offshore government.[39] Even once a request is submitted, the laws of the jurisdiction may cause more delays in the investigative process.[40]

For many years, the U.S. government primarily relied on self-reporting by U.S. taxpayers and financial institutions to report their offshore holdings. Pursuant to the Bank Secrecy Act of 1970, U.S. individuals and entities are required to report assets if they have "a financial interest in or signatory authority or foreign financial account" greater than $10,000.[41] In 2009, the IRS initiated the Offshore Voluntary Disclosure Programs to encourage U.S. taxpayers to self-report their offshore holdings.[42] Although the program has changed its requirements over the years, it has allowed U.S. taxpayers to identify their off-shore holdings for a penalty while avoiding criminal prosecution.[43] The U.S. government estimated that "43,000 U.S. taxpayers . . . have paid taxes, interest, and penalties totaling about $6 billion" from 2009 to 2013.[44]

In 2000, the U.S. government created the voluntary QI Program whereby a financial institution would sign an agreement with the IRS to report U.S. taxpayers' "U.S.-source income."[45] Under the QI Program, foreign financial institutions (FFIs) agreed to collect the required tax documents (e.g., Form W-9 and Form W-8) and adopt Know-Your-Customer (KYC) procedures to iden-tify U.S. beneficial owners.[46] If the financial institutions could not obtain the necessary information, they agreed to deduct 30 percent from their customers' U.S.-earned income.[47] These programs were a success, but they were not fully effective, as the U.S. government learned from whistleblowers, because they were based on trust.

To improve matters, the U.S. government has taken steps to facilitate the exchange of information between jurisdictions. After the series of enforcement actions against Swiss banks, in August 2013, the governments of the United States and Switzerland implemented a Swiss Bank Program, which allowed other Swiss banks to sign a non-prosecution agreement with the DOJ.[48] Under the Swiss Bank Program, the financial institutions agreed to disclose detailed infor-mation regarding their cross-border operations and account information about their U.S. clients. They also agreed to close accounts that do not comply with U.S. policies, implement a plan to comply with the Swiss Bank Program, and assign an independent examiner.[49]

By agreeing to these terms, the institutions would avoid criminal prosecu-tion but would have to pay a monetary penalty.[50] This program was available only to Swiss banks that were not under criminal investigation by the United States. The deadline to submit a letter of intent to participate in the Swiss Bank Program was December 31, 2013. In March 2015, BSI SA was the first Swiss bank to reach a resolution under the Swiss Bank Program, agreeing to pay a fine of $211 million and cooperate with related criminal and civil proceedings.[51] From March to December 2015, 75 more Swiss banks finalized their agreements with the DOJ and agreed to pay fines totaling $908 million.[52] After the dead-line passed, the Tax Division of the DOJ stated that it may initiate a criminal investigation at any time against Swiss banks that did not express their intent to participate in the program or if participating banks had not complied with the program's policies.[53]

There are countries other than Switzerland that provide a home for these abusive tax schemes. To combat the wider problem, the U.S. government introduced FATCA in 2010 as part of the Hiring Incentives to Restore Employment Act.[54]

FATCA Requirements

FATCA falls under Chapter 4 of the IRC and does not replace prior reporting and withholding requirements as stipulated under IRC's Chapters 3 and 61 and Section 3406.[55] Instead, FATCA builds upon these requirements by closing the gaps with these rules, and the IRS has released guidance on how to coordinate these regulations.[56] FATCA requires financial institutions, including banks, brokerage firms, mutual funds, hedge funds, and certain insurance companies outside the United States to report information on financial accounts[57] held by their U.S. account holders to the IRS. FATCA also places new withholding and reporting requirements on financial institutions, including U.S. withholding agents (USWA), with respect to payments they make to foreign entities. As part of this process, financial institutions have to collect W-9 and W-8 forms from customers. New W-9s went into effect starting March 14, 2014. New W-8s were made available on September 14, 2014, with the requirements for these forms to be used by entities and individuals starting on January 1, 2015.

If financial institutions do not comply with FATCA, they will be penalized with a 30 percent withholding tax imposed on withholdable payments[58] received from U.S. sources. This differs from the QI Program, which placed the penalty on the customer, not the financial institution. Additionally, in 2017, the FATCA penalty will be even stricter when the withholdable payment for noncompliant accounts will also apply to gross proceeds from the sale or disposition of any property that can produce U.S.-source interest or dividends.

The United States recognized that in some jurisdictions there were legal barriers to implementing FATCA. Due to some jurisdictions' bank secrecy laws, financial institutions were faced with the dilemma that being compliant with FATCA would mean violating the laws of their jurisdictions. As a result, extensive negotiations took place between the United States and foreign governments resulting in two types of model intergovernmental agreements—Model 1 IGA and Model 2 IGA—that were developed to overcome the legal issues and reduce some of the burden on the financial institutions.[59] Under the Model 1 IGA, financial institutions report the required information to their jurisdiction, and the jurisdiction automatically reports it to the IRS.[60] Under the Model 2 IGA, financial institutions are authorized to report the information directly to the IRS.[61] Under both types of IGA, financial institutions have the responsibility to identify accounts of U.S. nationals that in the aggregate are valued $50,000 or more.[62] Under FATCA, in addition to reporting requirements for payments, financial institutions must report to the IRS the U.S. clients' names, accounts, taxpayer identification numbers, and account values.[63]

Compliance Challenges

Financial institutions face significant challenges to comply with FATCA due to the operational impact of FATCA's implementation both domestically and internationally, the ongoing negotiation of the IGAs, and the fact that it took a few years for the U.S. government to issue implementing regulations.

Financial institutions are required to develop and implement a FATCA compliance program composed of detailed policies and procedures as well as a governance structure to ensure their procedures are implemented and enforced appropriately. Yet financial institutions find it difficult to understand the requirements, the processes, and the controls needed to be FATCA compliant.

FATCA requirements are highly complex; there are lengthy and technical tax forms that are difficult to interpret for financial institutions lacking FATCA or tax subject matter professionals. For instance, foreign entities have to complete an eight-page Form W-8BEN–E[64] and identify themselves as one out of the 31 FATCA classifications to determine their reporting and withholding requirements. Additionally, organizations will have difficulty performing a proper FATCA validation when collecting their clients' W-8 forms if the organizations do not understand the rules and do not have access to tools and professionals that do.

Smaller financial institutions are especially challenged by FATCA. Certain institutions, such as hedge funds and mutual funds, have outsourced their onboarding, reporting, and withholding requirements to third parties, such as administrators and transfer agents. Although FATCA allows these functions to be outsourced, firms retain the responsibility for the functions being performed. Proper due diligence and monitoring have to be performed on the third parties being leveraged for FATCA compliance. These institutions may not have a background and experience with these processes and are trying to understand the intricacies of FATCA to oversee these third parties' performance associated with FATCA.

It is a common misconception to think of FATCA solely as a tax issue, when in fact it coexists with other nontax legal and regulatory requirements such as AML and antifraud. This is evidenced in an indictment issued by the United States Eastern District of New York in September 2014. Six individuals and six corporations, operating in Belize, conspired to commit securities fraud, tax fraud, and money laundering as part of a $500 million asset protection scheme (see *U.S. v. Bandfield*, et al).[65] Legal commentators have stated that this was "the first time a FATCA violation has been charged as an 'overt act' in furtherance of a tax conspiracy and securities fraud."[66] This case demonstrates the way in which money laundering violations, such as manipulation of microcap stocks, can coexist with FATCA violations and how the failure to comply with FATCA legal and regulatory requirements can have adverse consequences.[67] FATCA affects many different areas (e.g., tax, operations, AML, compliance, legal, risk, IT). Existing processes related to AML/KYC and customer onboarding can be leveraged. However, if there are existing deficiencies in these functions, then a firm may have difficulty complying with FATCA.

Firms also require significant resources to remediate their existing payees to identify if there are U.S. indicia to their foreign entity clients. FATCA requires financial institutions (e.g., FFIs, USWAs) to perform FATCA validation of tax forms and enhanced due diligence (EDD) to ensure that clients are not U.S. persons.[68] However, this EDD does not apply only to new clients. Firms must also remediate existing clients. This identification process presents many challenges and costs for financial institutions in collecting, documenting, and reporting this information. U.S. financial institutions are equally affected by this detailed identification process, as they must ensure that their foreign account holders are exempt from FATCA. As a result, firms are spending significant amounts to enhance their processes and upgrade their systems to retain the necessary client information and track funds that may be subject to withholding. For instance, the *Wall Street Journal* reported in 2014 that the estimated cost of complying with FATCA for Canada's five biggest banks was almost $700 million.[69]

Another challenge for larger financial institutions is that functions (e.g., onboarding and tax departments) are decentralized, making it difficult to develop an enterprise-wide program to comply with FATCA. Many institutions find themselves trying to remediate inconsistent processes between departments while implementing FATCA. This exercise becomes more difficult if departments do not have an established infrastructure to identify, report, and withhold payments based on prior FATCA regulations (e.g., Chapter 3 and Chapter 61). Additionally, creating an enterprise-wide FATCA program presents an even greater challenge for multijurisdictional institutions since they may be faced with many different reporting processes when subject to Model 1 or Model 2 IGA regimes.[70] In the absence of enterprise-wide oversight, there is a risk that firms' FATCA processes will be inconsistent.

Given these challenges, what steps should financial institutions take to protect themselves from potential future enforcement actions? Firms can mitigate their regulatory risk by developing a robust compliance program and implementing controls that help prevent, detect, and respond to identified risks and potential violations. Since red flags associated with tax evasion could be identified by various departments in the organization such as tax, operations, customer onboarding, compliance, and front office functions, it is imperative that these controls are designed to define clearly each department's roles and responsibilities vis-à-vis the identification of tax evasion. Otherwise, weaknesses in one department may lead to weaknesses in other departments. As a result, financial institutions would be susceptible to increased regulatory penalties.

Compliance Program Controls

Preventative Controls

Preventative controls are designed to reduce the number of violations that occur. In terms of tax evasion, these violations are twofold. First, financial institutions' noncompliance with FATCA regulatory requirements may result in penalties. Second, firms want to ensure controls are in place so they are not unwitting participants in tax evasion schemes executed by clients.

Governance. FATCA involves a sizeable coordination effort requiring proper governance of the compliance program. The first preventative step is to build a strong governance program that addresses tax evasion and identifies the person responsible for overseeing this program. However, institutions are not required, under the legislation, to designate a specific department with the ultimate responsibility to oversee the implementation of FATCA. Some institutions have opted to designate, and sometimes create, a single department responsible for overseeing their FATCA compliance programs; others require each of the individual business groups to assume these responsibilities.

This governance program should involve developing policies, procedures, and processes to comply with FATCA requirements. As part of these policies, financial institutions could implement useful tools, such as checklists, to provide guidance to departments so they can support the tax subject matter professionals in their organization with the identification of entity classifications or the determination of whether payments fall under withholding requirements.

These policies and procedures should also guide various departments to identify customers who may present a high risk for tax evasion violations. Some firms may want to assess their customers' potential for tax-related risks. This profile would highlight potential red flags, such as high-risk jurisdictions or complex ownership structures. It would help determine whether a customer requires EDD to ensure its correct tax status under FATCA or if the customer's accounts should be monitored regularly for potential tax evasion or even money laundering violations. Companies that have a process to assess customer risk in their AML or Office of Foreign Assets Control (OFAC) programs may consider incorporating these tax-related risks into their programs since such risks may also warn of other potential money laundering violations.

Since the financial industry is always evolving, governance programs must be sufficiently flexible to address changes. When financial institutions develop and offer new financial products to clients, the institutions need to implement preventative controls to determine if new products fall under FATCA. Financial institutions should design a "change management process" to review the impact of any potential new products and determine what changes must be implemented to capture any payments that may be subject to reporting and withholding. The client's circumstances might alter, triggering the need for a reevaluation of a client's tax-related risk. Additionally, an effective governance program should establish processes to assess any regulatory changes, determine the impact those changes have on the firm, and update the firm's preventative, detective, and responsive controls accordingly.

All governance programs must also include a comprehensive training program to educate employees on the due diligence, reporting, and withholding requirements of FATCA as well as the importance and intricacies of proper documentation. The more educated the employees, the better they can service clients who may be confused by the new requirements. In addition, financial institutions should obtain a signed FATCA compliance certification from key personnel who should certify that they have attended FATCA training and familiarized themselves with FATCA principles. They should further certify their agreement to adhere to the firm's FATCA compliance program and that they will not, directly or indirectly, have any formal or informal policies, procedures, and processes to assist customers in avoiding FATCA. This can be incorporated in a firm's annual employee compliance certification.

Organizational Changes.   Governance is not the only step in establishing effective preventative controls. Firms may make changes in their organizational structure to avoid redundancies and streamline operations. One implementation that larger firms are considering is centralizing specific functions. For instance, due to FATCA's complexity, it may help to have one centralized tax operations department to service the enterprise. Having a centralized onboarding department also offers the added benefit of creating a one-stop data warehouse that is more effective not only for FATCA compliance but also for other regulatory compliance requirements.

Technology.   Depending on the size and complexity of the organization, compliance with FATCA may not be effective without the proper technology. Many organizations have selected tools and systems that will assist them in collecting, maintaining, and validating client information and tax documents. For instance, upgrading or creating a centralized onboarding system may ensure that a firm is addressing all the necessary requirements and consistently applying them across the firm.

Firms also need to identify payments affected by FATCA. Specific products generate payments from which the firm will need to withhold monies for tax purposes to meet the FATCA requirements. The logic is complex, involving multiple variables to determine an affected payment. Existing tools and systems may need to be upgraded to identify the treatment of the products that are reported under FATCA and calculate all the required withholding amounts under the IRC.

It is imperative that firms have adequate systems to archive documents. With the lines of bank secrecy fading, firms will be faced with multiple requests for customer information from the United States as well as from other jurisdictions. To save time and money, firms may want to ensure all their customers' information is electronically archived rather than stored in boxes and maintained at a warehouse.

Detective Controls

Preventative controls are meant to stop potential tax-related violations from occurring. Detective controls, by contrast, continuously monitor and test procedures and processes to ensure that preventative measures are being implemented effectively. With FATCA's recent implementation, firms should be testing their programs to ensure that the customer validation processes are properly applied and that the firms' systems are reporting and applying withholding requirements to their products. This means conducting tests more frequently than would normally be the case for more established functions. Firms should also establish strong detective controls to train employees to monitor customer accounts and behaviors and escalate any red flags.

Monitoring.   If a firm established a proper training program as part of its preventative controls, then its employees should have received adequate guidance to detect any red flags. For example, employees in the onboarding department must be able to identify discrepancies between a customer's tax documents versus their basic account information. After onboarding, customers' circumstances may change, and this may affect their tax-related status. As a result, employees who service accounts in the front office, operations, and compliance must monitor customers' behaviors and activities to detect issues that may heighten their tax risk or may indicate a potential violation of FATCA. This could be accomplished during periodic reviews (e.g., KYC updates, audits) or on a day-to-day basis (e.g., change in a customer's circumstances, daily transaction monitoring).

Effective monitoring will also include strong audit and testing processes continuously to assess that proper protocols are in place for all relevant departments, including onboarding, reporting, and withholding. For smaller financial institutions that outsource their onboarding, reporting, and withholding functions, this program should be designed to oversee and regularly test any third parties' processes.

Communication.   Detective controls will not be effective if departments are not transparent about their monitoring efforts. FATCA and tax evasion do not involve just the tax department, but also AML, KYC, onboarding, and the business lines. Information collected and observed by each of these departments can be leveraged to ensure that a firm is effectively monitoring for tax evasion red flags or potential FATCA violations. It also means deficiencies in one department could lead to deficiencies in other departments. In *U.S. v. Bandfield*, the U.S. government demonstrated that AML violations (e.g., microcap manipulation) could coincide with tax evasion and FATCA violations.[71] Firms must be on the lookout for fraudulent schemes that may be conducted through their institution.[72] Therefore, it is important that departments work together and maintain strong lines of communication regarding their detection efforts and findings to ensure that all departments are addressing and remediating potential tax evasion violations.

Data Analytics.   Firms should consider applying data analytics to measure the performance of their compliance program and identify areas of improvement. Firms will need to perform a validation of the tax forms for completeness and accuracy and due diligence of the tax forms to the data collected by the firms. The data may exist in hard copy or electronic form, but either way, firms need to compare the information to the tax forms. The ability of the organization to perform this EDD may rely on the firm's technology to identify the relevant data fields in the systems and extract the information for comparing the tax forms. The ability to use data analytics as part of the EDD will improve the firm's ability to identify clients and accounts affected by FATCA. It is important to note that data analytics is also needed to identify anomalies and outliers useful in detecting potential FATCA violations quickly and effectively. Data analytics may be used to gather necessary information from various sources to assist a firm in identifying any inconsistent information about a customer (e.g., information may indicate that the customer is not a U.S. citizen/resident, but other activity, such as wire transfers and checks, directed to the United States may indicate otherwise).

Responsive Controls

Finally, firms must also establish effective responsive controls so that potential violations are properly and quickly escalated, investigated, appropriately disclosed, and remediated.

Investigation.   Conducting an internal investigation should be a firm's first response when its detective controls have identified an issue. In regards to FATCA, this investigation could be on the client level (e.g., when there are difficulties validating a customer file), or it could be firm-wide (e.g., if there are systemic issues reporting withholding payments). If the investigation is firm-wide, it is necessary to verify that areas of the organization that are affected by FATCA are made aware of the investigation and its findings in accordance with a communication plan. There may be instances where certain information cannot be shared, such as when the investigation is ongoing. Once this information can be shared, it is important that all requisite parties participate in addressing any weaknesses with the firm's FATCA program.

Conducting an investigation to determine whether a customer is evading its U.S. tax obligations can be challenging and difficult. Firms should continue to be diligent as they investigate employee escalations reporting customers' suspicious behaviors and transaction activities in accordance with the firms' established AML programs. These investigations should be conducted with an understanding that customers associated with traditional AML concerns may be linked to potential tax evasion or FATCA violations.

As discussed, a U.S. government tax evasion investigation may take years because of the lengthy procedural processes to obtain all the necessary information to conduct an examination. However, this lengthy process does not mean that firms should delay their own internal investigations if they receive notice that the United States is investigating one of their customers. Firms should consider being proactive and conduct internal investigations on customers named in treaty requests and not delay until the government concludes its investigation. This way, firms may be able to identify any customers that pose a potential risk and remediate the issue prior to any U.S. government actions.

Firms, furthermore, should not have tunnel vision. They must be mindful that investigations of other departments (e.g., onboarding, KYC, tax, IT, and so on), which may seem to have no connection to tax, may affect a firm's ability to detect FATCA violations or customers avoiding their U.S. tax obligations. Therefore, if faced with regulatory inquiries or internal audit findings identifying weaknesses in these key departments, a firm should be aware of how these affect its FATCA programs or its internal controls in order to remediate the issue.

Disclosure.   It is important to ensure that there are escalation processes so that those responsible for the firm's governance are quickly made aware of any deficiencies in a firm's FATCA program or any control weaknesses. A firm's governance program should also have policies and procedures to set forth the conditions, methods, and timing for the disclosure of violations to appropriate government authorities.

Many firms may prefer to remediate the problem internally without involving regulators. But self-disclosing serious violations and cooperating with authorities may reduce regulatory penalties and ultimately mitigate reputational risk. Additionally, firms that have entered into agreements with the U.S.

government should consider whether self-disclosure is necessary to avoid violating the terms of those agreements.

Most important, after a firm investigates, remediates, and discloses a potential issue, responsive controls should include reviewing its preventative and detective controls and updating them to prevent future violations. Upon closing a matter, a firm should also review the lessons learned during an investigation and determine whether policies, procedures, and processes to respond to an inquiry were appropriate or whether enhancements are needed.

Remediation.   Investigation and disclosure are only as effective as the remediation. If the firm does not quickly and effectively respond to investigation findings, then they may exacerbate the problem. In November 2014, HSBC's Swiss private bank was fined $12.5 million by the SEC for engaging in a U.S. cross-border business from 2003 to 2011 without being registered with the SEC as an investment advisor.[73] As early as 2005, the bank's internal audit noted that the group was not complying with the bank's cross-border policies to monitor its compliance with U.S. regulation.[74] In the announcement of this settlement, the director of the SEC's Division of Enforcement, Andrew J. Ceresney, stated, "HSBC Private Bank's efforts to prevent registration violations ultimately failed because their compliance initiatives were not effectively implemented or monitored."[75] This case highlights how regulators will not tolerate companies that identify deficiencies with their controls but fail to remediate them.

Since FATCA did not go into effect until July 2014, it is too early to say how the U.S. government will respond to firms that delay remediating FATCA violations. However, based on previous enforcement actions involving tax evasion, it appears that the U.S. government will be aggressive in its enforcement of FATCA.[76] The U.S. government may be even more aggressive with its penalties given the amount of time firms have had to implement the FATCA initiatives.

A firm's remediation will vary depending on the issues identified. If the investigation is focused on a specific customer, it may mean terminating the relationship. However, if the investigation identifies deficiencies in controls, remediation would require firm-wide improvements such as enhancements to technological systems, improving controls, or conducting additional employee training. If a firm were to delay its response to an investigation, then it may be subject to increased regulatory risk and enforcement penalties.

Future Trends

Financial institutions should expect continued regulatory enforcement in the area of tax evasion. The U.S. government indicated that it would ease its enforcement actions in 2014, 2015, and possibly 2016 for those making a "good faith effort" to comply with FATCA and implement adequate controls for the prevention, detection, and response to tax evasion.[77] Once this "grace period" ends, however, the U.S. government will have more tools to detect tax evasion than before. Therefore, firms should take this opportunity to strengthen their preventative, detective, and responsive controls with respect to tax compliance. Otherwise, they may find themselves the target of enforcement.

Although FATCA may have initially been met with resistance outside the United States, its purpose has gained support in the international regulatory community. Countries are seeing the financial benefit to enacting FATCA-style legislation and are developing their own regulations to identify their nationals who may be hiding assets in foreign jurisdictions. The European Union (EU) has developed a program for the automatic exchange of information between its member states starting in 2017 and 2018; and, in May 2015, Switzerland entered into agreement with the EU to participate in its program.[78]

Drawing influence from FATCA, the OECD, with the support of the G20 Finance Ministers, released the *Standard for Automatic Exchange of Financial Account Information in Tax Matters* (Standard) in July 2014.[79] The Standard outlines the program for jurisdictions to participate in the AEOI on an annual basis. As of December 2015, 97 jurisdictions have committed to implement the Standard and 78 jurisdictions[80] have signed the Multilateral Competent Authority Agreement.[81] Some of the participating jurisdictions, such as British Virgin Islands, Switzerland, and the Cayman Islands, are well known for their bank secrecy laws. This exchange of information is also expected to be implemented in 2017 and 2018.

To coordinate this global effort and ensure consistency, the Standard incorporates the Common Reporting Standard (CRS), which specifies due diligence and reporting requirements that participating jurisdictions must comply with to implement the AEOI. Implementing this global standard has its challenges similar to FATCA, but there are also differences. For instance, preexisting accounts under $50,000 are excluded under FATCA, but not under the CRS.[82] Further, the CRS has a broader scope than FATCA as it covers identifying, collecting, and reporting information on citizens from multiple jurisdictions. Therefore, institutions will have to collect and report information on a larger scale, making it difficult to rely on manual controls.[83]

In August 2015, the OECD released guidance to help jurisdictions and financial institutions implement the Standard, namely *The Standard for Automatic Exchange of Financial Account Information in Tax Matters: Implementation Handbook* (also known as the CRS Handbook). It offers key information on due diligence requirements as well as IT infrastructure recommendations. The handbook also provides a comparison between the Standard and FATCA (Model I IGA) requirements.[84] The second reference guide released is the *Update on Voluntary Disclosure Programmes: A Pathway to Tax Compliance.* This document assesses 47 countries that have incorporated voluntary disclosure programs and provides guidance on establishing such programs based on these assessments.[85]

The increased international support for efforts to curb tax evasion may also be affecting the future of AML. The Financial Action Task Force (FATF), an intergovernmental organization that recommends policies to combat money laundering, released its latest recommendations in 2012. In its report, FATF added "tax crimes" to its list of designated categories of offenses that constitute a predicate offense to money laundering.[86] This allows law enforcement officials to add money laundering charges against those who have engaged in tax evasion. Some jurisdictions, such as Singapore, have adopted this FATF recommendation.[87] The Fourth EU AML Directive, effective in June 2015, also added tax crimes (relating to direct and indirect taxes) as a predicate offense for money laundering; however, Member States have until June 2017 to transpose the directive into local law.[88] The United States, one of the member jurisdictions of FATF, has not added tax evasion to the list of predicate offenses for money laundering (Specified Unlawful Activities).[89] However, *U.S. v. Bandfield* is an example of how the FATCA violations go hand in hand with AML violations, such as securities fraud, and may be a sign that tax evasion may become a predicate offense in the future.

One benefit of FATF's recommendation, in the eyes of governments, is that tax crimes would fall under the authorities of those investigating money laundering and encourage cross-border cooperation.[90] In addition, it would allow authorities to increase criminal penalties and fines. Yet this would increase the burden on financial institutions and their AML departments. AML departments would be faced with the difficulty of distinguishing between tax evasion and tax planning.[91] Adding tax evasion as a predicate offense to money laundering would also create strains on AML departments, especially at smaller financial institutions that lack resources to handle the complexities of these investigations.[92] It could also lead to additional fines and penalties for financial institutions and the accountability of BSA/AML officers if an institution failed to detect tax evasion.

Conclusion

For the past few years the spotlight has been on cross-border tax evasion, and it appears the shroud of bank secrecy is thinning as more jurisdictions agree to adopt the CRS. For instance, Panama and the United Arab Emirates, at first glance, were attractive to offshore account holders until they announced their agreement to adopt the CRS and to exchange information starting in 2018.[93]

But it is not disappearing entirely. Although account holders will continue to look for locations to hide assets, it is clear that finding a jurisdiction with a lax tax evasion regime will be increasingly difficult as it is expected that United States and international efforts will continue to combat tax evasion aggressively.

This new international environment might lead to fresh opportunities to establish a more rigorous compliance framework if it leads to the creation of centralized systems at financial institutions that address a range of regulatory requirements beyond FATCA, the Standard, and overall tax compliance.

Chapter 10

Fraud and Misconduct in Healthcare

Glen E. Moyers

The passage of the Patient Protection and Affordable Care Act (PPACA) in 2010 has had a significant impact on the healthcare industry, drawing attention to the way healthcare is delivered and patients are covered by healthcare services. At the same time, it has raised the level of regulatory scrutiny of the healthcare industry.

The healthcare industry is comprised of two segments, providers and payers, which have different operating models, operational challenges, and regulatory environments. Healthcare providers face a myriad of government regulations and increased enforcement activity. The vast majority of enforcement activity in the past decade has been aimed at providers who receive government funds. This chapter focuses on the unique regulatory risks and challenges faced by healthcare providers as they come under increased pressure to deliver higher quality care at lower costs in a changing regulatory landscape. We will look at the current environment in which healthcare providers are operating, significant enforcement areas, and ways in which an organization can prevent, detect, and respond to the risk of noncompliance.

Sarah Jacobs Beard was a major contributor to the content of this chapter. Ms. Beard is a director in KPMG's Forensic practice based in Atlanta. She specializes in providing regulatory compliance and investigative services to healthcare providers.

225

Regulatory Landscape

Government-funded healthcare spending per person has grown faster than the nation's economic output per person since 1985. Federal spending for Medicare and Medicaid rose from 1.8 percent of gross domestic product in 1985 to 4.6 percent in 2012,[1] and it is estimated that it will grow to 8 percent by 2038. In fiscal year 2015, the U.S. government spent $986 billion on healthcare with nearly two-thirds of this for Medicare,[2] and the amount is expected to grow. By 2030, one in five Americans will be a senior citizen, compared with one in eight in 2000. After combining private and government spending, total healthcare spending is projected to account for 19.3 percent of gross domestic product by 2023, up from 17.2 percent in 2012.[3] By 2023, government financed healthcare expenditures are projected to reach $2.5 trillion and account for 48 percent of national healthcare expenditure.

To continue to fund the cost of healthcare, the government must recoup spending. Since there is little political appetite to increase taxes, the government has looked to fund healthcare programs by expanding enforcement (recoupment of funds, fines, and penalties). This strategy of enforcement has strong government support since money spent on enforcement has a return on investment of 800 percent.[4]

In 2015, the government recovered $3.5 billion, marking the fourth consecutive year in which government recoveries exceeded $3.5 billion.[5] From January 2009 through the end of 2015, the government recovered $26.4 billion under the False Claims Act (FCA).

The healthcare industry is unique in its relationship with the federal government because the government is frequently the party paying for services rendered to a patient. Due to this relationship and links among the FCA, the Anti-Kickback Statute (AKS) and the Stark Law (which governs physician self-referral for Medicare and Medicaid patients),[6] business relationships and arrangements common in other industries are frequently found to be fraudulent in the healthcare industry. Arrangements that compensate a party for acquiring, referring, or retaining business reimbursed directly or indirectly by the federal government may be found to be illegal.

Further, consumers (i.e., patients) rarely have insight into the cost of the services they are seeking. Their buying decisions are made based on imperfect information regarding the factors of cost, quality, and time. Often in the healthcare industry, the consumer relies on a physician for referrals. However physicians cannot conduct business the same way service professionals in other industries can. Physicians who rely on government funds cannot reward loyal customers, nor offer incentives to patients to transfer from the care of one physician to another.

These physicians have very little, if any, influence over the price they get paid by the government for the services they offer.

In addition to the expense, settlements of alleged fraudulent conduct with the government often include extensive monitoring. This generally takes the form of a corporate integrity agreement (CIA), which requires the settling party to comply with requirements related to the conduct of its business and monitoring provisions. Frequently, a CIA requires the company to engage an independent review organization (IRO) to monitor, test, and attest to specific compliance matters.

Recently the government insisted on monitors for both quality of care and non–quality of care matters. Historically, monitors were employed by the U.S. Department of Justice (DOJ) when a deferred prosecution agreement (DPA) was entered into in connection with a settlement. The Office of Inspector General (OIG) at the Department of Health and Human Services also employs monitors, besides IROs, to address business conduct issues.

In at least one current CIA,[7] the government required the company to unwind certain business agreements. The monitor is often responsible for approving the modification of the business agreements before a company can enter or exit an arrangement or contract. Some CIAs require the approval of potential business partners to confirm they meet stated selection criteria, approval of the rationale used by the company in making its selection and the methodology used for determining the fair market value of the arrangement. Essentially, the monitor has a direct impact on the business decisions made by the company. These monitors are often selected by the government, but the fees are paid by the company. This is in contrast to a traditional IRO selected by the company and approved by the government.

Some CIAs specify compensation arrangements for sales personnel and/or executives. In a 2012 CIA,[8] the company was prohibited from compensating or disciplining its sales professionals based on product sales within the individual's territory. Rather, the employee could be compensated based on business acumen, scientific knowledge, and customer engagement. Such arrangements may directly affect a company's ability to attract and retain salespeople.

Besides specifying how an employee could be paid, some CIAs also specify when financial recoupment from officers or employees is required. Current CIAs allow for forfeiture and recoupment of up to three years of annual pay, including bonuses and long-term incentives, if the employee was involved in "significant misconduct."

Every CIA calls for an increased level of accountability by personnel associated with the settling entity, with certifications now extending further down the organization including middle management. Historically, board certifications were only required for repeat offenders; more recently, certification by the company's board of directors is included in most CIAs. If the company's compliance program does not address the board's involvement in compliance-related activities, the CIA will often require the compliance program to be updated.

Many in the industry believe that certifications may become the basis for future enforcement. The Park Doctrine (also known as the Responsible Corporate Officer Doctrine) allows the government to pursue both civil and criminal liability for corporate violations of public welfare. The liability does not depend on the officer's approval or knowledge of wrongdoing but on whether the officer had the responsibility or authority to prevent and correct the violation and did not do so. Besides fines and jail time, the officers convicted of a misdemeanor under the Park Doctrine may be subject to exclusion from federal healthcare programs.

Convergence Drives Enforcement

Healthcare enforcement is not only driven by the government; PPACA makes it easier for citizens to bring cases against healthcare providers on behalf of the government. The FCA allows citizens with knowledge of a fraud to bring suit in the name of the government and receive up to 30 percent of the amount recovered in fines. PPACA relaxed the public disclosure bar for *qui tam* relators.[9] Relators can now bring cases based partly on information in the public domain and partly on information that "materially adds" to public information. This opens the door for individuals who can mine and repackage publicly available information in a way that helps the government.

The amount of transactional data available to a relator is vast and increasing. This data can be mined and analyzed by relators to develop information that materially adds to public knowledge in a *qui tam* suit. As part of an effort to make the healthcare system more transparent, the Centers for Medicare and Medicaid Services (CMS) prepared a public data set. The Medicare Provider Utilization and Payment Data and the Physician and Other Supplier Public Use File provide information on services and procedures provided to Medicare beneficiaries by physicians and other healthcare professionals. The file contains information on utilization, payment (allowed amount and Medicare payment), and submitted charges, organized by National Provider Identifier, Healthcare Common Procedure Coding System (HCPCS), and place of service. Other available sources of data include the Physician Payment Sunshine Act, where pharmaceutical companies, medical device manufactures, biotech companies, and group purchasing organizations must collect and submit information on relationships they have with physicians and teaching hospitals. The information is published by CMS. A release of 2014 data showed that drug and medical device manufacturers made 11.4 million payments totaling $6.5 billion to physicians and teaching hospitals.[10] In addition to relators with access to vast amounts of data, law enforcement also has access to a vast, new pool of available transactional data.

New Concepts in Enforcement

In a new development of the FCA, the government recently started to enforce the concept of "worthless services." The theory is that certain healthcare providers have provided such poor quality of care that the services are ultimately worthless. In 2014, the government settled with one skilled nursing provider for $38 million, stating the services billed by the nursing home were of such poor quality that they were worthless and there was a "failure to care."

The FCA amended the AKS to state that a person need not have specific knowledge or intent to violate the AKS, making it easier for the government to prove intent. "Knowing" means that the presenter of the claim for reimbursement (1) has actual knowledge that information presented was false; (2) acts with deliberate ignorance of the truth or falsity of the information; and (3) acts in reckless disregard of the truth or falsity of the information. The FCA imposes penalties on any person who knowingly submits or causes someone to submit a false claim to the government.

Significant Enforcement Areas

Recent significant government enforcement has focused on the following areas:

- **Business Practices.** Despite the widespread practice of offering incentives to induce physicians to relocate their practices to a new area, doing so can expose both those offering, and physicians accepting, such incentives to severe civil and even criminal penalties if done in a way that violates federal or state healthcare fraud and abuse laws. A hospital organization in January 2015 agreed to pay $1.8 million to the U.S. government and the Commonwealth of Massachusetts to settle allegations of operating a recruitment program through which it allegedly paid kickbacks to its physician members in exchange for patient referrals.[11]
- **Lack of Medical Necessity.** Some healthcare providers bill Medicare and Medicaid for services or procedures that are not medically necessary. A San Francisco–based healthcare provider agreed in 2014 to pay $37 million to the U.S. government to settle allegations related to lack of medical necessity. It was alleged that the hospitals admitting patients for common diagnoses where admission as an inpatient was medically unnecessary.[12]

- **Third-Party Relationships.** Physician-owned distributorships have been an area of increased enforcement. Recent guidance makes it clear that the opportunity for a referring physician to earn a profit, including through an investment in an entity for which he or she generates business, could constitute illegal remuneration under the Anti-Kickback Statute. A hospital system in California agreed to pay $354,000 for allegedly paying remuneration to a healthcare company owned and operated by two physicians on staff.[13]
- **Compensation Models and Performance Incentives for Referral Sources.** Compensation models should be based on fair-market value of the services provided by the physician and not be tied to the actual or potential referrals the physician provides. A hospital system based in Florida agreed to pay the U.S. government $85 million to resolve allegations related to violations of the Stark Law. The government alleged that the hospital system executed contracts with six medical oncologists that provided an incentive bonus that improperly included the value of prescription drugs and tests that the oncologists ordered and the hospital system billed to Medicare.[14]

Compliance Program Controls

Preventive Controls

Prevention requires a new way of thinking about compliance. Historically, healthcare organizations looked to the compliance department and its various training and auditing programs to steer clear of potential violations of law. Now, compliance can no longer be the responsibility of the compliance department, but must become engrained in the thoughts and actions of all levels of an organization. The most effective way to stop a compliance issue is to prevent it. The first line of defense is frontline employees, those fulfilling the actual mission of the organization. Expectations must be clear that these employees understand and carry out their roles and responsibilities regarding compliance issues. The compliance program must be set by executive management, adopted by middle management, and carried out by frontline employees. The culture within the organization must set clear expectations that employees are encouraged to raise their hands and bring issues forward.

Organizations have limited resources in the face of ever-growing compliance requirements. Risk assessments can aid in determining how to allocate resources across the organization by examining:

- Physician compensation arrangements, structure, operation, and documentation
- Health information management standards, policies, and procedures

- Clinical practices and documentation
- Third-party arrangements, due diligence, and monitoring

There are several resources to assist organizations in determining the higher risk areas of focus. Each year the OIG publishes its work plan. The document summarizes new and ongoing reviews and activities that the OIG intends to pursue within the coming year. Riskier areas can also be identified by following emergent enforcement trends. These trends can be found in recent settlement agreements, CIAs, and other trade and industry publications. To complete a risk assessment, organizations should also look to historical audits. Internal and external compliance audits can be a very useful way of identifying and classifying specific risks to the organization.

The business practices an organization chooses can have a direct impact in preventing noncompliance. For example, physician recruitment should not focus on the physician's ability to generate referrals. Rather, the business must recruit particular physicians based on community needs, and an analysis of the fair market value of the compensation should be clearly documented.

Accountable care organizations (ACOs) are groups of providers who form relationships that tie provider reimbursements to quality metrics and reductions in the total cost of care for an assigned population of patients. Under the ACO model, physicians and providers may earn incentive bonuses if costs savings are realized. The risk to an ACO is that if an incentive bonus doesn't comply with certain safe harbors, it may be deemed to be a kickback to a physician.

Hospitals must fully understand who owns the companies from which they buy various medical devices. The OIG scrutinizes a business model common in the healthcare industry, whereby physician-owned medical device distributorships sell, or arrange for the sale of, implantable medical devices to healthcare providers, which may include the physician owners themselves. The OIG believes that when a physician controls the selection of a device that is provided by a distributor owned by the physician, there is too much of an incentive for the physician to favor that distributor over others.

Organizations should be very careful how they structure their compensations models and performance incentives. In the past, physician productivity and compensation were based on volume metrics attached to the number of patients seen or the revenue billed and collected. Today, productivity and compensation models are based on relative value units (RVUs). RVUs reflect the time, skills, training, and intensity required to provide a service and are a method of calculating the volume of work or effort spent by the physician. A well-patient visit has a lower assigned RVU then a complicated surgery. RVUs measure and reward "work" rather than the number of patients or billings. The key for an organization to remember when choosing an operating model is that there must be a legitimate business need. It is important to involve qualified legal counsel and the compliance department in business strategies and planning.

Besides business practices and models, an organization's clinical practices, decisions, and documentation can aid in preventing issues related to compliance. An organization's procedures, processes, and controls should allow the organization to correctly capture data that supports clinical and billing outcomes. Clinical documentation should adequately support all elements necessary to prove medical necessity. Procedures should be in place to capture and document the thought process and activities of the physician in real time, as opposed to after the fact and at the time of billing.

If the elements of medical necessity are clearly outlined and documented in the medical record, an organization is less likely to face an instance in which services are provided but are later found not to be medically necessary. It is also critical that the code assigned to an encounter be supported by the medical record. The organization should emphasize that employees assign the code supported by the medical records, not the code that will maximize reimbursement.

An organization's electronic health record (EHR) can help prevent compliance issues. The EHRs should be built to allow for necessary elements of care to be captured and concurrently documented. The better the quality of data, the easier it is to code correctly and seek reimbursement for services provided. Poorly designed EHRs may contribute to compliance concerns. An organization should confirm that macro-driven notes are not copied from one encounter to the next or one patient to the next. Healthcare professionals should contemporaneously document the particular encounter rather than select prepopulated information from a list.

Detective Controls

Detecting instances of noncompliance relies on the elements of risk assessment, data analytics, monitoring, and culture. The results of the risk assessment guide an organization in its detection mechanisms.

Once an organization inventories risks related to noncompliance, it should assess the controls in place to mitigate those risks. Effective controls are a very useful way to reduce risks. After the controls are compared against the risks, an organization can critically view which risks remain high and allocate resources to address those. The company should engage in a continuous process of monitoring and auditing to confirm that an effective compliance program exists.

Data analytics can help the organization identify an issue early. The amount of publicly available data is voluminous. Data analytics should be created to allow the organization to mine its own data, and publicly available data, to identify potential compliance violations. The analytics may address unusual relationships, including physician relationships. For example, data analytics can be used to assist in answering the following:

- Is the rate of one- and two-day inpatient admissions comparable to our peers?
- Are observation services being delivered and billed appropriately?
- What are the sources of high-risk admissions?
- Is the rate per square foot being paid or received commensurate with the industry standard?
- How many patients is a physician seeing in a day, and is it excessive?
- Are any referral sources in the vendor master list?
- Are the payments to those referral sources in line with the business arrangements?

Analytics may also identify medically unlikely edits (MUE) and National Correct Coding Initiative (NCCI) edits. CMS uses these edits to reduce the paid claim error rate. MUE limit the units coders can report with certain Current Procedural Terminology (CPT) or HCPCS[15] codes, and NCCI edits focus on combinations of codes that should not be reported together. Healthcare providers should develop policies around internally performing these edits on their own data prior to submitting it for reimbursement. Analytics can also be developed to identify outliers within the data. Not only can an organization's own data be mined, but with the wealth of publicly available data, organizations can benchmark their data with that of their peers. For example, is one of the organization's physicians performing a disproportionately high number of a procedure compared to his or her peers?

Monitoring and auditing should not reside solely in the compliance or internal audit functions of an organization. The organization should foster a culture where monitoring is driven back into the business. Similar to prevention, monitoring should be conducted as the first line of defense.

Each business or clinical unit within the organization should perform self-monitoring and auditing. Auditing business units is the tactical execution of a preventive culture. The clinical supervisor should routinely assess a sample of charts. This will allow the supervisor to detect issues, provide training, and monitor performance on a real-time basis. If business units own compliance, they will be committed to making the business compliant.

One of the most critical elements of effective detection is creating a culture that fosters an environment receptive to the reporting of concerns about business conduct. When an organization is made aware of an issue, it should address the concern, document the procedures and findings, and make any necessary behavioral changes. If the organization can demonstrate that it appropriately addresses concerns, the probability of a *qui tam* suit is reduced. Should an individual pursue a *qui tam* suit, the organization can demonstrate to the government the actions it took to address the behavior.

Responsive Controls

How a company responds to a compliance issue can directly affect the outcome of the event. If the organization can prove to the government that it adequately addressed the concern and incorporated corrective action, it is less likely to be assessed with the higher end of possible fines and may avoid a CIA.

When an organization learns of a compliance issue, it should determine if it is an isolated issue or more systemic. A root cause analysis, plus the use of data analytics, can aid the company in determining if there is a pattern of behavior. Analytics helps determine the extent of the issue and whether other areas of the organization need further investigation. The use of statistical sampling enables the organization to quantify the impact to the payer without the need of testing all the transactions.

The organization should also determine the root cause of the issue (e.g., business incentives, cost controls, staffing, other metrics). Was the unit under-staffed to keep costs down, leading to poor quality of care? Are physicians incentivized based on the patients seen or billings generated? Often a seemingly legitimate business incentive can cause a compliance problem.

The compliance issue may be related to a systemic cause. Are the organization's systems and processes enabling noncompliant behavior? Does the EHR either prepopulate visit notes or allow the physician to copy notes from one visit and paste into another visit? Or was the cause of the noncompliant behavior related to a control deficiency? The organization should undertake an analysis to determine if the control activity was not properly designed or functioning, or whether the control was evaded. Once the cause of noncompliant behavior is known, the organization can address it and reduce the likelihood of similar behavior in the future.

At this point, the organization should confirm that corrective measures were implemented. The corrective actions should be taken in a timely manner and address the cause of the behavior. The organization should clearly document the actions taken and provide additional training and education. To demonstrate that the corrective action is effective, the organization should undertake a process to test the operation of the new control. This monitoring and auditing will allow the company to determine if the behavior stopped. Besides corrective actions related to the control failure, the organization should determine whether any corrective actions are required for any individuals involved. Legal counsel and human resources should be involved in the corrective action procedures, especially if the individual might be a relator.

Reporting of noncompliant issues closes the feedback loop. The level and detail provided should vary based upon who is receiving the information. It is important that management and business unit leaders understand the details related to how the issue surfaced, what noncompliant actions occurred, how the matter was investigated, and what corrective actions were taken.

Does the organization understand what level of information is appropriate for the board? The message to the board may be different from the message to management. It will be interested in possible repercussions both legal and financial.

The organization should have a protocol for determining what governing bodies must be made aware of any compliance concerns and when. Engage legal counsel in this discussion as some states have specific reporting requirements. Another consideration is reporting to regulators. The organization should work with its legal counsel to determine if self-reporting is necessary and to which body it should self-report. Sometimes it may be acceptable to disclose the issue to a financial intermediary such as a Medicare contract organization, while in others it may be necessary to disclose to the government.

The benefit of self-reporting to a regulatory body may include a presumption against a CIA requirement or the benefit of a lower damages multiplier. However, the organization must provide detailed disclosures including an explanation of why the violation occurred and a full legal analysis. The organization must acknowledge that the conduct is a potential violation. Once a disclosure has been made, the organization has 90 days to complete its investigation and take the necessary corrective actions. Disclosure could trigger a criminal review because the OIG refers potential criminal conduct to the DOJ. The OIG may advocate that the disclosing party should receive a benefit for the disclosure, but it can offer no guarantees.

Conclusion

With the continued rise of healthcare costs, healthcare providers should expect to see an increase in enforcement actions. With an effective compliance program that is designed to prevent, detect, and respond to regulatory enforcement actions, a provider can minimize the impact of enforcement.

Chapter 11

Fraud and Misconduct in Life Sciences

Mark C. Scallon
Regina G. Cavaliere
Richard L. Zimmerer

Since the early 2000s, corporations and individuals in the life sciences industry have been the subject of heightened scrutiny and intensified regulatory enforcement for their alleged involvement in bribery and corruption, unlawful marketing practices, and research fraud. Since 2001, more than 35 pharmaceutical and biotechnology manufacturers and medical device companies have settled allegations with the U.S. government, many of them paying hefty fines and entering into expansive corporate integrity agreements (CIAs). For each fiscal year between 2009–2014, the U.S. government has recovered more than $2 billion from the life sciences industry.[1] Demands from both the government and the public at large have caused the industry to reshape its business practices at a fundamental operational level.

The initial wave of investigations in the 2000s focused on pricing and reimbursement issues. The first major settlement came in the case against TAP Pharmaceutical Products in 2001.[2] TAP agreed "to pay $875 million to settle criminal and civil charges that it had illegally manipulated the Medicare and Medicaid programs" and entered into a CIA that, among other things,

Kathy Tench was a major contributor to the content of this chapter. Ms. Tench is a director in KPMG's Forensic practice in New York City. Currently, Ms. Tench is on rotation to KPMG's Zurich office. She specializes in providing regulatory compliance services to life sciences companies.

"significantly changed the manner in which TAP supervised its marketing and sales staff, and ensured that TAP would report to the Medicare and Medicaid programs the true average sale price for drugs reimbursed by those programs."[3]

CIAs have become an important government vehicle for changing industry practices. The Office of Inspector General (OIG) for the U.S. Department of Health and Human Services negotiates CIAs with companies as part of the settlement of federal healthcare program investigations. In addition to penalties, companies agree to the CIA obligations, and in exchange, the OIG agrees not to seek their exclusion from participation in Medicare, Medicaid, or other federal healthcare programs. CIAs typically last five years and include sweeping requirements to implement compliance program components (for details, see Chapter 10).

Regulators soon broadened the scope of their enforcement scrutiny to include additional promotional activities, along with relationships and interactions with healthcare providers. From 2004 to 2009, settlements were reached with 11 manufacturers to resolve allegations of off-label promotion; by 2015 the list was more than 30. One impact of this new enforcement activity was the inclusion of additional CIA requirements that were aimed at multiple functions across the company. On top of the exorbitant settlements paid to resolve allegations related to misbranding—the highest was GlaxoSmithKline's (GSK) $3 billion settlement[4] with the U.S. Department of Justice (DOJ) in 2012 for off-label promotion and other allegations—the accompanying CIAs required companies to set up significant controls around commercial practices and strategies.

The new focus on industry relationships with healthcare professionals gave rise to unprecedented restrictions on promotional activities, including limitations on meals, entertainment, gift giving, and sample distribution, to name a few. Compliance monitoring of sales force personnel, speaker programs, and responses to medical information were standard CIA requirements that have since become routine across the industry. It has also become common for companies to conduct annual needs assessments and develop fair market value (FMV) frameworks to help ensure that healthcare professional (HCP) consultants are retained for legitimate services and paid at FMV. The drive toward transparency of financial relationships has resulted in state and federal laws as well as laws in European countries and other jurisdictions requiring pharmaceutical and medical device companies to publicly disclose payments to healthcare professionals.

Prosecutors have become more sophisticated in identifying a broader range of misconduct as seen by the evolving focus of their investigations. Past enforcement activity had targeted companies and behaviors that result in the biggest recoupments, but as the larger pharmaceutical and medical device companies have strengthened their compliance infrastructure, the government recognizes that the same risks may exist within small and mid-size companies.

Recent complaints have already begun to touch on medical and scientific activities, such as publications and investigator-sponsored research, and the DOJ has indicated that research and development issues will continue to be scrutinized. Interactions with payers and with patients are also receiving increased attention. Changes in the healthcare industry have led drug manufacturers to focus on the payer community to ensure that patients have access to their products and on patient education and support programs to differentiate their brand. The ongoing identification and exposure of fraudulent activities and conflicts of interest in the life sciences industry will continue to result in new and revised rules, regulations, and enforcement activity.

Industry Risk Areas and Enforcement Trends

Laws and regulations designed to ensure patient safety and prevent fraud and abuse of public healthcare programs are continuously being revised and updated, but the target risk areas have remained fairly constant since World War II. John Braithwaite's 1984 book *Corporate Crime in the Pharmaceutical Industry*[5] describes corporate misdeeds including bribing government officials, customs officers, and safety inspectors; fabricating clinical trial data; unsafe manufacturing practices; fraudulent government price reporting; expanding indications and inventing new diseases; kickbacks to physicians; misleading advertising; ghostwriting; and a host of other behaviors that are still under investigation 30 years later.

Government Pricing

In the United States, most healthcare providers, payers, and intermediaries are non-governmental commercial entities. Life sciences pricing to such commercial entities is largely unregulated and determined through negotiation in a manner broadly similar to other commercial industries.[6] Taxpayer dollars are, however, also used to pay for certain life science products, and the mechanism by which those prices are determined is known as "government pricing."

Government pricing programs are socially important in supporting the provision of drug access to tens of millions of people in need of the treatment regimen. These programs are financially significant with a large and increasing share of the market and large per-unit pricing impacts. They are also subject to significant risk for reasons including underlying complexity, uncertain guidance, executive certification, and massive oversight and enforcement.

Government pricing programs vary, but all share the same underlying approach whereby the government's prices are determined by reference to comparable commercial prices as reported by manufacturers. Specifically, participating manufacturers calculate and submit to the government average prices and/or lowest prices for various customer groups in a manner consistent with governmental guidance. This can be extremely difficult for a number of reasons including:

- Prices must be reported net of all discounts and other price concessions. The industry has a wide variety of relationships with entities in the distribution and pricing chains that could be considered price concessions in whole or in part.
- Prices are only for the designated customers and transaction types specific to each program. Criteria include customer type, customer location, distribution channel, transaction type (e.g., return, price correction, order adjustment), and price.
- Prices must be reported monthly, quarterly, and/or annually in 30 to 45 days, depending upon the program. Many relevant price concessions, such as rebates, are not paid, and the amounts are not known, until well after the reporting deadline.
- Governmental guidance varies by program. It is contained in a variety of statutes, regulations, and, significantly, in subregulatory sources. It is incomplete and not always clear or relevant, leaving the manufacturer to make significant assumptions.

Oversight and enforcement were relatively light during the early years of these programs. Then, in the late 1990s, a whistleblower filed the first of what became a flood of average wholesale price (AWP) lawsuits that extracted billions of dollars from the industry based on allegations that pharmaceutical manufacturers had manipulated their undiscounted prices in a scheme that caused payers to over-reimburse healthcare providers, which, in turn, promoted sales of the products.[7] These lawsuits revealed the challenges in compliance with government pricing programs, and a bevy of whistleblower lawsuits followed, along with various governmental actions, increased audit oversight, and other forms of scrutiny. It is difficult to quantify the amounts of money involved because individual settlements often address multiple issues and self-disclosures are generally not publicized.

The industry has responded by improving processes to avoid such lawsuits and providing visibility into potential areas of vulnerability (e.g., when guidance is unclear and assumptions are made). Corporate departments dedicated to government pricing have expanded, with many employing 20 or more people, and they are being led by more senior people. Dedicated government pricing attorneys have been brought in-house. Third-party systems costing tens of millions

"Government Pricing by Sub-Segment"

Government pricing affects life sciences subsegments inconsistently.

- The pharmaceutical subsegment receives most regulatory attention, with a significant portion of total sales being subjected to four separate major government pricing programs and scores of other smaller programs.
- The medical device subsegment is impacted by only one of the government pricing programs. But even though fewer sales are subject to government regulation, medical device pricing practices can make application of the program's provisions particularly challenging.
- The laboratory subsegment has historically been exempt from government pricing.

This changed, however, with the passage of the Protecting Access to Medicare Act in 2014, which turns industry pricing, and a significant portion of operations, on its head with the implementation of a government pricing program for laboratories beginning in 2016.

of dollars have been implemented at most large manufacturers, and the smaller ones are enhancing system capabilities as well.

Government pricing is based on commercial pricing, and compliance requires accurate and complete commercial data. Manufacturers have therefore adapted processes across numerous general business functions such as sales accounting, customer master, regulatory, and others. Robust internal certification processes have been put in place. Compliance audits led by external experts are conducted annually at many manufacturers. In 2015, the government settled a government pricing case with a manufacturer and included in the settlement agreement[8], for the first time, a comprehensive description of what a robust government pricing compliance program must include. The life sciences industry is in the process of assessing and revising its programs accordingly.

Kickbacks

The U.S. Anti-Kickback Statute (AKS)[9] prohibits drug and device companies from knowingly[10] and willfully offering or providing payments, other financial incentives, or items of value to healthcare professionals and organizations as inducements for prescribing, recommending, or using their drug or device that is reimbursed by federal health care programs. Improper industry influence over prescribing choices is a type of fraud that results in patient safety risks and excessive costs that are passed on to patients and payers, including the federal government.[11] Under the U.S. False Claims Act (FCA), a drug or device company may be held liable when its kickback schemes generate prescriptions that are reimbursed by federal health care programs. In 2010 the Patient Protection and Affordable Care Act (PPACA) made it official that claims submitted in violation of the AKS automatically constitute false claims for purposes of the FCA.

Purchasers

Contracting and discounting arrangements with purchasers of prescription drugs, biologics, and medical devices, including wholesalers, health maintenance organizations (HMOs), and other types of payers, are an area of potential kickback risk. Inducements offered to purchasers may fall under the AKS if the purchased products are reimbursable by a federal healthcare program.

In 2006 Schering-Plough paid $345 million to resolve charges for paying a kickback to an HMO in exchange for preferred treatment on the HMO's formulary and for failing to report to Medicaid the true best price for the product. Rather than agree to the HMO's request to reduce the price of a product, the pharmaceutical company had offered a $10 million package of added value that included an annual data fee equivalent to 2 percent of gross sales.[12] Other arrangements that have been identified in anti-kickback cases include stocking allowances, price protection payments, prebates,[13] market share payments, and free goods designed to induce retail pharmacy and wholesaler customers to purchase products.[14] Note that the AKS and the corresponding regulations establish a number of "safe harbors" into which arrangements can be structured to reduce or eliminate the risk of AKS violation.[15]

Healthcare Professionals

Regulators and the private sector recognize that there are legitimate and important reasons for drug and device companies to collaborate with physicians and healthcare professionals. However, there is a risk that these relationships may result in improper influence over medical decision making. This undue influence can come in the form of lavish dinners and vacations or be disguised in consulting arrangements. Repeated abuses of the AKS have resulted in numerous settlements and corporate integrity agreements and have led the government to demand greater transparency into financial relationships between industry and healthcare professionals.

Many of the largest settlements between the U.S. government and pharmaceutical companies consisted of alleged anti-kickback violations for making illegal payments to doctors and other health professionals.[16] The kickbacks included the use of speaker programs, preceptorships/mentorships, and improper gifts, such as entertainment and meals. One company allegedly "plied doctors with perks such as free spa treatments, Colorado ski trips, pheasant-hunting jaunts to Europe, and Madonna concert tickets."[17]

Medical device companies have also been scrutinized for some of their consulting arrangements. In September 2007, four major medical device manufacturers collectively paid the government $311 million to resolve allegations of providing kickbacks to physicians. The investigation identified certain arrangements designed to increase sales of artificial hip and knee implants used by the consulting surgeons. Some companies paid the surgeons a fee of $5,000 to provide a quarterly report on marketing trends; the reports were typically of little value and often duplicated from quarter to quarter. Sham product development agreements were also uncovered. These agreements, which yielded millions of dollars in royalty payments for up to 20 years, would include consultant physicians who were added midway through the project and who contributed little.

Potentially more nefarious, but less commonly seen, are investigations and settlements related to sham studies. In 2008, the biopharmaceutical company Biovail Pharmaceuticals pleaded guilty to conspiracy and to violating the anti-kickback statute for allegedly conducting a sham study. Physicians were paid up to $1,000 per enrollee to prescribe the company's drug, have the patient fill the prescription, conduct routine follow-ups, and complete a questionnaire. The work required was minimal, of limited to no scientific value, and the payment exceeded FMV.[18]

In 2009, in response to the increased scrutiny of interactions with HCPs, both the Pharmaceutical Research and Manufacturers of America (PhRMA) and the Advanced Medical Technology Association (AdvaMed) revised their codes on Interactions with Healthcare Professionals to include stricter limitations on the provision of gifts, meals, entertainment, support for conferences and education, and agreements related to speaker programs, consulting, and royalties. Both codes emphasize that HCP consultants should only be engaged for legitimate purposes unrelated to purchasing or prescribing behavior and that payments should be made at FMV.

Despite the heightened publicity of enforcement activity and industry guidance in this area, the industry continues to face litigation related to alleged kickbacks to healthcare professionals. In a January 2015 settlement against Daiichi

Sankyo, the government alleged that the company paid physicians improper kickbacks in the form of speaker fees. Physicians were allegedly compensated for "speaking" on duplicative topics over company-paid dinners. In one example cited, the dinner was "so lavish that its cost exceeded the company's own internal cost limitation of $140 per person"; in other instances, the inappropriate conduct involved payments to speakers for "speaking only to members of his or her own staff in his or her own office."[19] In addition, it was alleged that the same speaker program presentations were presented to the same audience several times in the same year.

Global Bribery and Corruption

Within the United States, bribery in the life sciences sector is prosecuted at both the federal and state levels. The OIG also has jurisdiction to investigate and oversee federal healthcare programs. For corruption matters involving foreign government officials outside of the United States, the U.S. Department of Justice (DOJ) and U.S. Securities and Exchange Commission (SEC) prosecute bribery cases under the Foreign Corrupt Practices Act (FCPA) across all industries including life sciences. The same activities prohibited by the AKS in the United States are prohibited by the FCPA when the recipient of the bribe is a government official. This includes health ministries, doctors, and other healthcare professionals in countries where the healthcare systems are government agencies. Siemens paid $1.7 billion to the United States and Germany in 2008 to settle allegations of corruption across a number of sectors including medical devices. Subsequent cases have included medical device companies, pharmaceutical manufacturers, and most recently a laboratory.

In remarks at a U.S. pharmaceutical industry conference in March 2015, SEC Director of Enforcement Andrew Ceresney said that FCPA enforcement in the pharmaceutical industry is a high priority. Ceresney provided examples of three types of misconduct that arise most often in FCPA enforcement actions in the pharmaceutical industry[20]:

- *Pay-to-prescribe.* Ceresney gave the example of Pfizer's $60 million settlement reached in 2012 with the SEC and DOJ to resolve charges that Pfizer subsidiaries bribed doctors in several countries to win business and increase sales. In Croatia, Pfizer employees created a "bonus program" for Croatian doctors who were employed in senior positions in Croatian government healthcare institutions. Once a doctor agreed to use Pfizer products, a percentage of the value purchased by a doctor's institution would be returned to the doctor in the form of cash, international travel, or free products.

- *Bribes paid to have products listed in a formulary.* In 2012, Eli Lilly reached a $29 million settlement with the SEC to resolve charges that the company's subsidiary in Poland made payments totaling $39,000 to a small foundation started by the head of a regional government health authority. In exchange, the official placed Lilly drugs on the government reimbursement list.

- *Bribes disguised as charitable contributions.* In 2013, medical technology company Stryker paid $13 million to the SEC to resolve charges that Stryker's subsidiary in Greece made a purported donation of nearly $200,000 to a public university to fund a laboratory that was set up by a public hospital doctor. In return, the doctor agreed to provide business to Stryker.

Many countries other than the United States have enforced their own anti-bribery and corruption laws in the pharmaceutical industry. In 2014, GSK was found guilty of bribery by a Chinese court and fined nearly $500 million for bribing government officials, hospitals, and doctors to sell drugs at higher prices.[21]

Off-Label Promotion

The Food, Drug and Cosmetic Act (FDCA) requires that a company must specify the intended uses of a product in its new drug application, 510K, or premarket approval application to the Food and Drug Administration (FDA). The FDA approves drugs for specific indications and clears devices for specific uses. Once approved or cleared, the product may not be marketed or promoted for any uses not specified in an application and approved or cleared by FDA (off-label uses).

Franklin v. Parke-Davis was the first case to link off-label promotion to the FCA, which allows private individuals to file whistleblower suits. Under the FCA, if the United States is successful in resolving or litigating the relator's (whistleblower's) claims, the relator may share in part of the recovery. The Parke-Davis complaint was initiated in 1996 by a physician who had been hired for a medical liaison role. Within four months, he left Parke-Davis and filed a whistleblower lawsuit alleging that the off-label marketing strategies employed by Parke-Davis resulted in federal reimbursement of drugs that were not prescribed for approved uses. In May 2004, Pfizer, Inc., which had acquired Parke-Davis and its parent company, Warner Lambert, settled the case for $430 million in civil fines and criminal penalties.

Since that case, there have been more than 30 FCA settlements against pharmaceutical and medical device companies for off-label promotion. These are often accompanied by CIAs requiring comprehensive controls and live monitoring around promotional and nonpromotional activities that have been linked to off-label marketing strategies.

Promotional Activities by Sales and Marketing

Off-label settlements usually identify a broad range of improper sales and marketing activities that support off-label marketing strategies. When used improperly, company-established sales goals and call plans have been cited as evidence supporting FDCA violations. These include call plans that target physician specialties unlikely to prescribe a product for an approved use and unrealistic sales representative incentive compensation plans whose targets could only be achieved with substantial off-label prescriptions.

Speaker programs for physicians have been criticized as kickback arrangements, and they also carry significant risk for off-label marketing activity. When speaking on behalf of a drug or device company, a physician is bound to the same regulatory requirements as a company's promotional employees. As a result, most companies attempt to control the program content by preparing the presentation materials for the speaker, with the expectation that the speaker will stay on message. However, oftentimes the audience will ask questions related to unapproved uses of the product.

In the past it was industry standard to allow speakers to provide narrow and tailored responses to audience questions about unapproved uses. However, FDA's 2011 guidance on Responding to Unsolicited Questions for Off-Label Information about Prescription Drugs and Medical Devices has led many companies to rethink that practice. Many companies now train their speakers not to answer off-label related questions, to address them one-on-one after the program, or to direct those questions to the company's medical affairs department. However, the risk remains that the speaker will add his or her own slides to the company's slide deck, respond broadly to unsolicited off-label questions, or proactively discuss off-label uses of the company's product.

Nonpromotional Activities

Nonpromotional activities include publishing scientific data, medical education, and research. These nonpromotional activities are meant to raise disease awareness and facilitate scientific exchanges between the industry and HCPs; they are usually conducted through a company's medical affairs (MA) department. The legal and regulatory basis for MA is limited. Although there is no statutory requirement to have a MA function, and no safe harbor for doing so, government and industry have provided some guidance. The 2003 OIG Compliance

Program Guidance for Pharmaceutical Manufacturers calls for the separation of commercial and MA functions. FDA's 2009 Reprint Guidance explicitly endorsed the role of MA in the dissemination of medical journal reprints along with a list of requirements.

Since 2009, many CIAs have required companies to follow the International Committee of Medical Journal Editors (ICMJE) requirements regarding authorship when developing policies and practices related to research and publications. These measures are in response to findings that research and publication planning have been used as key components of off-label marketing strategies. Evidence obtained in off-label investigations has shown corporate strategic plans to conduct research and create scientific literature specifically to enable the promotion of an unapproved use even when there was no intent to obtain approval for that use. A once common practice for developing a body of "scientific" information was to use company employees or professional medical writers to draft research publications and then identify prestigious doctors to put their names on the ghostwritten reports.[22]

Scientific Misconduct

The call for transparency into financial relationships has been mirrored by the requirement for greater insight into clinical research outcomes. National Institutes of Health (NIH) created clinicaltrials.gov in 1997, and since then, trial registration policies and requirements have been issued by FDA, ICMJE, World Health Organization, European Medicines Agency, and World Medical Association.[23]

Enforcement actions related to misconduct in research and development have primarily focused on individual researchers, but the impact of falsified research can have a devastating result for companies and the public at large. In 2010, a prominent Massachusetts doctor pleaded guilty to healthcare fraud and was sentenced to six months in prison for fabricating findings in 21 studies. This physician received funding from major drug companies, although it was not proven that the data were falsified at the instruction of those companies. Follow-up studies have found that although the main articles were retracted, articles citing the falsified findings remain in circulation.[24] Five years later, a scientist who faked acquired immune deficiency syndrome (AIDS) research funded by federal grant money entered guilty pleas to two felony charges of making false statements[25] was sentenced to 57 months in federal prison, fined $7.2 million, and will be subject to three years probation upon release.[26]

Consequences can be felt at the corporate level as well. In 2014–15, several European Union governments suspended the approval of drugs tied to alleged falsification of bioequivalence data used by a generic manufacturer to support product approval.[27] Further investigations are being conducted to determine the extent of the fraud. The proliferation of falsified research and publications is clearly dangerous to the public at large and will likely continue to draw interest from investigators.

Compliance Program Controls

The tenets of an effective compliance program have been described throughout this book, consisting of a strong tone at the top, robust written controls, excellent training and communication, monitoring and auditing, conducting investigations, and applying appropriate disciplinary action. All of these are relevant to the life sciences industry. For specific high-risk areas in life sciences, the approach to preventing, detecting, and responding to compliance violations has been reshaped in the past decade by government investigations and enforcement activity. Corrective plans for addressing risk areas that have been the focus of government investigations have been outlined in numerous CIAs, and many companies have looked to these CIAs for guidance in developing their own compliance programs. Another noteworthy external development is DOJ's retention of a full-time Compliance Counsel as of November 3, 2015. The Compliance Counsel will assist prosecutors with assessing "the existence and effectiveness of any compliance program that a company had in place at the time of the conduct giving rise to the prospect of criminal charges, and whether the corporation has taken meaningful remedial action, such as the implementation of new compliance measures to detect and prevent future wrongdoing."[28] In the coming months, companies can expect more guidance and benchmarking around metrics from DOJ's Compliance Counsel which can be used to gauge the effectiveness of a compliance program.

Preventative Controls

Effective prevention must begin with a strong ethical business culture that is demonstrated by leadership at all levels, from the executive team to first-line supervisors. During the height of enforcement activity in the mid to late 2000s, many drug and device companies—both with and without CIAs—assigned most, if not all, responsibility for compliance program development and implementation to the compliance department. By centralizing the responsibility, companies could quickly build a compliance program framework and bring policies and procedures in line with rapidly changing compliance requirements. The industry's approach to compliance, however, has become more holistic. Companies with more mature compliance programs recognize that the business needs to take ownership for compliance and to be compliance champions. The compliance program must be set by executive management, adopted by middle management, and carried out by frontline employees.

Central to risk prevention in the life sciences industry are ethical business practices related to HCP and healthcare institution (HCI)/healthcare organization (HCO) interactions. In general, almost any payment or transfer of value to an HCP/HCI/HCO poses a potential kickback risk and may also present an opportunity for off-label promotion. Employees who interact with these individuals and entities need clear guidelines regarding appropriate communications. It is not sufficient to say "stay on label." Each product and device has its own nuanced opportunities for straying into off-label territory.

Compliance departments need to work closely with their medical and commercial colleagues to understand these nuances and help the business develop approved responses to specific scenarios that field sales and field medical personnel encounter in day-to-day activities. Companies should also establish clear rules and responsibilities to govern interactions between medical and commercial field personnel during joint meetings with HCPs, internal account planning meetings, internal trainings, and so on.

Similar robust rules and training should be provided to HCPs who speak promotionally on behalf of the company. HCPs with expertise in a specific therapeutic area are often engaged by several companies that may have different rules about what they allow HCPs to communicate during a speaker program. While the industry is moving away from allowing speakers to respond to requests for off-label information, this practice was once widely accepted and is still allowed by some companies. It is important for speakers to be educated on a company's specific approach to this risk area.

Annual live speaker training should be supplemented with periodic follow-up training to ensure that the speaker is familiar with approved product messaging and compliance requirements. Before each program, the sales representative hosting the program should meet with the speaker and provide a quick review of messaging, compliance requirements, examples of potential off-label questions, and appropriate ways to respond to those questions.

Review and approval procedures should also be adopted to mitigate risk related to HCP/HCI/HCO relationships. Before a company engages HCPs as promotional speakers, consultants, advisors, investigators, and authors, a designated review committee should agree that there is a legitimate business need for the requested service based on well-defined selection criteria to meet a specific business need. For example, the number of speakers and programs required for an annual speaker bureau should be based on factors including the life cycle of the drug, availability of new data, and the size and location of the target audience. HCP speakers should be selected based on these needs as well as the HCP's expertise and geographic location. The invitation to participate as a speaker should not be a reward or incentive to prescribe drugs or use devices, so companies should be cautious about allowing sales personnel to influence the HCP selection process.

Likewise, companies should implement controls related to the award of educational grants, research grants, sponsorships, charitable contributions, and other donations to HCPs/HCI/HCOs. For example, an annual plan should predefine areas of interest for investigator-initiated research, and requests for funding should only be considered if they align with those interests. Proposed research protocols should be developed independently by HCPs without influence from the company and should be evaluated on their individual merit. Research grants should not be provided as rewards for promoting or prescribing a drug or device, so sales and marketing personnel are typically excluded from the review and approval process.

Drug and device companies should be careful how they structure their sales force compensation models. Sales representative bonuses are typically tied to the number of prescriptions generated by physicians within a sales representative's territory. Companies must be careful to create reasonable sales targets that can be achieved by selling products for approved uses to providers that are likely to treat patients with the diseases and conditions for which a drug or device is approved or cleared. Further, identifying mechanisms or controls to exclude any off-label use from compensation models is becoming a common practice.

Companies must also ensure that payments made to HCPs/HCIs/HCOs are at FMV for legitimate business needs. Physician fees should consider both HCP qualifications and the level of effort required for the proposed service. Payment terms and specific deliverables should be specified in contracts that are executed prior to the date that services are provided. Grants and sponsorships should only be awarded for purposes that advance the scientific and educational needs supported by the company, and these monies should be tied to specific, itemized budgets provided by the requesters and deemed appropriate and necessary by the review committee. Compliance departments should guide the business in establishing review and approval committees for grants and donations, but it is important for the business owners to be responsible for the process. Thus, compliance is usually not involved in the operational aspect of approval although they may be consulted by the review team as needed.

For companies with adequate resources, systems can be implemented to automate controls related to entering into these financial relationships. For example, web-based portals can be used to manage the request, review, and approval of grants for medical education and investigator-sponsored research.

Such systems can ensure that required needs assessment and budget documentation are provided and that each committee member approves before a grant is awarded. Systems can also be implemented to manage a broad range of compliance requirements related to HCP contracting. Comprehensive systems can be designed to manage annual needs assessments for HCP services, HCP selection criteria, determination of FMV rates, and annual payment caps.

Detective Controls

A strong compliance program will not prevent every compliance violation, so ongoing risk assessment and compliance monitoring are critical for detecting violations early before they become major issues. The most effective risk assessments will include strong participation from the business to identify and prioritize risk areas. With input from the business, the compliance department can develop a realistic plan for conducting monitoring and auditing.

Monitoring activities should also have a high level of involvement from the business. First-line monitoring of sales and medical field personnel can be performed by field managers. Compliance criteria should be a component of manager field rides (i.e., the observation by company representatives of sales calls or other interactions with HCPs[29]) to address appropriate messaging and use of promotional materials as well as adherence to company policy, such as those related to the provision of meals, handling of adverse events, provision of reprints, etc. Direct managers should also serve as first-line reviewers of expense reports. It may be easy for a direct manager to recognize a pattern of fraud, such as repeated submission of the same attendee sign-in sheets for multiple events or attendee sheets that do not reconcile to receipts. Active compliance involvement by the business is one of the defining components of a healthy culture of compliance.

However, monitoring conducted by the business should not replace live monitoring conducted by the compliance department. Interactions with HCPs are generally a high-risk area that should be included in any compliance monitoring plan. Field rides also provide an important opportunity for the compliance department to identify needs for policy revisions and specific training. With many companies downsizing their compliance departments, resource-intensive priorities, such as field rides with sales and medical personnel and live monitoring of speaker programs, may be effectively outsourced to a qualified third party.

Periodic review of documentation related to prioritized risk areas, such as HCP and HCI/HCO payments, should be conducted to evaluate compliance with processes related to review and approval, contracting, execution, and payment. Companies with reliable electronic information may employ data analytics to identify potential trends and outliers and focus their monitoring efforts. For example, many companies require employee expense reports to include the names of physicians and other HCPs who participated in a meal provided by the employee. This data can be mined to identify patterns of possible abuse such as "supper clubs" (a group of HCPs meeting for dinner under the guise of attending speaker programs). Medical information is another source of data that may be used to identify patterns of potential abuse. A regional spike in "unsolicited" requests for a specific off-label reprint may be indicative of a manager employing a specific strategy to promote for an unapproved use. Identifying such potential trends can help the compliance department focus its limited resources on higher risk areas.

One of the critical factors of effective monitoring is the ability to collate results and identify systemic issues and trends so they can be addressed in a timely manner. This means that findings from multiple sources of monitoring and auditing data (field rides, speaker program monitoring, expense report audits, email reviews, and so on) must be considered in aggregate to identify overarching trends. When designing monitoring programs, companies should proactively consider how to aggregate and analyze the various sources of audit and monitoring information. With proper planning, multiple data sources can be set up to feed into a single reporting platform. And compliance monitoring dashboards can be developed for quickly assimilating and communicating findings.

Responsive Controls

A strong compliance program, which includes the timely and appropriate response to a compliance issue, can be an important factor in the outcome of a government investigation. Companies should develop clear policies and procedures for handling compliance issues in an appropriate and consistent manner and assign roles and responsibilities for carrying out those policies.

When an issue is identified, either through monitoring or other reporting channels, a prompt investigation should be conducted to determine the magnitude of the problem. Is a single rogue employee promoting a product for an unapproved use? Or is there evidence of a broader off-label promotion strategy across a region or brand? The use of data analytics can help determine the extent of the issue and whether other areas within the organization need further investigation.

Additionally the company should identify gaps in controls that need to be addressed through corrective and preventative action plans. It is important for compliance to work with the business to identify root causes, but the business should be responsible for developing and implementing the action plans in a reasonable time frame. The company should track violations and responses to ensure that corrective and preventative action plans are carried out. Additionally, the company should ensure that multiple offenses by a particular employee or business unit can be identified and that increasing levels of discipline and corrective action plans can be implemented. For example, a valid corrective action plan for a first violation may be to retrain the employee on policies and processes; however, after multiple offenses a more robust plan should be developed.

The company should confirm that corrective and preventative measures were implemented in a timely manner and document all actions that were taken. Preventative actions should be subsequently tested and monitored to determine whether they were effective in preventing additional violations. In addition to corrective and preventative actions related to any business process, the company should address the conduct of all individuals involved in the matter. Lastly, significant findings should be communicated to executive management and external regulators when necessary.

Conclusion

Implementing mechanisms to help ensure that risks across the business are identified early, assessed thoroughly, and remediated promptly through additional controls, training, and communication are the hallmarks of an effective compliance program and provide value to the business. As this chapter outlines, the risk areas run the gamut; the areas implicated in prior settlements are illustrative and should not be viewed as the entirety of the risk areas. To provide the most value to their company, compliance programs are well advised to take a holistic approach—even if only through high-level oversight—when it comes to identifying areas of risk beyond the more common ones to assist the business with remediating gaps on their own. For example, understanding how many safety reports are received, from what channels, and how they are handled by the pharmacovigilance department is not inimical to a comprehensive compliance program, nor should other areas such as the use of third parties for manufacturing or assessing the accuracy of clinical trial investigator financial disclosure forms be off-limits. Business leaders generally prefer to address issues voluntarily; in this regard, a compliance program can be an asset to leadership by taking a wider view internally, raising awareness of areas for improvement and facilitating early resolution.

Endnotes

Introduction

1. McGraw-Hill, 2011.
2. KPMG analysis based on information sourced from LexisNexis and Factiva (accessed in October 2015).

Chapter 1

1. KPMG CEO Survey, US CEO Outlook 2105, The Growth Imperative in a More Competitive Environment, 19.
2. http://www.wsj.com/articles/goldman-reaches-5-billion-settlement-over-mortgage-backed-securities-1452808185.
3. http://conductcosts.ccpresearchfoundation.com/.
4. http://www.justice.gov/opa/pr/statement-attorney-general-loretta-e-lynch-agreement-principle-bp-settle-civil-claims.
5. http://www.sec.gov/News/Speech/Detail/Speech/1370543090864#_ftnref12.
6. https://www.congress.gov/bill/111th-congress/house-bill/4173.
7. http://www.cftc.gov/reports/afr/2014.
8. http://www.cfr.org/united-kingdom/understanding-libor-scandal/p28729.
9. http://www.nytimes.com/2015/05/21/business/dealbook/5-big-banks-to-pay-billions-and-plead-guilty-in-currency-and-interest-rate-cases.html?_r=0.
10. http://europe.newsweek.com/hsbc-embroiled-new-price-fixing-scandal-309156.
11. http://www.consumerfinance.gov/newsroom/written-testimony-of-cfpb-director-richard-cordray-before-the-senate-committee-on-banking-housing-and-urban-affairs-20150715/.

12. http://www.consumerfinance.gov/blog/category/enforcement/.
13. http://www.sec.gov/News/Speech/Detail/Speech/1370539872100.
14. https://www.sec.gov/about/secstats2015.pdf.
15. http://www.sec.gov/about/secstats2014.pdf (Revised June 01, 2015 from Total 99, as originally published, to 96).
16. https://www.sec.gov/about/secstats2013.pdf.
17. http://www.sec.gov/about/secpar/secafr2013, 29.
18. http://www.sec.gov/about/secpar/secafr2014.pdf.
19. https://www.sec.gov/news/pressrelease/2015-245.html.
20. http://www.justice.gov/opa/pr/health-care-fraud-prevention-and-enforcement-efforts-recover-record-4-billion-new-affordable.
21. http://www.hhs.gov/news/press/2011pres/01/20110124a.html.
22. http://www.justice.gov/opa/documents-and-resources-november-4-2013-johnson-johnson-jj-press-conference.
23. "Offshore Tax Evasion: The Effort to Collect Unpaid Taxes on Billions in Hidden Offshore Accounts," Majority and Minority Staff Report, U.S. Senate Permanent Subcommittee on Investigations Committee on Homeland Security and Governmental Affairs, February 26, 2014.
24. file:///C:/Users/Nigel/Downloads/REPORT%20-%20OFFSHORE%20 TAX%20EVASION%20(Feb%2026%202014,%208-20-14%20 FINAL)%20(1).pdf.
25. http://www.gibsondunn.com/publications/Pages/2015-Year-End-Update-Corporate-Non-Prosecution-Agreements-and-Deferred-Prosecution-Agreements.aspx.
26. http://www.wsj.com/articles/julius-baer-has-agreement-in-principle-in-u-s-tax-probe-1451458700.
27. http://www.oecd.org/tax/exchange-of-tax-information/automaticexchange.htm.
28. Fareed Zakaria, *The Post-American World: Release 2.0*, W. W. Norton & Company, 2011.
29. https://www.cov.com/files/Publication/446fa508-b853-4f88-a902-615eb62a28aa/Presentation/PublicationAttachment/1c4f86eb-6ce7-4115-aed6-67bd2d1e5ee6/Trends_and_Developments_in_Anti-Corruption_Enforcement_Winter_2015.pdf.
30. Wilczek, Bloomberg BNA, June 8, 2015.
31. Jaclyn Jaeger, "Petrobras Probe Means More Enforcement in Brazil," *Compliance Week*, May 2015, 55.
32. David Segal, "Brazil's Great Oil Swindle," *New York Times*, Sunday Business Section, August 9, 2105.
33. Press release, Office of Public Affairs, U.S. Department of Justice, September 17, 2014.

34. https://www.sec.gov/whistleblower/reportspubs/annual-reports/owb-annual-report-2015.pdf.

35. Thomas Fox, "Still Reading Tea Leaves on FCPA Enforcement," *Compliance Week*, May 2015.

36. http://www.sec.gov/news/pressrelease/2015-54.html.

37. http://www.gibsondunn.com/publications/Pages/2015-Mid-Year-False-Claims-Act-Update.aspx.

38. Ibid.

39. http://www.justice.gov/opa/pr/justice-department-recovers-over-35-billion-false-claims-act-cases-fiscal-year-2015.

40. http://www.gibsondunn.com/publications/Pages/2015-Year-End-False-Claims-Act-Update.aspx.

41. http://www.irs.gov/uac/The-Whistleblower-Law.

42. http://www.irs.gov/pub/whistleblower/WB_Annual_Report_FY_14_Final_Signature_June_11-signed%20corrected.pdf.

43. http://www.justice.gov/opa/speech/remarks-assistant-attorney-general-criminal-division-leslie-r-caldwell-taxpayers-against.

44. U.S. Commodity and Futures Trading Commission, Overview of the FY 2104 Budget and Performance Plan.

45. Stuart Gilleman, Financial Regulatory Forum, "'Big data' tools will improve regulatory oversight, FINRA's diFlorio says," Reuters, February 25, 2014.

46. Leslie R. Caldwell, Speech, U.S. Dept. of Justice, Assistant Attorney General for the Criminal Division, American Conference Institute 31st International Conference on the Foreign Corrupt Practices Act, November 19, 2014.

47. http://www.justice.gov/opa/pr/alstom-pleads-guilty-and-agrees-pay-772-million-criminal-penalty-resolve-foreign-bribery.

48. http://www.skadden.com/newsletters/Cross_Border_Investigations_051415.pdf.

49. http://www.wsj.com/articles/sec-escalates-financial-penalties-1436804327.

50. http://www.sec.gov/news/pressrelease/2015-209.html.

51. http://www.gibsondunn.com/publications/pages/SEC-Proposed-Amendments-to-Rules-Governing-Administrative-Proceedings.aspx.

52. http://www.wsj.com/articles/sec-trims-use-of-in-house-judges-1444611604.

53. Richard Strassberg and William Harrington, "Civil Enforcement Actions: Whither the Fifth Amendment?" *New York Law Journal*, May 30, 2014.

54. Ibid.

55. http://www.justice.gov/opa/speech/deputy-attorney-general-sally-quillian-yates-delivers-remarks-new-york-university-school.

56. http://www.gibsondunn.com/publications/Pages/2015-Mid-Year-Securities-Enforcement-Update.aspx.
57. http://www.corpcounsel.com/id=1202734361917/Is-the-SEC-Being-Too-Tough-on-Compliance-Officers?slreturn=20150718175759.
58. https://www.sec.gov/alj/aljdec/2015/id851ce.pdf.
59. http://www.reuters.com/article/2015/08/05/us-wells-far-sec-idUSKCN0QA2PG20150805.
60. http://www.sec.gov/News/Speech/Detail/Speech/1370541872207.
61. http://www.gibsondunn.com/publications/Pages/2015-Year-End-Update-Corporate-Non-Prosecution-Agreements-and-Deferred-Prosecution-Agreements.aspx.
62. http://globalinvestigationsreview.com/article/1016753/caldwell-settlement-%E2%80%9C-powerful-tool%E2%80%9D-convictions.
63. Offshore Tax Evasion: The Effort to Collect Unpaid Taxes on Billions in Offshore Accounts: Hearing Before the Permanent Subcommittee on Investigation of the Commission on Homeland Security and Government Affairs, 113th Congress 4-5 (2104) (joint statement of James M. Cole, Deputy Attorney General and Kathryn Keneally, Assistant Attorney General, Tax Division).
64. DOJ Memorandum issued by Acting Attorney General Craig S. Morford to the United States Attorneys on March 7, 2008. It was updated on May 25, 2010.
65. F. J. Warin, M. S. Daimant, and V. S. Root, "Somebody's Watching Me: FCPA Monitorships and How They Can Work Better," *University of Pennsylvania Journal of Business Law* 13 (2011): 2, 322.
66. Skadden, Arps, "Cross-Border Investigations Update," ibid.
67. Geoffrey P. Miller, "An Economic Analysis of Effective Compliance Programs," New York University Law and Economics Working Papers, New York University Law School, December 2014.
68. http://www.justice.gov/opa/speech/assistant-attorney-general-leslie-r-caldwell-delivers-remarks-compliance-week-conference.
69. http://www.ussc.gov/guidelines-manual/organizational-guidelines.
70. http://www.justice.gov/criminal-fraud/fcpa-guidance.
71. http://www.justice.gov/usam/usam-9-28000-principles-federal-prosecution-business-organizations.
72. http://www.justice.gov/criminal-fraud/file/790236/download.

Chapter 2

1. Money Laundering Enforcement Conference, Washington, DC, November 18, 2013.

2. Adapted from Jim DeLoach, "10 Questions to Help Shape the 2013 Risk Oversight Agenda," NACD Directorship, January 9, 2013.

3. The Sarbanes-Oxley Act, Section 301 requires that audit committees of issuers listed on U.S. exchanges "establish procedures" for (i) receipt, retention, and treatment of complaints regarding accounting, internal accounting controls, or auditing matters; and (ii) confidential, anonymous submission by employees of concerns regarding questionable accounting or auditing matters. Section 301 was codified as Exchange Act Section 10A(m), which the SEC implemented with Rule 10A-3(b)(3), which may be found at http://taft.law.uc.edu/CCL/34ActRls/rule10A-03.html.

4. Ethics Resource Center, "Leading Corporate Integrity: Defining the Role of the Chief Ethics & Compliance Officer (CECO)," August 2007, 18, http://www.ethics.org/files/u5/CECO_Paper_UPDATED.pdf.

5. See commentary to Section 8B2.1 of the Federal Sentencing Guidelines for Organizational Defendants.

6. Procter & Gamble CEO Bob McDonald, Compliance Week Conference 2012.

7. 22nd Annual Ethics and Compliance Conference, October 1, 2014.

8. Both the NYSE and the NASDAQ have adopted corporate governance rules that require U.S. listed companies to adopt and disclose codes of conduct for directors, officers, and employees, and disclose any code waivers for directors or executive officers.

9. Google Code of Conduct, https://investor.google.com/corporate/code-of-conduct.html.

10. One of the minimum requirements announced by the U.S. Sentencing Guidelines for Organizational Defendants calls for the entity to use reasonable efforts and exercise due diligence to exclude individuals from positions of substantial authority who have engaged in illegal activities. See United States Sentencing Commission, Guidelines Manual, §8B2.1(b)(3), http://www.ussc.gov/guidelines/2010_guidelines/Manual_HTML/8b2_1.htm.

11. Despite 73 percent of companies indicating they have a formal risk-based third-party onboarding process, only 45 percent have right to audit clauses in their third-party contracts, with slightly more than half (23 percent of the total) of those exercising these rights. Additionally, less than three-quarters said their companies have a formal process to identify third parties from an anti-bribery and corruption perspective. KPMG International, "Anti-Bribery and Corruption: Rising to the Challenge in the Age of Globalization," https://assets.kpmg.com/content/dam/kpmg/pdf/2015/09/anti-bribery-corruption-2015.pdf.

12. KPMG LLP, "Integrity Survey" http://www.kpmginstitutes.com/advisory-institute/insights/2013/pdf/integrity-survey-2013.pdf.

13. Association of Certified Fraud Examiners, 2014 Report to the Nations on Occupational Fraud and Abuse, http://www.acfe.com/rttn/docs/2014-report-to-nations.pdf.

14. Richard Girgenti and Ori Ben-Chorin, "Government Whistle-Blower Programs Are Here to Stay: 10 Tips to Help Ensure That Internal Reporting Programs Meet the Challenge," Bloomberg BNA (Bloomberg Law), April 2015, http://advisory.kpmg.us/content/dam/kpmg-advisory/PDFs/RiskConsulting/2015/bna-whistle-blower-programs.pdf?sf8971781=1.

15. KPMG LLP, "Integrity Survey."

16. Section 301 was codified as Exchange Act Section 10A(m), implemented by the U.S. Securities and Exchange Commission in Rule 10A-3(b)(3). See also Nasdaq Rule 5605(c)(3) and Section 303A.06 of the NYSE Listed Company Manual.

17. IBM website, "What Is Big Data," http://www-01.ibm.com/software/data/bigdata/what-is-big-data.html.

18. Marshall L. Miller, Principal Deputy Assistant Attorney General, U.S. Department of Justice, Criminal Division, The Global Investigation Review Program, September 17, 2014.

19. Marshall L. Miller, ibid.

20. These typically include the U.S. Department of Justice, the U.S. Securities and Exchange Commission, and the Office of Inspector General of Health and Human Services (OIG), the primary watchdog for healthcare providers and suppliers.

21. The term *government settlement agreement* is an umbrella term that describes the type of agreements that an offending organization may enter into with government enforcement entities, including, for example, deferred prosecution agreements, non-prosecution agreements, and corporate integrity agreements.

22. Institute of Internal Auditors, "The Three Lines of Defense in Effective Risk Management," January 2013, https://na.theiia.org/standards-guidance/Public%20Documents/PP%20The%20Three%20Lines%20of%20Defense%20in%20Effective%20Risk%20Management%20and%20Control.pdf.

23. Ibid.

Chapter 3

1. http://www.fcpablog.com/blog/2015/10/6/the-corporate-investigations-list-october-2015.html

http://www.fcpablog.com/blog/2016/1/4/the-2015-fcpa-enforcement-index.html

2. http://www.traceinternational.org/wp-content/uploads/2014/08/TRACE-Global-Enforcement-Report-2014.pdf.

3. http://web.worldbank.org/WBSITE/EXTERNAL/NEWS/0,,content MDK:20190295~menuPK:34457~pagePK:34370~piPK:34424~theSit ePK:4607,00.html.

4. "Anti-Bribery and Corruption: Rising to the Challenge in the Age of Globalization," KPMG International, September 2015.

5. http://www.oecd.org/corruption/oecdantibriberyconvention.htm. 34 OECD member countries and seven nonmembers, including Brazil and Russia, have adopted the convention.

6. https://www.unodc.org/unodc/en/treaties/CAC/. 172 countries are parties to the Convention, including the United States, the United Kingdom, Brazil, Russia, India. and China.

7. http://www.justice.gov.uk/downloads/legislation/bribery-act-2010-guidance.pdf.

8. http://www.bmz.de/en/what_we_do/issues/goodgovernance/korruption/index.html.

9. http://www.justice.gouv.fr/le-ministere-de-la-justice-10017/service-central-de-prevention-de-la-corruption-12312/.

10. http://www.rcmp-grc.gc.ca/ccb-sddc/international-corrup-eng.htm.

11. http://www.dfat.gov.au/issues/measures-against-corruption.html.

12. https://www.transparency.org/whatwedo/publication/exporting_corruption_progress_report_2015_assessing_enforcement_of_the_oecd.

13. http://www.skadden.com/eimages/WhiteCollarGroup_CrossBorderInvestig ationsUpdate_101414a.pdf.

14. http://www.justice.gov/opa/speech/attorney-general-holder-remarks-financial-fraud-prosecutions-nyu-school-law.

15. http://www.gibsondunn.com/publications/pages/2015-Year-End-FCPA-Update.aspx.

16. Hughes Hubbard & Reed LLP, Winter 2015 FCPA/Anti-Bribery Alert.

17. http://www.justice.gov/criminal/fraud/fcpa/guidance/.

18. Ibid., 71.

19. The United Kingdom ranked fourteenth out of 175 on Transparency International's Corruption Perceptions Index in 2014. The United States ranked seventeenth. See http://www.transparency.org/cpi2014/results.

20. http://www.skadden.com/eimages/WhiteCollarGroup_CrossBorderInvestig ationsUpdate_101414a.pdf.

21. Absolute legal responsibility for an injury that can be imposed on the wrongdoer without proof of carelessness or fault.

22. http://www.sfo.gov.uk/press-room/latest-press-releases/press-releases-2013/four-charged-in-'bio-fuel'-investigation.aspx.

23. http://www.sfo.gov.uk/press-room/latest-press-releases/press-releases-2013/statement---rolls-royce.aspx.

24. http://www.ft.com/cms/s/0/ce534256-93d6-11e3-bf0c-00144feab7de.html#axzz3HTKElk00.

25. http://www.gsk.com/en-gb/media/press-releases/2014/serious-fraud-office-investigation/.

26. https://www.gov.uk/government/speeches/a-balanced-approach-to-the-challenges-of-economic-crime.

27. http://www.justice.gov.uk/downloads/legislation/bribery-act-2010-guidance.pdf.

28. http://www.transparency.org/cpi2014/results.

29. http://www.cov.com/files/upload/E-Alert_Attachment_Brazilian_Clean_Companies_Act_Original.pdf.

30. http://www.nytimes.com/2015/08/09/business/international/effects-of-petrobras-scandal-leave-brazilians-lamenting-a-lost-dream.html.

31. http://www.transparency.org/country/#BRA.

32. http://media.mofo.com/files/Uploads/Images/130227-China-Anti-Corruption.pdf.

33. http://www.chinadaily.com.cn/china/2015twosession/2015-03/12/content_19788251.htm.

34. http://www.npc.gov.cn/englishnpc/Law/2007-12/13/content_1384075.htm.

35. http://www.npc.gov.cn/englishnpc/Law/2007-12/12/content_1383803.htm.

36. http://www.fcpablog.com/blog/2015/9/1/China -amends-its-criminal-law-impact-on-anti-bribery-enforce.html.

37. http://www.lexology.com/library/detail.aspx?g=240c32a2-7a7e-4195-b935-381040f4df04.

38. For a review of China's government departments responsible for anti-corruption enforcement, see Debevoise & Plimpton LLP, FCPA Update, September 2012.

39. http://www.skadden.com/eimages/WhiteCollarGroup_CrossBorderInvestigationsUpdate_101414a.pdf.

40. http://www.legalinfo.gov.cn/english/AboutMOJ/aboutmoj.htm.

41. http://www.gsk.com/en-gb/media/press-releases/2014/gsk-china-investigation-outcome/http://www.gsk.com/en-gb/media/press-releases/2014/gsk-china-investigation-outcome/.

42. http://www.reedsmith.com/China-Issues-New-Regulations-Prohibiting-Commercial-Bribery-in-the-Health-Care-Industry-01-30-2014/.

43. "A Resource Guide to the U.S. Foreign Corrupt Practices Act," ("Guide"), http//www.sec.gov/spotlight/fcpa/fcpa-resource-Guide.pdf.
44. Guide, 57.
45. COSO is a joint initiative of five private-sector organizations dedicated to provide reports on the development of frameworks and guidance on enterprise risk management, internal control, and fraud deterrence. See http://www.coso.org/.
46. Guide, 58.
47. Guide, 58.
48. http://www.sec.gov/News/PressRelease/Detail/PressRelease/ 1370541453075.
49. IIPF Practice Guide, *Auditing Anti-bribery and Anti-corruption Programs*, June 2014, 7.
50. Guide, 59.

Chapter 4

1. http://www.fincen.gov/statutes_regs/patriot/index.html?r=1&id=352#352.
2. Financial Crimes Enforcement Network: Anti-Money Laundering Program and Suspicious Activity Report Filing Requirements for Registered Investment Advisers, 31 CFR Chapter X (proposed August 25, 2015). http://www.fincen.gov/statutes_regs/frn/pdf/1506-AB10_FinCEN_IA_NPRM.pdf.
3. The NPRM allows for a 60-day comment period with publication of a final rule thereafter.
4. Remarks on financial regulation in New York City, delivered at Columbia Law School, February 25, 2015.
5. http://www.dfs.ny.gov/banking/bil-2014-10-10_cyber_security.pdf.
6. "U.S. Vulnerabilities to Money Laundering, Drugs, and Terrorist Financing: HSBC Case History." Permanent Subcommittee on Investigations, U.S. Senate, July 17, 2012, hearing.
7. https://www.kpmg.com/global/en/issuesandinsights/articlespublications/ global-anti-money-laundering-survey/pages/default.aspx.
8. Quantifying the strength of the elements is challenging and at the same time fairly straightforward. Institutions typically develop a scale that measures aspects of the risk at issue. For example, the firm may rely on severity of a violation as one factor. So the risk of failing to file appropriate SARs would be the highest severity, but it could be measured against strong controls that would bring the overall risk score to a midrange level. Some firms use a high/medium/low designation of residual risk; others might use number-based ratings (e.g., a risk that carries significant

consequences if mishandled, but when measured against strong controls might be designated a midrange score for residual risk).

9. The process must establish objective factors in setting these scores. Typical factors for scoring risk are the likelihood of an adverse event occurring and the severity of the consequences (dollar fine vs. exam letter findings, for example).

10. It is conceivable that data identified as high risk might be of poor quality, and the accompanying action item might call for enhancements to data collection, usage, and storage.

11. http://www.ffiec.gov/bsa_aml_infobase/pages_manual/olm_011.htm.

12. "Customer Due Diligence Requirements for Financial Institutions," *Federal Register 79*, no. 149, August 4, 2014.

13. Directive 2005/60/EC of the European Parliament and of the Council, October 26, 2005 (Third EU Money Laundering Directive), Chapter II, Section 1, Article 7.

14. OCC Bulletin 20011-12, *Supervisory Guidance on Model Risk Management*, 3.

Chapter 5

1. Information about these settlements and about all of OFAC's other enforcement actions can be found on OFAC's website, on the Civil Penalties and Enforcement Information page (http://www.treasury.gov/resource-center/sanctions/CivPen/Pages/civpen-index2.aspx).

2. See, for example, Statement of R. Richard Newcomb, Director, OFAC, before the U.S. Senate Committee on Governmental Affairs, July 31, 2003: "Economic sanctions are intended to deprive the target of the use of its assets and deny the target access to the U.S. financial system and the benefits of trade, transactions and services involving U.S. markets, businesses and individuals."

3. The statute of limitations for violations of OFAC's sanctions is five years. 28 U.S. Code §2462.

4. Under the International Emergency Economic Powers Act (IEEPA), criminal sanctions violations are punishable by a term of imprisonment of up to 20 years, and a fine of up to $1 million, per count of conviction. IEEPA underlies several of OFAC's sanctions programs, including those relating to Iran, Sudan, Syria, terrorists, and weapons of mass destruction proliferators, as well as the 2014 Ukraine-related sanctions.

5. See, for example, OFAC Enforcement Information for December 10, 2012, relating to a global settlement with Standard Chartered Bank involving several government agencies, including the New York County

District Attorney's Office; and OFAC Enforcement Information for December 11, 2013, relating to a global settlement with Royal Bank of Scotland, involving DFS and the Federal Reserve Board of Governors.

6. See OFAC Enforcement Information for November 26, 2013, relating to a global settlement with Weatherford International involving several government agencies, including BIS.

7. http://www.treasury.gov/resource-center/sanctions/SDN-List/Pages/default .aspx.

8. The SDN list is published on OFAC's website. As of the date of publication of this book, there are over 5,000 parties named on the list. Entries on the list provide the name of the designated party, and where known, aliases, variant spellings, dates of birth, addresses, and other identifying information. OFAC includes as much identifying information as possible, to increase the chances that persons checking the list will be able to determine if a prospective business partner is prohibited.

9. Directive 1 applied to the financial sector, and prohibited dealing in new short-term debt (debt of longer than 90 days maturity) or new equity for sanctioned parties. Directive 2 applied to the energy sector and prohibited dealing in new short-term debt (again, of longer than 90 days maturity) for sanctioned parties. No other business dealings were prohibited.

10. http://www.treasury.gov/resource-center/sanctions/SDN-List/Pages/ssi_list .aspx.

11. The sanctions relief granted by the P5+1 was highly specific. It involved, among other things, temporary suspension of certain sanctions involving Iran's purchase and sale of gold and other precious metals, its automotive industry, its export of petrochemical products, and certain services associated with each of those categories. In addition, the United States agreed to temporarily suspend its efforts to reduce Iran's crude oil exports and to enable Iran to access $4.2 billion in restricted funds.

12. OFAC also publishes and maintains a number of other lists, in addition to the SDN and SSI lists, including the Foreign Sanctions Evaders List and the Non-SDN Palestinian Legislative Council List. Companies should use a risk-based approach in deciding which lists to screen against. For the sake of simplicity, we will refer in the text only to the SDN list.

13. http://www.treasury.gov/press-center/press-releases/Pages/jl2223.aspx.

14. http://www.treasury.gov/about/organizational-structure/offices/Pages/ Office-of-Foreign-Assets-Control.aspx.

15. http://www.treasury.gov/about/organizational-structure/offices/Pages/ Office-of-Terrorism-and-Financial-Intelligence.aspx.

16. TEOAF administers the Treasury Forfeiture Fund (TFF), which is the receipt account for the deposit of nontax forfeitures. See the TFI website.

17. http://www.treasury.gov/about/organizational-structure/offices/Documents/ Strategic%20Direction%2008-13-12.pdf.

18. This point, and the following discussion of the focus on bad conduct and the private sector, and the use of intelligence information, is based on remarks by former Under Secretary of the Treasury Stuart Levey at "TFI@10," an event hosted by the Center for Strategic and International Studies on June 2, 2014, reflecting on the first 10 years of TFI's existence. See http://csis.org/node/50076/multimedia.

19. http://www.treasury.gov/resource-center/sanctions/documents/licensing_ guidance.pdf.

20. For violations of OFAC's IEEPA-based programs, for example, the maximum civil monetary penalty for each violation is the greater of twice the monetary value of the transaction constituting the violation, or $250,000. 50 U.S.C. section 1705(b). For violations of programs based on the Foreign Narcotics Kingpin Designation Act, the maximum penalty per violation is $1,075,000. 21 U.S.C. section 1906(b).

21. See 31 C.F.R. 560.417.

22. See 31 C.F.R. 538.407(a). The same provision further states that "[a] ctivity of a purely clerical or reporting nature that does not further trade or financial transactions with Sudan or the Government of Sudan is not considered prohibited facilitation."

23. The maximum monetary penalty for a single violation under an IEEPA-based sanctions program, including the Iran, Sudan, and Ukraine-related sanctions, is the greater of twice the monetary value of the transaction constituting the violations, or $250,000.

24. Enforcement Guidelines, pages 57602-04.

25. See OFAC's Enforcement Guidelines, 31 CFR Part 501, Appendix A, pages 57601 and following, http://www.treasury.gov/resource-center/ sanctions/Documents/fr74_57593.pdf.

26. "Voluntary self-disclosure" is defined at pages 57601–02, and "egregiousness" is explained at pages 57604–05, of the Enforcement Guidelines.

27. The General Factors are set forth at pages 57602–04 of the Enforcement Guidelines.

28. Page 57601 of the Enforcement Guidelines.

29. See, for example, OFAC's public announcements of its settlement with Bank of America on July 24, 2014, for violations that occurred between 2006 and 2009; its settlement with American International Group on May 8, 2014, for violations that occurred between 2006 and 2009; and its settlement with GAC Bunker Fuels on March 31, 2014, for a violation

that occurred in November 2008. http://www.treasury.gov/resource-center/sanctions/CivPen/Documents/20140724_bofa.pdf; http://www.treasury.gov/resource-center/sanctions/CivPen/Documents/20140508_aig.pdf; http://www.treasury.gov/resource-center/sanctions/CivPen/Documents/20140331_gac_bunker.pdf.

30. Where the target makes no VSD but substantially cooperates with OFACs investigation, "the base penalty amount generally will be reduced between 25 and 40 percent." Enforcement Guidelines, page 57606. This reduction "is intended to approximate the significant mitigation provided for voluntary self-disclosure cases in the base penalty amount itself. This reduction is intended to afford parties whose conduct was reported to OFAC by others (for example, through a blocking or reject report) the opportunity to obtain, by providing substantial cooperation, much (but not all) of the benefit they would have obtained had they voluntarily self-disclosed the apparent violation." Ibid., Specific Responses to Comments, page 57598.

31. Where OFAC seeks to impose a penalty under the authority of the Trading With the Enemy Act ("TWEA"), its regulations provide a target with the opportunity to request a hearing before an ALJ, in which OFAC will be required to prove its case by a preponderance of the evidence. See 31 CFR subpart D, TWEA Penalties, sections 501.700 and following. OFAC's Cuba sanctions program is predicated on TWEA, and is therefore subject to these provisions. No such procedure is provided for in any of OFAC's other programs, all of which are predicated on authorities other than TWEA.

Chapter 6

1. http://www.sec.gov/News/Speech/Detail/Speech/1370539841202.
2. Note that in this chapter, market power is discussed exclusively on a single firm/individual basis. It is important to note, however, that market power can also exist for a subset of firms or individuals in a market. That is, on an individual basis, each firm may not have market power, but through collusion or tacit coordination between certain firms, market power for a subset of these cooperating firms can be achieved. When this occurs, antitrust concerns, in addition to market manipulation concerns, may be raised; for the sake of brevity and clarity, we refrain from an in-depth discussion of such multifirm market power in this chapter.
3. http://www.cmegroup.com/education/glossary.html.
4. An example of market manipulation via the exercise of market power is Sumitomo Corporation's attempt to corner the copper market in 1986.

See *In the Matter of Sumitomo Corporation*, http://www.cftc.gov/ogc/oporders98/ogcfsumitomo.htm.

5. Note that the types of fraud listed here are by no means exhaustive and are meant to illustrate prevalent types of market manipulation via fraudulent schemes.

6. An example of market manipulation through fraud is Zenergy's reverse merger with Paradigm Tactical Products in 2009. See *SEC v. Nenad Jovanovich, et al.*, Case No. 13-C-5513 (August 16, 2013), http://www.sec.gov/litigation/complaints/2013/comp1-pr2013-143.pdf.

7. In this chapter, uneconomic trading/bidding is discussed exclusively on a single firm or individual basis. Nonetheless, it is important to note that uneconomic trading/bidding can also occur if multiple firms are involved. In such situations, the uneconomic behavior would typically involve some aspect of collusion in the market, meaning that antitrust concerns may also be raised.

8. See the CFTC's settlements with Lloyds Bank (http://www.cftc.gov/ucm/groups/public/@lrenforcementactions/documents/legalpleading/enflloydsorderdf072814.pdf), Barclays (http://www.cftc.gov/ucm/groups/public/@lrenforcementactions/documents/legalpleading/enfbarclaysorder062712.pdf), and RBS (http://www.cftc.gov/ucm/groups/public/@lrenforcementactions/documents/legalpleading/enfrbsorder020613.pdf).

9. http://www.cftc.gov/PressRoom/PressReleases/pr7181-15.

10. Bank of International Settlements Triennial Central Bank Survey, September 2013, 4, http://www.bis.org/publ/rpfx13fx.pdf.

11. Bloomberg Visual Data, *Forex Investigation a Global Affair*, December 19, 2014, http://www.bloomberg.com/infographics/2014-08-13/forex-investigation-a-global-affair.html.

12. Bloomberg Visual Data, *Forex Investigation a Global Affair*, May 20, 2015, http://www.bloomberg.com/infographics/2014-08-13/forex-investigation-a-global-affair.html.

13. The full definition of all financial products to which the term "security" refers is given by the Securities Exchange Act of 1934, pg. 11–12. See: https://www.sec.gov/about/laws/sea34.pdf.

14. Maxwell K. Muller, "Open Market Manipulation Under SEC Rule 10b-5 and Its Analogues: Inappropriate Distinctions, Judicial Disagreement and Case Study: FERC's Anti-manipulation Rule," *Securities Law Journal*, Summer 2011, 97, http://www.dinsmore.com/files/Uploads/Documents/SRLJ%20-%20Multer.pdf.

15. For example, insider trading charges are typically brought under Rule 10b-5 as well.

16. 17 C.F.R. § 240.10b-5.

17. 18 C.F.R. § 1c.

18. 16 C.F.R. Part 317.

19. For a comprehensive legal definition of "swap," please refer to 7 U.S.C. §1a(47) and 17 C.F.R. 1.3.

20. http://www.cftc.gov/ucm/groups/public/@newsroom/documents/file/amaf_factsheet_final.pdf.

21. Fines from the DOJ and FTC have not been included because these agencies do not provide specific information related to the amount of fines stemming from only market manipulation. The Office of the Comptroller of the Currency (OCC) was included in 2014, due to a total of $950 million in fines stemming from the foreign exchange investigation; the OCC's role, however, is likely to be a one-off event.

22. For the CFTC's definition of "recklessness," please see: CFTC Adopting Release, 76 Fed. Reg. at 41404.

23. *CFTC Manipulation Rule*, 17 C.F.R. Part 180.1.

24. *CFTC Manipulation Rule*, 17 C.F.R. § 180.2.

25. CEA section 4c(a)(5).

26. CFTC Interpretive Guidance and Policy Statement on Disruptive Practices, http://www.cftc.gov/ucm/groups/public/@newsroom/documents/file/dtpinterpretiveorder_qa.pdf.

27. http://www.sec.gov/answers/insider.htm.

28. http://www.sec.gov/news/speech/2008/spch021908lct.htm.

29. Ibid.

30. 17 C.F.R. § 240.10b5-1(b).

31. *TSC Industries, Inc. v. Northway, Inc.*, 426 U.S. 438, 449 (1976); see *Basic v. Levinson*, 485 U.S. 224, 231 (1988).

32. Thomas C. Newkirk and Melissa A. Robertson, *Speech by SEC Staff: Insider Trading—A U.S. Perspective*, 16th International Symposium on Economic Crime, Jesus College, Cambridge, England, September 19, 1998, http://www.sec.gov/news/speech/speecharchive/1998/spch221.htm.

33. *United States v. O'Hagan*, 117 S. Ct. at 2207.

34. Harry S. Davis, *Insider Trading and Compliance Answer Book 2014*, Ch. 1, "Overview of the Law of Insider Trading," 18.

35. *United States v. O'Hagan*, 117 S. Ct. at 2207.

36. https://www.sec.gov/news/speech/2008/spch021908lct.htm.

37. Ibid.

38. For an important court decision regarding tipping, see *U.S. v. Newman*, No. 13-1837, 2014 WL 6911278 (2d Cir. Dec. 10, 2014).

39. http://www.justice.gov/usao/priority-areas/financial-fraud/securities-fraud.

40. Rule 14-3e, insider trading liability does not necessarily require a breach of fiduciary duty or of trust or confidence as does insider trading brought under Section 10(b) of the Securities Exchange Act of 1934.
41. 15 U.S.C. § 78j(b).
42. 17 CFR 240.10b-5.
43. 17 CFR 240.10b5-1.
44. 17 CFR 240.10b5-2.
45. 17 CFR 240.10b5-2.
46. 15 U.S. Code § 78o(g).
47. 15 U.S. Code § 80b-4a.
48. Rule 10b5-1(c) sets forth the parameters under which an individual who is aware of material nonpublic information may still transact in the security in question; satisfying these parameters can provide an affirmative defense for trading while in possession of such information. As a whole, the affirmative defenses laid out in Rule 10b5-1(c) are designed to cover situations where an individual can demonstrate that the material nonpublic information was not a factor in his or her decision to buy or sell.
49. Marc E. Elovitz and Ida. Draim, *Insider Trading and Compliance Answer Book 2011-12*, Ch. 21, "Protecting Firms Through Policies and Procedures, Training, and Testing," 532.
50. Morrison Foerster, *2014 Insider Trading Annual Review*, 12.
51. Ibid. 11.

Chapter 7

1. See Audit Analytics 2010 Financial Statements, A Ten Year Comparison (May 2011).
2. http://www.sec.gov/News/Speech/Detail/Speech/1370541342996#.VL2orivF_aY.
3. http://www.sec.gov/News/Speech/Detail/Speech/1370541872207.
4. See http://www.sec.gov/news/studies/soxoffbalancerpt.pdf, page 10.
5. GAAP includes rules, procedures, and conventions that make up accepted accounting practices.
6. May 20, 2014, http://www.sec.gov/News/Speech/Detail/Speech/1370541872065.
7. Earnings press releases often contain excerpts of financial statements, and earnings calls include financial presentations. Issuer websites publish the company's financial information.
8. Foreign issuers file annual reports on Form 20-F and furnish quarterly reports on Form 6-K. Public companies also disseminate financial information in other SEC filings, including (1) registration statements

filed in connection with capital raising efforts; (2) current reports on Form 8-K that must be filed when certain material events occur; and (3) proxy statements describing insider compensation.

9. An unqualified audit report (or so-called "clean opinion") states than the financial statements are presented fairly in all material respects. Auditors review Forms 10-Q, but do not opine on them.

10. http://www.sec.gov/news/studies/soxoffbalancerpt.pdf, page 15. See also http://www.sec.gov/rules/interp/33-8350.htm and http://www.sec.gov/news/press/2003-179.htm. The MD&A is required by Section 303 of the Regulation S-K.

11. *TSC Ind. v. Northway, Inc.*, 426 U.S. 438, 449 (1976) and *Basic, Inc. v. Levinson*, 485 U.S. 224 (1988).

12. See SEC Staff Bulletin 99 regarding qualitative materiality factors.

13. http://www.sec.gov/interps/account/sab99.htm.

14. TSC Industries, 426 U.S. at 450.

15. The Supreme Court has defined *scienter* as "a mental state embracing intent to deceive, manipulate, or defraud." See *Ernst & Ernst v. Hochfelder*, 425 U.S. 185, 194 n. 2 (1976). See also Section 17(a)(1) of the 33 Act and Section 10(b) of the 34 Act.

16. The SEC alleged that the company's former senior managers engineered a scheme that created more than 6,000 phony invoices and then used bogus bank statements to reflect payment of the sham invoices, resulting in more than $1 billion in fictitious cash. See http://www.sec.gov/news/press/2011/2011-81.htm.

17. http://www.sec.gov/litigation/complaints/2011/comp21915.pdf.

18. Every Court of Appeals has held that a plaintiff may meet the scienter requirement by showing recklessness. See https://www.sec.gov/divisions/corpfin/guidance/wksi-waivers-interp.htm.

19. Nonaccountants often argue that they relied on the company's CPAs or independent auditors for accounting interpretation or were not otherwise involved in accounting determinations.

20. Companies, large and small, have transactions with customers, suppliers, and other business partners going on every day. Some have multiple products and services and/or business locations, including many with global operations involving overseas subsidiaries. Public companies must "account" for these business transactions by recording, accumulating, and summarizing the data and then translating it into financial statements so that users can digest the information on a quarterly basis. Inevitably, due to the complexities of the financial reporting process and volumes of data, errors may occur in compiling and calculating amounts.

21. Various 2007 credit crisis–related SEC Enforcement actions in which
    it alleged that investors were misled regarding exposures to subprime
    mortgage risks. American Home misled investors about the company's
    deteriorating financial condition as the subprime crisis emerged; Fannie/
    Freddie misled investors about the extent of each company's holdings
    of higher-risk mortgage loans; and Countrywide misled investors about
    significant credit risks taken in efforts to build and maintain the company's
    market share (http://www.sec.gov/spotlight/enf-actions-fc.shtml).

22. At HealthSouth, the SEC alleged that it engaged in a financial reporting
    fraud in which it overstated earnings by at least $1.4 billion. The founder,
    CEO, and chairman, Richard Scrushy, insisted that the company should
    make false entries to meet or exceed earnings expectations established
    by Wall Street analysts. http://www.sec.gov/litigation/complaints/
    comphealths.htm.

23. A lengthy report by Anton Valukas, the examiner in Lehman Brothers
    Holdings Inc., bankruptcy proceedings, highlighted an off–balance sheet
    scheme referred to as "Repo 105." The scheme involved treating certain
    repurchase agreements as "sales" rather than "financings" to get the
    associated debt off Lehman's books, thereby making its leverage appear
    better. Lehman's collapse and bankruptcy precipitated the 2007 credit
    crisis. Although Lehman was not prosecuted for engaging in Repo 105
    transactions, the Valukas report raised questions about whether Repo
    105 was an improper window dressing scheme designed to artificially
    reduce debt levels. See the report of Anton R. Valukas, Examiner, In re
    Lehman Brothers Holdings Inc., et al. 3/11/10. http://jenner.com/lehman/
    VOLUME%203.pdf. In the case of Enron, the SEC alleged that a series
    of complex structured finance transactions preceding Enron's bankruptcy
    were structured as "asset sales" for accounting and financial reporting
    purposes, allowing Enron to hide the true extent of its borrowings from
    investors and rating agencies (http://www.sec.gov/litigation/litreleases/
    lr18517.htm).

24. Fannie Mae portrayed volatile earnings as stable by booking adjustments
    less than required by accounting rules, resulting in the company not only
    exceeding Wall Street expectations, but also hitting the earnings per share
    targets necessary to trigger maximum bonuses. See AAER 2433 5/23/06
    and http://www.sec.gov/litigation/litreleases/2006/lr19710.htm.
    Diamond Foods hid the impact of higher costs it paid to nut suppliers by
    treating certain payments to growers as "advances" instead of inventory
    costs which boosted profits by improperly understating expenses (AAER
    3527 1/9/14). See also http://www.sec.gov/litigation/litreleases/2014/
    lr22902.htm.

25. Stock options Backdating Enforcement Actions, including Broadcom, UnitedHealth Group and Comverse. SEC Enforcement investigated over 100 companies in and around 2006 regarding stock options backdating schemes that instantly provided grantees with guaranteed profits because certain grants were made retroactively without disclosure when the price had already risen. http://www.sec.gov/news/testimony/2006/ts090606lt .htm, http://www.sec.gov/news/speech/2006/spch103006lct.htm. In the case of Tyco, the SEC alleged that the CEO, the CFO, and the chief legal officer failed to disclose multimillion-dollar loans they received from the company that they used for personal expenses including yachts, fine art, jewelry, luxury apartments, and vacations (AAER 1627 9/12/02).

26. SEC enforcement actions are public. Financial reporting cases are assigned Accounting and Auditing Enforcement Release (AAER) numbers. The SEC has AAERs going back to 1999 on its website.

27. In the case of HealthSouth, false accounting entries were made that primarily consisted of reducing a contra revenue account, called "contractual adjustment," and/or decreasing expenses and correspondingly increasing assets or decreasing liabilities. See http://www.sec.gov/litigation/ complaints/comphealths.htm.

28. See SEC's Report Pursuant to Section 704 of the Sarbanes-Oxley Act, page 25. In the case of AIG, the SEC alleged that AIG entered into two sham reinsurance transactions with Gen Re that had no economic substance but were designed to allow AIG improperly to add a total of $500 million in phony loss reserves to its balance sheet, which was done to quell analysts' criticism of AIG for a prior reduction of the reserves (http:// www.sec.gov/news/press/2006-19.htm).
In the case of Time Warner, the SEC alleged that it engaged in fraudulent round-trip transactions that boosted its online advertising revenue to mask the fact that it also experienced a business slowdown. See AAER 2216 3/21/05, http://www.sec.gov/litigation/litreleases/lr19147.htm.

29. Under GAAP, revenue is generally not recognized until it is earned and realized (or realizable), which means that a good or service must be delivered or performed and the amounts collected or collectible. For example, accounting rules generally would not allow a company to record revenue if the customer did not yet accept the product, the seller had future performance obligations, or the sales were subject to significant future contingencies. Alternatively, if the customer did not intend to pay because it was dependent upon resale by the customer to a third party, revenue recognition would generally be inappropriate.

30. Although GAAP may permit certain bill and hold transactions, the requirements are very strict. Raytheon's senior management held "executive

review sessions," in which they identified unfinished planes in the production process that could be "pulled forward" for a "financial delivery" to "bridge" certain "gaps" or "shortfalls" in performance targets (AAER 2449 6/28/06, http://www.sec.gov/litigation/admin/2006/33-8715.pdf). Diebold had customers sign contracts containing boilerplate bill and hold language and then recognized revenue on sales to its own company warehouses when customers had not requested bill and hold arrangements (http://www.sec.gov/litigation/complaints/2010/comp21543-diebold.pdf).

31. The SEC alleged that Sensormatic turned back its computer clock that recorded shipment dates (AAER 1017 3/25/98).

32. McKesson used side letters to hide contingencies, such as rights to cancel and continuing negotiations software sales (AAER 1467 10/15/01).

33. Xerox improperly shifted revenue from servicing and financing equipment leases, which was supposed to be recognized over the entire lease term, to periods earlier than permitted under GAAP (AAER 1542 4/11/02). Microstrategy assigned all the value of its software contracts to licenses, allocating nothing to servicing components, which were a substantial part of the arrangements, thus shifting all the revenue into earlier quarters (AAER 1350 12/14/00).

34. 704 Report, page 13, footnote 34. Expenses are outflows of a company's assets resulting in purchasing goods or services or otherwise incurring certain liabilities.

35. This could occur simply by making false entries or by treating an expense, such as a repair cost, as an addition to fixed assets, which would then be depreciated over time rather than reflected as a current period expense (generally, if the cost does not extend the asset's useful life, then accounting rules would require the cost to be expensed immediately, not capitalized). WorldCom engaged in what may be the largest capitalization scheme of all time, according to the SEC's amended complaint alleged that WorldCom overstated its net income by approximately $9 billion by improperly capitalizing and deferring, rather than immediately expensing, line costs (AAER 1585 6/27/02).

36. Waste Management improperly deferred current period expenses by extending the estimated useful lives of the company's garbage trucks and making unsupported increases to the trucks' salvages values. An unusual aspect of this case was that its independent auditor, Arthur Andersen, was aware of the scheme (AAER 1532 3/26/02 and 1410 6/19/01, http://www.sec.gov/litigation/complaints/complr17435.htm).

37. United Commercial Bank delayed including newer and lower appraisals in the valuations of collateral, despite knowing that certain loans or collateral

were nearly worthless (http://www.sec.gov/litigation/complaints/2011/comp22121.pdf).

A director of remediation at Ashland Oil reduced environmental reserves via large, across-the-board cuts that were undocumented and where no evidence existed that the estimates had been overstated before making arbitrary reductions (http://www.sec.gov/litigation/admin/2006/34-54830.pdf).

38. "Big bath" charges are also a form of earnings management whereby large write-downs are booked in an accounting period when performance may already be poor and analysts have already lowered expectations, or possibly during a period when the company is doing so well that it could record the charges and still meet expectations. This "clears the road" for lower future expenses. Sunbeam padded restructuring charges and created cookie-jar reserves (AAER 1395 5/15/01). Conagra improperly used tens of millions of excess post acquisition interest reserves to offset unrelated, unplanned-for, and unreserved-for losses and transferred excess reserves to "general" reserve accounts to be used to improperly reduce current legal and environmental expenses (http://www.sec.gov/litigation/complaints/2007/comp20206.pdf). Kimberly-Clark Corporation reallocated excess merger related reserves to other merger-related programs or new programs rather than reducing them, thus avoiding current period expenses, and released certain amounts of these reserves into earnings without adequate support (AAER 1533 3/27/02).

39. Rather than record a shrinkage of its inventory, the CFO of Rite Aid made adjusting entries to lower the cost of goods sold (AAER 1579 6/21/02). MiniScribe repackaged scrap and obsolete inventory and improperly included the costs in its ending inventory (AAER 1150 1999). Sinotech lied about the value of its primary operating drilling assets, including unsuccessfully trying to get its supplier to falsely justify the inflated values (AAER 3383 4/23/12, http://www.sec.gov/litigation/litreleases/2012/lr22341.htm).

40. Enron Corporation improperly used special purpose entities in off–balance sheet arrangements in order to keep certain debt off its books (AAER 1640 10/2/02). Adelphia improperly shifted liabilities onto off–balance sheet entities (704 Report page 29 and AAER 1599 6/24/02).

41. At Koss, the principal account and a senior accountant embezzled over $30 million by taking advantage of lax internal controls and hiding their actions by making many false journal entries (http://www.sec.gov/litigation/complaints/2011/comp22138.pdf).

42. SEC 704 Report, page 44.

43. Many SEC disclosure cases do not allege GAAP accounting violations, only false or misleading statements (or omissions) in sections of SEC filings (or other documents) that are not technically part of the financial statements. Segment reporting cases include Navistar and Paccar, in which the SEC alleged that the companies failed to comply with segment reporting requirements (AAER 3165 and 3462). Related parties—China Northeast Petroleum engaged in over one hundred undisclosed related party transactions that diverted millions in offering proceeds to insiders and their family members (AAER 3481). Classification of balances/revenue misclassification—Elan classified revenue from nonrecurring transactions as product revenue creating the false impression that revenue growth was due to drug sales in the normal course of business (http://www.sec .gov/litigation/complaints/comp19066.pdf). Expenses misclassification— Ashford.Com incorrectly classified certain marketing expenses as depreciation and amortization expenses because it excluded such expenses from non-GAAP financial metrics that it touted (AAER 1573 6/10/02). Cash flow misclassifications—Dynegy reported certain loan transactions as operating cash flow (AAER 1632 9/25/02); Enron improperly reported structured financing proceeds as operating cash flows rather than cash flow from financing activities (http://www.sec.gov/litigation/admin/2008/34-57210.pdf).

44. Fair presentation—Elan failed to disclose that its revenue was generated through "round-trip" transactions, in which its joint venture partners paid it license fees using money that Elan had provided, thus obscuring the true demand for technology and the company's ability to generate license revenue in the future. It thereby misled investors about the quality of the revenue, earnings, and cash flow that it generated from its joint venture program. Edison Schools—the company failed to disclose that a substantial portion of its revenues consisted of payments that it ultimately never got. The SEC indicated that even if Edison's accounting technically complied with GAAP, that such technical compliance would not insulate an issuer from enforcement action (AAER 1555 5/14/02). Channel stuffing—Involves accelerating revenue by selling to customers that already have a sufficient supply of inventory on hand. Unlike improper revenue recognition schemes in which accelerated revenue violates GAAP, disclosure-based channel stuffing frauds are "robbing Peter to pay Paul" omission cases as investors don't know that future performance will suffer because the company front-loaded sales by offering discounts to customers (http://www.sec.gov/news/press/2004-105.htm). Non-GAAP measures— Trump Hotels issued a press release announcing non-GAAP pro forma earnings that excluded a one-time charge, but failed to disclose the results

also had included a one-time gain, creating the misleading impression that the positive had been achieved through recurring operations (AAER 1499 1/16/02).

45. While most of these investigations are done on a parallel basis with the SEC, simultaneous, but separate, cooperation and communication typically occurs. During the Enron and WorldCom investigations, accounting cases became important for criminal authorities. However, criminal cases are much harder to prove because of the higher burden of proof ("beyond a reasonable doubt" versus the lower "preponderance of the evidence" in a civil case). The lack of criminal cases involving the 2007 credit crisis illustrates the difficulties in prosecuting individuals for criminal violations when the issues involve business judgment accounting estimates and valuation judgments. Criminal prosecutors are more likely to get involved in accounting cases when they may involve willful violations and intentional acts such as obstruction, self-dealing, collusion, misappropriation, embezzlement, and bribery.

46. http://www.sec.gov/News/Speech/Detail/Speech/1370541253621. Other SEC divisions with major role in financial reporting include the Office of the Chief Accountant and Division of Corporation Finance.

47. There is no specialized unit for accounting fraud cases as is the case for other areas including insider trading, FCPA, and asset management, among others.

48. The SEC publishes Select SEC and Market Data each year which contains a chart listing enforcement actions by primary classification. The classification for accounting and auditing related actions is called Issuer Reporting and Disclosure. Prior to 2011, Issuer Reporting and Disclosure actions included FCPA cases, however, in 2011, the SEC began reporting FCPA cases as a separate category. The chart reflects Issuer Reporting and Disclosure statistics adjusted to exclude FCPA for 2002 through 2010. In 2015, the SEC began disclosing the number of enforcement actions that were substantive (i.e. independent actions for violations, versus non-substantive delinquent filings or actions seeking bars). The enforcement director was quoted in a news article as stating that for accounting cases in 2014, 79 of the 96 were substantive; and that in 2015, 113 out of the 134 cases were substantive. See SEC Enforcement Chief Looks Back Over the Past Year, Think Advisor, October 19, 2015. The SEC complaints and administrative orders for these actions can be found on the SEC's website under Accounting and Auditing Enforcement Releases (AAERs).

49. http://www.wsj.com/articles/sec-gets-busy-with-accounting-investigations-1421797895?KEYWORDS=securities.

50. http://www.sec.gov/News/Speech/Detail/Speech/1370539845772.

51. http://www.sec.gov/whistleblower/reportspubs/annual-reports/owb-annual-report-2015.pdf.

52. In 2006, the stock options backdating scandal arose after Erik Lie, a finance professor at the University of Iowa, published a study that showed an uncanny number of cases where companies granted stock options to executives just before a sharp increase in their stocks (https://www.biz .uiowa.edu/faculty/elie/Grants-MS.pdf).

53. The SEC's Division of Economic Risk and Analysis works with Enforcement to develop analytic tools that can be used to identify potential issues.

54. SEC formed a Cross-Border Working Group that worked internally with other SEC Divisions and externally with the PCAOB and stock exchanges. The author of this chapter was a co-head of the Cross-Border Working Group.

55. http://s.wsj.net/public/resources/documents/BARRONS-SEC-050411.pdf.

56. http://www.sec.gov/News/PressRelease/Detail/PressRelease/1370539850572.

57. *Wall Street Journal*, January 20, 2015, http://www.wsj.com/articles/sec-gets-busy-with-accounting-investigations-1421797895.

58. http://www.wsj.com/articles/sec-gets-busy-with-accounting-investigations-1421797895.

59. According to a November 4, 2014, *Wall Street Journal* article, total restatements among companies reporting to the SEC have more than halved since a 2006 peak of nearly 1,850, but the number has decreased over the past six years. Audit Analytics, a service that analyzes financial information, has reported that the severity of measures (such as the amount restated, negative impact on net income, average number of issues restated, average number accounting periods restated) has also declined.

60. At the beginning of most financial reporting investigations, unless there has been a restatement that occurred involving fictitious accounting or admissions (which rarely occur), it is generally unclear whether financial statement errors came about due to fraud.

61. The nature of the investigation conducted by the SEC will differ depending on whether a company has restated or not. If a restatement has already occurred, the focus may in large part be on establishing who was responsible and their intent, although they will be on the lookout for other material errors. If the company decides to "dig in" and vigorously defend against any allegations, the dynamics will be different because the staff will also need to establish that GAAP violations occurred.

62. A 2010 COSO report indicated that 50 percent of the companies committing accounting fraud traded on Nasdaq, 27 percent on the NYSE/Amex, and the rest OTC (bulletin board and pink sheets).

63. http://www.coso.org/IC.htm.

64. See Staff Accounting Bulletins 99 regarding materiality and 108 regarding error corrections.

65. It is possible that the SEC may target violations of Section 303 of Sarbanes Oxley, which prohibits any officer or director, or person acting under their direction, to take any action to fraudulently influence, coerce, manipulate, or mislead any independent accountant.

66. While the SEC has mostly limited clawback actions to CEOs and CFOs that engaged in misconduct, in the future, the SEC may be more aggressive in seeking them from innocent officers.

Chapter 8

1. Federal Reserve Board, Office of the Comptroller of the Currency, Federal Deposit Insurance Corporation, Office of Thrift Supervision, National Credit Union Administration, Federal Trade Commission, Department of Housing and Urban Development. Excluded from CFPB oversight were entities supervised by state insurance agencies, the SEC and the CFTC, as well as insurance- and securities-related products and services regulated by these agencies.

2. http://www.treasury.gov/initiatives/Documents/FinalReport_web.pdf, *Financial Regulatory Reform: A New Foundation*, 2009, page 7.

3. Dodd-Frank Act § 1021(b) (codified at 12 U.S.C. § 5511).

4. Dodd-Frank Act § 1021(c) (codified at 12 U.S.C. § 5511).

5. http://www.consumerfinance.gov/newsroom/prepared-remarks-of-cfpb-director-richard-cordray-on-the-bank-of-america-enforcement-action-press-call/.

6. http://www.consumerfinance.gov/newsroom/cfpb-capital-one-probe/.

7. 15 U.S. C § 45.

8. Wheeler-Lea Act of 1938, P.L. 75-447, 52 Stat. 111 (1938).

9. https://www.ftc.gov/public-statements/1980/12/ftc-policy-statement-unfairness.

10. https://www.ftc.gov/public-statements/1983/10/ftc-policy-statement-deception.

11. FTC Improvement Act of 1994—added Section 5(n) to 15 U.S.C. § 45.

12. In determining whether an act or practice is unfair, the FTC may consider established public policies as evidence to be considered with all other evidence, though such public policy considerations may not serve as a primary basis for such determination. 15 U.S.C. § 45(n).

13. http://www.ftc.gov/public-statements/2003/05/ftcs-use-unfairness-authority-its-rise-fall-and-resurrection. Public statement of J. Howard

Beales, former director of the FTC Bureau of Consumer Protection, May 30, 2003, *The FTC's Use of Unfairness Authority: Its Rise, Fall, and Resurrection.* In his remarks, Director Beales stated, "Commission precedent incorporated in the statutory codification makes clear that deception is properly viewed as a subset of unfairness." And at footnote 44 states, "The Commission's unfairness jurisdiction provisions a more general basis for action against acts or practices which cause significant consumer injury. This part of our jurisdiction is broader than that involving deception, and the standards for its exercise are correspondingly more stringent. It requires the complete analysis of a practice which may be harmful to consumers. To put the point another way, unfairness is the set of general principles of which deception is a particularly well-established and streamlined subset."

14. Kathlyn L. Farrell, "Managing UDAAP Compliance Risk in Financial Institutions," *Journal of Taxation and Regulation of Financial Institutions*, November/December 2013, Vol27/No 2.

15. Including national banks, state member banks, state nonmember banks, federal branches, and agencies of foreign banks. 15 USC 54(f).

16. OTS authority was subsumed by the OCC following enactment of the Dodd-Frank Act.

17. This authority was subsequently repealed by the Dodd-Frank Act.

18. Subpart B of the Federal Reserve's Regulation AA is referred to as the Credit Practices Rule and is intended to declare certain acts or practices as unlawful. It covers unfair credit contract provisions, unfair or deceptive practices involving cosigners, unfair late charges, and exemptions for states (which may be granted by the Federal Reserve Board if "the state administers and enforces a state law that provides consumers with protection equivalent to or greater than the Board's rule"). The Dodd-Frank Act repealed the Federal Reserve Board's rule-writing authority under the FTC Act, and the Federal Reserve Board published a proposed rule on August 27, 2014, to repeal its Regulation AA (79 FR 51115).

19. An example is dishonoring credit card convenience checks without notice. The OTS and FDIC brought enforcement actions against a credit card issuer that sent convenience checks with stated credit limits and expiration dates to customers. For a significant percentage of consumers, the issuer reduced credit lines after the checks were presented, and then the issuer dishonored the consumers' checks.
Substantial injury. Customers paid returned-check fees and may have experienced a negative impact on credit history.
Not outweighed by benefits. The card issuer later reduced credit limits based on credit reviews. Based on the particular facts involved in the case, the

harm to consumers from the dishonored convenience checks outweighed any benefit of using new credit reviews.

Not reasonably avoidable. Consumers reasonably relied on their existing credit limits and expiration dates on the checks when deciding to use them for a payment. Consumers had received no notice that the checks they used were being dishonored until they learned from the payees. Thus, consumers could not reasonably have avoided the injury. CFPB Supervision and Exam Manual, October 2012. Case cited as footnote 8 on page UDAAP 4 "*In re American Express Bank, FSB* (Cease and Desist Order WN-09-016, and Order of Assessment of a Civil Money Penalty for $250,000, WN-09-017, June 29, 2009) OTS Docket No. 15648; *In re American Express Centurion Bank* (Cease and Desist Order, June 30, 2009) Docket FDIC-09-251b, available at http://www.fdic.gov/news."

An example from a federal enforcement action involves misrepresentation about loan terms.

In 2004, the FTC sued a mortgage broker advertising mortgage refinance loans at "3.5% fixed payment 30-year loan" or "3.5% fixed payment for 30 years," implying that the offer was for a 30-year loan with a 3.5% fixed interest rate. Instead, the FTC claimed that the broker offered adjustable rate mortgages (ARMs) with an option to pay various amounts, including a minimum monthly payment that represented only a portion of the required interest. As a result, unpaid interest was added to the principal of the loan, resulting in negative amortization.

Practice likely to mislead. The FTC claimed that the advertisements were misleading because they compared payments on a mortgage that fully amortized to payments on a nonamortizing loan with payments that increased after the first year. In addition, the FTC claimed that after application, the broker provided Truth in Lending Act (TILA) disclosures that misstated the annual percentage rate (APR) and that failed to state that the loan was a variable rate loan.

Reasonable consumer perspective. It was reasonable for consumers to believe that they would obtain fixed-rate mortgages, based on the representations.

Material representation. The representations were material because consumers relied on them when making the decision to refinance their fully amortizing 30-year fixed loans. As a result, the consumers ended up with adjustable rate mortgages that would negatively amortize if they made payments at the stated 3.5% payment rate. CFPB Supervision and Exam Manual, October 2012. Case cited as footnote 13 on page UDAAP 8. "FTC v. Chase Financial Funding, Inc., No. SACV04-549 (C.D.Cal. 2004), Stipulated Preliminary Injunction, available at http://www.ftc.gov/os/caselist/0223287/0223287.shtm." Also footnote 14 makes clarification regarding negative amortization—"In 2008, amendments to the Truth in Lending Act's Regulation Z were adopted to prohibit certain advertising practices, such as misleading advertising of fixed rates and payments, for credit secured by a dwelling. Similar practices could be identified as deceptive in other product lines. See 73 Fed. Reg. 44522 (July 30, 2008) (promulgating 12 CFR 226.24), which has since been recodified as 12 CFR 1026.24."

20. Section 1001 of the Dodd-Frank Act.

21. Section 1011 of the Dodd-Frank Act.

22. Section 1021 of the Dodd-Frank Act.

23. Section 1025 of the Dodd-Frank Act.

24. Section 1024 of the Dodd-Frank Act.

25. Section 1024 of the Dodd-Frank Act.

26. Sections 1031 and 1036 of the Dodd-Frank Act.

27. CFPB Supervision and Exam Manual, page UDAAP 5, footnote 10 references FTC Policy Statement on Deception, available at http://www .ftc.gov/bcp/policystmt/ad-decept.htm, and instructs examiners to be informed by the FTC's standard for deception.

28. CFPB has offices to address these groups that were mandated as part of Title X of the Dodd-Frank Act.

29. Kate Davidson, "Trying to Stay Above Politics: A Conversation with Richard Cordray," *American Banker*, March 23, 2013.

30. CFPB Supervision and Examination Manual, October 2012, pages UDAAP 3 and UDAAP 7.

31. For example, the CFPB announced an enforcement action against Capital One to address the CFPB's findings of UDAAP violations related to credit card "add-on" products. As part of the press statement, the CFPB also announced the release of two Consumer Advisories and one Compliance Bulletin (2012-06) that the CFPB stated "puts other institutions on notice that the CFPB will not tolerate deceptive marketing practices, and institutions will be held responsible for the actions of their third-party vendors." http://www.consumerfinance.gov/newsroom/cfpb-capital-one-probe/.

32. Became effective July 2012—though follows from NASD Suitability Rules.

33. FINRA Rule 2111 (a) http://finra.complinet.com/en/display/display_main .html?rbid=2403&element_id=9859.

34. http://files.consumerfinance.gov/f/201503_cfpb_consumer-response-annual-report-2014.pdf.

35. They were: (1) Capital One Bank, July 2012, $140 million restitution, $25 million CMP, 2 million customers; coordination with OCC. (2) Discover Bank, September 2012, $200 million restitution, $14 million CMP,

3.5 million customers; coordination with FDIC. (3) American Express, October 2012, $85 million restitution, $27.5 million CMP, 250,000 customers; coordination with FDIC.

36. http://www.consumerfinance.gov/newsroom/cfpb-state-authorities-order-ocwen-to-provide-2-billion-in-relief-to-homeowners-for-servicing-wrongs/.

37. The CFPB was statutorily required to establish an Office of Servicemember Affairs, an Office of Older Americans, and an Office of the Student Ombudsman.

38. www.consumerfinance.gov/guidance/supervision/manual Overview p4.

39. Some examination objectives cited here have been paraphrased. For actual wording, go to http://www.consumerfinance.gov/guidance/supervision/manual/.

40. See page 5 of CFPB Supervisory Highlights, August 2013. http://files.consumerfinance.gov/f/201308_cfpb_supervisory-highlights_august.pdf.

41. CFPB Supervision and Examination Manual, v2, Compliance Management Review CMR 1.

42. http://files.consumerfinance.gov/f/201210_cfpb_supervisory-highlights-fall-2012.pdf, page 4.

43. CFPB Supervision and Examination Manual, v2, Compliance Management Review, CMR 2.

44. CFPB Bulletin 2013-06, June 25, 2013, *Responsible Business Conduct: Self-Policing, Self-Reporting, Remediation, and Cooperation.*

45. http://www.consumerfinance.gov/newsroom/prepared-remarks-of-cfpb-director-richard-cordray-at-the-national-association-of-attorneys-general/.

46. LIBOR scandals.

47. U.S. mortgage servicing and foreclosures actions (jointly by State AGs and prudential regulators).

48. CFPB Supervision and Examination Manual, Version 2, October 2012, page CMR 1.

49. Kathlyn L. Farrell, "Managing UDAAP Compliance Risk in Financial Institutions," *Journal of Taxation and Regulation of Financial Institutions*, November/December 2013, Vol27/No 2.

50. Latham & Watkins Client Alert White Paper number 1782.

51. 12 C.F.R.1080 6 (c).

Chapter 9

1. Henry, James S., Tax Justice Network, *The Price of Offshore Revisited: New Estimates for "Missing" Global Private Wealth, Income, Inequality, and Lost Taxes*, July 2012, 5, http://www.taxjustice.net/2014/01/17/price-offshore-revisited/.

2. It is a criminal offense for any person to willfully attempt to evade paying taxes. (Internal Revenue Code (IRC) 26 U.S. Code § 7201). Yet it is not illegal for individuals to use legal means to avoid paying taxes. Tax avoidance does not involve concealment or misrepresentation, whereas tax evasion is taking some form of "affirmative act . . . such as deceit, subterfuge, camouflage, concealment, attempts to color or obscure events, or make things seem other than they are." See Internal Revenue Services (IRS) Manual, Part 25: Special Topics, Chapter 1: Fraud Handbook, Section 25.1.1.2.4, Definitions of Fraud: Avoidance vs. Evasion, January 23, 2014.

3. U.S. Senate Permanent Subcommittee on Investigations, *Offshore Tax Evasion: The Effort to Collect Unpaid Taxes on Billions in Hidden Offshore Accounts*, Majority and Minority Staff Report, February 26, 2014, final August 20, 2014 (Washington, D.C.), 9.

4. "Six Corporate Executives and Six Corporate Entities Indicted for Orchestrating a $500 Million Offshore Asset Protection, Securities Fraud, and Money Laundering Scheme," press release, September 9, 2014, on FBI's website, http://www.fbi.gov/newyork/press-releases/2014/six-corporate-executives-and-six-corporate-entities-indicted-for-orchestrating-a-500-million-offshore-asset-protection-securities-fraud-and-money-laundering-scheme.

5. U.S. Senate Permanent Subcommittee on Investigations, *Crime and Secrecy: The Use of Offshore Banks and Companies Hearings before the Permanent Subcommittee on Investigations*, Sr. Hrg. 98-151, 98th Cong., 1st sess., May 15, 16, and 24, 1983, 7, https://www.ncjrs.gov/App/Publications/abstract.aspx?ID=91139.

6. U.S. Government Accountability Office ("GAO"), Report to the Committee on Finance, U.S. Senate, *Tax Administration Additional Time Needed to Complete Offshore Tax Evasion Examinations*, GAO-07-237 (Washington, D.C.), March 2007, 7–8.

7. U.S. Senate Permanent Subcommittee on Investigations, *Tax Haven Abuses: The Enablers, the Tools, and the Secrecy*, Majority and Minority Staff Report, August 1, 2006, final January 2007 (Washington, D.C.), 11, http://www.hsgac.senate.gov/subcommittees/investigations/hearings/tax-haven-abuses-the-enablers-the-tools-and-secrecy.

8. Ibid.

9. Ibid.

10. IRS, "Abusive Offshore Tax Avoidance Schemes—Talking Points," http://www.irs.gov/Businesses/Small-Businesses-&-Self-Employed/Abusive-Offshore-Tax-Avoidance-Schemes-Talking-Points, accessed November 23, 2014.

11. U.S. GAO Report, Testimony Before the Committee on Finance, U.S. Senate, *Tax Compliance Offshore Financial Activity Creates Enforcement Issues for IRS*, Statement of Michael Brostek, Director Strategic Issues Team, GAO-09-478T (Washington, D.C.), March 17, 2009, 4.

12. Ibid.

13. IRS, "Abusive Offshore Tax Avoidance Schemes—Talking Points," http://www.irs.gov/Businesses/Small-Businesses-&-Self-Employed/Abusive-Offshore-Tax-Avoidance-Schemes-Talking-Points, accessed November 23, 2014.

14. IRS defines an offshore promoter as "a person or entity who markets offshore arrangements to the public. The promoter can be financial institution, lawyer, accountant, broker, financial planner, or other individual." See IRS, "Abusive Offshore Tax Avoidance Schemes—Glossary of Offshore Terms," http://www.irs.gov/Businesses/Small-Businesses-&-Self-Employed/Abusive-Offshore-Tax-Avoidance-Schemes-Glossary-of-Offshore-Terms.

15. U.S. GAO, Report to the Committee on Finance, U.S. Senate, *Tax Administration Additional Time Needed to Complete Offshore Tax Evasion Examinations*, GAO-07-237 (Washington, D.C.), March 2007, 7.

16. A "John Doe summons is any summons where the name of the taxpayer under investigation is unknown and therefore not specifically identified." See IRS website, http://www.irs.gov/irm/part25/irm_25-005-007.html#d0e81, accessed March 22, 2015.

17. U.S. GAO, Report to the Committee on Finance, U.S. Senate, *Tax Administration Additional Time Needed to Complete Offshore Tax Evasion Examinations*, GAO-07-237, (Washington D.C.), March 2007, p. 7–8; U.S. Senate Permanent Subcommittee on Investigations, *Offshore Tax Evasion: The Effort to Collect Unpaid Taxes on Billions in Hidden Offshore Accounts*, Majority and Minority Staff Report, February 26, 2014, final August 20, 2014 (Washington D.C.), p. 144.

18. U.S. GAO, Report to the Committee on Finance, U.S Senate, *Tax Administration Additional Time Needed to Complete Offshore Tax Evasion Examinations*, GAO-07-237, (Washington D.C.), March 2007, p. 8.

19. Ibid., 9.

20. Ibid., 8.

21. 26 U.S. Code Chapter 3 and 26 U.S. Code Chapter 61.

22. U.S. Senate Permanent Subcommittee on Investigations, *Tax Haven Banks and U.S. Tax Compliance*, Staff Report, July 17, 2008, final September 26, 2008 (Washington, D.C.), 9, http://www.hsgac.senate.gov/subcommittees/investigations/issues/tax-havens-and-abusive-tax-schemes. In 2008, Birkenfeld pleaded guilty to conspiracy to defraud the IRS to

hide $200 million offshore and evade $7.2 million for a U.S. client. In 2012, Birkenfeld received a whistleblower award of $104 million for the information he supplied to the U.S. regarding UBS AG. (See David Kocieniewski, "Whistle-Blower Awarded $104 Million by IRS," NYTimes .com, September 11, 2012).

23. U.S. Senate Permanent Subcommittee on Investigations, *Tax Haven Banks and U.S. Tax Compliance*, Staff Report, July 17, 2008, final September 26, 2008 (Washington, D.C.), p. 2, 9–15.

24. *United States v. UBS AG*, Case No. 09-60033-CR-COHN (S.D. Fla. 2009), Deferred Prosecution Agreement, 2/18/09 (hereafter referred to "UBS DPA")—UBS AG paid $780 million in fines; "Swiss Bank Pleads Guilty in Manhattan Federal Court to Conspiracy to Evade Taxes," press release, January 3, 2013, on U.S. DOJ website, http://www.justice.gov/ usao/nys/pressreleases/January13/WegelinPleaPR.php, accessed November 28, 2014—Wegelin & Co. paid $74 million in fines; "Credit Suisse Sentenced for Conspiracy to Help U.S. Taxpayers Hide Offshore Accounts from Internal Revenue Service," press release, November 21, 2014, on U.S. DOJ website, http://www.justice.gov/opa/pr/credit-suisse-sentenced-conspiracy-help-us-taxpayers-hide-offshore-accounts-internal-revenue, accessed December 9, 2014—Credit Suisse AG paid $2.6 billion in fines and restitutions.

25. UBS DPA, 3.

26. "Credit Suisse Pleads Guilty to Conspiracy to Aid and Assist U.S. Taxpayers in Filing False Returns" press release, May 19, 2014, on DOJ website, http://www.justice.gov/tax/2014/txdv14531.htm.

27. Ibid.; "Remarks as Prepared for Delivery by Deputy Attorney General James M. Cole Announcing Guilty Plea in Credit Suisse Offshore Tax Evasion Case Washington, D.C.," press release, May 19, 2014, on DOJ website, http://www.justice.gov/tax/pr/remarks-prepared-delivery-deputy-attorney-general-james-m-cole-announcing-guilty-plea-credit.

28. "Swiss Bank Pleads Guilty in Manhattan Federal Court to Conspiracy to Evade Taxes," press release, January 3, 2013, on U.S. DOJ website, http:// www.justice.gov/usao/nys/pressreleases/January13/WegelinPleaPR.php.

29. The $74 million includes a 2012 forfeiture of $16.2 million from Wegelin's correspondent bank account. "Swiss Bank Pleads Guilty in Manhattan Federal Court to Conspiracy to Evade Taxes," press release, January 3, 2013, on U.S. DOJ website, http://www.justice.gov/usao/nys/ pressreleases/January13/WegelinPleaPR.php; Rupert Neate, "Oldest Swiss Bank Wegelin to Close After Admitting Aiding U.S. Tax Evasion," *The Guardian*, January 4, 2013.

30. UBS DPA, Exhibit C, Statement of Facts; *United States v. Credit Suisse AG*, Plea Agreement (E.D. Va Alexandria Div. No. 1:14-CR-1:14CR2188, 2014), Statement of Facts, May 19, 2014.

31. Form W-8BEN (for individuals) and Form W-8BEN-E (for entities) are the "Certificate of Status of Beneficial Owner for U.S. Tax Withholding and Reporting," which are completed to certify the foreign status for U.S. tax treaty benefits and U.S. tax withholding purposes.

32. UBS DPA, Exhibit C, Statement of Facts; *United States v. Credit Suisse AG*, Plea Agreement (E.D. Va Alexandria Div. No. 1:14-CR-1:14CR2188, 2014), Statement of Facts, May 19, 2014; and "Swiss Bank Pleads Guilty in Manhattan Federal Court to Conspiracy to Evade Taxes," press release, January 3, 2013, on U.S. DOJ website, http://www.justice.gov/usao/nys/pressreleases/January13/WegelinPleaPR.php.

33. UBS DPA, Exhibit C, Statement of Facts; U.S. Senate Permanent Subcommittee on Investigations, *Tax Haven Banks and U.S. Tax Compliance*, Staff Report, July 17, 2008, final September 26, 2008 (Washington, D.C.), 99; *United States v. Credit Suisse AG*, Plea Agreement (E.D. Va Alexandria Div. No. 1:14-CR-1:14CR2188, 2014), Statement of Facts, May 19, 2014; and "Swiss Bank Pleads Guilty in Manhattan Federal Court to Conspiracy to Evade Taxes," press release, January 3, 2013, on U.S. DOJ website, http://www.justice.gov/usao/nys/pressreleases/January13/WegelinPleaPR.php.

34. UBS DPA, Exhibit C, Statement of Facts, and *United States v. Credit Suisse AG*, Plea Agreement (E.D. Va Alexandria Div. No. 1:14-CR-1:14CR2188, 2014), Statement of Facts, May 19, 2014.

35. Ibid.

36. U.S. DOJ, "Offshore Compliance Initiative," http://www.justice.gov/tax/offshore_compliance_intiative.htm.

37. U.S. Senate Permanent Subcommittee on Investigations, *Offshore Tax Evasion: The Effort to Collect Unpaid Taxes on Billions in Hidden Offshore Accounts*, Majority and Minority Staff Report, February 26, 2014, final August 20, 2014 (Washington D.C.), 10.

38. Ibid., 10–11.

39. Ibid., 147–149.

40. Ibid.

41. 31 C.F.R. § 103.24—taxpayers must file the Report of Foreign Bank and Financial Accounts (currently Form 114, formerly known as Form TD F 90.22-1) every year with the Department of Treasury.

42. U.S. Senate Permanent Subcommittee on Investigations, *Offshore Tax Evasion: The Effort to Collect Unpaid Taxes on Billions in Hidden Offshore*

Accounts, Majority and Minority Staff Report, February 26, 2014, final
August 20, 2014 (Washington D.C.), p. 19.

43. Ibid.

44. Ibid., citing a Subcommittee briefing by the U.S. DOJ (dated December 17, 2013).

45. Ibid., 13—"U.S.-source income refers to income that originates in the United States, such as dividends paid on U.S. stock; capital gains paid on sales of U.S. stock or real estate; royalties paid on U.S. assets; rent paid on U.S. property; interest paid on U.S. deposits; and other types of 'fixed, determinable, annual, or periodic income.'"

46. Ibid., 14.

47. Ibid., 13.

48. "United States and Switzerland Issue Joint Statement Regarding Tax Evasion Investigations," press release, August 29, 2013, on U.S. DOJ website, http://www.justice.gov/tax/2013/txdv13975.htm.

49. Joint Statement Between U.S. DOJ and Swiss Federal Department of Finance, August 29, 2013, http://www.justice.gov/iso/opa/resour ces/7532013829164644664074.pdf.

50. Ibid.

51. "BSI SA of Lugano, Switzerland, Is First Bank to Reach Resolution Under Justice Department's Swiss Bank Program," press release, March 30, 2015, on U.S. DOJ website, http://www.justice.gov/opa/pr/bsi-sa-lugano-switzerland-first-bank-reach-resolution-under-justice-department-s-swiss-bank.

52. U.S. DOJ, "Tax Division Press Releases," http://www.justice.gov/tax/tax-division-press-releases.

53. U.S. DOJ, "The Tax Division's further comments about the Program for Non-Prosecution Agreements or Non-Target Letters for Swiss Banks," June 5, 2014, 1, http://www.justice.gov/tax/2014/Further_Comments_on_Program_for_NonProsecution_Agreements_NonTarget_Letters_%20 for_Swiss_Banks.pdf.

54. 26 U.S. Code Chapter 4.

55. "Chapter 3 contains reporting and withholding rules relating to payments of certain U.S. source income (e.g., dividends on stock of U.S. companies) to non-U.S. persons. Chapter 61 and Section 3406 address the reporting and withholding requirements for various types of payments made to certain U.S. persons (U.S. non-exempt recipients)." U.S. Treasury Department. Office of Public Affairs, "Fact Sheet: FATCA Amendments and Coordination Regulation," February 20, 2014, https://www.treasury .gov/resource-center/tax-policy/treaties/Documents/022014%20-%20 FATCA%20Fact%20Sheet.pdf.

56. U.S. Treasury Department. Office of Public Affairs, "Fact Sheet: FATCA Amendments and Coordination Regulation," February 20, 2014, https://www.treasury.gov/resource-center/tax-policy/treaties/Documents/022014%20-%20FATCA%20Fact%20Sheet.pdf.

57. 26 U.S. Code § 1471 (d)(2)—"financial account" means, with respect to any financial institution, (a) any depository account maintained by such financial institution,(b) any custodial account maintained by such financial institution, and (c) any equity or debt interest in such financial institution [other than interests which are regularly traded on an established securities market]."

58. Aside from a few exceptions for grandfathered payments, the term "withholdable payment" generally means a payment of U.S.-source fixed determinable annual or periodic (FDAP) income, such as interest, dividends, services, and so on, which is made after June 30, 2014.

59. U.S. Senate Permanent Subcommittee on Investigations, *Offshore Tax Evasion: The Effort to Collect Unpaid Taxes on Billions in Hidden Offshore Accounts*, 17–18.

60. Ibid.

61. Ibid.

62. The financial thresholds may vary depending on joint filing or U.S. residency status. See IRS, "Do I Need to File Form 8938, Statement of Specified Foreign Financial Assets," updated November 19, 2014, http://www.irs.gov/Businesses/Corporations/Do-I-need-to-file-Form-8938-Statement-of-Specified-Foreign-Financial-Assets.

63. IRC 26 U.S. Code § 1471(c).

64. Certificate of Status of Beneficial Owner for U.S. Tax Withholding and Reporting, for Entities.

65. To accomplish this scheme, the defendants created shell companies in Belize, Nevis, and West Indies that were controlled by nominees in order to conceal the companies' true owners and their ownership in microcap securities. With this anonymity, the defendants were able to manipulate a penny stock's price and hide the ownership of the security's sale proceeds. See "Six Corporate Executives and Six Corporate Entities Indicted for Orchestrating a $500 Million Offshore Asset Protection, Securities Fraud, and Money Laundering Scheme," press release, September 9, 2014, on FBI's website, http://www.fbi.gov/newyork/press-releases/2014/six-corporate-executives-and-six-corporate-entities-indicted-for-orchestrating-a-500-million-offshore-asset-protection-securities-fraud-and-money-laundering-scheme.

66. Miriam L. Fisher, Brian C. McManus, Latham & Watkins LLP, "Bandfield Confirms Aggressive FATCA Enforcement Tactics," *Law360 .com*, September 16, 2014, http://www.law360.com/articles/577558/ bandfield-confirms-aggressive-fatca-enforcement-tactics.

67. Ibid.

68. If a financial intuition has information or knowledge that a reasonably prudent person would question the accuracy and completeness of a W-8 Form, then the financial institution is required to conduct further due diligence. See IRS, "Instructions for the Requester of Forms W–8BEN, W–8BEN–E, W–8ECI, W–8EXP, and W–8IMY, http://www.irs.gov/ pub/irs-pdf/iw8.pdf.

69. Rita Tricher, Paul Vieira (contributor), "Canada Banks Tally Their Tax-Compliance Tab," *Wall Street Journal*, July 27, 2014.

70. Joe Harpaz, "With Clock Ticking on FATCA, Financial Firms Brace for Headaches," *Forbes*, April 2, 2014, quoting Kevin Sullivan, head of North American tax operations for BNP Paribas.

71. Miriam L. Fisher, Brian C. McManus, Latham & Watkins LLP, "Bandfield Confirms Aggressive FATCA Enforcement Tactics," *Law360 .com*, September 16, 2014, http://www.law360.com/articles/577558/ bandfield-confirms-aggressive-fatca-enforcement-tactics.

72. Ibid.

73. From 2003 to 2011, HSBC Swiss private bank division was not registered as a brokerage or advisory business with the SEC but engaged in a cross-border banking business advising U.S. taxpayers. "SEC Charges HSBC's Swiss Private Banking Unit with Providing Unregistered Services to U.S. Clients," press release, November 25, 2014, on SEC website, http://www .sec.gov/News/PressRelease/Detail/PressRelease/1370543534789.

74. *In the Matter of HSBC Private Bank (Suisse), SA*, SEC File No. 3-16288, November 25, 2014, 5–7, http://www.sec.gov/litigation/admin/2014/34-73681.pdf. In 2003, HSBC Private Bank created a desk to service North American clients and to consolidate accounts with a small number of relationship managers in order to monitor U.S. registration requirements. In 2005, Internal Audit determined there were deficiencies in complying with the cross-border policy. For example, there were 76 accounts that did not transfer to the North American desk, and investment instructions were being sent by clients residing in the United States. In 2007, the HSBC compliance department conducted a review and determined that the firm was still not fully compliant with firm's cross-border policy.

75. "SEC Charges HSBC's Swiss Private Banking Unit with Providing Unregistered Services to U.S. Clients," press release, November 25,

2014, on SEC website, http://www.sec.gov/News/PressRelease/Detail/ PressRelease/1370543534789.

76. Miriam L. Fisher, Brian C. McManus, Latham & Watkins LLP, "Bandfield Confirms Aggressive FATCA Enforcement Tactics," *Law360 .com*, September 16, 2014, http://www.law360.com/articles/577558/ bandfield-confirms-aggressive-fatca-enforcement-tactics.

77. John D. McKinnon, "U.S. Initials Deal with China to Curb Offshore Tax Evasion," *Wall Street Journal*, June 26, 2014.

78. Neil Maclucas, "Switzerland, EU to Share Tax Information," *Wall Street Journal*, May 27, 2015.

79. OECD, "Standard for Automatic Exchange of Financial Account Information in Tax Matters," July 21, 2014, http://www.oecd.org/tax/ exchange-of-tax-information/standard-for-automatic-exchange-of-financial-information-in-tax-matters.htm.

80. OECD, Global Forum on Transparency, "AEOI: Status of Commitments," December 11, 2015, http://www.oecd.org/tax/ transparency/AEOI-commitments.pdf; OECD, "Signatories of the Multilateral Competent Authority Agreement and Intended First Information Exchange Date," December 21, 2015, http://www.oecd.org/ tax/exchange-of-tax-information/MCAA-Signatories.pdf.

81. Multilateral Competent Authority Agreement outlines the scope of information that jurisdictions will exchange, as well as the agreement to comply with the common standards of due diligence outlined by the CRS. OECD, Global Forum on Transparency, "AEOI: Status of Commitments," December 11, 2015, http://www.oecd.org/tax/ transparency/AEOI-commitments.pdf; OECD, "Signatories of the Multilateral Competent Authority Agreement and Intended First Information Exchange Date," December 21, 2015, http://www.oecd.org/ tax/exchange-of-tax-information/MCAA-Signatories.pdf.

82. KPMG. "Automatic Exchange of Information. The Common Reporting Standard," Publication number 131579, September 2014.

83. Ibid.

84. OECD, "Standard for Automatic Exchange of Financial Account Information in Tax Matters: Implementation Handbook," August 7, 2015, http://www.oecd.org/tax/exchange-of-tax-information/implementation-handbook-standard-for-automatic-exchange-of-financial-account-information-in-tax-matters.htm.

85. OECD, "Update on Voluntary Disclosure Programmes: A Pathway to Tax Compliance," August 7, 2015, http://www.oecd.org/ctp/exchange-of-tax-information/update-on-voluntary-disclosure-programmes-a-pathwaypto-tax-compliance.htm.

86. FATF, "International Standards on Combating Money Laundering and the
     Finance of Terrorism and Proliferation. The FATF Recommendations,"
     February 16, 2012, Recommendation 3, p. 34–35 and Definitions
     ("Designated Categories of Offenses"), p. 112–113.

87. Alan Lau and Chua Kong Ping, KPMG, "Devil's in the Details with Tax
     Cheats," *The Business Times*, September 12, 2013, http://www.kpmg.com/
     sg/en/pressroom/pages/mc20130912.aspx.

88. Valerie Chianuri, Davis Wright Tremaine LLP, "The Fourth European
     Union Anti-Money Laundering Directive and its effects on financial
     institutions operating in the EU," *Lexology.com*, August 25, 2015, http://
     www.lexology.com/library/detail.aspx?g=51b9e399-0f2f-471b-b930-
     d688bf6dfe65.

89. 18 U.S.C. § 1956 (c) (7).

90. FATF, "FATF Recommendations. Media Narrative," p. 2, http://www
     .fatf-gafi.org/media/fatf/documents/Press%20handout%20FATF%20
     Recommendations%202012.pdf.

91. Alan Lau and Chua Kong Ping, KPMG, "Devil's in the Details with Tax
     Cheats," *The Business Times*, September 12, 2013, http://www.kpmg.com/
     sg/en/pressroom/pages/mc20130912.aspx.

92. Christopher M. Matthews, "FATF Nears Proposal for Tax Evasion
     Coverage by AML Laws," *WSJBlogs*, December 21, 2011; and Alan Lau
     and Chua Kong Ping, KPMG, "Devil's in the Details with Tax Cheats,"
     The Business Times, September 12, 2013, http://www.kpmg.com/sg/en/
     pressroom/pages/mc20130912.aspx.

93. Vanessa Houlder, "Switzerland Pledges to Lift Veil on Tax Secrecy,"
     Financial Times, May 6, 2014; OECD, CRS by jurisdiction 2018, http://
     www.oecd.org/tax/automatic-exchange/crs-implementation-and-assistance/
     crs-by-jurisdiction/crs-by-jurisdiction-2018.htm, accessed January 21,
     2016.

Chapter 10

1. http://www.cbo.gov/publication/44582.

2. www.nationalpriorities.org/budget-basics/federal-budget-101/spending/.

3. http://www.cms.gov/Research-Statistics-Data-and-Systems/Statistics-
    Trends-and-Reports/NationalHealthExpendData/NHE-Fact-Sheet.html.

4. http://www.hhs.gov/news/press/2014pres/02/20140226a.html.

5. http://www.justice.gov/opa/pr/justice-department-recovers-over-35-billion-
    false-claims-act-cases-fiscal-year-2015.

6. Starklaw.org.

7. http://www.justice.gov/opa/pr/davita-pay-350-million-resolve-allegations-illegal-kickbacks.
8. http://www.justice.gov/opa/pr/glaxosmithkline-plead-guilty-and-pay-3-billion-resolve-fraud-allegations-and-failure-report.
9. Qui tam cases are different from other types of lawsuits, such as those involving personal injuries, because the person bringing the lawsuit is not the one who has been harmed.
10. http://www.policymed.com/2015/06/physician-payments-sunshine-act-cms-posts-2014-open-payments-data-totaling-649-billion.html.
11. http://www.justice.gov/usao-ma/pr/south-shore-physicians-hospital-organization-pay-1775-million-alleged-kickbacks-patient.
12. http://www.justice.gov/opa/pr/dignity-health-agrees-pay-37-million-settle-false-claims-act-allegations.
13. https://oig.hhs.gov/fraud/enforcement/cmp/kickback.asp.
14. http://www.justice.gov/opa/pr/florida-hospital-system-agrees-pay-government-85-million-settle-allegations-improper.
15. CPT (Current Procedural Terminology) is a five digit numeric code that is used to describe medical, surgical, radiology, laboratory, anesthesiology, and evaluation/management services of physicians, hospitals, and other healthcare providers. HCPCS (Healthcare Common Procedure Coding System) is a standardized coding system that is used primarily to identify products, supplies, and services, such as ambulance services and durable medical equipment, prosthetics, orthotics, and supplies.

Chapter 11

1. http://www.justice.gov/opa/pr/justice-department-recovers-nearly-6-billion-false-claims-act-cases-fiscal-year-2014.
2. http://www.nytimes.com/2001/10/04/business/2-drug-makers-to-pay-875-million-to-settle-fraud-case.html.
3. http://www.justice.gov/archive/opa/pr/2001/October/513civ.htm.
4. http://www.justice.gov/opa/pr/glaxosmithkline-plead-guilty-and-pay-3-billion-resolve-fraud-allegations-and-failure-report.
5. Routledge Kegan & Paul.
6. FDA approval of new products generally provides the manufacturer with a period of market exclusivity. There is reasonable debate about whether, in all such circumstances, the normal laws of supply and demand apply, the commercial marketplace is equipped to maintain price reasonableness, and the current market is setting prices at levels that are in the best interest of the public. The case of Gilead's hepatitis C drugs Sovaldi and Harvoni have sharpened the debate and are a good place for the interested reader

to start. This debate is outside the scope of this book, however, and is not addressed further.

7. While most of the lawsuits have settled, there are continuing issues around the difference between undiscounted "full" prices and net prices. Many manufacturers manage this risk through their government pricing groups, but further discussion of this matter is beyond the scope of this chapter.

8. http://oig.hhs.gov/newsroom/news-releases/2015/sandoz.asp.

9. 42 U.S.C. §1320a-7b(b).

10. The Affordable Care Act clarified that "a person need not have actual knowledge of this section or specific intent to commit a violation of this section."

11. Testimony of: Gregory E. Demske, Office of Counsel to the Inspector General, U.S. Department of Health and Human Services, "Examining the Relationship Between the Medical Device Industry and Physicians," Hearing before the Senate Special Committee on Aging, United States Senate, February 27, 2008, page 4.

12. http://www.justice.gov/archive/opa/pr/2004/July/04_civ_523.htm.

13. A rebate paid in advance of payment for a product.

14. http://www.justice.gov/archive/opa/pr/2007/September/07_civ_782.html.

15. https://oig.hhs.gov/authorities/docs/03/050503FRCPGPharmac.pdf.

16. http://www.coloradoattorneygeneral.gov/press/news/2009/09/02/attorney_general_announces_colorado_will_receive_35_million_part_settlements_o.

17. http://www.wsj.com/articles/SB10001424052702304299704577502642401041730.

18. *Health Care Fraud and Abuse: Practical Perspectives: 2nd Edition—2009 Cumulative Supplement*, Ch.11.II.A.2.b., p. 436.

19. http://www.justice.gov/opa/pr/daiichi-sankyo-inc-agrees-pay-39-million-settle-kickback-allegations-under-false-claims-act.

20. http://www.sec.gov/news/speech/2015-spch030315ajc.html.

21. https://www.gsk.com/en-gb/media/press-releases/2014/gsk-china-investigation-outcome/.

22. http://www.nytimes.com/2008/04/15/business/15cnd-vioxx.html?pagewanted=all.

23. https://clinicaltrials.gov/ct2/about-site/history#WorldHealthOrganization.

24. http://www.cbsnews.com/news/doc-who-faked-pfizer-studies-gets-6-months-in-prison-showing-why-gift-bans-are-a-good-idea/. Another infamous clinical trial fraud case involved Dr. Richard Borison and Pharmacologist Bruce Diamond; see http://www.cbsnews.com/news/drug-money-31-07-2000/.

25. http://www.desmoinesregister.com/story/news/2015/02/25/dong-pyou-han-iowa-state-university-guilty-plea/23996449/.

26. http://www.nature.com/news/us-vaccine-researcher-sentenced-to-prison-for-fraud-1.17660.
27. http://www.pharmaceutical-journal.com/news-and-analysis/news-in-brief/ema-recommends-suspending-licences-for-700-drugs-manufactured-by-gvk-biosciences/20067710.article.
28. See DOJ Announcement, http://www.justice.gov/criminal-fraud/file/790236/download.
29. Life sciences sales representatives routinely visit assigned doctors in their territory. There is a certain amount of risk associated with these unsupervised discussions, and the notion of "ride alongs" pertains to having their manager and/or compliance accompany the sales representatives during the visits in order to monitor their interactions with the doctor. In companies with a robust compliance program, these ride alongs are done by compliance and the business unit. The term "manager field rides" pertains to the act of a business manager conducting the ride along instead of compliance.

Index